De Smith's Judicial Review

Third Cumulative Supplement to the 7th Edition

SWEET & MAXWELL

 THOMSON REUTERS

First edition	1959
Second impression	1960
Third impression	1961
Second edition	1968
Third edition	1973
Fourth edition	1980
Second impression	1986
Third impresion	1987
Fifth edition	1995
Supplement to the fifth edition	1998
Sixth edition	2007
Supplement to the sixth edition	2009
Seventh edition	2013
Supplement to the seventh edition	2014
Second Supplement to the seventh edition	2015
Third Supplement to the seventh edition	2016

Published in 2016 by Thomson Reuters (Professional) UK Limited,
trading as Sweet & Maxwell, 5 Canada Square, Canary Wharf,
London E14 5AQ
(Registered in England & Wales, Company No.1679046).

For further information on our products and services, visit
www.sweetandmaxwell.co.uk

Typeset by LBJ Typesetting Ltd
Printed and bound in the UK by CPI Group (UK) Ltd, Croydon, CR0 4YY.

No natural forests were destroyed to make this product; only farmed
timber was used and re-planted.
A CIP catalogue record for this book is available for the British Library.

ISBN 9780414060104

Thomson Reuters and the Thomson Reuters logo are trademarks of
Thomson Reuters.

Sweet & Maxwell® is a registered trademark of Thomson Reuters
(Professional) UK Limited.

Crown copyright material is reproduced with the permission of the
Controller of the HMSO and the Queen's Printer for Scotland.

DE SMITH'S JUDICIAL REVIEW

THIRD CUMULATIVE SUPPLEMENT TO THE SEVENTH EDITION

EDITORS

Professor Andrew Le Sueur
Professor of Constitutional Justice, University of Essex
Barrister, Brick Court Chambers

Catherine Donnelly
Associate Professor and Fellow, Trinity College, Dublin
Barrister, Blackstone Chambers and Law Library, Dublin

Ivan Hare
Barrister, Blackstone Chambers
Former Fellow of Trinity College Cambridge

ASSISTANT EDITORS

Anna Hardiman-McCartney
Lecturer in Law, University of Essex

Jo Moore
Barrister

CONSULTANT EDITORS

The Rt Hon the Lord Woolf
Professor Sir Jeffrey Jowell QC

London
Sweet & Maxwell
2016

PREFACE

The 7th edition of *de Smith's Judicial Review* was published in 2013. The law was stated as it stood on January 31, 2013 (although some later developments were incorporated at proof stage). A *First Supplement* followed, stating the law as at August 1, 2014; a *Second Cumulative Supplement* stated the law as at September 30, 2015; this *Third Cumulative Supplement* brings the main work up to date to September 30, 2016.

As in the main work, we have been selective in the cases that have been included. They either develop a principle or provide a particularly useful illustration of a principle or practice. Although some unreported judgments have been included, we have focused on analysis of reported decisions.

Following the pattern of the *First Supplement*, we have not systematically updated the comparative law material.

Andrew Le Sueur and Anna Hardiman-McCartney worked on Chapters 1–5, 11 and 12. Maura Kavanagh provided research assistance with Chapters 6–10 and 14, and Jo Moore worked on drafts of Chapters 13 and 16–18.

We are grateful to Harry Woolf and Jeffrey Jowell for their oversight of this Supplement.

Editors: Andrew Le Sueur; Catherine Donnelly; Ivan Hare
September 2016

TABLE OF CONTENTS

Supplementary Table of Cases

Supplementary Table of Statutes

Supplementary Table of Statutory Instruments

Supplementary Table of European and International Legislation

Supplementary Table of Civil Procedure Rules

Part I

THE CONTEXT OF JUDICIAL REVIEW

CHAPTER 1

THE NATURE OF JUDICIAL REVIEW

INTRODUCTION

The value and significance of judicial review

[Delete all text in para.1–005, but retain existing n.26, and substitute]   1–005

Notwithstanding these restrictions on access, in December 2012 the Ministry of Justice published a Consultation Paper setting out further proposals for reform in three areas: (i) shortening the three-month time limit for bringing proceedings in certain procurement cases to 30 days and in certain categories of planning decisions to six weeks, bringing them into line with the statutory appeal timetable which applied to those cases; (ii) tightening the procedural rules for granting permission to bring judicial review proceedings by removing the right to an oral renewal where there had already been a prior judicial process involving a hearing on substantially the same issue or where the judge, on written submissions, had determined the case to be "totally without merit"; and (iii) increasing the court fee for an oral renewal hearing where permission had already been refused by a judge on the papers but the claimant asked for the decision to be reconsidered at a hearing.[26] The Government expressed concern that the judicial review process was subject to abuse and was used as a delaying tactic, added to the cost of public services, stifled innovation and frustrated much needed reforms aimed at stimulating growth and promoting economic recovery. It sought to justify its proposals by reference in particular to the significant growth in judicial review applications: 160 applications in 1974, increasing to nearly 4,250 by 2000 and over 11,000 by 2011 (largely attributable to challenges in immigration and asylum matters). The proposals were heavily criticised by academics and practitioners.[26a]

[26a] For a critique of the proposals, see Public Law Project, *Briefing on response to consultation Judicial Review: Proposals for Reform* (January 9, 2013); V. Bondy and M. Sunkin, "Judicial Review Reform: Who is Afraid of Judicial Review? Debunking the Myths of Growth and Abuse", UK Const. L. Blog, January 10, 2013; R. Gordon, "Judicial Review – Storm Clouds Ahead?" [2013] J.R. 1. The new time limits for bringing procurement or planning challenges where the grounds for review arose on or after July 1, 2013 and removal of the right to seek an oral hearing where the case was

assessed by a judge as being without merit on the papers were given effect on July 1, 2013 by an amendment to the Civil Procedure Rules. See Civil Procedure (Amendment No. 4) Rules 2013 (SI 2013/1412). A Planning Fast-Track was also put in place in the Administrative Court in July 2013. The court fee for seeking an oral renewal hearing after the initial judicial review application has been turned down was increased from £60 to £215. Certain proposals were not pursued: where there was a series of linked administrative acts, commencement of time limit for seeking judicial review to be when the first such act was committed; and removal of the right to an oral renewal where there had already been a prior judicial process involving a hearing on substantially the same matter.

1–005A *[Add new para.1–005A after para.1–005]*

The Ministry of Justice subsequently published consultation papers proposing, inter alia, reforms to reduce the use of legal aid to fund weak judicial reviews and proposals for further reform of judicial review.[26b] The proposals included: (i) the creation of a Specialist Planning Chamber in the Upper Tribunal to hear planning judicial reviews and statutory challenges; (ii) extending leapfrog appeals to the Supreme Court in important cases – implemented by ss 63–68 of the Criminal Justice and Courts Act 2015; (iii) limits on the ability of local authorities to challenge decisions on nationally significant infrastructure projects (subsequently abandoned); (iv) narrowing of the test for standing where the claimant has little or no interest in the matter (subsequently abandoned); (v) strengthening the court's powers where a procedural flaw would have made no difference to the original outcome – implemented by s.84 of the Criminal Justice and Courts Act 2015; (vi) consideration of mechanisms other than judicial review for enforcing the public sector equality duty under the Equality Act 2010; and (v) revisions to legal aid for judicial review cases, oral permission hearings, Protective Costs Orders, Wasted Costs Orders, interveners' costs and third party funding – provision for which is made in ss 85–90 of the Criminal Justice and Courts Act 2015.[26c]

[26b] Ministry of Justice, *Transforming Legal Aid: Delivering a More Credible and Efficient System*, CP14/2013; Ministry of Justice, *Judicial Review: Proposals for Further Reform*, Cm 8703. For a critique of the proposals, see Public Law Project, *Judicial Review: Proposals for Further Reform* (October 2013); V. Bondy and M. Sunkin, "How Many JRs are Too Many? An Evidence Based Response to Judicial Review: Proposals for Further Reform", UK Const. L. Blog (October 26, 2013); Joint Committee on Human Rights, *The Implications for Access to Justice of the Government's Proposals to Reform Judicial Review*, 13th Report of the 2013–2014 Session, HL 74/HC 868; M. Elliott, "Judicial Review Reform – The Report of the Joint Committee on Human Rights", UK Const. L. Blog (May 1, 2014); J. McGarry, "The

Importance of an Expansive Test of Standing" [2014] J.R. 60; Bingham Centre for the Rule of Law, *Response to Ministry of Justice Consultation Paper CM 8703: Judicial Review: Proposals for Further Reform* (available at *http://www.biicl.org/files/6618_bingham_centre_response_jr-pffr_cm_8703_2013-11-01.pdf*); M. Fordham, M. Chamberlain, I. Steele and Z. Al-Rikabi, *Streamlining Judicial Review in a Manner Consistent with the Rule of Law* (Bingham Centre Report 2014/01, Bingham Centre for the Rule of Law, BIICL, London, February 2014).

26c In July 2015, the Ministry of Justice opened a consultation on provision of financial information to the court, on applications for judicial review or when applying for a costs capping order: see Ministry of Justice, *Judicial Review: Proposal for the provision and use of financial information* (Cm 9117). The Ministry of Justice published a response to the consultation submissions in July 2016, indicating that the government intended to retain the general approach upon which it consulted and inviting further views on the provision of financial information to other parties: see Ministry of Justice, *Reform of judicial review: Proposals for the provision and use of financial information* (Cm 9303). New rules on when legally aided claimant solicitors will be paid in judicial review claims were brought into force under the Civil Legal Aid (Remuneration) (Amendment) (No.3) Regulations 2014 (SI 2014/607), reg.5A, which prevent legal aid payments unless permission is granted by the Administrative Court or no order is made and the Lord Chancellor considers it reasonable to make a payment.

[Add to end of para.1–007]   1–007

Recent judgments of the UK Supreme Court have, however, emphasised the continuing vitality and importance of common law principles and approaches in contexts where European law also applies.[29a]

29a See, e.g. *Osborn v Parole Board* [2013] UKSC 61; [2014] A.C. 1115, [57] (Lord Reed: "The importance of the [Human Rights] Act is unquestionable. It does not however supersede the protection of human rights under the common law or statute, or create a discrete body of law based upon the judgments of the European court. Human rights continue to be protected by our domestic law, interpreted and developed in accordance with the Act when appropriate); *R. (on the application of HS2 Action Alliance Ltd) v Secretary of State for Transport* [2014] UKSC 3; [2014] 1 W.L.R. 324, [207] (Lord Neuberger P.S.C. and Lord Mance J.S.C., lamenting at [158] that "the issues that have had to be addressed only arise as a result of decisions of the European Court of Justice, which we have found problematic and which call for some further observations" went on to say "The common law itself also recognises certain principles as fundamental to the rule of law. It is, putting the point at its lowest, certainly arguable (and it is for United Kingdom law and courts to determine) that there may be fundamental principles, whether contained in other constitutional instruments or recognised at common law, of which Parliament when it enacted the European Communities Act 1972 did not either contemplate or authorise the abrogation".); *Kennedy v The Charity Commission* [2014] UKSC 20; [2015] A.C. 455 (Lord Mance J.S.C. at [46] "Since the passing of the Human Rights Act 1998, there has too often been a tendency to see the law in areas touched on by the Convention solely in terms of the Convention rights. But the Convention rights represent a threshold protection; and, especially in view of the contribution which common lawyers made to the Convention's inception, they may be expected, at least generally even if not always, to reflect and to find their homologue in the common or domestic statute law" and Lord Toulson J.S.C. at [133] "The growth of the state has presented the courts with new challenges to which they have responded by a process of gradual adaption and development of the common law to meet current needs. This has always been the way of the common law and it has not ceased on the enactment of the Human Rights Act 1998, although since then there has sometimes been a baleful and unnecessary tendency to overlook the common law. It needs to be emphasised that it was not the purpose of the Human Rights Act that the common law should become an ossuary"); *Pham v Secretary of State for the Home Department (Open Society Justice Initiative intervening)* [2015] UKSC 19; [2015] 1 W.L.R. 1591, [97]–[98] (Lord Mance J.S.C.: "The present appeal concerns a status which is as fundamental at common law as it is in European and international law, that is that status of citizenship . . . It is therefore improbably that the nature, strictness or outcome of such a review would differ according to whether it was conducted under domestic principles or whether it was also required to be conducted by reference to a principle of proportionality derived from [European] Union law") and [110] (Lord Sumption J.S.C: urging SIAC "to take the common law test as its starting point and then say in what respects (if any) its conclusions are different applying art.8 of the Human Rights Convention or EU law"). See further para.1–117 below.

THE CONSTITUTIONAL CONTEXT OF JUDICIAL REVIEW

Justification by constitutional principle

1–023 *[Add to end of n.65]*

See further, J. Sumption, "The Limits of Law", 27th Sultan Azlan Shah Lecture, November 20, 2013 (available at *http://www.supremecourt.uk/docs/speech-131120.pdf*).

JUSTICIABILITY: THE LIMITS OF JUDICIAL REVIEW

[Add new n.93a after ". . . institutional capacity"]   1–032

[93a] In *Khaira v Shergill* [2014] UKSC 33; [2015] A.C. 359, the Supreme Court reviewed the application of the principle of non-justiciability in the context of the interpretation and validity of the trust deeds of Sikh religious charities. Lord Neuberger PSC observed:

> "[41] . . . the term non-justiciability refers . . . to a case where an issue is said to be inherently unsuitable for judicial determination by reason only of its subject matter. Such cases generally fall into one of two categories.
>
> [42] The first category comprises cases where the issue in question is beyond the constitutional competence assigned to the courts under our conception of the separation of powers. Cases in this category are rare, and rightly so, for they may result in a denial of justice which could only exceptionally be justified either at common law or under ECHR art.6. The paradigm cases are the non-justiciability of certain transactions of foreign states and of proceedings in Parliament. The first is based in part on the constitutional limits of the court's competence as against that of the executive in matters directly affecting the United Kingdom's relations with foreign states . . . The second is based on the constitutional limits of the court's competence as against that of Parliament . . . The distinctive feature of all these cases is that once the forbidden area is identified, the court may not adjudicate on the matters within it, even if it is necessary to do so in order to decide some other issue which is itself unquestionably justiciable. Where the non-justiciable issue inhibits the defence of a claim, this may make it necessary to strike out an otherwise justiciable claim on the ground that it cannot fairly be tried . . .
>
> [43] The basis of the second category of non-justiciable cases is quite different. It comprises claims or defences which are based neither on private legal rights or obligations, nor on reviewable matters of public law. Examples include domestic disputes; transactions not intended by the participants to affect their legal relations; and issues of international law which engage no private right of the claimant or reviewable question of public law. Some issues might well be non-justiciable in this sense if the court were asked to decide them in the abstract. But they must nevertheless be resolved if their resolution is necessary in order to decide some other issue which is in itself justiciable. The best-known examples are in the domain of public law. Thus, when the court declines to adjudicate on the international acts of foreign sovereign states or to review the exercise of the Crown's prerogative in the conduct of foreign affairs, it normally refuses on the ground that no legal right of the citizen is engaged whether in public or private law: *R. (Campaign for Nuclear Disarmament) v Prime Minister* [2002] EWHC 2777 (Admin); *R. (Al-Haq) v Secretary of State for*

Foreign and Commonwealth Affairs [2009] EWHC 1910 (Admin). . . . But the court does adjudicate on these matters if a justiciable legitimate expectation or a Convention right depends on it: *R. (Abbasi) v Secretary of State for Foreign and Commonwealth Affairs* [2003] UKHRR 76. The same would apply if a private law liability was asserted which depended on such a matter. As Lord Bingham of Cornhill observed in *R. (Gentle) v Prime Minister* [2008] A.C. 1356, para.8, there are 'issues which judicial tribunals have traditionally been very reluctant to entertain because they recognise their limitations as suitable bodies to resolve them. This is not to say that if the claimants have a legal right the courts cannot decide it'."

Limitations inherent in the courts' constitutional role

1–033 *[Add to end of n.94]*

In *R. (on the application of Reilly and Wilson) v Secretary of State for Work and Pensions* [2013] UKSC 68; [2014] A.C. 453; [2013] EWCA Civ 66; [2013] 1 W.L.R. 2239, in a successful challenge to the legality of the Jobseeker's Allowance (Employment, Skills and Enterprise Scheme) Regulations 2011, Sir Stanley Burnton stated in the Court of Appeal:

"I emphasise that this case is not about the social, economic or other merits of the Employment, Skills and Enterprise Scheme. Parliament is entitled to authorise the creation and administration of schemes that . . . are designed to assist the unemployed to obtain employment . . . Parliament is equally entitled to encourage participation . . . by imposing sanctions . . . on those who without good cause refuse to participate in a suitable scheme. The appeal is solely about the lawfulness of the Regulations . . ."

Both the Court of Appeal and the Supreme Court held the regulations to be ultra vires.

[Add to end of n.105]

In *R. (on the application of Reilly and Wilson) v Secretary of State for Work and Pensions* [2013] UKSC 68; [2014] A.C. 453, the Supreme Court upheld the decision of the Court of Appeal that the Jobseeker's Allowance (Employment, Skills and Enterprise Scheme) Regulations 2011 were ultra vires because the Scheme did not have a "prescribed description" as required by s.17A(1) of the Jobseekers Act 1995. Retrospective legislation (the Jobseekers (Back to Work Schemes) Act 2013) to negate the financial effects of that decision was subsequently made the subject of a declaration of incompatibility in *R. (on the application of Reilly (No.2) and Hewstone) v Secretary of State for Work and Pensions* [2014] EWHC 2182 (Admin) (July 4, 2014) as being incompatible with ECHR, art.6.

[Add to end of n.110]   1–037

And see, e.g. *R. (on the application of Lord Carlile) v Secretary of State for the Home Department* [2014] UKSC 60; [2015] A.C. 945, [28]–[29] (Lord Sumption: "The Human Rights Act 1998 did not abrogate the constitutional distribution of powers between the organs of the state which the courts had recognised for many years before it was passed. . . . However, traditional notions of the constitutional distribution of powers have unquestionably been modified by the Human Rights Act 1998. In the first place, any arguable allegation that a person's Convention rights have been infringed is necessarily justiciable").

[Add new n.112a after ". . . democracy"]

112a In *R. (on the application of Nicklinson) v Ministry of Justice* [2014] UKSC 38; [2015] A.C. 657 a nine-member Supreme Court engaged in a discussion of these issues in the context of the imposition of criminal liability under s.2 of the Suicide Act 1961 on those who assisted suicide. Lord Neuberger stated:

> "[72] . . . even under our constitutional settlement, which acknowledges parliamentary supremacy and has no written constitution, it is, in principle, open to a domestic court to consider whether s.2 infringes art.8. The more difficult question . . . is whether we should do so.
>
> . . .
>
> [76] . . . while I respect and understand the contrary opinion, so well articulated by Lord Sumption and Lord Hughes, I am of the view that, provided that the evidence and the arguments justified such a conclusion, we could properly hold that section 2 infringed article 8. . . . More specifically, where the court has jurisdiction on an issue falling within the margin of appreciation, I think it would be wrong in principle to rule out exercising that jurisdiction if Parliament addresses the issue . . . . such an approach would be an abdication of judicial responsibility . . . . given the potential for rapid changes in moral values and medicine, it seems to me that such an approach may well turn out to be inappropriate in relation to this particular issue."

Having said that, Lord Neuberger concluded that it would not be appropriate to grant a declaration of incompatibility at this time. Lords Sumption, Clarke, Reed and Hughes considered that it would be institutionally inappropriate, or only institutionally appropriate if Parliament refused to address the issue, for a domestic court to consider whether s.2 infringed the ECHR. Lady Hale and Lord Kerr, however, did consider it to be institutionally appropriate at the current time and concluded that s.2 was not Convention compliant. On September 11, 2015, the House of Commons rejected a private member's bill on assisted dying by 330 to 180. On July 18, 2015 the House of Lords was split in a debate on Lord Falconer's private member's bill.

9

1–039 *[Add to end of n.116]*

See also *Wheeler v Office of the Prime Minister* [2014] EWHC 3815 (Admin); [2015] 1 C.M.L.R 46 at [44]–[47] (enforcement of a legitimate expectation that a parliamentary vote would be held concerning European Arrest Warrants would involve a breach of art.9 of the Bill of Rights 1689, a breach of parliamentary privilege and breach the separation of powers).

Limitations inherent in the courts' institutional capacity

Matters in relation to which the court lacks expertise

1–041 *[Add to end of n.121]*

; *R. (on the application of Lord Carlile) v Secretary of State for the Home Department* [2014] UKSC 60; [2015] A.C. 945, [49], in a case concerning the exclusion from the UK of a dissident Iranian politician resident in France (Lord Sumption: "There is no challenge to the primary facts. We have absolutely no evidential basis and no expertise with which to substitute our assessment of the risks to national security, public safety and A the rights of others for that of the Foreign Office. We have only the material and the expertise to assess whether the Home Secretary has set about her task rationally, by reference to relevant matters and on the correct legal principle. Beyond that, in a case like this one, we would be substituting our own decision for that of the constitutional decision-maker without any proper ground for rejecting what she had done. All the recent jurisprudence of this court has rejected that as an inappropriate exercise for a Court of review, even where Convention rights are engaged").

[Add to end of n.130]

; *R. (on the application of Lord Carlile) v Secretary of State for the Home Department* [2014] UKSC 60; [2015] A.C. 945.

[Add to para.1–041 after ". . . power to exclude a person from the UK"]

; "secret" trials in the context of terrorist prosecutions;[131a]

[131a] *Guardian News and Media Ltd v AB*, Court of Appeal (Criminal Division), June 12, 2014; *The Times*, June 18, 2014. On the use of closed material procedures in recent years, see paras 8–009 to 8–014.

THE INCIDENCE AND IMPACT OF JUDICIAL REVIEW

The case load

[Add new footnote after "claims brought in relation to immigration and 1–047
asylum decision-making (in 2011, over 75 per cent).]

160a See further R. Thomas, "Mapping Immigration Judicial Review Litigation: An Empirical Legal Analysis" [2015] P.L. 652.

Central government responses to judicial review

[Add to end of n.184] 1–053

See also *R. (on the application of Chester) v Secretary of State for Justice* [2013] UKSC 63; [2014] A.C. 271, where the Supreme Court agreed that the blanket ban on convicted prisoners' rights was ECHR incompatible but dismissed the appeals of the particular applicants that their rights had been infringed and declined to make a further declaration of incompatibility. On August 12, 2014, the European Court of Human Rights found the United Kingdom to be in violation of ECHR Protocol 1 art.3 in having primary legislation preventing all prisoners voting in the June 2009 European Parliament elections; the court held that the finding of a violation consti-tuted sufficient just satisfaction for any non-pecuniary damage sustained by the applicants and therefore declined to award compensation and also rejected the applicants' claim for legal costs (*Firth v United Kingdom*, Application no. 47784/09).

[Add to end of para.1–053]

In November 2012, the Voting Eligibility (Prisoners) Bill was drafted to give Members of Parliament three options on which to vote.184a In a letter to the chairman of the Joint Committee on the Bill dated February 25, 2014, the Secretary of State for Justice, Chris Grayling MP, gave an assurance that "the matter is under active consideration within Government". The Committee of Ministers of the Council of Europe deferred any further discussion of the issue until after September 2015. Prisoners had no right to vote in the May 2015 General Election.

184a Option 1 would retain the ban for prisoners jailed for over four years; option 2 would retain the ban for prisoners jailed for over six months; option 3 would retain the current ban with minor amendments.

Local government responses

1–058 *[Add to end of para.1–058 after ". . . general power of competence"]*

, which allows councils to do anything an individual can do unless specifically prohibited by law.

[Add to end of n.198]

The Localism Act 2011 was brought into force earlier than originally planned by the Secretary of State for Communities and Government Minister, Eric Pickles MP, following the decision of the High Court in *R. (on the application of the National Secular Society) v Bideford Town Council* [2012] EWHC 175 (Admin); [2012] 2 All E.R. 1175, where Ouseley J. held that the saying of Christian prayers as part of the formal business at the start of council meetings was ultra vires the Local Government Act 1972 s.111.

The impact of judicial review on the quality of decision making

1–059 *[Add to end of n.201]*

R. Thomas "Administrative justice, better decisions, and organisational learning" [2015] P.L. 111; V. Bondy, L. Platt and M. Sunkin *The Value and Effects of Judicial Review: The Nature of Claims, their Outcomes and Consequences* (2015). In 2014, the Nuffield Foundation granted funding for three years to multi-disciplinary team of academics working at the University of Essex and elsewhere to create the UK Administrative Justice Institute ("UKAJI"), which has a remit to link the policy, practice and research communities, develop a coordinated research agenda, and identify and tackle capacity constraints on empirical research about law and administration.

ADMINISTRATIVE JUSTICE AND PROPORTIONATE DISPUTE RESOLUTION

Internal complaints systems

1–066A *[Add new para.1–066A after para.1–066]*

In 2013, the Department of Work and Pensions introduced a policy of mandatory reconsideration, requiring all benefit decisions to be re-examined internally before a claimant may appeal to the First-tier Tribunal.[223a] This reform aims, *inter alia*, to promote early resolution of disputes and reduce demand on HMCTS.[223b] A recent consultation conducted by the Social

Security Advisory Committee suggests that, while mandatory reconsideration has potential, the process does not work as well as it should; and makes a series of recommendations for improvement.[223c]

[223a] Empowered by the Welfare Reform Act 2012, s.102.

[223b] Department for Work and Pensions, *Appeals Reform: An Introduction* (August 2013).

[223c] Social Security Advisory Committee, *Decision Making and Mandatory Reconsideration* (July 2016).

[Add to end of n.226]   1–068

See, e.g. *R. (on the application of Bhatti) v Bury MBC* [2013] EWHC 3093 (Admin); (2014) 17 C.C.L. Rep. 64 (application to reinstate judicial review proceedings in community care proceedings dismissed. It would not be right to grant permission for the proceedings where there was an adequate alternative remedy and where the proceedings could be used as a mechanism for a challenge to new decisions).

[Add to end of n.228]

This is a general requirement. In certain cases, stricter time limits apply.

[Add to end of n.233]   1–069

On the meaning of "civil rights and obligations", see *Ali v Birmingham City Council* [2010] UKSC 8; [2010] 2 A.C. 39 where, unlike the entitlement to benefits in *Tsfayo*, the provision of housing to the homeless under the 1996 Housing Act did not engage a "civil right" within ECHR art.6. The award of services or benefits in kind which was dependent upon a series of evaluative judgments by the provider as to whether the statutory criteria had been satisfied and how the need for it ought to be met did not give rise to "civil rights".

Ombudsman

[Add after 1–071]   1–071A

In 2015 the Gordon Report recommended reform of the ombudsman sector and the creation of a new Public Service Ombudsman (PSO) uniting the existing jurisdictions of the Parliamentary and Health Service Ombudsman, Local Government Ombudsman and Housing Ombudsman.[241a] The report makes a range of recommendations as to the role and powers of the proposed PSO, among them giving the PSO the task of promoting standards in public sector complaint-handling and improving access to the Ombudsman, including the suggestion that the PSO be furnished with "own initiative" powers to investigate complaints.[241b]

[241a] R. Gordon *Better to Serve the Public: Proposals to restructure, reform, renew and reinvigorate public services ombudsman* (2015), at para.57.

[241b] R. Gordon *Better to Serve the Public: Proposals to restructure, reform, renew and reinvigorate public services ombudsman* (2015), at paras 137–138. The Cabinet Office's Consultation Paper on the creation of a Public Service Ombudsman, while accepting the need for enhanced access, did not seek views on "own initiative" powers: see Cabinet Office, *A Public Service Ombudsman- A Consultation* (March 2015).

1–076 *[Add to end of para.1–076]*

The Gordon Report recommended the removal of the MP filter, allowing the public to address the proposed PSO directly.[250a]

[250a] para.131.

Judicial review of ombudsmen

1–085 *[At end of para.1–085, delete "and applying the wrong standard of proof to the question whether a consultant surgeon had acted unreasonably in the management of a patient after his discharge from hospital.[273]", but retain existing n.273, and substitute]*

applying the wrong standard of proof to the question whether a consultant surgeon had acted unreasonably in the management of a patient after his discharge from hospital;[273] and then recommendation of financial compensation following the investigation of a complaint where the complainant had a remedy in damages in a court of law.[273a]

[273a] *JR55 v Northern Ireland Commissioner for Complaints* [2016] UKSC 22; (2016) 150 B.M.L.R. 26.

Overlap of jurisdiction between judicial review and the ombudsmen

1–089 *[Add to n.287]*

See *R. (on the application of ER) v Commissioner for Local Administration in England (Local Government Ombudsman)* [2014] EWCA Civ 1407; [2015] E.L.R. 36 (LGO has no jurisdiction to investigate the *consequences* of a decision if investigation of the decision itself is excluded by s.26(6) because of right of appeal to Special Educational Needs and Disability Tribunal).

Tribunals

Review and appeal in the new tribunal system

[Add to end of para.1–098 after ". . . or re-make a decision itself.³¹⁶"] 1–098

The Upper Tribunal has no jurisdiction to review its own refusal of permission to appeal.³¹⁶ᵃ The approach of the Court of Appeal and Supreme Court to considering appeals on points of law from the First-tier Tribunal is "that judicial restraint should be exercised when the reasons that a tribunal gives for its decision are being examined".³¹⁶ᵇ

³¹⁶ᵃ *Samuda v Secretary of State for Work and Pensions* [2014] EWCA Civ 1; [2014] 3 All E.R. 201.

³¹⁶ᵇ *Jones (by Caldwell) (Respondent) v First Tier Tribunal* [2013] UKSC 19; [2013] 2 A.C. 48 at [25] per Lord Hope.

PUBLIC INQUIRIES AND INQUESTS

Other public inquiries

[Add to end of para.1–102] 1–102

In March 2014, a House of Lords Select Committee reported on post-legislative scrutiny of the Inquiries Act 2005. Noting that no inquiry had been set up under the 2005 Act since 2011, but a number of non-statutory inquiries had been established, the committee recommended: "Ministers have at their disposal on the statute book an Act and Rules which, subject to the reservations we have set out, in our view constitute a good framework for such inquiries. Ministers should be ready to make better use of these powers, and should set up inquiries under the Inquiries Act unless there are overriding reasons of security or sensitivity for doing otherwise."³²⁸ᵃ The Government rejected this recommendation (and several others), arguing that "Ministers should not feel constrained from considering other options which may be better suited to the circumstances".³²⁸ᵇ

³²⁸ᵃ House of Lords Select Committee on the Inquiries Act 2005, *The Inquiries Act 2005: Post-legislative Scrutiny*, HL Paper 143, para.300.

³²⁸ᵇ Ministry of Justice, *Government Response to the Report of the House of Lords Select Committee on the Inquiries Act 2005*, Cm 8903 (June 2014). For commentary on the Select Committee recommendations see Lord Thomas, "The Future of Public Inquiries" [2015] P.L. 225.

1–104 *[Add to end of para.1–104]*

In *R. (on the application of Litvinenko) v Secretary of State for the Home Department*, the Secretary of State refused the coroner's request to replace an inquest with an inquiry under the Inquiries Act 2005, to permit account to be taken of closed material that the coroner was not permitted to consider. The Divisional Court held that the Secretary of State's refusal was irrational.[332a]

[332a] [2014] EWHC 194 (Admin); [2014] H.R.L.R. 6 (for criticism of the court's approach, see Jason N.E. Varuhas, "Ministerial Refusals to Initiate Public Inquiries: Review or Appeal?" [2014] C.L.J. 238, arguing that the court had erroneously approached its task "as though it was hearing an appeal from the Minister's decision rather than exercising a supervisory jurisdiction").

CATEGORIES OF JUDICIAL REVIEW

Convention rights protected by the HRA

1–117 *[Add new n.357a after ". . . away from purely domestic standards"]*

[357a] But the courts are increasingly asserting the power of common law human rights protection independently of the Human Rights Act 1998 and the ECHR. See *Osborn v Parole Board; Booth v Parole Board* [2013] UKSC 61; [2014] A.C. 1115 at [57] per Lord Reed: "The importance of the [Human Rights] Act is unquestionable. It does not however supersede the protection of human rights under the common law or statute, or create a discrete body of law based on the judgments of the European Court. Human rights continue to be protected by our domestic law, interpreted and developed in accordance with the Act when appropriate." The Convention was not to be treated "as if it were Moses and the prophets" (at [56]); and other cases discussed at para.1–007, above. See also: Lady Hale, "UK Constitutionalism on the March?" [2014] J.R. 201 (". . . there is emerging a renewed emphasis on the common law and distinctively UK constitutional principles as a source of legal inspiration"); and Lord Neuberger P.S.C., "The Role of Judges in Human Rights Jurisprudence: A Comparison of the Australian and UK Experience", Conference speech given at the Supreme Court of Victoria, Melbourne, August 8, 2014, para.29 (available at *http://www.supremecourt.uk/docs/speech-140808.pdf*) (". . . the Judges have tried to bring the common law back to centre stage. The most dramatic example of this is . . . *Kennedy v Charity Commission* ([2014] UKSC 20; [2015] A.C. 455. A journalist wished to see the results of a Charity Commission inquiry into the affairs of a charity . . . and based the claim on article 10 . . . we sent

the claim back to the trial judge on the basis that we thought that there was a stronger case based on common law . . ."). Compare however the recent decision of *Moohan v Lord Advocate (Advocate General for Scotland intervening)* [2014] UKSC 67; [2015] A.C. 901 in which both Lord Hodge (at [34]) and Baroness Hale (at [56]) rejected the existence of a common law right to vote. *Moohan*, together with other recent jurisprudence on common law rights, is considered in M. Elliott, "Beyond the European Convention: Human Rights and the Common Law" (2015) 68 C.L.P.

CHAPTER 2

CLAIMANTS, INTERESTED PARTIES AND INTERVENERS

CONSTITUTIONAL SIGNIFICANCE OF STANDING RULES

[Add new para.2–002A after para.2–002] 2–002A

In 2013, the Ministry of Justice expressed concern[8a] that judicial review is sometimes used as a delaying tactic in cases that have little prospect of success. The Ministry of Justice claimed that unmeritorious applications could delay government reforms and the progress of major infrastructure projects intended to stimulate growth and promote economic recovery. The courts' wide approach to standing, it said, "has tipped the balance too far, allowing judicial review to be used to seek publicity or otherwise to hinder the process of proper decision-making".[8b] The Ministry of Justice considered that claimants for judicial review should have a more direct interest in the matter to which the application related, to exclude those who had only a political or theoretical interest, such as campaigning groups. Faced with opposition from many quarters, including the senior judiciary, proposals for a stricter test of standing were abandoned (though proposals for financing judicial review may have an equivalent effect).

[8a] Ministry of Justice, *Judicial Review: Proposals for Further Reform*, Cm 8703 (September 2013), paras 67–90. See further para.1–005 above. For a critique of the proposals, see J. McGarry, "The Importance of an Expansive Test of Standing" [2014] J.R. 60.

[8b] Ministry of Justice, *Judicial Review: Proposals for Further Reform*, Cm 8703, para.79.

IN FAVOUR OF RESTRICTED ACCESS

[Delete all text in n.12 and substitute] 2–004

On recent government proposals to restrict standing for claimants without a direct interest, in particular pressure groups, see para.2–002 above.

IN FAVOUR OF A MORE OPEN APPROACH

2–005 *[Add to end of n.17]*

Time limits in certain procurement and planning cases have been shortened to 30 days and six weeks respectively by an amendment to the Civil Procedure Rules: Civil Procedure (Amendment No. 4) Rules 2013 (SI 2013/1412).

CAPACITY AND STANDING

Capacity and standing of public authorities

2–014 *[Add to end of para 2–014]*

The fact that the decision in question is one which a public authority could itself have made does not preclude the authority from bringing judicial review. A recent decision of the Administrative Court upheld the possibility of a challenge by an NHS Trust to a decision which the Trust was empowered to take but had delegated to another body.[55a]

[55a] *South Staffordshire and Shropshire Healthcare NHS Foundations Trust v St George's Hospital Managers* [2016] EWHC 1196 (Admin); [2016] Med. L.R. 283. The claim failed on the merits.

ASSESSING THE CLAIMANT'S INTEREST

The legislative framework

2–028 *[Add new n.87a at end of para.2–028]*

[87a] See e.g., *R. (Nationwide Association of Fostering Providers) v Bristol CC and others* [2015] EWHC 3615 (Admin); [2016] P.T.S.R. 932 (in a challenge to local authorities' approach to decision-making under the Children Act 1989, s.22C about the "most appropriate placement" for looked after children, William J. held that the claimant trade association "can legitimately be said to have more than purely commercial interests at heart" in relation to the s.22C administrative process, and declined to refuse judicial review on the basis that the claimant did not have sufficient interest.

Impact and proximity interests

2–030 *[Add to end of n.93]*

R. (Project Management Institute) v Minister for the Cabinet Office [2016] EWCA Civ 21; [2016] 1 W.L.R. 1737 (claimant had sufficient interest because it would be adversely affected by the grant of a Royal Charter to a competitor).

[Add after ". . . restoration to the cottage to be dismantled.[101]"   2–031

A former student of the University of Oxford, who alleged that another student had raped her, was held at the permission stage not to have standing to challenge the application of a new policy adopted by the university on investigation of such complaints.[101a]

[101a] *R. (on the application of Ramey) v University of Oxford* [2014] EWHC 4847 (Admin), Edis J ("It appears to me that it is inappropriate for the claimant to be granted permission to bring judicial review to question not the terms of the policy itself but its application in circumstances where it has never actually been applied so far as the court knows. No doubt it has been applied but the court has no evidence about the way in which that has been done or the circumstances in which it is being done or whether indeed its application has caused anybody to suffer any sense of grievance. So the court is ill-equipped to take a decision on that question and that directly relates to the question of standing").

The role of campaign and interest groups as claimants

[Add to n.122 after ". . . lived in Cumbria)."   2–036

Gibraltar Betting and Gaming Association Ltd v Secretary of State for Culture, Media and Sport [2014] EWHC 3236 (Admin); [2015] A.C.D. 10 (a trade association's challenge to the introduction of a new regulatory framework for gambling).

[Add new n.132a after ". . . within three months of the impugned decision"]   2–042

[132a] In *R. (on the application of Plantagenet Alliance Ltd) v Secretary of State for Justice* (unreported, August 15, 2013), the claimant was a not-for profit entity comprised of the collateral descendants Richard III (king of England 1483–1485), which was formed in response to the discovery of the king's remains during an archaeological excavation in a local authority carpark. The Alliance was granted permission to apply for judicial review of the Secretary of State's decision to grant an exhumation licence on the ground that he had failed to comply with a duty to consult relevant interests as to how and where the remains should be reburied, either prior to issuing the licence or subsequently. Although the application was made after the

three-month time limit, additional time was granted. The Alliance was held to have standing and to have an arguable case. *R. v Secretary of State for the Environment, ex p. Rose Theatre Ltd* [1990] 1 Q.B. 504 was not cited. In *R. (on the application of Plantagenet Alliance Ltd) v Secretary of State for Justice* [2013] EWHC 3164 (Admin); [2014] A.C.D. 26, the court upheld a protective costs order made in respect of the judicial review proceedings brought by the Alliance (which had no assets) on the basis that the proceedings raised matters of general public importance. At the full hearing of the claim for judicial review, it was held that there were no public law grounds to interfere with the Secretary of State's decision and the application was dismissed: *R (on the application of the Plantagenet Alliance Ltd) v Secretary of State for Justice* [2014] EWHC 1662 (QB). The Ministry of Justice estimated its unrecoverable costs at around £90,000. The University of Leicester and Leicester City Council (the second and third defendants) were also unable to recover their costs from the Alliance. This case was used by the government to justify its proposed reforms to protective costs orders contained in the Criminal Justice and Courts Bill 2014.

HUMAN RIGHTS ACT 1998 AND THE VICTIM REQUIREMENT

Strasbourg case law on meaning of "victim"

2–054 *[Add to end of n.152]*

On determining the governmental status of a body, see *Transpetrol v Slovakia* Application 28502/08 [2011] E.C.H.R 2004. Transpetrol was a joint-stock company which specialised in transporting, storing, buying and selling oil. At the time of the contested judgment of the national Constitutional Court, which the applicant complained had breached its ECHR art.6 right to a fair hearing, the state owned 51 per cent of the shares in the company. The remainder were owned by private parties. The applicant had features of both a governmental and a non-governmental body. The court noted, at [65], that the applicant was a commercial joint-stock company operating exclusively under the private-law regime, governed by the Commercial Code, with no privileges or special rights or rules concerning enforcement of judgments against it; subject to the jurisdiction of the ordinary courts; not participating in the exercise of any government power and, in the past, partly owned by private entities (it had since become entirely state-owned). On the other hand (at [66]), the state had always been a major shareholder and at present was the sole shareholder in the company; on account of its national strategic economic importance it used to be excluded by law from privatisation; it had a "natural monopoly" and an unrivalled market position in the state. However, rather than weighing these elements against each other, the decisive considerations for the determination of the applicant's standing under

ECHR art.34 lay in "the assessment of the overall procedural and substantive context of the application and of its underlying facts". The genuine issue behind the proceedings was the ownership of the shares in the applicant company, which primarily concerned the rights and interests of other shareholders rather than those of the company itself. In the circumstances, the interests of the applicant company and the government were the same and the application did not strive to further interests other than those that were concurrent interests of the state. The state had also joined the applicant as an intervener in separate proceedings involving essentially the same issues. The application was declared inadmissible for lack of standing under art.34. The court noted, however, that this was without prejudice to the applicant company's art.34 standing should the relevant circumstances be different. But see *Olympic Delivery Authority v Persons Unknown* [2012] EWHC 1012 (Ch), where, in a claim in private and public nuisance, the ODA sought injunctions to restrain protestors from entering or occupying land that was being developed as part of the Olympic site. The ODA was established by statute under the London Olympic Games and Paralympic Games Act 2006, s.3. In exercising its functions it must obey any directions given by the Secretary of State (Sch.1, para.18(1)(b)) who appointed its members and chairman (Sch.1, para.1(1)). It was undoubtedly a public authority (whether core or hybrid) within HRA s.6. Arnold J., however, considered himself bound to balance the rights of the protestors under ECHR arts 10 and 11 with the ODA's rights to peaceful enjoyment of property under art.1 of Protocol 1 (which he did in favour of the ODA). This aspect of the decision is open to criticism on the basis that the ODA, as a public authority, could not argue Convention rights.

Application of "victim" requirement in the HRA

Victim status

[Add new para.2–056A after para.2–056]   2–056A

In a Northern Irish case, the applicant for judicial review (a detained patient) challenged the compatibility of arts 32 and 36 of the Mental Health (Northern Ireland) Order 1986 relating to the appointment of his "nearest relative" with Convention rights. The applicant wanted to change his nearest relative from his sister to his cousin (who lived in Northern Ireland and with whom he had more regular contact) but the legislation did not provide a procedure for achieving this. Identically, legislation in England and Wales had been acknowledged to be incompatible but the respondent was reluctant to bring forward amendments in Northern Ireland. Surprisingly, the respondent contended that the applicant did not have victim status, a submission rejected by the court.[159a]

[159a] *An Application by HM for Judicial Review v In the Matter of Articles 32 and 36 of the Mental Health (Northern Ireland) Order 1986* [2014] NIQB 43, Treacy J. ("The applicant submits that his article 8 rights are infringed by the lack of a mechanism allowing him to apply to change his nearest relative as evidenced at sections 32 and 36 of the 1986 order. It is common case that the 1986 order does not in fact contain any such mechanism. Therefore, if it is found that the relevant sections do infringe the applicant's rights then clearly he will fulfil the victim requirement as his rights will actually have been infringed by the impugned provisions").

Not a victim

2–057 *[Add to end of n.160]*

Cf. *Re Northern Ireland Human Rights Commission's Application for Judicial Review* [2012] NIQB 77; [2012] Eq. L.R. 1135, where the Commission brought an application on behalf of unmarried couples in a challenge to the Adoption (Northern Ireland) Order 1987 arts 14–15, which provided that adoption orders could only be made on the application of married couples or individuals who were neither married nor in a civil partnership. The Commission had standing under the Northern Ireland Act 1998 s.71(2B)(c) provided there was or would be one or more victims of the unlawful act (which was established).

[Add to para.2–057 before "In Somerville v Scottish Ministers . . ."]

In *R (on the application of Broadway Care Centre Ltd) v Caerphilly CBC*,[161a] where a local authority decided to terminate a care home's contract, the care home was not a victim in bringing a claim to protect its residents' ECHR art.8 rights. Nor did the responsibilities in respect of closure of care homes give rise to a responsibility of the local authority towards the care home such that the care home would itself be a victim of any breach.

[161a] [2012] EWHC 37 (Admin); (2012) 15 C.C.L. Rep. 82.

STANDING OF "PERSONS AGGRIEVED"

2–064 *[Add to end of n.186]*

Some members of the Supreme Court expressed the caveat that there was, however, also a wide discretion to refuse a remedy even though the applicant had successfully established a breach of European Union law, see R. McCracken, "Standing and Discretion in Environmental Challenges:

Walton, a Curate's Egg" [2014] J.P.L. 304; Baroness Hale of Richmond, "Who Guards the Guardians?" (2014) 3 C.J.I.C.L. 100 at 101–104.

[Add to end of n.187]

In *R (on the application of Cherkley Campaign Ltd) v Mole Valley DC* [2013] EWHC 2582 (Admin); [2014] 1 P. & C.R. 12 in a challenge to the grant of planning permission for the development of a luxury golf course in the Cherkley estate, an area of great landscape value and part of which was also within an area of outstanding natural beauty, proof of participation in the process of objection was said (per Haddon-Cave J.) not to be a *sine qua non* to standing, but merely strong evidence that such persons would ordinarily be regarded as aggrieved. Numerous of the directors of and individual subscribers to Cherkley Campaign Ltd not only lived in the area (and could be said thereby to be "aggrieved") but were also involved in the process of objecting to the proposal through bodies such as the Surrey Branch of the Campaign for the Protection for Rural England. Further, there was nothing unfair or improper about a group of aggrieved individuals forming a limited company to bring a claim. Haddon-Cave J. quashed the decision (reversed on appeal [2014] EWCA Civ 567; [2014] P.T.S.R. D14).

INTERESTED PARTIES AND INTERVENERS

Interveners

[Add to end of n.204]   2–068

See S. Knights, "Interventions in Public Law Proceedings" [2013] J.R. 200.

[Add to end of n.205]

See also S. Shah, T. Poole and M. Blackwell, "Rights, Interveners and the Law Lords" (2014) 34 O.J.L.S. 295 which, inter alia, tests the hypothesis that the HRA led to an increase in third party interventions. For a comparative analysis with the Supreme Court of the United States and the Supreme Court of Canada, see L. Neudorf, "Intervention in the UK Supreme Court" (2013) 2 C.J.I.C.L. 16.

[Add to end of n.209]

See also Baroness Hale of Richmond, "Who Guards the Guardians?" (2014) 3 C.J.I.C.L. 100 at 104: "Once a matter is in court, the more important the subject, the more difficult the issues, the more help we need to try and get the right answer."

[Add to end of n.211]

In *R. (on the application of British American Tobacco UK Ltd) v Secretary of State for Health* [2014] EWHC 3515 (Admin); [2015] A.C.D. 6 an application to intervene was refused where it was considered that the interests of the proposed interveners were not discernibly different from those of the claimant: as such, their intervention would offer little assistance to the court.

[Add to end of para.2–068]

An intervener may seek a protective costs order in its application for permission to be heard and/or file evidence, though costs are within the court's discretion.[211a]

[211a] The Criminal Justice and Courts Act 2015 s.87 introduced a provision that the applicant and defendant (or any interested party) to judicial review proceedings shall not be required to pay the intervener's costs in connection with the proceedings, although the court may make such an order if it considers there are exceptional circumstances. Further, on an application to the High Court or Court of Appeal by the applicant, defendant or interested party, the court must order the intervener to pay any costs specified in the application which the court considers have been incurred as a result of the intervener's involvement in the proceedings. Again, the court has a discretion in exceptional circumstances. During the Bill's second reading in the House of Lords, Lord Carlile commented: "The inevitable consequence of this is that charitable and not-for-profit organisations will no longer be prepared to provide their expertise to assist the court in cases of wide public importance" (HL Deb, June 30, 2014, col.1604).

CHAPTER 3

DEFENDANTS AND DECISIONS SUBJECT TO JUDICIAL REVIEW

SCOPE

[In n.1, delete "3rd edn (2005)" and substitute]   3–001

4th edn (2010)

RANGE OF PUBLIC AUTHORITIES SUBJECT TO JUDICIAL REVIEW

Criminal justice system

[Add to end of n.29]   3–006

R. (S) v Crown Prosecution Service; R. (S) v Oxford Magistrates' Court [2015] EWHC 2868 (Admin); [2016] 1 W.L.R. 804 (refusing permission to proceed and holding that procedural propriety did not require consultation with the suspect when the prosecution decided to prosecute following a request for review by an alleged victim under the Victims' Right to Review scheme).

Courts

[Add to end of n.43]   3–009

Though note that the High Court has considered the restriction ineffective where the trial judge has acted without jurisdiction: *R. v Maidstone Crown Court, ex p. Harrow LBC* [2000] Q.B. 719; *R. (DPP) v Sheffield Crown Court)* [2014] EWHC 2014 (Admin); [2014] 1 W.L.R. 4639; *R. (M) v Crown Court at Kingston upon Thames* [2014] EWHC 2702 (Admin); [2016] 1 W.L.R. 1685 ("an error so severe that it deprived the [Crown Court] of jurisdiction" to make the impugned order).

Legislation

[Add to end of n.50]   3–011

R. (on the application of Reilly and Wilson) v Secretary of State for Work and Pensions [2013] UKSC 68; [2014] A.C. 453 (Jobseeker's Allowance (Employment, Skills and Enterprise Scheme) Regulations (SI 2011/917) were ultra vires bcause the Scheme did not have a "prescribed description" as required by s.17A(1) of the Jobseekers Act 1995); *R. (on the application of SG) v Secretary of State for Work and Pensions (Child Poverty Action Group intervening)* [2015] UKSC 16; [2015] 1 W.L.R. 1449 (Benefit Cap (Housing Benefit) Regulations 2012 (SI 2012/2994) held not incompatible with Convention rights); *R. (on the application of Cushnie) v Secretary of State for Health* [2014] EWHC 3626 (Admin); [2015] P.T.S.R. 384 (National Health Service (Charges to Overseas Visitors) Regulations 2011 (SI 2011/1556) unlawful due to the Secretary of State's failure to comply with the public sector equality duty).

[Add after ". . . by affirmative resolution of Parliament.⁵¹"]

Challenges may be made to draft orders not yet considered by Parliament.[51a]

[51a] See e.g., *R. (Public Law Project) v Lord Chancellor (Office of the Children's Commissioner intervening)* [2016] UKSC 39; [2016] 3 W.L.R. 387 (draft order laid before Parliament concerning restrictions on legal aid).

[Add to end of n.52]

In relation to illegality as a ground of review, the UK Supreme Court has approved the proposition that "[a]lthough Henry VIII powers are often case in very wide terms, the more general the words used by Parliament to delegate a power, the more likely it is that an exercise within the literal meaning of the words will nevertheless be outside the legislature's contemplation" (*R. (Public Law Project) v Lord Chancellor (Office of the Children's Commissioner intervening)* [2016] UKSC 39; [2016] 3 W.L.R. 387 at [26], citing D. Greenberg (ed), *Craies on Legislation* 10th edn (2012), para.1.3.9).

[Add to end of para.3–011]

The Immigration Rules (formally, the Statement of Changes in Immigration Rules (1994), HC 395, as amended from time to time) made by the Home Secretary under s.1(4) of the Immigration Act 1971 "do not constitute 'rules' in the sense that a statute or a statutory instrument do" and are not subject to all the public law constraints on policies and discretionary powers, including the non-fettering principle.[54a]

[54a] *R. (Sayaniya v Upper Tribunal)* [2016] EWCA Civ 85; [2016] 4 W.L.R. 58.

JURISDICTION, JUSTICIABILITY AND DISCRETION

Jurisdiction of the Administrative Court

Public functions outside the court's jurisdiction

[Add to end of n.69]   3–017

Wheeler v Office of the Prime Minister [2014] EWHC 3815 (Admin); [2015] 1 C.M.L.R 46 at [44]–[47] (enforcement of a legitimate expectation that a parliamentary vote would be held concerning European Arrest Warrants would involve a breach of art.9 of the Bill of Rights 1689, a breach of parliamentary privilege and breach the separation of powers).

[Add to end of "(a) . . . the administration of Parliament', which is not.[72]*"]*

Parliamentary privilege did not impede the UK Supreme Court from considering in detail the hybrid bill procedure and whether it was in accordance with an EU directive.[72a]

[72a] *R. (on the application of Buckingham County Council) v Secretary of State for Transport* [2014] UKSC 3; [2014] 1 W.L.R. 324, [95] (Lord Reed S.C.J.: "I am mindful of the importance of refraining from trespassing upon the province of Parliament or, so far as possible, even appearing to do so. The court can however consider the effect of the Directive under EU law without in my opinion affecting or encroaching upon any of the powers of Parliament. The parliamentary authorities have not thought it necessary to seek to intervene in these proceedings, although the court was told that they have been kept informed of the parties' cases").

[Correction to n.77]

Thorburn should read *Thoburn*.

[Add after "This reflects the dualist character . . . until such time as a treaty   3–019
provision is expressly incorporated into domestic law.[92]*]*

In the UK Supreme Court, Lord Kerr of Tonaghmore J.S.C has, however, called into question the rationale for this "dualist conception" of the restriction on the use of unincorporated treaty provisions in the human rights context, holding that art.3.1 of the United Nations Convention on the Rights of the Child should be directly enforceable in UK domestic law (a minority view with which the other Justices did concur).[92a]

[92a] *R. (on the application of SG) v Secretary of State for Work and Pensions (Child Poverty Action Group intervening)* [2015] UKSC 16; [2015] 1 W.L.R. 1449, [256] ("Standards expressed in international treaties or conventions dealing with human rights to which the United Kingdom has subscribed must be presumed to be the product of extensive and enlightened consideration. There is no logical reason to deny to United Kingdom citizens domestic law's vindication of the rights that those conventions proclaim. If the Government commits itself to a standard of human rights protection, it seems to me entirely logical that it should be held to account in the courts as to its actual compliance with that standard").

[Add to end of n.93]

R. (on the application of Khan) v Secretary of State for Foreign and Commonwealth Affairs [2014] EWCA Civ 24; [2014] 1 W.L.R. 872 (refusal of permission to seek judicial review of the alleged provision of intelligence by GCHQ officers to the United States for use in drone strikes in Pakistan. The claims involved serious criticism of the acts of a foreign state and there were no exceptional circumstances to justify the court sitting in judgment on those acts); *R. (on the application of Sandiford) v Secretary of State for Foreign and Commonwealth Affairs* [2014] UKSC 44; [2014] 1 W.L.R. 2697 (the government's blanket policy of refusing to provide funding for legal representation of British nationals facing criminal proceedings abroad was lawful. There was no necessary implication that a blanket policy was inappropriate, or that there must always be room for exceptions, when a policy was formulated for the exercise of a prerogative and not a statutory power. However, the Secretary of State should review the blanket policy in the light of information that the Indonesian proceedings appeared to raise the most serious issues as to the functioning of the local judicial system). In *Belhaj v Straw* [2013] EWHC 4111 (QB) the High Court struck out claims for damages and declarations of illegality relating to alleged unlawful rendition from Bangkok to Libya by agents of the US in which the defendants had allegedly participated by providing intelligence.

[Add to end of para.3–019]

However, the conduct of foreign states in gross violation of established principles of international law or fundamental human rights can impact upon the legality of actions by the UK government.[93a]

[93a] *Othman v Secretary of State for the Home Department* [2013] EWCA Civ 277 (the defendant, also known as Abu Qatada—a Jordanian national resident in the United Kingdom—could not be deported to Jordan to stand trial on terrorism charges as there was a real risk that evidence previously obtained by torture would be admitted at his trial. He was eventually

deported to Jordan on July 7, 2013, after the United Kingdom and Jordanian governments agreed and ratified a treaty satisfying the requirement that evidence obtained through torture would not be used against him).

NO DECISION OR DECISIONS WITHOUT LEGAL EFFECT

Decisions without direct legal effect

Chains of decisions

[Delete "or what purports to be a second decision may in reality be only a   3–026
confirmation of an initial decision and so not itself reviewable.[118]", but retain
existing n.118, and substitute]

what purports to be a second decision may in reality be only a confirmation of an initial decision and so not itself reviewable[118]; or the legislative framework may make it unnecessary for a decision-maker to wait for an inspector's report before taking a decision.[118a]

[118a] See *R. (Cruelty Free International) v Secretary of State for the Home Department* [2015] EWHC 3631 (Admin); [2016] P.T.S.R. 431 (claimant unsuccessfully argued that it was necessary under the Animals (Scientific Procedures) Act 1986 for the Minister to wait for final report from Home Office's Animals in Science Regulation Unit before imposing sanctions on license holder).

AMENABILTY TESTS BASED ON THE SOURCE OF POWER

Prerogative powers

Nature of prerogative powers

[Add new paragraph after ". . . in accordance with the Fixed-term Parliaments   3–030
Act 2011"]

Many exercises of prerogative powers are also regulated by constitutional conventions (rules of political behaviour which are regarded as binding by those to whom they apply) and new conventions continue to emerge to accommodate new or changing political times. Under the royal prerogative, the Prime Minister has power to order the deployment of the armed forces overseas. However, it became a political practice to open up such decisions to Parliamentary debate. In February 2006, Tony Blair sought the approval of the House of Commons before authorising military intervention in Iraq.

In September 2013, David Cameron sought the approval of the House of Common before deciding on military intervention in Syria. When the Commons did not vote in favour, Cameron declined to intervene militarily. In 2008 Gordon Brown's government had suggested that Parliament's role should be formalised in a resolution to be passed by the House of Commons, but that proposal was not implemented. In July 2013, the House of Lords Constitution Committee stated that there was now an "existing convention – that, save in exceptional circumstances, the House of Commons is given the opportunity to debate and vote on the deployment of armed forces overseas".[135a]

[135a] House of Lords Constitution Committee, *Constitutional Arrangements for the Use of Armed Force*, Second Report of 2013–2014, HL Paper 46, para.64.

Shift from jurisdiction to justiciability to set limits on court's powers to supervise legality of prerogative powers

3–033 *[Add new n.143a after ". . . or a refusal to dissolve Parliament"]*

[143a] The prerogative power of dissolution of Parliament prior to a general election has been overtaken by the Fixed Term Parliaments Act 2011: see para.3–030 above.

[Add to end of n.150]

; *R. (on the application of Rahman) v Secretary of State for the Home Department* [2015] EWHC 1146 (Admin) (refusal to renew the claimant's passport was quashed as irrational given the findings of an Immigration Appeal Tribunal that his late father had been a British citizen).

[Add to para.3–033 after ". . . excluding a person from the United Kingdom;[151]"]

inclusion of a person on the United Nations Security Council's list of persons associated with terrorist organisations and the European Union's sanctions list;[151a]

[151a] *R. (on the application of Youssef) v Secretary of State for Foreign and Commonwealth Affairs* [2013] EWCA Civ 1302; [2014] Q.B. 728.

[Add to end of n.153]

In an answer to a Written Question, the Secretary of State for Northern Ireland revealed that the Royal Prerogative of Mercy had been used "in

Northern Ireland 365 times between 1979 and 2002, but this total does not include the period between 1987 and 1997 for which records cannot currently be found" and "There are no cases where the RPM has been granted since the current Government came to office in May 2010, and the records indicate that there are no instances where the RPM was granted after 2002" (HC Deb, May 1, 2014, c762W). It was not clear how many of those pardoned were members of paramilitary groups or members of the security services, but the Northern Ireland Office said that the vast majority were not terrorism-related and examples of use "included driving offences, assault, burglary, theft and non-payment of national insurance contributions" (BBC News, "Royal Prerogative of Mercy: Over 350 issued in Northern Ireland", May 2, 2014 (available at *http://www.bbc.co.uk/news/ uk-northern-ireland–27260596*)). The NIO also highlighted that the prerogative of mercy had been used much more frequently before the establishment of the Criminal Cases Review Commission in 1997. In December 2013 the wartime code breaker, Alan Turing, was granted a posthumous pardon by the Queen at the request of the Secretary of State for Justice (Chris Grayling MP). Turing had been convicted of an offence of gross indecency in 1952 for engaging in homosexual activity and had been chemically castrated (Ministry of Justice, "Press Release: Royal Pardon for WW2 code-breaker Dr Alan Turing", December 24, 2013 (available at *https://www.gov.uk/ government/ news/royal-pardon-for-ww2-code-breaker-dr-alan-turing*)).

[Add to end of n.154]

This duty does not extend to the provision of funding for legal representation of British nationals facing criminal proceedings abroad. *R. (on the application of Sandiford) v Secretary of State for Foreign and Commonwealth Affairs* [2014] UKSC 44; [2014] 1 W.L.R. 2697.

Prerogative powers in respect of which the court may not have supervisory jurisdiction

[Add to end of n.159] 3–034

The conduct of foreign policy through the United Nations is not amenable to judicial review in the domestic courts – but logically prior decisions of a Minister about an individual living in the United Kingdom was assumed not to be immune from judicial review, though it would be an area in which the courts should proceed with caution: see *R. (Youssef) v Secretary of State for Foreign and Commonwealth Affairs* [2016] UKSC 3; [2016] 2 W.L.R. 509.

[At end of n.161, delete "3rd edn (2005)" and substitute]

4th edn (2010)

JUDICIAL REVIEW OF PUBLIC FUNCTIONS

Bodies held not to be amenable to judicial review

3–040 *[Add to end of n.194]*

In *R. (Holmcroft Properties Ltd) v KPMG LLP* [2016] EWHC 323 (Admin); [2016] A.C.D. 67, it was held that a company appointed by the Financial Services Authority to provide redress to customers who had been mis-sold financial products was not amenable to review.

AMENABILITY OF FUNCTIONS RELATING TO PRECONTRACTUAL AND CONTRACTUAL POWERS

Amenability tests for contractual situations

3–057 *[Add to end of n.239]*

R. (on the application of Trafford) v Blackpool BC [2014] EWHC 85; [2014] P.T.S.R. 989 (decision not to renew lease to firm of solicitors who had acted for claimants in personal injuries claims against the council held to be amenable to judicial review). Per H.H. Judge Stephen Davies: "At the very least there is a sufficient public element or connection to render the decision amenable to judicial review on the ground of abuse of power, whether categorised as improper or unauthorised power." See also para.11–072 n.259.

Identifying the "additional public element"

Situations where there was a sufficient "additional public element"

3–062 *[Add to end of para.3–062]*

Also, where a sub-contractor to run a breakdown recovery service for the police was refused a vetting clearance without reasons.[259a]

[259a] *R. (on the application of A) v Chief Constable of B* [2012] EWHC 2141; [2012] A.C.D. 125.

Employment situations

3–063 *[Add to end of n.262]*

Tucker was distinguished in *R. (on the application of Woods) v Chief Constable of Merseyside Police* [2014] EWHC 2784 (Admin); [2015] 1 W.L.R. 539, where the decision to subject a police officer to a "service confidence procedure" was held to have a sufficient public law element to be amenable to judicial review and was not merely a deployment or operational decision.

AMENABILITY AND THE HUMAN RIGHTS ACT

"Functions of a public nature" under the HRA

The YL decision in the House of Lords

[Add to end of n.319]   3–078

A. Williams, "A Fresh Perspective on Hybrid Public Authorities under the Human Rights Act 1998: Private Contractors, Rights-stripping and 'Chameleonic' Horizontal Effect" [2011] P.L. 139.

[Add new paragraph at end of 3–079]   3–079

Section 145 afforded protection to those whose care was arranged under the National Assistance Act 1948 but not those whose care was arranged outside the 1948 Act—for example, those who receive care in a home but pay for it themselves and those who receive care at home by an independent provider. This loophole was closed by s.73 of the Care Act 2014.[324a]

[324a] Section 73 reads:

"Human Rights Act 1998: provision of regulated care or support etc a public function

(1) This section applies where—
    (a) in England, a registered care provider provides care and support to an adult or support to a carer, in the course of providing—
        (i) personal care in a place where the adult receiving the personal care is living when the personal care is provided, or
        (ii) residential accommodation together with nursing or personal care;
    (b) in Wales, a person registered under Part 2 of the Care Standards Act 2000 provides care and support to an adult, or support to a carer, in the course of providing—
        (i) personal care in a place where the adult receiving the personal care is living when the personal care is provided, or
        (ii) residential accommodation together with nursing or personal care;

(c) in Scotland, a person provides advice, guidance or assistance to an adult or support to a carer, in the course of providing a care service which is registered under section 59 of the Public Services Reform (Scotland) Act 2010 and which consists of the provision of—

    (i) personal care in a place where the adult receiving the personal care is living when the personal care is provided, or

    (ii) residential accommodation together with nursing or personal care;

(d) in Northern Ireland, a person registered under Part 3 of the Health and Personal Social Services (Quality, Improvement and Regulation) (Northern Ireland) Order 2003 provides advice, guidance or assistance to an adult or services to a carer, in the course of providing—

    (i) personal care in a place where the adult receiving the personal care is living when the personal care is provided, or

    (ii) residential accommodation together with nursing or personal care.

In this section "the care or support" means the care and support, support, advice, guidance, assistance or services provided as mentioned above, and "the provider" means the person who provides the care or support.

(2) The provider is to be taken for the purposes of section 6(3)(b) of the Human Rights Act 1998 (acts of public authorities) to be exercising a function of a public nature in providing the care or support, if the requirements of subsection (3) are met.

(3) The requirements are that—

(a) the care or support is arranged by an authority listed in column 1 of the Table below, or paid for (directly or indirectly, and in whole or in part) by such an authority, and

(b) the authority arranges or pays for the care or support under a provision listed in the corresponding entry in column 2 of the Table."

Overview of the case law

3–080 *[Add to end of n.335]*

See also *R. (on the application of Bevan & Clarke LLP) v Neath Port Talbot CBC* [2012] EWHC 236 (Admin); [2012] B.L.G.R. 728 (private sector operators of care homes applied for judicial review of local authority's decision to award a 5.7 per cent increase in the rate to be paid to them. The decision was amenable to judicial review. The mere fact that it concerned the setting of a fee under a contract did not characterise it as a private act. The application failed on other grounds).

Judicial review of public functions exercised outside the United Kingdom

[Add to end of n.420]   3–092

Though note *R. (on the application of Barclay) v Lord Chancellor and Secretary of State for Justice (No. 2) (Attorney General and another intervening)* [2014] UKSC 54; [2015] A.C. 276 in which the Supreme Court, although confirming its earlier conclusion that the UK courts *could* review the making of an Order in Council giving assent to legislation made by the Bailiwick of Guernsey, nevertheless considered that they should decline to do so in the circumstances before it. *Per* Baroness Hale at [37]: "For the courts of England and Wales to entertain challenges to the compatibility of Island legislation with the Convention rights would clearly be to subvert the scheme of the Islands' own human rights legislation. It would also be to subvert the method by which the United Kingdom extended the European Convention to the Channel Islands. This was not by extending the 1998 Act to them: amendments to that effect were resisted in the United Kingdom Parliament. It was by extending the scope of the Convention in international law by a declaration under article 56, and leaving it to the Islands to legislate to incorporate the rights contained in the Convention into Island law. They happened to adopt the same model as the 1998 Act but they did not have to do so. It would be inconsistent with that scheme for the definition of 'primary legislation' in the 1998 Act to cover any form of primary Island legislation as defined in the Human Rights (Bailiwick of Guernsey) Law 2000."

TERRITORIAL REACH OF JUDICIAL REVIEW AND THE HRA

Territorial jurisdiction and the HRA

[Delete text in n.427 from "For UK case law, see: Smith and others v Ministry   3–094
of Defence [2012] EWCA Civ 1365; [2013] 2 W.L.R. 27 ..." and
substitute]

For UK case law, see *Smith v Ministry of Defence* [2013] UKSC 41; [2014] A.C. 52 (in civil claims brought by families of British soldiers killed in Iraq, arguing that they had not been provided with adequate protective equipment, the Supreme Court, following the decision of the Grand Chamber in *Al-Skeini v United Kingdom* (above) held, reversing the decision of the Court of Appeal [2012] EWCA Civ 1365; [2013] 2 W.L.R. 27, that the United Kingdom's jurisdiction under art.1 of the ECHR extended to securing the protection of art.2 to members of the armed forces when serving outside its territory. The statement in *Al-Skeini* that "whenever the state through its agents exercises control and authority over an individual, and thus jurisdiction" stated the circumstances in which the state could be held to exercise jurisdiction extraterritorially. The state was under an obligation under art.1 to secure to the individuals over whom it had such authority and control the rights and freedoms under art.1 of the Convention relevant to their situation. The previous decision of the Supreme Court in *R. (on the application of Smith) v Oxfordshire Assistant Deputy Coroner* [2010] UKSC 29; [2011] 1 A.C. 1 that, unless they were on a UK military base, British troops on active service overseas were not within Convention jurisdiction was not followed). In *R. (on the application of Sandiford) v Secretary of State for Foreign and Commonwealth Affairs* [2014] UKSC 44; [2014] 1 W.L.R. 2697, S, who was facing the death penalty in Indonesia following her conviction for drug trafficking, was not within the jurisdiction of the United Kingdom for the purposes of ECHR art.1 and so no part of ECHR art.6 could impose an obligation on the United Kingdom to provide funding for legal representation in an application to the Indonesian Supreme Court to re-open her case or an application to the President for clemency in order to avoid execution.

PUBLIC LAW ARGUMENTS IN CIVIL CLAIMS, TRIBUNALS AND CRIMINAL PROCEEDINGS

Procedural exclusivity

The justification for procedural exclusivity under RSC, Ord.53

3–104 *[Add to end of n.455]*

R. (on the application of NE) v Birmingham Magistrates' Court [2015] EWHC 688 (Admin); [2015] 1 W.L.R. 4771 (court was disadvantaged on a judicial review application in comparison with an appeal by way of case stated as it did not have a complete note of the evidence before the magistrate; noting that the similar case of *R. (on the application of Hamill) v Chelmsford Magistrates' Court* [2014] EWHC 2799 (Admin); [2015] 1 W.L.R. 1798 had proceeded by way of judicial review without comment, it would not have been appropriate to deprive the claimants of a remedy).

CHAPTER 4

CONCEPTS OF JURISDICTION AND LAWFUL ADMINISTRATION

STATUTORY RESTRICTION OF JUDICIAL REVIEW

[Add to para.4–016 after ". . . or to a provision that conferred exclusive juris- 4–016
diction on the Investigatory Powers Tribunal.⁴⁰"]

By comparison, a provision that, in given circumstances, conferred jurisdiction over exclusion and naturalisation decisions on the Special Immigration Appeals Commission rather than the High Court, did not enable the Secretary of State to stay existing judicial review proceedings challenging such decisions and transfer them to SIAC. The statutory provisions were too general to confer such a power on the Secretary of State. Specific and express language was expected.[40a]

[40a] See *R. (on the application of Ignaoua) v Secretary of State for the Home Department* [2013] EWCA Civ 1498; [2014] 1 W.L.R. 651, reversing [2013] EWHC 2512 (Admin); [2014] A.C.D. 37 on the interpretation of the Justice and Security Act 2013 s.15, which reads:
"(1) Subsection (2) applies in relation to any direction about the exclusion of a non-EEA national from the United Kingdom which—
　(a) is made by the Secretary of State wholly or partly on the ground that the exclusion from the United Kingdom of the non-EEA national is conducive to the public good,
　(b) is not subject to a right of appeal, and
　(c) is certified by the Secretary of State as a direction that was made wholly or partly in reliance on information which, in the opinion of the Secretary of State, should not be made public—
　　(i) in the interests of national security,
　　(ii) in the interests of the relationship between the United Kingdom and another country, or
　　(iii) otherwise in the public interest.
(2) The non-EEA national to whom the direction relates may apply to the Special Immigration Appeals Commission to set aside the direction.
(3) In determining whether the direction should be set aside, the Commission must apply the principles which would be applied in judicial review proceedings."

The judicial review proceedings were, however, subsequently stayed by the Divisional Court itself and transferred to SIAC: *R. (on the application of Ignaoua) v Secretary of State for the Home Department* [2014] EWHC 1382 (Admin).

Time-limited clauses

4–025 *[Add new n.77a after ". . . in any legal proceedings whatsoever"]*

[77a] New time limits for bringing a judicial review in certain planning cases (six weeks) and in certain procurement cases (30 days) were given effect on July 1, 2013 by an amendment to the Civil Procedure Rules: see Civil Procedure (Amendment No.4) Rules 2013 (SI 2013/1412):

"Amendments to the Civil Procedure Rules 1998
4. In Part 54—

(a) in rule 54.5—
(i) before paragraph (1), insert—

'(A1) In this rule—
'the planning acts' has the same meaning as in section 336 of the Town and Country Planning Act 1990(1);
'decision governed by the Public Contracts Regulations 2006(2)' means any decision the legality of which is or may be affected by a duty owed to an economic operator by virtue of regulation 47A of those Regulations (and for this purpose it does not matter that the claimant is not an economic operator); and
'economic operator' has the same meaning as in regulation 4 of the Public Contracts Regulations 2006.';

(ii) in paragraph (2), for 'limit' substitute 'limits'; and
(iii) after paragraph (3), insert—

'(4) Paragraph (1) does not apply in the cases specified in paragraphs (5) and (6).
(5) Where the application for judicial review relates to a decision made by the Secretary of State or local planning authority under the planning acts, the claim form must be filed not later than six weeks after the grounds to make the claim first arose.
(6) Where the application for judicial review relates to a decision governed by the Public Contracts Regulations 2006, the claim form must be filed within the time within which an economic operator would have been required by regulation 47D(2) of those Regulations (and disregarding the rest of that regulation) to start any proceedings under those Regulations in respect of that decision.'"

THE ANISMINIC CASE

Criminal proceedings

[Add new n.111a after ". . . subject now to the Criminal Justice Act 2003 **4–038**
Pt 10"]

[111a] For the position in Scotland, see the Double Jeopardy (Scotland) Act
2011.

Review of courts and tribunals

[Add to end of para.4–040]   **4–040**

The second-tier appeals test places the emphasis on important points of law
or principle or other compelling reasons.[127a]

[127a] On the application of the second-tier appeals test, see *PR (Sri Lanka) v
Secretary of State for the Home Department* [2011] EWCA Civ 988; [2012]
1 W.L.R. 73 (the "other compelling reasons" test was to be an exceptional
remedy; "compelling" meant legally compelling, rather than politically or
emotionally though extreme consequences might exceptionally add weight
to the legal arguments); *JD (Congo) v Secretary of State for the Home
Department* [2012] EWCA Civ 327; [2012] 1 W.L.R. 3273 (the fact that an
appellant had succeeded in the First-tier Tribunal (FTT) but failed in the
Upper Tribunal (UT) or that the FTT's decision had been set aside and
remade by the UT could be a relevant factor in applying the "other compelling reason" test; further, approving *PR*, in the absence of a strongly arguable
error of law on the part of the UT, extreme consequences could not of
themselves amount to a free-standing "compelling reason"); *R. (on the
application of HS) v Upper Tribunal (Immigration and Asylum Chamber)*
[2012] EWHC 3126; [2013] Imm. A.R. 579 (the second-tier appeals criteria
were to be satisfied at the permission stage; it was not sufficient to establish
that they would be satisfied at the substantive hearing; if permission was
granted on that basis, the test was spent and the Court of Appeal had to
apply the established grounds for judicial review in determining whether the
decision of the UT to refuse permission to appeal should be set aside); cf. *A
v Secretary of State for the Home Department* [2013] EWHC 1272 (Admin)
(applicants wrongly treated as non-EU nationals and made subject to deportation orders; multiple failures by the FTT and the UT amounted to a
"compelling reason").

JURISDICTION AND VIRES TODAY

Precedent fact

4–052 *[Add to end of para.4–052]*

However, a mistaken but reasonable belief that a person was over 18 did not render detention pending removal from the United Kingdom in breach of the Home Secretary's statutory duty regarding the welfare of children unlawful.[176a]

[176a] *R. (AA (Afghanistan)) v Secretary of State for the Home Department* [2013] UKSC 49; [2013] 1 W.L.R. 2224 (Borders, Citizenship and Immigration Act 2009 s.55, required the Home Secretary to make arrangements for ensuring that her immigration functions were discharged having regard to the need to safeguard and promote the welfare of children; an initial local authority age assessment had concluded that the person was over 19 years of age on which basis the Home Secretary refused an asylum claim and made a detention order; a subsequent local authority age assessment concluded that the person was 17 and the Home Secretary conceded that, had she known this, she would not have made the order).

FROM "VOID AND VOIDABLE" TO "LAWFUL AND UNLAWFUL"

The situation today

Presumption of validity

4–059 *[Correction to n.190]*

Delete "Smith v East Elloe RDC [1986] A.C. 736" and replace with "Smith v East Elloe RDC [1956] A.C. 736"

[Add to end of n.190]

See also D. Feldman, "Error of Law and Flawed Administrative Acts" [2014] C.L.J. 273, where it is argued that seven principles operate alongside the proposition that all legal flaws make a decision void as a matter of law and "can mitigate its potential to operate in anti-social ways in some circumstances".

Residual categories

4–061 *[Add new n.200a after "The Prevention of Terrorism Act 2005"]*

[200a] Repealed by the Terrorism Prevention and Investigation Measures Act 2011, which replaced "control orders" with "Terrorism Prevention and Investigation Measures" (TPIMs).

The Effect of a Judgment that a Decision is Unlawful

[Add to end of n.202]   4–062

See also R. *(Mohammed (Shapoor)) v Secretary of State for the Home Department* [014] EWHC 4317 (Admin); [2015] 1 W.L.R. 3349, in which it was held that the Home Secretary could not have "reasonable grounds for suspecting" that the claimant could be removed from the United Kingdom, where those grounds were based on a mistake of law.

Part II
GROUNDS OF JUDICIAL REVIEW

CHAPTER 5

ILLEGALITY

DISCRETIONARY POWER: A BRIEF HISTORY OF JUDICIAL ATTITUDES

Change of approach

[Add to para. 5–018 after ". . . that included a substantial subjective element"] 5–018

The *Padfield* principle also applies to a failure to exercise a power.[44a]

[44a] In *M v Scottish Ministers* [2012] UKSC 58; [2012] 1 W.L.R. 3386 the Mental Health (Care and Treatment) (Scotland) Act 2003 enabled patients compulsorily detained in hospital to apply to a mental health tribunal for a declaration that they were being held in conditions of excessive security. The provisions applied, inter alia, to "qualifying patients" in "qualifying hospitals", to be defined in ministerial regulations. The Act provided that the provisions were to come into force no later than May 1, 2006 but no regulations were ever made. In an application for judicial review, the Scottish Ministers argued a distinction between a statute coming into force and a statute coming into operation and that the failure to make regulations had not defeated the intention of the Scottish Parliament in defining the date when the statute should come into force. The Lord Ordinary refused the petition and the Inner House of the Court of Session refused the petitioner's reclaiming motion. But the Supreme Court allowed the petitioner's appeal— in the judgment of the court, Lord Reed held at [42]–[43], [47]:

"It has long been a basic principle of administrative law that a discretionary power must not be used to frustrate the object of the Act which conferred it . . . it follows that, although the Ministers had a discretion as to the manner in which they exercised their power to make the necessary regulations, they were under a duty to exercise that power no later than 1 May 2006 . . . although (the relevant sections) are technically in force, they have no more practical effect today than they had . . . when the 2003 Act received the Royal Assent. The Ministers' failure to make the necessary regulations has thus thwarted the intention of the Scottish Parliament . . . The importance of *Padfield's case* [1968] AC 997 was its reassertion that, even where a statute confers a discretionary power, a failure to exercise the power will be unlawful if it is contrary to Parliament's intention. That intention may be to create legal rights which can only be made effective if the power is exercised . . . It may however be to bring about some other result which is similarly dependent upon the exercise of the power . . . In the present case, the exercise of the power to make regulations by 1 May 2006 was necessary in order to bring (the relevant part) of the 2003 Act into effective operation by that date, as the Scottish Parliament intended. The Ministers were therefore under an obligation to exercise the power by that date."

Cf. *R. (on the application of Great Yarmouth Port Co. Ltd) v Marine Management Organisation* [2014] EWHC 833 (a discretionary power to make a harbour revision order if certain preconditions were met did not compel the making of such an order once the preconditions were met. There remained a residual discretion to refuse to make an order).

STATUTORY INTERPRETATION

5–020 *[Add after "residing in or resorting to the area[52]"]*

and "ordinary residence".[52a]

[52a] In *R. (on the application of Cornwall Council) v Secretary of State for Health* [2015] UKSC 46; [2015] 3 W.L.R. 213, the Supreme Court was required to determine the meaning of "ordinary residence" in s.24 of the National Assistance Act 1948, for the purpose of ascertaining which local authority had responsibility for a severely incapacitated adult, the majority coming to a conclusion that no party had contended for at any stage of the proceedings. Lord Carnwath held that in construing the relevant words, "context is critical" and drew a distinction between a provision the purpose of which is purely "administrative and fiscal" (allocating responsibility between local authorities) and a context where the provision was directed to a person's entitlement to a benefit (at [57]). Dissenting, Lord Wilson emphasised that "in deploying a phrase, Parliament understands the meaning which the courts have ascribed to it . . . No doubt Parliament understands that in the future the courts may refine and develop their interpretation of a phrase. Subject to that however, Parliament in 1948 intended that the courts should construe the phrase in s.24(1) by reference to its established meaning" (at [67]).

[Add to para.5–020 after ". . . has also been construed in various contexts.[53]"]

The Supreme Court was called upon to determine the meaning of "stateless" in the British Nationality Act 1981.[53a]

[53a] *Al-Jedda v Secretary of State for the Home Department* [2013] UKSC 62; [2014] A.C. 253 (under s.40(2) of the British Nationality Act 1981, the

Secretary of State may not make an order depriving a person of citizenship if "satisfied that the order would make a person stateless". It was not open to the Secretary of State to argue that the cause of statelessness was a failure on the part of the applicant to apply for restoration of Iraqi nationality rather than the making of the order).

[Add to end of para.5–020]

Where wording of a statute is equivocal, the phrase is to be given a purposive construction.[56a]

Where the Secretary of State appointed a trust special administrator to a failing NHS trust pursuant to the statutory regime contained in Ch.5A of the National Health Service Act 2006, the words "action . . . in relation to the trust" meant the trust special administrator could make recommendations only in relation to that specific NHS trust and the Secretary of State accordingly acted unlawfully in accepting recommendations relating to a neighbouring NHS trust.[56b] The Supreme Court has held (by a majority) that the phrase "a map drawn to the prescribed scale" in relation to an application for modification orders in respect of a local authority's definitive map and statement of vehicular rights of way under the Wildlife and Countryside Act 1981, s.53(5) was not confined to the restrictive meaning of "originally drawn" but should be given a meaning that embraced later map production techniques synonymous with "produced" or "reproduced".[56c]

[56a] See e.g., *R. (on the application of J) v Worcestershire County Council (Equality and Human Rights Commission intervening)* [2014] EWCA Civ 1518; [2015] 1 W.L.R. 2825 (Children Act 1989, s.17(1) was to promote the welfare and best interests of children in need; since it was not expressly limited as to where the services could be provided, a local authority had the power (but no duty) to provide services to a child who had been in its area at the time of assessment but who had subsequently moved).

[56b] *R. (on the application of Lewisham LBC) v Secretary of State for Health; R. (on the application of Save Lewisham Hospital Campaign Ltd) v Secretary of State for Health* [2013] EWCA Civ 1409; [2014] 1 W.L.R. 514.

[56c] *R. (on the application of Trail Riders Fellowship) v Dorset County Council (Plumbe intervening)* [2015] UKSC 18; [2015] 1 W.L.R. 1406.

[Add to end of first paragraph]   5–021

Where a Henry VIII clause seeks to empower a Minister to amend primary legislation by use of delegated legislation, a purported exercise of that power that is within the literal meaning of the general words may nevertheless be outside Parliament's contemplation and the court will resolve any doubt about its scope by a restrictive reading of the clause.[60a]

[60a] R. *(Public Law Project) v Lord Chancellor (Office of the Children's Commissioner intervening)* [2016] UKSC 39; [2016] 3 W.L.R. 387.

Non-statutory sources of power and the Ram doctrine

5–027 *[Delete all text in n.86 and substitute]*

See House of Lords Constitution Committee, *The pre-emption of Parliament*, 13th Report of 2012–2013, HL Paper 165. The Committee found no widespread or egregious use of pre-emption but made the following recommendations:

(i) All instances of pre-emption must be governed by certain fundamental constitutional principles, including the rule of law and effective parliamentary scrutiny.

(ii) The Treasury plays an important role in policing this area within Government. However, the Treasury's practices carry no constitutional force, and should not be described so as to suggest otherwise. In particular, its practice of authorising certain expenditure once a bill has been given a second reading in the House of Commons is not a constitutional convention and has not been endorsed by Parliament.

(iii) As there is no standard procedure at present, the Government must do more to inform Parliament of their pre-emptive activities. Written statements should be made to Parliament in a timely manner, setting out details of each instance of pre-emption and justifying it; and a statement should be made at the end of each session giving an annual summary of pre-emptive activities.

(iv) Similarly, a written ministerial statement should be made at the end of each session on the number of ministerial directions issued in the session.

(v) Where pre-emption occurs, the Government must always state clearly the power under which they consider themselves authorised to act.

(vi) The principles and practices governing pre-emption should be consolidated into a single, authoritative restatement for inclusion in the Cabinet Manual.

(vii) The common law powers of the Crown are restrained by public law and constitutional principle. This should be made clear in all Government publications mentioning these powers.

(viii) The so-called "Ram doctrine", which has been invoked to support pre-emption, is misleading and inaccurate, and should no longer be used.

(ix) Pre-emption of Parliament should not be undertaken when it would threaten the principle of effective parliamentary scrutiny. The Government's response in October 2013 accepted "that the advice in the Ram opinion is necessarily incomplete because it predates important developments in public law, as well as the Human Rights Act. Nor can it have the force of law. But the Government believes that principle described in the Ram opinion does remain valid. That is, the Crown does have common law powers which may be exercised subject to overarching legal constraints" (see *http://www.parliament. uk/documents/lords-committees/constitution/GovernmentResponse/ Government%20response%20-%20report%20on%20pre-emption% 20of%20parliament.pdf*).

The discovery of Parliament's intent and use of Hansard

[Delete text in n.101 from "At the time of writing . . ." and substitute] 5–032

For Parliament's response to the European Court of Human Right's judgment, see para.1–053 above.

Overarching statutory duties

[Add to end of n.120] 5–039

The main question in relation to the PSED is not whether the outcome is justifiable, but whether, in the process leading to the making of the decision, the decision-maker had "due regard" to the relevant considerations. For a summary of the case law on the correct approach, see *R. (on the application of Bracking) v Secretary of State for Work and Pensions* [2013] EWCA Civ 1345; [2014] Eq. L.R. 60 at [25] (McCombe L.J.) and see para.5–072 below.

Interpretation in relation to constitutional principles and constitutional rights

[Add to end of n.124] 5–040

In *Osborn v Parole Board* [2013] UKSC 61; [2014] A.C. 1115 at [57], Lord Reed stated: "The importance of the [Human Rights] Act is unquestionable. It does not however supersede the protection of human rights under the common law or statute, or create a discrete body of law based on the judgments of the European Court. Human rights continue to be protected by our domestic law, interpreted and developed in accordance with the Act when appropriate." See also para.1–117 above.

[Add to end of n.130]

In *R. (on the application of Richards) v Teeside Magistrates' Court* [2015] EWCA Civ 7; [2015] 1 W.L.R. 1695, the Court of Appeal upheld a requirement in a sexual offences prevention order (SOPO) that the claimant wear an electronic tag, considering that the order had been "imposed pursuant to a specific power" in the Sexual Offences Act 2003 and moreover that there was a "necessary implication" that many standard prohibitions in SOPOs would interfere with fundamental rights of the person subject to them.

[Add to end of n.137]

See also *Pham v Secretary of State for the Home Department (Open Society Justice Initiative intervening)* [2015] UKSC 19; [2015] 1 W.L.R. 1591, [119] (Lord Reed J.S.C.: ". . . where Parliament authorises significant interferences with important legal rights, the courts may interpret the legislation as requiring that any such interference should be no greater than is objectively established to be necessary to achieve the legitimate aim of the interference: in substance, a requirement of proportionality".)

5–041A *[Add new para.5–041A after para.5–041]*

A vivid case study of how emphasising different constitutional principles can lead to different outcomes is provided by the UK Supreme Court in *R. (on the application of Evans) v Attorney General (Campaign for Freedom of Information intervening)*.[121a] The Court had to consider the circumstances in which it was lawful for the Attorney General to issue a certificate under s.53(3) of the Freedom of Information Act 2000 that he had "reasonable grounds" for forming the opinion that there had been no breach of the Act, effectively overriding the judgment of the Upper Tribunal (part of the judiciary under the s.3(5) of the Constitutional Reform Act 2005). The background to the litigation was a request under the 2000 Act by a journalist for copies to the so-called "black spider" letters written to ministers by the Prince of Wales on matters of public policy. Lord Neuberger of Abbotsbury P.S.C. (with whom Lord Kerr of Tonaghmore and Lord Reid JJ.S.C. agreed) suggested that a statutory provision that entitled a member of the executive "to overrule a decision of the judiciary merely because he does not agree with it would be unique in the laws of the United Kingdom" and would "cut across two constitutional principles which are also fundamental components of the rule of law" (at [51]) – the basic principle that a decision of a court is binding as between the parties and cannot be ignored and that decisions of the executive are reviewable by the court (at [52]). It was not "crystal clear" to Lord Neuberger that Parliament intended these fundamental constitutional principles to be disapplied (at [90]). Against this constitutional background, the expression "reasonable grounds" did not permit the Attorney General to issue a certificate "simply because, on the same facts and admittedly reasonably, he takes a different view from that adopted by" the Upper Tribunal "after a full public hearing" (at [88]). The ambit of s.53(3) was confined to issues that were not before the Tribunal (at [89]). Dissenting, Lord Wilson J.S.C. was critical of the Court of Appeal – and Lord Neuberger – for "rewriting" s.53(3): "It invoked precious constitutional principles but among the most precious is that of parliamentary sovereignty, emblematic of our democracy" (at [169]). Lord Wilson agreed that a power of the executive to override decisions on issues of law "would have been an unlawful encroachment on the principle of separation of powers" but "issues relating to the *evaluation of the public interest* is entirely different" (at [171]). Agreeing in large part with Lord Wilson J.S.C., Lord Hughes J.S.C. said "The rule of law is of the first importance. But it is an integral part of the rule of law that courts give effect to Parliamentary intention" (at [154]) and concluded that Parliament had "plainly shown" an intention to empower a member of the executive to override a decision of a court on where the balance in the public interest lay.

[121a] [2015] UKSC 21; [2015] 2 W.L.R. 813. The judgments of Lord Mance J.S.C. (with which Baroness Hale of Richmond DPSC agreed) did not expressly emphasise constitutional principles. See further M. Elliott, "A tangled constitutional web: the black-spider memos and the British constitution's relational architecture" [2015] P.L. 539.

[Add to end of n.141]   5–042

R. (on the application of the Public Law Project) v Lord Chancellor [2016] UKSC 39; [2016] 3 W.L.R. 387 (an amendment by secondary legislation to the Legal Aid, Sentencing and Punishment of Offenders Act 2012 introducing a residence test for eligibility to legal aid was ultra vires. The power to make delegated legislation had to be construed in the context of the statutory policy and aims. The primary objective of the Act was based on funding those with a priority need. The residence test was focussed entirely on reducing cost).

[Add to n.144 before "See also ECHR art.6 . . ."]

But see *Guardian News and Media Ltd v AB*, Court of Appeal (Criminal Division), June 12, 2014; *The Times*, June 18, 2014, where Gross L.J. stated at [2]: "Open justice is both a fundamental principle of the common law and a means of ensuring public confidence in our legal system: exceptions are rare and must be justified on the facts. Any such exceptions must be necessary and proportionate. No more than the minimum departure from open justice will be countenanced." However, open justice must give way to "the yet more fundamental principle that the paramount object of the Court is to *do* justice" (at [5]). This case was "exceptional" and, as a matter of necessity, the *core* (emphasis supplied) of the trial must be heard *in camera*. See also paras 8–009 to 8–014.

[Add to text after n.155]

Note however the Supreme Court's denial of a common law right to vote in *Moohan v Lord Advocate (Advocate General for Scotland intervening).*[155a]

[155a] [2014] UKSC 67; [2015] A.C. 901

Interpretation and international law

Incorporated treaties

5–048 *[Add to end of n.177]*

And see *Pham v Secretary of State for the Home Department (Open Society Justice Initiative intervening)* [2015] UKSC 19; [2015] 1 W.L.R. 1591, [38] (Lord Mance J.S.C., "I would accept that the question arising under art.1(1) of the 1954 Convention [relating to the Status of Stateless Persons] in this case is not necessarily to be decided solely by reference to the text of the nationality legislation of the state in question, and that reference may also be made to the practice of the government, even if not subject to effective challenge in the courts").

Unincorporated treaties

5–049 *[Add to end of n.180]*

In *R. (on the application of SG) v Secretary of State for Work and Pensions (Child Poverty Action Group intervening)* [2015] UKSC 16; [2015] 1 W.L.R. 1449, Lord Kerr (dissenting at [254]–[257]) argued explicitly for "an exception to the dualist theory in human rights Conventions" and that he considered "that article 3.1 of the [United Nations Convention on the Rights of the Child] is directly enforceable in United Kingdom domestic law." See further para.3–019 above.

[Add to end of n.181]

In *R. (Yam) v Central Criminal Court* [2015] UKSC 76; [2016] A.C. 771, the Supreme Court rejected an argument that a court's discretionary common law power was constrained by the United Kingdom's international obligations, emphasising that while a domestic decision-maker exercising a general discretion may have regard to the United Kingdom's international obligations, he is not bound to do so.

MANDATORY AND DIRECTORY DUTIES AND POWERS

[Add to end of n.199] 5–057

R. v Stocker [2013] EWCA Crim 1993; [2014] 1 Cr. App. R. 18 (appeal against rape conviction on the basis that the defendant had been indicted under the wrong Act dismissed even though the Criminal Procedure Rules 2013 stated that the indictment "must" identify the legislation that created the offence. The clear purpose of the relevant rule was to ensure that an accused had sufficient information to know the case he had to meet. The error was a pure technicality that had caused no prejudice. It was not so fundamental as to render the proceedings a nullity and the draftsman would not have intended such an outcome for such a breach); *Aylesbury Vale DC v Call a Cab Ltd* [2013] EWHC 3765 (Admin); [2014] P.T.S.R. 523 (although the Local Government (Miscellaneous Provisions) Act 1976 s.45(3) clearly made it mandatory for a district council to give notice to each parish council of its intention to pass a resolution to bring the hackney carriage licensing provisions into force for the whole of its area, reading the statute as a whole and recognising the complete lack of prejudice to the defendants from non-compliance with the statutory requirements beyond the fact that non-compliance might give them an argument whereas validity would deprive them of it, if there was substantial compliance with the statutory provision, the act was not invalid).

[Add to end of n.210]

Cf. *R. v Stocker* [2013] EWCA Crim 1993; [2014] 1 Cr. App. R. 18.

Marginal failures by individuals to comply with requirements

[Add to end of n.240] 5–067

R. (on the application of Hafeez) v Secretary of State for the Home Department [2014] EWHC 1342 (Admin) (the fact that H's leave to remain in the United Kingdom expired in November 2011 and his university course finished in January 2012 was not a "near miss" justifying the grant of leave; the absence of a near-miss principle in such cases was well established).

Duties owed to the public generally

5–069 *[Add to end of n.248]*

Note however, *R. (on the application of West) v Rhondda Cynon Taff* CBC [2014] EWHC 2134 (Admin); [2015] A.C.D. 9, where a breach of duty was found when a local authority failed to give regard to its duties under s.17(1) and s.18 (provision of day care for children in need) of the 1989 Act; similar breaches were found in respect of the local authority's duties under s.118 of the School Standards and Framework Act 1998 (duty to secure nursery education) and s.22 of the Childcare Act 2006 (duty to secure sufficient childcare for working parents).

5–071A *[Add new para.5–071A after para.5–071]*

Making good unlawfulness

Where a public body has failed in the past to fulfil a statutory duty, the question may arise as to what if any duty it has to make things right. The Court of Appeal has held that "There is no general rule that, wherever it has acted unlawfully, a local authority must undo its past errors to the fullest extent that it can" – rather it was a matter of discretion depending all the circumstances, including countervailing considerations of public interest.[258a]

[258a] See *R. (on the application of GE (Eritrea)) v Secretary of State for the Home Department* [2014] EWCA Civ 1490; [2015] P.T.S.R. 854: GE, an asylum seeker, claimed to be 16½ years old but the local authority determined her to be an adult and consequently performed none of the duties that would have arisen under the Children Act 1989. A court subsequently held that GE had been a child at the relevant time. The issue before the CA was whether GE should be treated as a "former relevant child" with continuing rights to support. The majority held that it was not open to the court to "deem" accommodation to have been provided to GE so bringing her within the scope of the statutory definition.

Duties to "have regard to" the desirability of something

5–072 *[Add new n.260a after ". . . persons who do not share it"]*

[260a] For a summary of the correct approach to be taken to the public sector equality duty, see *R. (on the application of Bracking) v Secretary of State for Work and Pensions* [2013] EWCA Civ 1345; [2014] Eq. L.R. 60 at [25] (McCombe L.J.), followed in *R. (on the application of MA) v Secretary of State*

for Work and Pensions [2014] EWCA Civ 13; [2014] P.T.S.R. 584. In *R. (on the application of Cushnie) v Secretary of State for Health* [2014] EWHC 3626; [2015] P.T.S.R. 384 at [114] Singh J. drew an analogy between the PSED and "the well known principle of administrative law that a public authority must have regard to all relevant considerations. If it fails to do so, it will breach that duty and in principle that failure in its decision-making process will vitiate the resulting decision. The failure may be an 'innocent' one. Nevertheless, the fact that the decision-maker has not had regard to a relevant consideration is a breach of one of the most basic requirements of administrative law". In *R. (West Berkshire DC and another) v Secretary of State for Communities and Local Government* [2016] EWCA Civ 441; [2016] P.T.S.R. 982, the court accepted an an equality statement that "takes a relatively broad brush approach" and emphasised that "[t]he requirement to pay due regard to equally impact under s.149 is just that. It does not require a precise mathematical exercise to be carried out in relation to particular affected groups or, for example, urban areas as opposed to rural areas" (at [83]).

[Add to end of n.265]

In *R. (Logan) v Havering LBC* [2015] EWHC 3193 (Admin); [2016] P.T.S.R. 603, there was a lack of due regard: "There must be conscientious consideration of the impact of the proposals on relevant groups, whether by diligent reading of the EIA or some other evidence based assessment"; on the facts, there was "insufficient evidence to indicate that the decision-makers [each member of the full council] had accessed the EIA attached to the officers' report or had understood the importance of reading it in order to discharge their statutory obligation. It was not sufficient to assume that they could have done so and therefore would have done so" (at [53]).

[Add new para.5–073A after para.5–073] 5–073A

Obligations to "have regard to" may also be created by ministerial guidance: for example, the Secretary of State issued a circular to local authorities under the Local Authority Social Services Act 1970 s.7(1) in which it was said that "councils should have due regard to the actual costs of providing care and other local factors" in setting rates they would pay providers of residential accommodation and care for people for whom the local authorities were responsible. Duties such as this, in a circular or other non-statutory guidance, are not to be equated with statutory duties to "have regard to" and the courts will not "read across" to apply the detailed, structured approach to decision-making developed in relation to the statutory duties.[272a]

[272a] *R. (on the application of Members of the Committee of Care North East Northumberland) v Northumberland CC* [2013] EWCA Civ 1740; [2014] P.T.S.R. 758.

Discretionary power in the context of law enforcement

5-079 *[Add to end of n.295]*

(the DPP was required to promulgate an offence-specific policy identifying the facts and circumstances that he would take into account in deciding whether to consent to a prosecution under s.2(1) of the Suicide Act 1961). Cf. *Nicklinson v Ministry of Justice* [2014] UKSC 38; [2014] 3 W.L.R. 200 (the court should not involve itself with the terms of the DPP's policy; it was one thing for the court to decide that the DPP must publish a policy, but quite another for it to dictate what should be in that policy, reversing the Court of Appeal [2013] EWCA Civ 961; [2014] 2 All E.R. 32 on this point).

EXERCISE OF A DISCRETIONARY POWER FOR EXTRANEOUS PURPOSE

Bad faith and improper motive

5-084 *[Add to end of para.5–084]*

In a case concerning the refusal to accept advertisements from a Christian campaign group stating "Not gay! Ex-gay, post-gay and proud. Get over it!", the Court of Appeal held that there was uncertainty as to who had made the refusal decisions—Transport for London (the defendant) or the Mayor of London (not a party); the court ordered further inquiry by the Administrative Court to be conducted as to whether the decision was instructed by the Mayor and whether it was made for the improper purpose of advancing his election campaign.[324a]

[324a] *R. (Core Issues Trust) v Transport for London (Secretary of State for Culture, Media and Sport and Minister for Women and Equalities intervening)* [2014] EWCA Civ 34; [2014] P.T.S.R. 785.

Incidental powers

5-098 *[Add to para.5–098 after ". . . the discharge of those limited powers.[355]"]*

In *R. (on the application of the National Secular Society) v Bideford Town Council* a parish council's practice of saying prayers as part of the formal business of full meetings of the council was not authorised by s.111 of the 1972 Act.[355a]

[355a] [2012] EWHC 175 (Admin); [2012] 2 All E.R. 1175. See para.5–100 below

Unspecified purposes

[Add to end of para.5–103] 5–103

In R. *(on the application of Ben Hoare Bell Solicitors) v Lord Chancellor* a regulation introducing a "no permission, no fee" arrangement for making a legally aided judicial review application was held to be incompatible with the purposes of the enabling legislation, as it did not further the Act's purpose of incentivising legal aid providers to reflect on the merits of a case before applying for judicial review.[370a] In R. *(on the application of Rights of Women) v Lord Chancellor and Secretary of State for Justice,* a regulation provided that legal aid would only be available to victims of domestic violence where documentary evidence of domestic violence was available in the 24-month period before the application for legal aid. The Court of Appeal held that this regulation frustrated the purpose of the relevant provision of the Legal Aid, Sentencing and Punishment of Offenders Act 2012, which was to save money through withdrawal of civil legal services from certain categories of case, while continuing to provide civil legal services to the most deserving cases. The 24-month requirement rendered legal aid unavailable to many victims of domestic violence who were in need of it.[370b]

[370a] [2015] EWHC 523 (Admin); [2015] A.C.D. 93.

[370b] [2016] EWCA Civ 91, [2016] 1 W.L.R. 2543.

[Add to end of para.5–105] 5–105

In R. *(on the application of Gordon-Jones) v Secretary of State for Justice,* the High Court considered that the effect of a Prison Service Instruction in restricting prisoners' access to books in pursuance of an incentive scheme was to undercut the rehabilitative purpose of that scheme.[377a]

[377a] [2014] EWHC 3997 (Admin); [2015] A.C.D. 42.

[Add to end of para.5–106] 5–106

In another immigration case, the claimants were the wife and adult children of a person assessed by the Home Secretary to be an Islamist extremist. They sought naturalisation as British citizens and though they met the statutory requirements, the Home Secretary refused their application.[378a]

[378a] R. *(MM and others) v Secretary of State for the Home Department* [2015] EWHC 3513 (Admin); [2016] 1 W.L.R. 2858.

DECISIONS BASED UPON IRRELEVANT CONSIDERATIONS OR FAILURE TO TAKE ACCOUNT OF RELEVANT CONSIDERATIONS

5–122 *[Add to end of para.5–122]*

In some contexts, written statements of reasons for a decision may be "set out in brief form and their brevity does not indicate a failure to take account of any material considerations".[410a] Where the question is whether due regard was had to all material facts in making delegated legislation, the court may consider parliamentary material: there was no objection to referring to parliamentary debates in *Hansard* and select committee reports simply in relation to any relevant information contained in them, so long as there was no attempt to analyse or criticise anything contained in the material contrary to art.9 of the Bill of Rights 1689.[410b]

[410a] *R. (on the application of Evans) v Cornwall Council* [2013] EWHC 4109 (Admin); [2014] P.T.S.R. 556.

[410b] *R. (Hurley) v Secretary of State for Work and Pensions* (Equality and Human Rights Commission intervening) [2015] EWHC 3382 (Admin); [2016] P.T.S.R. 636 at [15]–[27], Collins J. noting that "I should not make my view prevail over the informed view of both Houses of Parliament as expressed in the democratic process".

Government policy as a relevant consideration

5–131 *[Add to end of n.450]*

In *R. (on the application of Winder) v Sandwell Metropolitan Borough Council (Equality and Human Rights Commission intervening)* [2014] EWHC 2617 (Admin); [2015] P.T.S.R. 34 the defendant council was considered to have acted unlawfully, when, in designing a council tax reduction scheme, it failed to take into account stated government policy objectives relating to the localisation of support for council tax.

Financial considerations and relevancy

Excessive expenditure

5–137 *[Add to end of para.5–137]*

In *Charles Terence Estates Ltd v Cornwall CC* a local authority raised its own alleged breach of fiduciary duty to its local taxpayers as a defence to an action in private law proceedings for recovery of rent due under lease agreements. The Court of Appeal held that there had been no breach of fiduciary duty but, in any case, such a breach would only render an act ultra vires and void and so provide a defence to a claim in private law if it went to legal capacity.[479a]

[479a] [2012] EWCA Civ 1439; [2013] 1 W.L.R. 466, reversing [2011] EWHC 2542 (QB); [2012] 1 P. & C.R. 2. If the decision of Cranston J. in the High Court was correct then, in the words of Maurice Kay L.J. in the Court of Appeal, Cornwall had succeeded "in ridding itself of what it considered to be bad bargains".

Limited resources

[Add to end of n.483]   5–138

Cf. *R. (on the application of Rose) v Thanet Clinical Commissioning Group* [2014] EWHC 1182 (Admin). A 25-year-old woman suffering from Crohn's disease was refused funding for oocyte cryopreservation before undergoing chemotherapy with the probable consequence of infertility and early onset of menopause. R was not considered by T to be clinically exceptional. Jay J., at [113], refused to accept that the policy was a blanket policy that permitted of no exceptions: "In the present case the wording of the exceptionality policy . . . cannot be regarded as potentially discriminatory; the issue is the more limited one of whether it could ever be fulfilled by someone in the claimant's position, and if not whether that matters." An argument based on ECHR arts 8, 12 and 14 also failed.

[Add to para.5–138 after n.485]

Similarly, in *R. (Kebede) v Newcastle City Council,* the Court of Appeal held that a local authority is not permitted to take into account restrictions on its own resources in decision-making under the Children Act 1989 s.23C(4)(b) to give assistance to relevant children "to the extent that his welfare and his educational needs require it".[485a]

[485a] [2013] EWCA Civ 960; [2014] P.T.S.R. 82.

DELEGATION OF POWERS

Delegation of "administrative powers"

[Add to n.546]   5–157

A scheme of delegation may lawfully provide for dual and concurrent delegation to both a regulatory board and officers – delegation need not be a simple hierarchical structure: see *R. (on the application of Couves) v Gravesham BC* [2015] EWHC 504 (Admin); [2015] J.P.L. 1193 (QBD (Admin).

[Add at end of paragraph after ". . . assurances or other conduct.[548]]

Where under s.37 of the Local Government Act 2000 a local authority has adopted and published a constitution detailing its executive arrangements, it acts unlawfully if it departs from the scheme of delegation.[548a]

[548a] See *R. (on the application of Bridgerow Ltd) v Cheshire West and Chester Borough Council* [2014] EWHC 1187 (Admin); [2015] P.T.S.R. 91 (power to determine renewal of licences had been sub-delegated to a panel "comprising" three members drawn from the licensing committee; "comprising" was prescriptive rather than permissive so the full licensing committee acted unlawfully when it purported to make the determination).

The Carltona principle

5–172 *[Add to end of n.592]*

Castle v Crown Prosecution Service [2014] EWHC 587 (Admin); (2014) 178 J.P. 285 (one of the questions posed in an appeal by way of case stated against a speeding conviction was whether an order imposing temporary and variable speed limits was ultra vires because it was signed and/or made by an employee of the Highways Agency (which was not part of the Minister's department); it was held that the *Carltona* principle allowed this delegation of power; the Agency was the alter ego of the Secretary of State in the areas for which he accepted responsibility in Parliament just as he did for the actions of civil servants housed under his departmental roof).

5–176 *[Add to end of n.609]*

Haw was applied by the Divisional Court in *R. (on the application of Hamill) v Chelmsford Justices* [2014] EWHC 2799 (Admin); [2015] 1 W.L.R. 1798, which held that the delegation of the Chief Constable's duty to determine a review under s.91C of the Sexual Offences Act 2003 could properly be delegated to an officer of superintendent rank or above.

[Add to end of para.5–176]

Moreover, the purpose for which a power is conferred may prevent delegation. In *R. (on the application of Bourgass) v Secretary of State for Justice*

(Howard League for Penal Reform intervening) it was held that the purpose of a power to review the continued segregation of prisoners was to act as a safeguard for prisoners; as this safeguard could only be meaningful if exercised by an official independent of the management of the prison, it was not possible to delegate the power from the Secretary of State to the prison governor.[612a]

[612a] [2015] UKSC 54; [2015] 3 W.L.R. 457.

[Add to end of para.5–177]   5–177

However, in *R. (on the application of Bourgass) v Secretary of State for Justice (Howard League for Penal Reform intervening)* the Supreme Court held that *Carltona* cannot apply to the holder of a statutory office who is himself constitutionally responsible for the manner in which he discharges his office and is thus constitutionally demarcated from the Secretary of State. As such the principle could not operate to permit the delegation of the power to segregate prisoners from the Secretary of State to a prison governor.[619a]

[619a] [2015] UKSC 54; [2015] 3 W.L.R. 457.

[Add to n.622 after "... (validity of council's Minutes of Delegation)]   5–178

; *Noon v Matthews* [2014] EWHC 4330 (Admin); [2015] A.C.D. 53; (validity of delegation of decision to bring a prosecution to enforce byelaws relating to a river).

CHAPTER 6

PROCEDURAL FAIRNESS: INTRODUCTION, HISTORY AND COMPARATIVE PERSPECTIVES

THE CONCEPT OF NATURAL JUSTICE

[Add new n.26a after "... as phrases which express the same idea"]   6–010

[26a] These expressions are not always regarded as helpful however. See, e.g., *Secretary of State for Communities and Local Government v Hopkins Developments* [2014] EWCA Civ 470 at [48] for concern about use of the expression "fair crack of the whip".

HISTORICAL DEVELOPMENT SINCE THE 1960s

The duty to act fairly

[Add to end of n.174]   6–047

; see also *R. (on the application of L) v West London Mental Health NHS Trust* [2014] EWCA Civ 47; (2014) 158(6) S.J.L.B. 37 at [68], [69] (Beatson L.J. expressing concern that the emphasis on flexibility could lead to an inappropriate drawing together of the concepts of procedural and substantive fairness and undue uncertainty). See also *Secretary of State for Communities and Local Government v Hopkins Developments* [2014] EWCA Civ 470 at [85] ("it does not generally matter whether what is at issue is characterised as 'natural justice' or 'procedural fairness'"). See also *R. (on the application of Moseley) v Haringey LBC* [2014] UKSC 56; [2014] 1 W.L.R. 3947 at [24]: "[f]airness is a protean concept, not susceptible of much generalised enlargement."

European influences

The ECHR

[Add to end of n.175]   6–048

See also *R. (on the application of TH (Bangladesh) v Secretary of State for the Home Department* [2016] EWCA Civ 815 at [22] (Beatson LJ observing that his "starting point is that the history of procedural fairness shows it to be the result of implying into broadly-phrased powers and procedures the requirements of procedural fairness reflected in the principles of natural justice and, since the enactment of the Human Rights Act 1998, the duty of the court where possible to construe such powers, if necessary by reading them down, as compatible with the Convention rights. It is in that context and in that sense that it can be said that procedural fairness is . . . a well-established principle ingrained in public administration".).

[Add to end of n.188]

Where other rights of the Convention are engaged, there may also be procedural requirements specific to the engagement of that particular right. For example, a discussion of the influence of ECHR art.5(4) on procedural requirements in the context of parole board hearings can be found in *Re. Reilly's Application for Judicial Review* [2013] UKSC 61; [2013] 3 W.L.R. 1020 at [54]–[63] (noting that Convention law permeates the domestic legal system and that domestic law is interpreted and developed in accordance with the Convention as appropriate).

The national security challenge

6–050 *[Add to end of n.194]*

The power may be necessarily implied into the statutory framework: *Bank Mellat v HM Treasury (No. 1)* [2013] UKSC 38; [2014] A.C. 700 at [37]–[43] (since s.40(2) of the 2005 Act provides that an appeal lies to the Supreme Court against "any" judgment of the Court of Appeal, that must extend to parts of a closed judgment as justice will not be able to be done in some cases if the appellate court cannot consider the closed material). For comment, see C. Sargeant, "Two Steps Backward, One Step Forward—the Cautionary Tale of Bank Mellat (No 1)" [2014] 3(1) C.J.I.C.L. 111.

[In para.6–050, delete "at present, it seems likely that Parliament will respond to this judgment by introducing a statutory basis for use of closed material procedures.[195]" and substitute]

the Justice and Security Act 2013 now extends the possibility of using a CMP to all civil proceedings.[195]

[In n.195, delete "Justice and Security Bill 2012–2013 and"]

CHAPTER 7

PROCEDURAL FAIRNESS: ENTITLEMENT AND CONTENT

SCOPE

[Add to end of n.4]   7–001

Where other rights of the Convention are engaged, there may also be procedural requirements specific to the engagement of that particular right. For example, a discussion of the influence of ECHR art.5(4) on procedural requirements in the context of parole board hearings can be found in *Re Reilly's Application for Judicial Review* [2013] UKSC 61; [2013] 3 W.L.R. 1020 at [54]–[63] (noting that Convention law permeates the domestic legal system and that domestic law is interpreted and developed in accordance with the Convention as appropriate). For a similar approach, see *Re P* [2015] EWCOP 59; and in the context of a fair hearing for a disabled person before an employment tribunal, see *Galo v Bombardier Aerospace UK* [2016] NICA 25.

ENTITLEMENT TO PROCEDURAL FAIRNESS: OVERVIEW

From "natural justice" to "the duty to act fairly"

[Add to n.17 after ". . . ("simple fairness");"]   7–003

Re Reilly's Application for Judicial Review [2013] UKSC 61; [2013] 3 W.L.R. 1020 at [2], [65]–[71] (reference to "the common law duty to act fairly"); *R. (on the application of L) v West London Mental Health NHS* [2014] EWCA Civ 47; (2014) 158(6) S.J.L.B. 37 at [67] ("the common-law principles of natural justice or fairness").

[Add to n.17 after ". . . [2008] B.L.G.R. 267 at [6]"]

; *Secretary of State for Communities and Local Government v Hopkins Developments* [2014] EWCA Civ 470 at [85] ("it does not generally matter whether what is at issue is characterised as 'natural justice' or 'procedural fairness'").

[Add to end of n.20]

See also *R. (on the application of LH) v Shropshire Council* [2014] EWCA Civ 404; [2014] P.T.S.R. 1052 at [28] ("the duty to consult will arise when a person has an interest which the law decides is one which is to be protected by procedural fairness").

[Add new n.22a after ". . . the costs of uncertainty"]

[22a] See, e.g. *R. (on the application of L) v West London Mental Health NHS Trust* [2014] EWCA Civ 47; (2014) 158(6) S.J.L.B. 37 at [68], [69] (Beatson L.J. expressing concern that the emphasis on flexibility could lead to an inappropriate drawing together of the concepts of procedural and substantive fairness and undue uncertainty).

[Add to end of n.23]

See also *R. (on the application of L) v West London Mental Health NHS Trust* [2014] EWCA Civ 47; (2014) 158(6) S.J.L.B. 37 (in which the Court of Appeal overturned the procedural requirements specified by the lower court for the decisions of managers of a medium security hospital contemplating referring a detainee to high security conditions as the requirements turned what was largely a clinical decision into an inappropriately adversarial process which went beyond what fairness required).

The recognition of a general duty of fairness

7–009 *[Add to n.49 after ". . . the arbiter of that is fair')"]*

; *Re Reilly's Application for Judicial Review* [2013] U.K.S.C. 61; [2013] 3 W.L.R. 1020 at [64] (the court's function is "not merely to review the reasonableness of the decision-makers judgment of what fairness required"); *R. (on the application of LH) v Shropshire Council* [2014] EWCA Civ 404 at [29] ("[f]airness is a matter for the Court not the Council to decide"); *R. (on the application of Flatley) v Hywel Dda University Local Health Board* [2014] EWHC 2258 (Admin) at [88] ("[i]t is a matter for the court to decide whether a fair procedure was followed").

STATUTORY REQUIREMENTS OF FAIR PROCEDURES

Express statutory requirements

7–011 *[Add to n.56 after ". . . [2006] 1 W.L.R. 3315"]*

; *R. (on the application of Flatley) v Hywel Dda University Local Health Board* [2014] EWHC 2258 (Admin) (limiting the extent of the duty of consultation to that provided for in Community Health Councils (Constitution, Membership and Procedures) (Wales) Regulations 2010 reg.27(7)).

Supplementing statutory procedures

[Add to n.57 after ". . . [2004] EWHC 1220"]   7–012

; *Uprichard v Scottish Ministers* [2013] UKSC 21; [2013] P.T.S.R. D37 at [47]; *Garlick v Secretary of State for Communities and Local Government* [2013] EWHC 1126 (Admin); *Farah v Hillingdon LBC* [2014] EWCA Civ 359; [2014] H.L.R. 24. In a different context, see *Nzolameso v Westminster City Council* [2015] UKSC 22; [2015] 2 All ER 942 (a decision on a temporary accommodation offer must clearly show that "proper" or "serious" consideration was given to the local authority's obligations under the statutory framework).

[Add to end of n.58]

See also *R. (on the application of Moseley) v Haringey LBC* [2014] UKSC 56; [2014] 1 W.L.R. 3947 at [25]; *R. (on the application of United Company Rusal plc) v London Metal Exchange* [2014] EWCA Civ 1271; [2015] 1 W.L.R. 1375.

[Add to n.59 after ". . . to ensure its fair and workable operation);"]   7–013

Bank Mellat v HM Treasury [2013] UKSC 39; [2014] A.C. 700 at [32] (unless the Act expressly or impliedly excluded any relevant duty of consultation, fairness required an opportunity to make representations before a direction was made);

[Add to para.7–013 after ". . . the courts have supplemented a statutory scheme.[59]"]

Indeed, recently, a majority of the Supreme Court expressed the following view:

> "The duty of fairness governing the exercise of a statutory power is a limitation on the discretion of the decision-maker which is implied into the statute. But the fact that the statute makes some provision for the procedure to be followed before or after the exercise of a statutory power does not of itself impliedly exclude either the duty of fairness in general or the duty of prior consultation in particular, where they would otherwise arise."[59a]

[59a] *Bank Mellat v HM Treasury* [2013] UKSC 39; [2014] A.C. 700 at [35].

[In n.60 delete "Bank Mellat v HM Treasury (No.2) [2011] EWCA Civ 1; [2012] Q.B. 101 at [135] (express statutory procedure, including laying instrument before Parliament and right of subsequent judicial review; Parliament had intentionally excluded a duty to hear representations);"]

[Add to end of n.63]

Secretary of State for Communities and Local Government v Hopkins Developments [2014] EWCA Civ 470 at [62] (observing that the Town and Country Planning Appeals (Determination by Inspectors) (Inquiries Procedure) (England) Rules 2000 were *"not a complete code for achieving procedural fairness"*); *R. (on the application of LH) v Shropshire Council* [2014] EWCA Civ 404.

[Add to para.7–013 after ". . . the attainment of fairness'.[63]"]

More recently, in *Bank Mellat v HM Treasury*, Lord Sumption observed that he found it hard to envisage cases in which the maximum expression unios exclusion alterius could suffice to exclude so basic a right as that of fairness.[63a]

[63a] [2013] UKSC 39; [2014] A.C. 700 at [35].

7–014 *[In n.66 delete "; Bank Mellat (No. 2) [2011] EWCA Civ 1; [2012] Q.B. 101 at [135]"]*

FAIRNESS NEEDED TO SAFEGUARD RIGHTS AND INTERESTS

7–018 *[Add to end of n.73]*

Re. Reilly's Application for Judicial Review [2013] U.K.S.C. 61; [2013] 3 W.L.R. 1020 at [54]–[62], [80]–[96] (noting that a parole board's common law duty to act fairly was influenced by the requirements of ECHR art.5(4) and outlining the circumstances in which oral hearings would be required).

[Add to n.74]

For the limits of the obligation of common law fairness, see *EK (Ivory Coast) v Secretary of State for the Home Department* [2014] EWCA Civ 1517 (the Secretary of State for the Home Department was not responsible for a college's administrative error in withdrawing a letter of confirmation of acceptance for studies before an application for leave to remain had been determined and where the Secretary of State saw that the letter had been withdrawn, the general public law duty of fairness had not obliged her to adjourn any decision to give the applicant notice of the problem and an opportunity to rectify it).

The scope of interests protected by fair procedures

[Add to para.7–023 after ". . . proposal to close a local public library?"]   7–023

[87a] Does a local authority, having consulted widely on the need to close a certain number of day care centres, owe a specific duty to then consult with users of individual centres?[87b]

[87a] See *R. (on the application of L) v Warwickshire County Council* [2015] EWHC 203 (Admin); [2015] B.L.G.R. 81 at [42] (government would not be possible if every decision-maker were required in every case to consult everyone who might be affected by his decision and a duty to consult was not imposed on a local authority before it made the political decision in a meeting of its full council to approve a budget which cuts funding to certain services supplied to vulnerable members of the community; this was an example of democratic power being properly, lawfully and constitutionally exercised).

[87b] *R. (on the application of LH) v Shropshire Council* [2014] EWCA Civ 404 (finding that a local authority had breached its common law duty in failing to consult with the users of a particular day care centre).

Resource allocation decisions

[Add to end of n.94]   7–024

; *Re Reilly's Application for Judicial Review* [2013] UKSC 61; [2013] 3 W.L.R. 1020. See also *R. (on the application of Foster) v Secretary of State for Justice* [2015] EWCA Civ 281.

[Add to end of para.7–024]

It has also been held that where a local authority decided to close a day care centre as a result of budgetary constraints, even though there was no express or implied statutory duty to consult, the obligation stemmed from the expectation that a public body, making decisions affecting the public, would act fairly.[96a]

[96a] *R. (on the application of LH) v Shropshire Council* [2014] EWCA Civ 404; [2014] P.T.S.R. 1052 at 21 (Longmore L.J. observing that "[i]f . . . a local authority withdraws a benefit previously afforded to the public, it will

usually be under an obligation to consult with the beneficiaries of that service before withdrawing it"; see also [26] (describing the closure as "undoubtedly a serious step")).

Legislative decisions

[Add to n.100 after ". . . of a statutory function")"]

; see also *R. (on the application of Moseley) v Haringey LBC* [2014] UKSC 56; [2014] 1 W.L.R. 3947, in which Lord Reed JSC referred at [35] to the fact that there is no "general common law duty to consult persons who may be affected by a measure before it is adopted" save where "there is a legitimate expectation of such consultation").

Legitimate expectations

7–030 *[Add to end of n.112]*

; see also *R. (on the application of Badger Trust) v Secretary of State for the Environment, Food and Rural Affairs* [2014] EWCA Civ 1405. See further the dictum of Lord Wilson JSC in *R. (on the application of Moseley) v Haringey LBC* [2014] UKSC 56; [2014] 1 W.L.R. 3947 at [23] on the duty of consultation: "[t]he search for the demands of fairness in this context is often illumined by the doctrine of legitimate expectation."). See also *R. (on the application of Plantagenet Alliance Ltd) v Secretary of State for Justice* [2014] EWHC 1662 (Admin) at [98] (where a public authority charged with a duty of making a decision promises to follow a certain procedure before reaching that decision, good administration requires that it should be bound by its undertaking as to procedure provided that this does not conflict with its statutory duty); *British Dental Association v General Dental Council* [2014] EWHC 4311 at [36] (Admin) (specific public announcements can give rise to a legitimate expectation that a consultation would be conducted); *R. (on the application of Telefonica Europe Plc) v Revenue and Customs Commissioners* [2016] UKUT 173 (TCC) (even where there is no legitimate expectation, a duty to consult may arise where an abrupt change of policy would be so unfair as to amount to an abuse of power).

FAIR PROCEDURES UNDER ECHR ART 6: THRESHOLD ISSUES

7–031 *[Add to end of n.115]*

; see also J. Varuhas, "The Reformation of English Administrative Law? Rights, Rhetoric and Reality" [2013] 72(2) C.L.J. 369.

[Add to end of n.123]   7–033

; *Perry v Nursing and Midwifery Council* [2013] EWCA Civ 145; [2013] 1 W.L.R. 3423 at [15]–[16] (assumed though not determined that ECHR art.6 rights were engaged by an interim investigation and suspension decision taken by the Nursing and Midwifery Council).

[Add to n.136 after ". . . 4 E.H.R.R. 1."]   7–034

; see also *McCarthy v Visitors to the Inns of Court* [2015] EWCA Civ 12 (a material non-disclosure of a witness statement in disciplinary proceedings against a barrister was procedurally unfair, and it was immaterial in this context whether the question was answered using the common law or ECHR art.6).

[Add to n.136 after ". . . Lloyd's Rept. Med. 250 at [33]–[35]"]

; *Perry v Nursing and Midwifery Council* [2013] EWCA Civ 145; [2013] 1 W.L.R. 3423;

[Add to end of n.136]

Christou v Haringey London Borough Council [2013] EWCA Civ 178.

[Correction to n.141]

For *Pomieschowski* read *Pomiechowski*.

[Add to end of n.145]

R. (on the application of Ali) v Secretary of State for Justice [2013] EWHC 72 (Admin); [2013] 1 W.L.R. 3536 at [66]–[72] (doubting if a statutory scheme for compensation for reversal of a conviction engaged ECHR art.6).

[Add to end of n.148]

; *R (YA) v Secretary of State for the Home Department* [2013] EWHC 3229 (Admin) at [103] ("not only is it the decision on the part of the administrative authority to refuse leave to an alien to enter but also the decision to impose conditions on an alien's leave to stay which does not involve a determination of civil rights and obligations"); *R. (on the application of Rahman) v Secretary of State for the Home Department* [2015] EWHC 1146 (Admin) at [32]. But see *R. (on the application of Gudanaviciene) v Director of Legal Aid Casework* [2014] EWCA Civ 1622; [2015] 1 W.L.R. 2247 at [181] (the Lord Chancellor's guidance on exceptional civil legal aid funding pursuant to s.10(3)(a) of the Legal Aid, Sentencing and Punishment of Offenders Act 2012 impermissibly stated that only in rare and extreme cases, and in no immigration cases, would a refusal of legal aid amount to a breach of ECHR art.6(1), and hence the guidance itself was incompatible with ECHR art.6(1) and ECHR art.8). See also *R. (on the application of S) v Director of legal Aid Casework* [2016] EWCA Civ 464; [2016] 3 Costs L.R. 569.

[Add to end of n.149]

; see also *BB v Secretary of State for the Home Department* [2015] EWCA Civ 9 (ECHR art.6 was not used in quashing a subsequent deportation decision in respect of the same appellant as in *RB*). See also *R. (on the application of Gudanaviciene) v Director of Legal Aid Casework* [2014] EWCA Civ 1622; [2015] 1 W.L.R. 2247.

[Add to end of n.151]

See also *Hargreaves v Revenue and Customs Commissioners* [2016] EWCA Civ 174; [2016] 1 W.L.R. 2981; *Walapu v Revenue and Customs Commissioners* [2016] EWHC 658 (Admin); [2016] S.T.C. 1682.

[Add to n.155 after ". . . [66]"]

; see also *Klausecker v Germany* (2015) 60 E.H.R.R. SE9; *Boyraz v Turkey* (2015) 60 E.H.R.R. 30.

[Add to n.156 after ". . . in the context of financial restrictions"]

(overturned though not on this ground in *Bank Mellat v HM Treasury* [2013] UKSC 39; [2014] A.C. 700). Lord Hope proceeded on the assumption (at [129]) that art.6 applies, albeit that this was not decided.

[Add to n.157 after ". . . interferes with his human rights")]

; see also *Bank Mellat v HM Treasury* [2013] UKSC 39; [2014] A.C. 700 at [157] per Lord Hope (dissenting) ("it is not disputed that the Bank's right to carry on its business was a civil right and that the effect of the direction was to greatly impede the exercise of that right").

7–035 *[Correction to n.160]*

For *Pomieschowski* read *Pomiechowski*.

FAIR PROCEDURES REQUIRED BY ECHR ART.2:
THRESHOLD ISSUES

[Add to end of n.168]   7–036

However, where a person detained had committed suicide while in hospital, the State was not required, in fulfilling its procedural obligation under art.2, to perform an immediate and independent investigation into the circumstances of the death prior to an inquest: *R. (on the application of Antoniu) v Central and North West London NHS Foundation Trust* [2013] EWHC 3055; [2014] A.C.D. 44.

[In para.7–036 delete "soldiers of the territorial army, provided they are within the United Kingdom's jurisdiction" and substitute]

those under the authority or control of the state and its agents, as well as those affected a state's agents when exercising authority and control on the state's behalf.

[In n.169 delete from "R (on the application of Smith . . ." and substitute]

Smith v Ministry of Defence [2013] UKSC 41; [2014] A.C. 52. In this case, the Supreme Court took the step of departing from its earlier decision in *R. (on the application of Smith) v Oxfordshire Assistant Deputy Coroner (Equality and Human Rights)* [2010] UKSC 29; [2011] 1 A.C. 1. In the earlier case, it had been held that unless they were on a UK military base, British troops on active service overseas were not within the jurisdiction of the United Kingdom. However, in light of the ruling in *Al-Skeini*, the State could be held to exercise jurisdiction extraterritorially wherever the State through its agents exercised control and authority over an individual. See also G. Junor, "A Soldier's (Human) Rights when Fighting Abroad: The Supreme Court Decides" [2013] 37 S.L.T. 251. The jurisdiction test in *Al-Skeini* has also been applied in *Jaloud v Netherlands* (2015) 60 E.H.R.R. 29 (see [154]).

[Add to end of n.170]

See also *Smith v Ministry of Defence* [2013] UKSC 41; [2014] A.C. 52 at [65], [75]–[76], [81] in which the Supreme Court held that the extent to which the application of the substantive obligation under art.2 could be held impossible or inappropriate would vary according to context and that procurement decisions, although remote from the battlefield, would not always be appropriate for review. The court had to avoid imposing unrealistic positive obligations on the state regarding the planning and conduct of military operations, but it had to give effect to obligations where it was reasonable to expect the protection of ECHR art.2.

[Add to end of n.171]

; *Keyu v Secretary of State for Foreign and Commonwealth Affairs* [2015] UKSC 69; [2015] 3 W.L.R. 1665 (declining to decide whether *In re McKerr* remains good law in circumstances in which the Supreme Court had not reached a clear and unanimous view).

[Add to n.172 after ". . . [2012] 1 AC 725"]

; *McCaughey v United Kingdom* (2014) 58 E.H.R.R. 13.

[In n.172, delete "Janowiec v Russia App. Nos 55508/07 and 29520/09 (April 16, 2012)" and substitute]

Janowiec v Russia (2014) 58 E.H.R.R. 30 at [132]–[133], [144]–[148]. See also *R. (on the application of Keyu) v Secretary of State for Foreign and Commonwealth Affairs* [2015] UKSC 69; [2015] 3 W.L.R. 1665.

[In n.172, delete "Varnava v Turkey App. Nos 16064/90–16066/90 and 16068/90–16073/90 (September 18, 2009)" and substitute]

Varnava v Turkey (2010) 50 E.H.R.R. 21.

[Add to end of n.173]

The criteria were held not to have been satisfied in *R. (on the application of Keyu) v Secretary of State for Foreign and Commonwealth Affairs* [2015] UKSC 69; [2015] 3 W.L.R. 1665 in respect of the deaths of 24 unarmed civilians killed by British soldiers in colonial Malaya in 1948. Baroness Hale dissented on the issue of identifying the "critical date" for the operation of the requirement for a genuine connection between the death and the entry into force of the Convention, with the majority regarding the relevant date as being the date of recognition of the right of individual petition to the Strasbourg court (for the United Kingdom, 1966), and Baroness Hale regarding the date as being the date of entry into force of the Convention (for the United Kingdom, 1953).

[Add to para.7–036 after ". . . under art.2 applied to the death.[172]"]

However, this obligation arises in relation to the applicable standards for an ongoing investigation, rather than to the question of whether there is an obligation to commence an investigation into an historic death.[172a]

[172a] *Keyu v Secretary of State for Foreign and Commonwealth Affairs* [2015] UKSC 69; [2015] 3 W.L.R. 1665.

[Add to n.173 after ". . . 49 E.H.R.R. 996 at [163]"]

; *Janoweic v Russia* (2014) 58 E.H.R.R. 30 at [132]–[133].

[Add to end of n.174] 7–037

; see also *Jaloud v Netherlands* (2015) 60 E.H.R.R. 29; *R. (on the application of Letts) v Lord Chancellor* [2015] EWHC 402; [2015] 1 W.L.R. 4497 at [95] (case law identified a variety of circumstances and types of case of real public importance and significance where the duty arose independently of the existence of such evidence).

[Add to n.176 after ". . . 28 E.H.R.R. 408 at [100]"]

; *R. (on the application of Litvinenko) v Secretary of State for the Home Department* [2014] EWHC 194 (Admin); [2014] H.R.L.R. 6 at [50]–[52] (here the ECHR art.2 obligation was discharged by an "extremely thorough" and "exceptionally detailed" police investigation into the death of a man in a London restaurant from radiation poisoning and the attempted extradition of two named suspects).

[Add to n.179 after ". . . the common law")] 7–038

; *Guardian News and Media Ltd v Incedal* [2014] EWCA Crim 1861; [2015] 1 Cr. App. R. 4 at [11] (no difference in substance between common law and ECHR art.6 in relation to the principle that "[t]he Court does not require a party to destroy the right it is seeking to assert or protect as the price of its vindication").

[Add to end of n.179]

See also *R. (on the application of B) v Westminster Magistrates' Court* [2014] UKSC 59; [2015] A.C. 1195 at [28] and [34] (ECHR art.6 did not require in the determination of extradition proceedings a further exception, on the basis of "the protective nature of the bars to extradition which exist in cases of extraneous circumstances, potential human rights violations and abuse of process", to the ordinary principles of open inter partes justice, beyond those identified by Lord Dyson JSC in *Al Rawi*).

CONTENT OF PROCEDURAL FAIRNESS: OVERVIEW

A flexible and evolving concept

[Add to end of n.183] 7–039

; *Secretary of State for Communities and Local Government v Hopkins Developments* [2014] EWCA Civ 470 (Jackson L.J. noting at [85] that "[f]airness is thus a flexible concept"). However, caution was expressed in respect of an emphasis on procedural fairness being "flexible" in *R. (on the application of L) v West London Mental Health NHS Trust* [2014] EWCA Civ 47; (2014) 158(6) S.J.L.B. 37 at [68]–[69]. Beatson L.J. was concerned that the emphasis could lead to an inappropriate drawing together of the concepts of procedural and substantive fairness and undue uncertainty.

[Add to n.187 after ". . . [2004] 1 A.C. 604"]

Secretary of State for Communities and Local Government v Hopkins Developments [2014] EWCA Civ 470 at [85].

[In n.187 delete "Bank Mellat [2010] EWCA Civ 483; [2012] Q.B. 91" and substitute]

Bank Mellat v HM Treasury [2013] UKSC 39; [2014] A.C. 700.

[Add to end of n.187]

See, e.g., *Re W (Children) (Care Proceedings: Summary Disposal at Case Management Hearing)* [2015] EWCA Civ 27; [2015] 2 F.L.R. 136 (while family law reforms were intended to resolve children's cases without delay, this was not at the expense of fairness and the right to a fair trial; interim care orders ought not therefore normally be made final at case management hearings).

[Add to end of n.193]

See also *R. (on the application of Foster) v Secretary of State for Justice* [2015] EWCA Civ 281 at [30].

7-041 *[Add to end of n.194]*

Secretary of State for Communities and Local Government v Hopkins Developments [2014] EWCA Civ 470 at [62] (the Town and Country Planning Appeals (Determination by Inspectors) (Inquiries Procedure) Rules 2000 "are not a complete code for achieving procedural fairness").

Consequences of following flawed procedures

7-042 *[Add to end of n.198]*

; *Natt v Osman* [2014] EWCA Civ 1520; [2015] 1 W.L.R. 1536 at [25] and [33] ("[t]he modern approach is to determine the consequence of non-compliance as an ordinary issue of statutory interpretation, applying all the usual principles of statutory interpretation" and, in cases involving the acquisition of property rights by private persons pursuant to statute, the intention of the legislature is to be ascertained in the light of the statutory scheme as a whole).

PRIOR NOTICE OF THE DECISION

The importance of prior notice

[Add to end of n.200]   7–043

R. (on the application of Reilly) v Secretary of State for Work and Pensions [2013] UKSC 68; [2014] A.C. 453 at [65] (invocation of a statutory power in a way which will or may impose a requirement to perform work on a jobseeker allowance claimant and which may have serious consequences on the claimant's ability to meet his or her living needs required the claimant to have access to such information as needed to make an informed and mean-ingful representation before the decision). See also *Ware Homes Ltd v Secretary of State for Communities and Local Government* [2016] EWHC 103 (Admin) (fairness required that parties to a planning inquiry should be aware of the points to be addressed and have a reasonable opportunity to deal with them).

[Add to n.201 after ". . . and, if appropriate, challenge it')"]

(the holding in this case was affirmed in [2014] UKSC 17; [2014] 2 W.L.R. 558 at [28]–[31] on the basis of an interpretation of the relevant statutory provision).

[Add to end of n.201]

; *R. (on the application of B) v Westminster Magistrates' Court* [2014] UKSC 59; [2015] A.C. 1195 (an appeal of a refusal of judicial review of a decision not to order a closed material procedure was dismissed, on the basis that the sought exception to the principles of open inter partes justice would deny the ability of the Rwandan Government, which was involved in extradition proceedings against the appellant, to hear evidence in relation to these proceedings).

[Add to end of para.7–043]

The Court of Appeal has recently characterised the principle of natural justice or procedural fairness as requiring that any participant in adversarial proceedings is entitled to know the case which he has to meet and to have a reasonable opportunity to adduce evidence and make submissions in relation to that opposing case.[203a]

[203a] *Secretary of State for Communities and Local Government v Hopkins Developments* [2014] EWCA Civ 470 at [47] (holding that it was not a breach of natural justice for a planning inspector to base her decision on issues which emerged in evidence during the course of a planning inquiry but which she had not previously identified as issues in statements produced pursuant to the relevant rules).

The degree of notice required

7–046 *[In n.208 delete "(General Development Procedure) Order 1190 (SI 1995/419)" and substitute]*

(Development Management Procedure) Order 2010 (SI 2010/2184)

7–047 *[Add to end of n.220]*

See also R. *(on the application of Joicey) v Northumberland CC* [2014] EWHC 3657 (Admin); [2015] P.T.S.R. 622; [2015] B.L.G.R. 1 (where information which was statutorily required to be accessible to members of the public is not available in a timely fashion to enable them to participate effectively in democratic decision-making, a claimant is entitled to have the decision quashed unless the decision-maker can demonstrate that it would inevitably have come to the same conclusion even if the information had been available).

Statutory requirements for notice

7–050 *[In n.231 delete "School Organisation (Establishment and Discontinuance of Schools) Regulations 2013" and substitute]*

School Organisation (Establishment and Discontinuance of Schools) Regulations 2013 (SI 2013/3109)

[In para.7–050 delete "a number of interested parties, including: any schools which are proposed to be discontinued;[232] and any local education authority which may be affected by the establishment of the new school.[233] It must also hold at least one public meeting to inform the public of the proposals.[234]" (including footnotes) and substitute]

interested parties that the local authority thinks appropriate.[232]

[232] SI 2013/3109 reg.5(4)(d).

[In para.7–050 delete "in at least one newspaper circulating in the area" and substitute]

on the website of the local authority as well as in both a national and local newspaper

[In n.235 delete "SI 2007/1288 reg.5(1)(h)" and substitute]

SI 2013/3109 reg.5(2)

[In n.236 delete "SI 2007/1288 reg.10(6)(h)" and substitute]

SI 2013/3109 reg.10(4)

Consequences of inadequate notice

[Add to end of para.7–051]   7–051

[240a] But see *McCarthy v Visitors to the Inns of Court* [2015] EWCA Civ 12 (a judge had erred in concluding that, although the Bar Standards Board's failure to disclose a witness statement in disciplinary proceedings against a barrister had breached the rules governing tribunal proceedings and had been procedurally unfair, the outcome of the proceedings had not been affected by the non-disclosure).

[Add to n. 240 after first sentence]

For an application of s.288, see *Powys County Council v Welsh Ministers* [2015] EWHC 3284 (Admin).

[Add to end of n.240]

See also *Secretary of State for Communities and Local Government v Hopkins Developments Ltd* [2014] EWCA Civ 470 at [62] (noting that if there is procedural unfairness which materially prejudices a party to a planning inquiry that may be a good ground for quashing the Inspector's decision).

[Add to end of n.241]

; *R. (on the application of Foster) v Secretary of State for Justice* [2015] EWCA Civ 281 (no oral hearing required in the context of a home detention curfew decision).

81

CONSULTATION AND WRITTEN REPRESENTATIONS

Standards of consultation

7–053 *[Add after the first sentence]*

It has been observed that for a non-statutory consultation process, the question of whether there has been a breach of procedural fairness, is fact and context sensitive, with the test being whether the process has been so unfair as to be unlawful.[245a] Indeed, whether the duty to consult has been satisfied depends in all cases on an intensely case-sensitive analysis.[245b] Overall, the consultation has to be fair, but it does not have to be perfect, since with the benefit of hindsight, it will no doubt often be possible to show that a consultation could have been carried out rather better.[245c]

[245a] *R. (on the application of West Berkshire DC) v Secretary of State for Communities and Local Government* [2016] EWCA Civ 441; [2016] P.T.S.R. 982.

[245b] *R. (on the application of Steven Sumpter) v Secretary of State for Works and Pensions* [2015] EWCA Civ 1033 at [50] (citing from *R. (on the application of United Company Rusal Plc) v The London Metal Exchange* [2014] EWCA Civ 1271 at [28]).

[245c] *R. (on the application of Steven Sumpter) v Secretary of State for Works and Pensions* [2015] EWCA Civ 1033 at [50] (citing from *R. (on the application of United Company Rusal Plc) v The London Metal Exchange* [2014] EWCA Civ 1271 at [28]).

[Add to n.245 after "See, e.g.,"]

R. (on the application of Moseley) v Haringey LBC [2014] UKSC 56; [2014] 1 W.L.R. 3947 *per* Lord Reed JSC. For a recent very comprehensive analysis of the duty to consult, both of when it arises and of what it entails, see: *R. (on the application of Plantagenet Alliance Ltd) v Secretary of State for Justice* [2014] EWHC 1662 (Admin) at [84]–[86] and [98] (noting in particular that a duty to consult will arise in four circumstances: where there is a statutory duty; where there has been a promise to consult; where there has been an established practice of consultation; and where a failure to consult would lead to conspicuous unfairness).

[Add to end of n.245]

R. (on the application of Flatley) v Hywel Dda University Local Health Board [2014] EWHC 2258 (Admin) at [98] (Community Health Councils

(Constitution, Membership and Procedures) (Wales) Regulations 2010 reg.27(7) is solely concerned with the health board's duty to consult with the community health council and not with the public).

[Add to n.246 after "84 L.G.R. 168;"]

the Supreme Court affirmed these requirements in *R. (on the application of Moseley) v Haringey LBC* [2014] UKSC 56; [2014] 1 W.L.R. 3947 at [25].

[Add to end of n.246]

See also *R. (on the application of LH) v Shropshire Council* [2014] EWCA Civ 404 at [21] (the obligation to consult "requires that there be a proposal, that the consultation takes place before a decision is reached and that responses be conscientiously considered"); *R. (on the application of Flatley) v Hywel Dda University Local Health Board* [2014] EWHC 2258 (Admin) at [88]; *R. (on the application of United Company Rusal plc) v London Metal Exchange* [2014] EWCA Civ 1271; [2015] 1 W.L.R. 1375 at [25].

[Add to end of n.247]   7–054

See also *R. (on the application of United Company Rusal plc) v London Metal Exchange* [2014] EWCA Civ 1271; [2015] 1 W.L.R. 1375 at [26].

[Add to end of n.248]

; *R. (on the application of Flatley) v Hywel Dda University Local Health Board* [2014] EWHC 2258 (Admin) at [88] (there is no need for a "pre-consultation consultation"); but see *R. (on the application of Moseley) v Haringey LBC* [2014] UKSC 56; [2014] 1 W.L.R. 3947 at [40] (the question is generally whether the provision of information on alternative options is required by the statutory duty to consult in the context of the statute concerned, in other words whether such information is necessary in order for the particular consultees to whom that statutory duty is owed to be able to express meaningful views on the proposal, but the duty does not require a detailed discussion of the alternatives or of the reasons for their rejection; *Vale of Glamorgan* distinguished on the basis that such information was not considered necessary there, having regard to the nature and purpose of the particular consultation exercise at issue in that case (Lord Reed JSC); "[s]ometimes, particularly when statute does not limit the subject of the requisite consultation to the preferred option, fairness will require that interested persons be consulted not only upon the preferred option but also upon arguable yet discarded alternative options" (Lord Wilson JSC at [27])).

[Delete "although there should be consultation on every viable option" and substitute]

although the decision-maker is entitled to narrow the options prior to consultation, provided the proposed course can still be altered as a result of the consultation, there may be a necessity to deal with alternative options where it would be unfair not to do so.

[Add to beginning of n.249]

R. (on the application of United Company Rusal Plc) v London Metal Exchange [2014] EWCA Civ 1271 [2015] 1 W.L.R. 1375 (a public body is not required to consult on proposals which it had discarded unless there were very specific reasons for doing so); but see now *R. (on the application of Moseley) v Haringey LBC* [2014] UKSC 56; [2014] 1 W.L.R. 3947 at [29] and [39] (consultation inevitably involves inviting and considering views about possible alternatives; those consulted were the most economically disadvantaged residents in the borough to whom real hardship would in all likelihood be caused by the proposed scheme and fairness demanded brief reference in the consultation document to other ways of absorbing the short-fall and the reasons why (Lord Wilson JSC); the content of the statutory duty to consult can vary greatly from one statutory context to another and, in the context of such a statutory duty the purpose of which is to ensure mean-ingful public participation in the decision-making process; what was required was not only information about the draft scheme but also the provision of an outline of the realistic alternatives and an indication of the main reasons for the adoption of the draft scheme (Lord Reed JSC)); *R. (on the application of T) v Trafford MBC* [2015] EWHC 369 (Admin); [2015] A.C.D. 101.

[Add to end of n.254]

; *R (United Company Rusal plc) v London Metal Exchange* [2014] EWCA Civ 1271; [2015] 1 W.L.R. 1375 at [85] ("the explanation provided by a consultant body in its consultation document is not unfair unless something material has been omitted or something has been materially misstated").

[Add to end of n.255]

R. (on the application of Save our Surgery Limited v Joint Committee of Primary Care Trusts [2013] EWHC 439 (Admin); [2013] P.T.S.R. D16 at [27], [109] (sub-scores in assessments of cardiac centres were not "under-lying workings" which did not need to be disclosed).

[Add to end of n.259]

It has also been held that explaining why three units were not used instead of 10 units in the context of a consultation on affordable housing involved descending into a level of particularity and a detailed analysis of options that was not necessary: *Secretary of State for Communities and Local Government v West Berkshire District Council* [2016] EWCA Civ 441; [2016] P.T.S.R. 982 at [63].

[Add to n.263 after ". . . [43]–[47]"]

; *R. (on the application of Moseley) v Haringey LBC* [2014] UKSC 56; [2014] 1 W.L.R. 3947 at [40] *per* Lord Reed (the content of a statutory duty to consult in circumstances in which meaningful public participation was required depended, in the context of providing information on rejected options, on whether the provision of such information was necessary in order for the consultees to express meaningful views on the proposal).

[Add to end of n.265]

R. (on the application of M) v Haringey LBC [2013] EWCA Civ 116; [2013] P.T.S.R. 1285 (announcement of a transitional grant scheme after a consultation for a council tax reduction scheme did not require further consultation as it was not a change of such significance that the council would have been required to draw it to the attention of what would have been a much broader category of consultees than the 36,000 current council tax benefit claimant households in its area; decision on the transitional grant scheme affirmed on appeal [2014] UKSC 56; [2014] 1 W.L.R. 3947 but Lord Wilson JSC noted at [32] the council's "illuminating concession" that, had it known of the scheme when it commenced its consultation exercise, it would have referred to it; the duty to consult normally requires brief reference to other discarded options).

[Add to end of n.267]

; *R. (on the application of Silus Investments SA) v Hounslow LBC* [2015] EWHC 358 (Admin); [2015] B.L.G.R. 291.

Considering the representations

[Add after ". . . consulted parties.[270]"]   7–055

It is also not a duty to adopt the submissions of respondents to the consultation; the decision-maker is entitled to consider the whole range of responses and to form his own conclusion independently of the view of any particular section of consultees or indeed the views of his own advisers.[270a]

[270a] *Secretary of State for Communities and Local Government v West Berkshire District Council, Reading Borough Council* [2016] EWCA Civ 441; [2016] P.T.S.R. 982 at [62].

The increasing importance of consultation

7–056 *[In n.274, delete "http://www.cabinetoffice.gov.uk/resource-library/consulta-tion- principles-guidance (last accessed December 28, 2012)" and substitute]*

https://www.gov.uk/government/publications/consultation-principles-guidance.

7–059 Exceptions

[Add to end of n.293]

See also *Evans v Royal Wolverhampton Hospitals NHS Foundation Trust* [2014] EWHC 3185 (QB); [2015] 1 All E.R. 1091; [2014] 6 Costs L.O. 899 at [29] (Leggatt J noting that ". . . adherence to the principle of natural justice is not an optional feature of litigation from which a court has power to derogate because it considers that in the particular circumstances the need to follow a fair procedure is outweighed by a conflicting public or private interest. Subject only to certain established and tightly defined exceptions, the right to participate in proceedings in accordance with the principle of natural justice is absolute").

HEARING

7–062 *[Add to n.314 after ". . . a just decision)"]*

; see also *R. (on the application of Foster) v Secretary of State for Justice* [2015] EWCA Civ 281 at [38] (the requirements of procedural fairness are flexible and context-dependent and in this case did not require the flexibility of oral presentation or evidence to determine the truth of the appellant's account; the context of home detention curfew meant the appellant had been under detention by other means and had been released on the discretion of the Secretary of State subject to compulsory curfew).

[Add to end of n.316]

Re Reilly's Application for Judicial Review [2013] UKSC 61; [2013] 3 W.L.R. 1020 generally at [80]–[96] and in particular at [85]–[86] (guidance on the necessity for oral hearings before parole boards, which are required in particular where facts which appear to be important are in dispute or where a significant explanation or mitigation is advanced which needs to be heard orally to be accepted, including where an assessment may depend on the view formed by the board of the characteristics of a prisoner which can best be judged by seeing or questioning him in person, where a psychological assessment is disputed or where the board may be materially assisted by hearing evidence, for example, from a psychologist or psychiatrist). For comment, see P. Murray, "Procedural Fairness, Human Rights and the Parole Board" [2014] 73(1) C.L.J. 5.

[In n.317 delete "R. (on the application of Osborn) v Parole Board [2010] EWCA Civ 1409; [2011] U.K.H.R.R. 35 at [35];"

[Add to end of n.317]

For comprehensive guidelines on when oral hearings will be required in respect of decisions affecting the prospective liberty of prisoners or the conditions in which they are detained, see: *Re Reilly's Application for Judicial Review* [2013] UKSC 61; [2014] A.C. 1115 at [2]; *Foster v Secretary of State for Justice* [2015] EWCA Civ 281 at [25] and *R. (on the application of Whiston) v Secretary of State for Justice* [2014] UKSC 39; [2015] A.C. 176. See also *R. (on the application of King) v Secretary of State for Justice* [2015] UKSC 54; [2015] 3 W.L.R. 457 at [93] (fairness at common law required that prisoners should usually have a meaningful opportunity to make representations before a decision was made to impose further segregation of 14 days). For application of *Re Reilly's Application* in the context of a hearing involving a disabled person before an employment tribunal, see *Galo v Bombardier Aerospace UK* [2016] NICA 25.

[Add to end of n.318]

Similarly, if the defendant or his duly authorised advocate agrees (in a voluntary, informed and unequivocal way) that a member of the tribunal can be absent for a part of the hearing and read a transcript of evidence and contribute to the decision, there is no breach of the rules of natural justice: *R. (on the application of Hill) v Chartered Accountants in England and Wales* [2013] EWCA Civ 555; [2014] 1 W.L.R. 86 at [23].

Requirements at an oral hearing

[Add to end of n.321]   7–063

R. (on the application of Hill) v Chartered Accountants in England and Wales [2013] EWCA Civ 555; [2014] 1 W.L.R. 86 at [15] (if it is decided that a defendant or a witness will give oral evidence, then that evidence will be "heard" and it is important that each member of the tribunal should if at all possible "hear" all the evidence; reading the transcript is normally no substitute for hearing evidence from a live witness given oral and for a tribunal member, juror or judge to absent himself without consent while oral evidence is given is usually a breach of the *audi alteram partem* rule).

7–064 *[Add to n.325 after ". . . [2008] EWCA Civ 811"]*

Bank Mellat v HM Treasury [2013] UKSC 39; [2014] A.C. 700 at [67]–[74]; *Guardian News and Media Ltd v Incedal* [2014] EWCA Crim 1861; [2015] 1 Cr. App. R. 4 at [31].

Adjournments

7–066 *[Add to end of n.331]*

R. (on the application of Gatawa) v Nursing and Midwifery Council [2013] EWHC 3435 (Admin) at [18]–[19] (decision not to adjourn a Nursing and Midwifery Council disciplinary hearing to allow more time for a lay representative to prepare on behalf of a nurse, who was suffering from mental illness and was absent, had not been procedurally unfair, where her representative had been given many opportunities to ask for more time).

Failure to appear at an oral hearing

7–068 *[In n.343 delete "Town and Country Planning (Appeals) (Written Representations Procedure) (England) Regulations 2000 (SI 2000/1628)" and substitute]*

Town and Country Planning (Appeals) (Written Representations Procedure) (England) Regulations 2009 (SI 2009/452) as amended by the Town and Country Planning (Appeals) (Written Representations Procedure and Advertisements) (England) (Amendment) Regulations 2013 (SI 2013/2114).

RIGHT TO LEGAL REPRESENTATION AND OTHER ASSISTANCE

Right to Legal Representation and Other Assistance

7–074 *[Add to n.359]*

See also *Re BP's Application for Judicial Review* [2015] NICA 20 (there was no overriding principle that everyone giving evidence to an inquiry was entitled to legal representation; procedural fairness may often not require it, as it would increase the inquiry's costs and duration, and encourage the proliferation of side issues).

RIGHT TO REASONS

Reasons as an aspect of procedural fairness

[Add to end of n.405]   7–087

See also *Re S-W (Children) (Care Proceedings: Summary Disposal at Case Management Hearing)* [2015] EWCA Civ 27; [2015] 1 W.L.R. 4099; *Weymont v Place* [2015] EWCA Civ 289; [2015] C.P. Rep. 29; *Re V (A Child) (Inadequate Reasons for Findings of Fact)* [2015] EWCA Civ 274. But see the dicta of Lord Phillips MR in *English v Emery Reimbold & Strick Ltd* [2002] EWCA Civ 605; [2002] 1 W.L.R. 2409 at [24] that while judges should not "have a second bite at the cherry", the Court of Appeal was "much less attracted at the prospect of expensive appellate proceedings on the ground of lack of reasons", noting that the successful party would suffer an injustice if a rational judgment were set aside because the judge did not include adequate reasons in the judgment.

Advantages of a duty to give reasons

[Add to end of n.428]   7–090

; see also *Re S-W (Children) (Care Proceedings: Summary Disposal at Case Management Hearing)* [2015] EWCA Civ 27; [2015] 1 W.L.R. 4099 at [46]; *Re V (A Child) (Inadequate Reasons for Findings of Fact)* [2015] EWCA Civ 274 at [31] (noting that the parties needed to know why the judge preferred the evidence of one against the other, which was important "not simply as a matter of justice and a matter of having a fair trial which comes to a clear and transparent conclusion" but, as this was a family law case, in order to enable the father to undertake counselling or therapy on the basis of the findings made).

[Add to end of n.429]

Secretary of State for the Home Department v CC [2014] EWCA Civ 559 at [38]–[39] (control orders quashed for material non-disclosure where provision of reasons for rejecting abuse allegations in closed judgment prevented the public from knowing the extent to which their allegations had been accepted or rejected).

[Add to end of n.432]   7–091

Horada v Secretary of State for Communities & Local Government [2016] EWCA Civ 169 at [34]. Of course, whether the reasons provided demonstrate error of fact or law is separate from the question of the adequacy of the reasons: see *R. (on the application of C) v Financial Services Authority* [2013] EWCA Civ 677 at [48].

Disadvantages of a duty to give reasons

7–093 *[Add to end of n.438]*

; *Uprichard v Scottish Ministers* [2013] UKSC 21; [2013] P.T.S.R. D37 at [48] (observing that it was important to maintain a sense of proportion when considering the duty to give reasons and not to impose a burden on decision-makers which is unreasonable having regard to the purpose intended to be served and noting that "[i]f the ministers were to be expected to address, line by line, every nuance of every matter raised in every objection, the burden imposed in such circumstances would be unreasonable").

Circumstances in which reasons will be required

To enable an effective right of appeal

7–098 *[Add to end of n.458]*

; *R. (on the application of T) v Legal Aid Agency* [2013] EWHC 960 (Admin); [2013] 2 F.L.R. 1315 at [14] (fairness dictates that reasons be given for a decision by the Legal Aid Board not to grant prior authority for the preparation of an expert report and an absence of resources did not excuse the lack of reasons).

The standard of reasons required

7–102 *[Add to end of n.488]*

; *Re V (A Child) (Inadequate Reasons for Findings of Fact)* [2015] EWCA Civ 274 at [15] (in a straightforward fact-finding exercise, there is no need for an elaborate distillation of every point; what is required is a straightforward explanation of the key factors that the judge has taken into account and his or her reasons for preferring one part of the evidence over another).

[In n.490 delete "R. (on the application of C) v Financial Services Authority [2012] EWHC 1417; [2012] A.C.D. 97" and substitute]

R. (on the application of C) v Financial Services Authority [2013] EWCA Civ 677 at [44]–[51]

[Add to end of n.493]

; *Nzolameso v Westminster City Council* [2015] UKSC 22; [2015] 2 All ER 942 (a "standard paragraph" would not suffice but the Supreme Court accepted that there are various ways for an authority to ensure that its decisions are properly evidenced and properly explained); see also *Ajilore v Hackney LBC* [2014] EWCA Civ 1273.

[Correction to para.7–102]

Delete the double inverted commas before[197].

[Add to end of n.497]

; *Uprichard v Scottish Ministers* [2013] UKSC 21; [2013] P.T.S.R. D37 at [48].

[Add to end of n.498]

; *Re. S-W (Children) (Care Proceedings: Summary Disposal at Case Management Hearing)* [2015] EWCA Civ 27; [2015] 1 W.L.R. 4099 at [46] ("[t]he reasons may be brief but they must be explanatory").

[Add to n.505]   7–103

Lavis v Nursing and Midwifery Council [2014] EWHC 4083 (Admin); [2015] A.C.D. 64 at [24] (it is not necessary for a judge to deal with every argument presented by counsel in support of its case).

[Add to end of para.7–103]

Where a decision-maker is disagreeing with a recommendation, such as with a planning inspector's report, there will be a duty to explain why the inspector's view is rejected.[507a]

[507a] *Horada v Secretary of State for Communities & Local Government* [2016] EWCA Civ 169 at [40] (finding that the Secretary of State had failed to explain why he disagreed with the inspector, beyond merely stating his conclusion that he did). However, there is no obligation on the majority of a tribunal to explain their disagreement with the dissenting majority, any more than there is an obligation on the Court of Appeal or the Supreme Court for the majority to examine and address directly the views of the dissenting minority (*Federation of Independent Practitioner Organisations v Competition and Markets Authority* [2016] EWCA Civ 777).

7–112 *[Add to end of n.529]*

; *Re V (A Child) (Inadequate Reasons for Findings of Fact)* [2015] EWCA Civ 274.

7–113 *[Add to end of n.533]*

See also *R. (on the application of Jedwell) v Denbighshire County Council* [2015] EWCA Civ 1232; [2016] P.T.S.R. 715 at [42], noting that even if a reasonable time has elapsed for the provision of reasons, the competent authority may still cure the deficiency by supplying reasons or further reasons before the application to the court is actually made. However, a local authority which had issued an inadequately reasoned negative screening opinion could not rectify its breach of duty to give proper reasons by supplying the information in a witness statement made in the course of judicial review proceedings challenging the screening opinion. On the facts of the case, it was held that cross-examination ought to have been conducted to assess whether the contents of a witness statement entailed *ex post facto* rationalisation of the decision.

ECHR Art.6: Content

Fair hearing

7–118 *[Add to end of n.551]*

Retrospective legislation affecting the result of pending proceedings may also infringe ECHR art.6(1): *R. (on the application of Reilly) v Secretary of State for Work and Pensions* [2016] EWCA Civ 413.

[Correction to n.551]

For *Willams* read *Williams*.

[Add to n.552]

; see also *R. (on the application of Gudanaviciene) v Director of Legal Aid Casework* [2014] EWCA Civ 1622; [2015] 1 W.L.R. 2247 (guidance on the Legal Aid, Sentencing and Punishment of Offenders Act 2012 stating that the refusal of legal aid would amount to a breach of ECHR art.6 only in rare and extreme cases was unsupported by case law and incompatible with ECHR art.6).

7–119 *[Add to end of n.559]*

Cf. the application of the common-law principle in *Weymont v Place* [2015] EWCA Civ 289; [2015] C.P. Rep. 29 (a re-trial was ordered on the basis of a judge's unreasoned judgment, in which there had been blanket acceptance of one party's evidence and blanket rejection of the evidence produced by the other party's witnesses, and not one sentence was provided in the judgment on the facts with the judge's specific findings of fact or the reasons for making them).

Hearing within a reasonable time

[Add to n.579 after first sentence] 7–123

O'Neill v HM Advocate (No 2) [2013] UKSC 36; [2013] 1 W.L.R. 1992 at [25] (noting that art.6(1) of the ECHR contains four separate rights that can and should be considered separately and a complaint that one of them has been breached cannot be answered by showing that the other rights were not breached; see also [36]).

[Add to end of n.581]

See also *R. v Kerrigan (David Joseph)* [2014] EWCA Crim 2348 (the delay at issue, while it might not have been ideal, was far from excessive and there was a satisfactory explanation for it).

[Add to end of n.582] 7–124

R. v Duncan Evans [2016] EWCA Crim 671.

[Add to end of 585]

For rejection of an attempt to use ECHR art.6 to create a duty on administrative decision-makers to make decisions within a reasonable time, see *R. (on the application of C) v Secretary of State for Work and Pensions* [2015] EWHC 1607 (Admin).

[Add new n.586a after ". . . the stage of the proceedings at which the breach 7–125 *was established"]*

586a See, e.g. *R. (on the application of Sturnham) v Secretary of State for Justice* [2013] UKSC 23; [2013] 2 A.C. 254 (detention beyond a tariff period caused by delay would warrant damages if it could be shown that an earlier hearing would result in earlier release, or had caused sufficiently serious frustration and anxiety).

7–126 *[Add to end of n.589]*

; *Beggs v United Kingdom* (2013) 56 E.H.R.R. 26 (violation of ECRH art.6 where appeal proceedings had lasted for over 10 years).

ECHR ART.2: CONTENT

The requirements of art.2

7–127 *[Add to para.7–127 after ". . . to protect their legitimate interests.[597]"]*

It has also been held that an art.2 investigation must encompass broader issues such as planning and control of operations and all surrounding circumstances, not just the actions of State agents who directly used lethal force, and must include "lessons learned" from the identification of wider or systemic issues.[597a]

[597a] *R. (on the application of Mousa) v Secretary of State for Defence* [2013] EWHC 1412 (Admin); [2013] A.C.D. 84 at [147].

[Add to para.7–127 after ". . . collusion in an incident.[602]"]

Excessive investigative delay will violate ECHR art.2.[602a]

[602a] *McCaughey v United Kingdom* (2014) 58 E.H.R.R. 13 at [121]–[140] (prompt response by the authorities in investigating the use of lethal force was essential to maintain public confidence in adherence to the rule of law and in preventing any appearance of collusion in or tolerance of unlawful acts; there had been excessive delay where an inquest began over 21 years after the deaths in question).

[Add to end of para.7–127]

It has been held that there are only two realistic ways in which the State can fulfil its ECHR art.2 obligations in respect of deaths in custody, namely, by setting up an overarching public inquiry or by developing a procedure based on coroner's inquests,[607a] which are now discussed.

[607a] *R. (on the application of Mousa) v Secretary of State for Defence* [2013] EWHC 1412 (Admin); [2013] A.C.D. 84 at [197]–[202], [210] (refusing to

direct a public inquiry into deaths of Iraqi civilians in the custody of British armed forces).

[Add to end of n.592]

; *R. (on the application of Mousa) v Secretary of State for Defence* [2013] EWHC 1412 (Admin); [2013] A.C.D. 84 at [108]–[123] and [147].

[Add to end of n.593]

See also *R. (on the application of Delezuch) v Chief Constable of Leicestershire* [2014] EWCA Civ 1635 (police guidance provisions were not unlawful for failing to require the immediate separation of officers who used force or who witnessed its use; whether such a failure to separate impairs the adequacy of an investigation depends on the circumstances, including the other safeguards in place, and on an overall assessment of relevant factors, of which the risk of collusion is only one).

[Add to end of n.594]

; *Mocanu v Romania* (2015) 60 E.H.R.R. 19.

[Add to end of n.596]

; *McCaughey v United Kingdom* (2014) 58 E.H.R.R. 13.

[Add to end of n.599]

; *Jaloud v Netherlands* (2015) 60 E.H.R.R. 29 at [197]–[203]; [209]–[211].

[Add to end of n.600]

; *Jaloud v Netherlands* (2015) 60 E.H.R.R. 29 at [197]–[203]; [206]–[208].

[Add to end of n.601]

; *Jaloud v Netherlands* (2015) 60 E.H.R.R. 29 at [212]–[220].

[Add to end of n.602]

See also *R. (on the application of Litvinenko) v Secretary of State for the Home Department* [2014] EWHC 194 (Admin); [2014] H.R.L.R. 6 at [57]–[73] (deficiencies in the reasons *"so substantial"* that a decision for refusing to launch a public inquiry into a death due to radiation poisoning in suspicious circumstances could not stand).

CHAPTER 8

PROCEDURAL FAIRNESS: EXCEPTIONS

EXPRESS STATUTORY EXCLUSION

[In n.15 delete "Criminal Procedure Rules 2002 (SI 2012/1726) r.65.6" and   8–003
substitute]

Criminal Procedure Rules 2002 (SI 2013/1554) r.56.6.

[Add to end of n.16]

See also *Walapu v Revenue and Customs Commissioners* [2016] EWHC 658
(Admin) (ruling that the provisions applicable to a power on the part of
HMRC to issue an accelerated payment notice pursuant to the Finance Act
2014 was perfectly fair and adequate).

LEGISLATION REQUIRES FAIRNESS FOR SOME BUT NOT OTHER PURPOSES

[Add after ". . . not listed in the regulations.²⁸"]   8–005

Furthermore, where the recognition of additional fair procedure requirements to those specified in the legislation would frustrate the purpose of the
statutory scheme or its practical operation, additional fair procedures will
not be implied into the statutory scheme.[28a]

[28a] *R. (on the application of Rowe) v Revenue and Customs Commissioners*
[2015] EWHC 2293 (Admin) at [70].

[Add to end of n.24]

Bank Mellat v HM Treasury (No.2) [2013] UKSC 39; [2014] A.C. 700 at
[35] (Lord Sumption observing: "Like Lord Bingham in *R (West) v Parole
Board [2005]* 1 W.L.R. 350 at para 29, I find it hard to envisage cases in
which the maximum expression unius exclusion alterius could suffice to
exclude so basic a right as that of fairness"); *EK (Ivory Coast) v Secretary of
State for the Home Department* [2014] EWCA Civ 1517 at [26] (the Secretary
of State accepting, correctly, that the Immigration Rules do not exclude the

general public law duty to act fairly which rests upon the Secretary of State in exercising her functions). A different approach is taken with respect to appeals against refusal of permission to appeal. In *Sarfraz v Disclosure and Barring Service* [2015] EWCA Civ 544, it was held that while there was force in an argument that exceptions on the right of appeal were set out exhaustively in the legislation and there was no room for further exception, the court could not ignore the long-standing principle, established by *Lane v Esdaile* [1891] A.C. 210, that, in the absence of express statutory language to the contrary, a provision giving a court the power to grant or refuse permission to appeal should be construed as not extending to an appeal against a refusal of permission to appeal. See also *R. (on the application of Rowe) v Revenue and Customs Commissioners* [2015] EWHC 2293 (Admin) at [59] (observing that where Parliament has prescribed a set of procedural protections, the courts should generally be slow to impose a further set of obligations as a matter of common law).

RISK TO THE PUBLIC INTEREST

Risks to national security

8–007 *[Add to n.40 after "... given to that material) at [87]"]*

; *Bank Mellat v HM Treasury (No.1)* [2013] UKSC 38; [2014] A.C. 700 at [52] (ECHR art.6 is the principled control mechanism on what the legislature can prescribe, and it is for the courts to decide, within parameters set down by the legislature, how the tension between the need for natural justice and confidentiality is to be resolved in the natural interest).

8–008 *[Add to para.8–008 after "... restrict such a right[44]"]*

As has recently been observed: "It is no answer that terrorism is horrendous ... However grave the case, there can come a point where 'the court's sense of justice and propriety is offended'."[44a]

[44a] *Secretary of State for the Home Department v CC and CF* [2014] EWCA Civ 559 at [16] (Kay L.J.).

Disclosure

8–009 *[Add to end of n.46]*

See also *Kiani v Secretary of State for the Home Department* [2015] EWCA Civ 776; [2016] Q.B. 595 at [39]–[40].

[In n.47 delete "Employment Tribunals (Constitutional and Rule of Procedure) Regulations 2004 (SI 2004/1861) Sch.1, para.54)" and substitute]

Employment Tribunals (Constitutional and Rule of Procedure) Regulations 2013 (2013/1237) Sch.1, reg.94.

[Add to end of n.48]

Justice and Security Act 2013. See also *R. (on the application of Sarkandi) v Secretary of State for Foreign and Commonwealth Affairs* [2014] EWHC 2359 (Admin) at [30] (in deciding whether an application for public interest immunity rather than a closed material procedure was the more appropriate course, it was necessary to consider whether the claim could fairly be tried without the sensitive material; see now [2015] EWCA Civ 687). For an example in the immigration context, see: *BB, PP, W, U and Others v Secretary of State for the Home Department* [2015] EWCA Civ 9.

[Add to end of n.49]

For a comparative perspective, see A. Gray, "A Comparison and Critique of Closed Court Hearings" [2014] E. & P. 230.

[Add to end of n.50]

See also K Clubb " 'Secret Justice': a critical review of closed material proceedings and the Justice and Security Act 2013" (2014) 2 *Covert Policing, Terrorism and Intelligence Law Review* 75.

[Add to para.8–009 after ". . . to the other side.⁵⁰ᶜ]

It has been observed that the process of considering an application to withhold information from disclosure on the grounds of public interest, and the closed material procedure are very different, and in their essence may be thought of as conflicting.[50a]

[50a] *F v Security Service* [2013] EWHC 3402; [2014] 1 W.L.R. 1699 (QB) at [15] (Irwin J. also referring to *Al Rawi v Security Service* [2011] 1 A.C. 531, in which Lord Dyson J.S.C. described (at [41]) a closed procedure as "the very antithesis of PII").

[Add to n.51 after ". . . a substitute for public interest immunity ([192])"]

; *R. (on the application of British Sky Broadcasting Ltd.) v Central Criminal Court* [2014] UKSC 17; [2014] A.C. 885 at [30]–[31].

[In n.51 delete "[2012] EWHC 2837 (Admin)" and substitute]

[2014] EWCA Civ 559

[Add to end of n.51]

R. *(on the application of B) v Westminster Magistrates' Court* [2014] UKSC 59; [2015] A.C. 1195 at [28]–[34] (holding that extradition proceedings did not fall within the special category of cases which justified or called for a further qualification of the principle of open justice). Here the argument was rejected that by reference to two categories of potential exception to the normal rule identified in the judgment of Lord Dyson JSC in *Al Rawi*—child welfare cases and intellectual property cases where full disclosure would undermine the whole object of the proceedings—a departure from the normal rule could be justified in extradition proceedings. The Court reasoned that there was no express statutory power. Furthermore, there was no triangulation of interests (such as where a witness is at risk) such as to warrant recourse to the closed material procedure. For comment, see T Garner, "Behind closed doors?" (2014) 164 New Law Journal 164 and Lord Kerr "'Only Parliament can do that'? The reliance of British jurisprudence on the common law in the national security context" (2015) 34 C.J.Q. 244. See also R. *(on the application of Immigration Law Practitioners' Association) v Tribunal Procedure Committee* [2016] EWHC 218 (Admin); [2016] 1 W.L.R. 3519 at [14] (finding statutory power to introduce a rule which permitted the First-tier Tribunal to give a direction prohibiting the disclosure of a document or information to a person, if satisfied that such disclosure would be likely to cause that person or some other person serious harm and having regard to the interests of justice that it was proportionate to give such a direction). It has also been held in *Da Costa v Sargaco* [2016] EWCA Civ 764; [2016] C.P. Rep. 40 at [51] (the decision in *Al-Rawi v Security Service* [20111] UKSC 34; [2012] 1 A.C. 531 was not authority for the proposition that, in order to a party to have a fair trial, there was an absolute requirement that he or she had to have the opportunity to be present throughout the hearing).

[In para. 8–009 delete "although it is not clear" and add after "to conduct a closed material procedure,[51]*"*

although the power to conduct a closed material procedure is necessarily implied into the statutory right to appeal decisions where a closed material procedure has been used.[51a] It remains unclear

[51a] *Bank Mellat v HM Treasury (No. 1)* [2013] UKSC 38; [2014] A.C. 700 at [37]–[43] (since s.40(2) of the 2005 Act provides that an appeal lies to the Supreme Court against "any" judgment of the Court of Appeal, that must extend to parts of a closed judgment as justice will not be able to be done in

some cases if the appellate court cannot consider the closed material). For comment, see C. Sargeant, "Two Steps Backward, One Step Forward—the Cautionary Tale of Bank Mellat (No 1)" [2014] 3(1) C.J.I.C.L. 111.

[In para 8–009 delete "At the time of writing,[53] the Justice and Security Bill 2012–2013 has just passed through Parliament and will extend the possibility of using a CMP to all civil proceedings" and substitute]

The Justice and Security Act 2013 now extends the possibility of using a CMP to all civil proceedings.[53] It is not necessary that a public immunity process be concluded before a closed material procedure.[53a]

[53] For discussion of the Bill as it passed through Parliament, see T. Hickman, "Justice and Security Bill: Defeat or Not a Defeat: That is the Question", UK Const. L. Blog (November 27, 2012). See also, generally J. Jackson, "Justice, Security and the Right to a Fair Trial: Is the Use of Secret Evidence Ever Fair?" (2013) P.L. 720. The central provision in the legislation is s.6, which sets out the conditions in which the court may make a declaration that the proceedings are proceedings in which the closed material application may be made to the court. For application of the legislation, see *CF v Security Service and Mohamed v Foreign and Commonwealth office* [2013] EWHC 3402 (QB); [2014] 1 W.L.R. 1699; *R. (on the application of Sarkandi) v Secretary of State for Foreign and Commonwealth Affairs* [2014] EWHC 2359 at [30] (Admin) (in deciding whether an application for public interest immunity rather than a closed material procedure was the more appropriate course, it was necessary to consider whether the claim could fairly be tried without the sensitive material; see now [2015] EWCA Civ 687).

[53a] In *CF v Security Service and Mohamed v Foreign and Commonwealth office* [2013] EWHC 3402 (QB); [2014] 1 W.L.R. 1699 the court made its first ruling on the use of the Justice and Security Act 2013, accepting that the government could make a closed material application to the court in a civil claim for damages. It was unnecessary that a public immunity process should be concluded before the court accepted a closed material application. The validity of the closed material procedure could not turn on objections which would arise in every case and therefore which would, if successful, subvert Parliament's intention. The courts have criticised the uneasy coexistence of the closed material and public interest immunity procedures (see [2014] 1 W.L.R. at [56]). See also *R. (on the application of Sarkandi) v Secretary of State for Foreign and Commonwealth Affairs* [2014] EWHC 2359 (Admin) at [9] (it was agreed that CPR 82.23(4), which gives effect to s.6 of the legislation and which allows for a hearing in the absence of the specially represented party and the specially represented party's legal representative, ought to be interpreted as allowing such a hearing "so far as necessary"); see now [2015] EWCA Civ 687.

8–010 *[Add to end of n.54]*

; and the guidance given by the court in *Commissioner of Policy of the Metropolis v Bangs* [2014] EWHC 546 (Admin); (2014) 178 J.P. 158 at [30]–[51], [59] (Beatson J noting at [40] that "[i]n all cases where the issue of PII is raised, what has to be balanced are the public interest which demands the material be withheld as against the public interest in the administration of justice that the individual and the court should have the fullest possible access to all relevant material"). See also *R. (on the application of X) v Chief Constable of Y* [2015] EWHC 484 (Admin) at [23].

[Add to end of n.56]

Commissioner of Policy of the Metropolis v Bangs [2014] EWHC 546 (Admin); (2014) 178 J.P. 158 at [58]. See also *R. v Ryan (Veronica)* [2014] NICA 72 at [16] (where convictions had been found to be unsafe on account of the prosecution having failed at trial to disclose certain confidential information, the setting aside of those convictions was all that was required to satisfy the public interest and it was not in the interests of fairness and justice for the court to provide a fully reasoned judgment on what material had been withheld, why it had been withheld, and by whom; the public interest would be undermined not advanced by the disclosure of material covered by the PII certificate which the court had found to be properly issued).

[Add new n.56a after ". . . in the interests of justice"]

56a However, it has been held that the appropriate question is not whether disclosure "would" result in the harm identified but rather whether there is a real risk of the harm occurring: *Commissioner of Policy of the Metropolis v Bangs* [2014] EWHC 546 (Admin) at [50].

[Add to end of n.57]

; *Bank Mellat* [2013] 4 All E.R. 495 at [68]–[69]; *Bangs* [2014] EWHC 546 (Admin) at [34]–[35], [50]–[51]; *CF v Security Service* [2013] EWHC 3402 (QB); [2014] 1 W.L.R. 1600 at [45]; *Secretary of State for the Home Department v CC and CF* [2014] EWCA Civ 559 (withholding of Secretary of State's case on a potentially dispositive issue and total confinement of reasons for rejecting applicant's case on those issues to the closed judgment invalid).

[Add at end of para.8–010]

In short, any denial of disclosure or inspection must be limited to circumstances where such denial is strictly necessary, and where some restriction is necessary, consideration should be given to the use of redaction, confidentiality rings, anonymity orders and other steps to respect protected interests.[57a]

[57a] *R. (on the application of X) v Chief Constable of Y* [2015] EWHC 484 at [40].

[Add new n.59a after ". . . especially important"]   8–011

[59a] For discussion of the difference in the balancing in the civil and criminal context, see *Commissioner of Policy of the Metropolis v Bangs* [2014] EWHC 546 at [39]–[40].

[Add to end of n.60]

See also D Heaton *"Carnduff, Al Rawi, the 'unfairness' of public interest immunity and sharp procedure"* (2015) 34 Civil Justice Quarterly 191.

[Add a new n.64a after ". . . recent years."]   8–013

[64a] For an interesting discussion of the difference between closed material procedures and in camera proceedings, see *Guardian News and Media Ltd v Incedal* [2014] EWCA Crim 1861 at [11]–[12] (the former involving a departure from natural justice and the latter a departure from open justice).

[Add after first sentence]

It is accepted that the closed material procedure is a serious departure from the fundamental principles of open justice and natural justice, but that it is a departure authorised by Parliament in defined circumstances for the protection of national security.[64b] It has been described as "certainly an exceptional procedure", which "in the nature of things one would expect . . . to be used only rarely".[64c] However, the relevant statutory provisions are not to be given a narrow or restrictive construction, save for any reading down that may be required, in accordance with the terms of the statute itself, for compliance with art.6 ECHR.[64d]

[64b] *R. (on the application of Sarkandi) v Secretary of State for Foreign and Commonwealth Affairs* [2015] EWCA Civ 687 at [57]. See also *McGartland v Attorney General* [2015] EWCA Civ 686 at [34]; *Guardian News and Media Ltd v Incedal* [2014] EWCA Crim 1861. It has been observed that open justice "is an important principle of the common law" but it is not absolute and must "sometimes bow to other rights such as the right to life, or other elements of the public interest such as national security": *R. (on the application of Yam) v Central Criminal Court* [2014] EWHC 3558 (Admin); [2016] 3 W.L.R. 1050 (affirmed on appeal in [2015] UKSC 76; [2016] A.C. 771).

[64c] *R. (on the application of Sarkandi) v Secretary of State for Foreign and Commonwealth Affairs* [2015] EWCA Civ 687 at [58]. See also *McGartland v Attorney General* [2015] EWCA Civ 686 at [35].

[64d] *R. (on the application of Sarkandi) v Secretary of State for Foreign and Commonwealth Affairs* [2015] EWCA Civ 687 at [58]. See also *McGartland v Attorney General* [2015] EWCA Civ 686 at [35].

[Add after ". . . take it on trust.[67]"]

It has also been held that the standard in *F(No.3)*, rather than any lower standard, applied where financial restrictions had been imposed which had an utterly damaging effect on an Iranian bank's ability to function.[67a]

[67a] *Bank Mellat v HM Treasury* [2015] EWCA Civ 1052; [2016] 1 W.L.R. 1187.

[At end of n.66, delete "Bank Mellat v Her Majesty's Treasury [2010] EWCA Civ 483; [2012] Q.B. 91" and substitute]

Bank Mellat v HM Treasury (No.1) [2013] UKSC 38; [2013] 4 All E.R. 495; *Secretary of State for the Home Department v CC and CF* [2014] EWCA Civ 559 at [16] (use of closed material procedure in abuse of process proceedings against the Secretary of State which would have led to quashing of control orders involved "a radical departure from procedural and constitutional normality" as the closed material procedure limited the obligation of disclosure and permitted much of the detail to be dealt with only in a closed judgment).

[Add to end of n.66]

See also *R. (on the application of the Immigration Law Practitioners' Association) v Tribunal Procedure Committee* [2016] EWHC 218 (Admin); [2016] 1 W.L.R. 3519 (use of a closed material procedure in the context of the First-tier Tribunal was lawful as it could only be ordered where the judge considered it to be proportionate and it was improbable that a judge would not properly direct himself as to the requirements of fairness in making this assessment. Nonetheless, the Court suggested that the very existence of the power was troubling, ad that this was an issue that the Chamber President or the Senior President of Tribunals would wish to consider issuing guidance on). It has also been held that directions which required financial institutions to cease business relationships or transactions with all Iranian banks had the effect of shutting an Iranian bank out of the UK financial market and which thereby involved serious restrictions on the bank's freedom of action and a serious impact on its banking business required the application of the *AF*

(No.3) standard of disclosure: *Bank Mellat v Her Majesty's Treasury (No 4)* [2015] EWCA Civ 1052; [2016] 1 W.L.R. 1187 at [25].

[In n.69, delete "Bank Mellat [2011] EWCA Civ 1; [2012] Q.B. 101" and substitute]

Bank Mellat (No.1) [2013] UKSC 38; [2014] A.C. 700 at [5]–[6]; *Secretary of State for the Home Department v CC and CF* [2014] EWCA Civ 559 at [43].

[In n.69, add after "[2012] Q.B. 101"]

; *R. (on the application of X) v Chief Constable of Y Police* [2015] EWHC 484 (Admin) at [35] (while the art.6 right to a fair trial is a powerful factor in the balancing exercise the court is to undertake when determining a claim for public interest immunity, that factor is not decisive of the question of whether a party is entitled to disclosure of the gist of allegations against him, being capable of being overridden by other compelling factors).

[Add to end of n.69]

D Kelman "Closed trials and secret allegations: an analysis of the 'gisting' requirement" (2016) (80) J of Criminal L 264.

[Add to end of para.8–013]

In summary, therefore, the requirements of art.6 depend on context and all the circumstances of the case, such as: whether the case involves the liberty of the subject; whether the claimant has been provided with a degree of information as to the basis for the decision; whether there is real scope for the special advocate to test the issues without obtaining instructions on the facts and the extent of art.6 rights applicable. For example, in a security vetting case, the Strasbourg jurisprudence indicates that an individual is not entitled to full ECHR art.6 rights if to accord him such rights would jeopardise the efficacy of the vetting regime itself.[69a] It has also been confirmed that, in a case not directly affecting the liberty of the subject, there is no irreducible minimum of disclosure or necessary minimum revelation by summary or gist of the defendant's case, which the court would require despite the consequences for national security.[69b] It has been held that a refusal by the English courts to permit disclosure to the ECtHR of material heard in camera during a murder trial does not breach the courts' obligations under ECHR art.6.[69c]

It has also been held that, in principle, a protective costs order may be made where an individual who brought a claim had been accused of terrorism and reliance was placed on closed evidence, rendering it impossible for him to determine the merits of his claim.[69d] The granting of such an order is dependent on satisfaction of four conditions: first, the case has to be of real benefit to the individual bringing it; secondly, the applicant has to be able to assess the prospects of success in the ordinary way; thirdly, having regard to the individual's financial resources and the amount of likely costs, it has to be fair and just to make the order; and fourthly, it has to be shown that if the order is not made, the applicant would probably discontinue the proceedings and would be acting reasonably in doing so.[69e] To avoid unfairness, the second condition must be considered prior to the making of disclosure, since otherwise, an individual would be required to embark on an appeal without the protection of a protective costs order, at least until the Treasury had served its evidence, including any gisting of the closed material.[69f]

[69a] *Kiani v The Secretary of State for the Home Department* [2015] EWCA Civ 776; [2016] Q.B. 595 at [23].

[69b] *CF v Ministry of Defence* [2014] EWHC 3171 at [23] (noting that as the case before the Court was a claim for compensation, it was in a category where the Court must conduct a balancing exercise, bearing in mind the competing principles of maximising the fairness of the trial and protecting the public through the preservation of national security).

[69c] *R. (on the application of Yam) v Central Criminal Court* [2015] UKSC 76; [2016] A.C. 771.

[69d] *Begg v HM Treasury* [2016] EWCA Civ 568; [2016] C.P.Rep. 39.

[69e] *Begg v HM Treasury* [2016] EWCA Civ 568; [2016] C.P.Rep. 39 at [15].

[69f] *Begg v HM Treasury* [2016] EWCA Civ 568; [2016] C.P.Rep. 39 at [27].

8–013A *[Add new para.8–013A after para.8–013]*

Consideration has also been given recently to the use of a closed material procedure in the appeal context. In *Bank Mellat v HM Treasury (No 2)*, the Supreme Court concluded that, while the Supreme Court rules contained no express power to conduct a closed material procedure, it nonetheless had the power to adopt such a procedure in an appeal under the Counter Terrorism Act 2008 if justice required it and provided guidance on the judicial approach to adopt.[69g]

Meanwhile, the ECJ has suggested that pursuant to art.47 of the Charter of Fundamental Rights of the European Union, the person must be informed of the essence of the grounds which constitute the basis of the decision in question in a manner which takes due account of the necessary confidentiality of the evidence and secondly, to draw, pursuant to national law, the appropriate conclusions from any failure to comply with that obligation to inform him.[69h]

It has also been held that where there has been an open and a closed hearing and a judge gives an open and a closed judgment, it is highly desirable in the open judgment to identify every conclusion in that judgment which has been reached in whole or in part in the light of points made in evidence referred to in the closed judgment and state that this is what has been done.[69i] In addition, where closed material has been relied on, the judge should, in the open judgment, say as much as can properly be said about that closed material.[69j] The principles governing an appeal against an open and closed judgment have recently been considered.[69k] An appellate court should only be asked to conduct a closed hearing if it is strictly necessary for fairly determining the appeal, so that any party who is proposing to invite the appellate court to take such a course should consider very carefully whether it really is necessary to go outside the open material in order for the appeal to be fairly heard.[69l] If the appellate court decides that it should look at closed material, careful consideration should be given by the advocates and the court to the question whether it would nonetheless be possible to avoid a closed substantive hearing.[69m] If a court decides that a closed material procedure appear to be necessary, the parties should try and agree a way of avoiding or minimising the extent of a closed hearing.[69n] If there is a closed hearing, the lawyers representing the party who is relying on the closed material, as well as that party itself, should ensure that, well in advance of the hearing of the appeal: (i) the excluded party is given as much information as possible about any closed documents (including any closed judgment) relied on; and (ii) the special advocates are given as full information as possible as to the nature of the passages relied on in such closed documents and the arguments which will be advanced in relation thereto.[69o] Appellate courts should be robust about acceding to applications to go into closed session or even to look at closed material. Given that the issues will have already been debated and adjudicated upon, there must be very few appeals where any sort of closed material procedure is likely to be necessary. And, in those few cases where it may be necessary, it is hard to believe that an advocate seeking to rely on closed material or seeking a closed hearing, could be unable to articulate convincing reasons in open court for taking such a course.[69p]

[69g] *Bank Mellat v HM Treasury (No.2)* [2013] UKSC 39; [2014] A.C. 700 at [67]–[74].

[69h] *ZZ (France) v Secretary of State for the Home Department (C–300/11)* EU:C:2013:363 at [68] (see generally also [53]–[69] for discussion on the EU position). See also *Bank Mellat v HM Treasury* [2014] EWHC 3631; [2015] H.R.L.R. 6 at [19] (Admin) (describing *ZZ* as a "bad decision") (judgment affirmed without considering EU law in [2015] EWCA Civ 1052; [2016] 1 W.L.R. 1187). See also *S1 v Secretary of State for the Home Department*

[2016] EWCA Civ 560 (finding that the disclosure made satisfied the "essence of the grounds" obligations, albeit that EU law did not apply). It has also been observed that, while the right in art.41 of the Charter of Fundamental Rights of the European Union reflects a general principle of Union law, Member States are entitled to withhold disclosure, and hence restrict the right to make representations, on grounds of national security: *R (AZ) v Secretary of State for the Home Department* [2015] EWHC 3695 (Admin) (involving refusal of a travel document which was not as serious as interference with the free movement of EU nationals or refoulement); *R. (on the application of XH) v Secretary of State for the Home Department* [2016] EWHC 1898 (Admin) at [116].

[69i] *Bank Mellat (No.1)* [2013] UKSC 38; [2014] A.C. 700 at [68].

[69j] *Bank Mellat (No.1)* [2013] UKSC 38; [2014] A.C. 700 at [69].

[69k] *Bank Mellat (No.1)* [2013] UKSC 38; [2014] A.C. 700.

[69l] *Bank Mellat (No.1)* [2013] UKSC 38; [2014] A.C. 700 at [70].

[69m] *Bank Mellat (No.1)* [2013] UKSC 38; [2014] A.C. 700 at [71].

[69n] *Bank Mellat (No.1)* [2013] UKSC 38; [2014] A.C. 700 at [72].

[69o] *Bank Mellat (No.1)* [2013] UKSC 38; [2014] A.C. 700 at [73].

[69p] *Bank Mellat (No.1)* [2013] UKSC 38; [2014] A.C. 700 at [74].

The role of special advocates in closed material procedures

8–014 *[Add to end of n.70]*

; C. Murphy, "Counter-Terrorism and the Culture of Legality: The Case of Special Advocates" (2013) 24 K.L.J 19.

8–015 *[Add to end of n.74]*

; *ZZ v Secretary of State for the Home Department* [2014] EWCA Civ 7; [2014] 2 W.L.R. 791 at [37], [39].

[Add to end of n.77]

See also *CC and CF* [2014] EWCA Civ 559; *ZZ (France) v Secretary of State for the Home Department* (C–300/11) EU:C:2013:363; ZZ (France) [2014] EWCA Civ 7; [2014] 2 W.L.R. 791 (in the context of the EU Charter of rights, any failure to disclose precisely and in full the grounds on which the decision is based is limited to that which is strictly necessary).

[Add new para.8–015A after para.8–015]   **8–015A**

In the context of financial restrictions, the relationship between the position under Union law and the standard applied pursuant to the Convention has also been explored.[77a] It has been suggested that there is difficulty in discerning that there was any practical difference between the requirement under Union law, as identified in the ZZ case, that the essence of the grounds be disclosed, and the Convention position. However, it may be that the requirement under Union law to inform the person concerned of the essence of the grounds, limited to that which was strictly necessary, required only limited disclosure and set a standard which might be below set by the Convention, as applied in *F (No.3)*.[77b]

[77a] *Bank Mellat v HM Treasury* [2014] EWHC 3631; [2015] H.R.L.R. 6 (judgment affirmed without considering Union law in [2015] EWCA Civ 1052; [2016] 1 W.L.R. 1187).

[77b] *Bank Mellat v HM Treasury* [2014] EWHC 3631; [2015] H.R.L.R. 6 at [16]. See also [19] (observing that ZZ was "*a bad decision*") (judgment affirmed without considering Union law in [2015] EWCA Civ 1052; [2016] 1 W.L.R. 1187).

[Add to end of n.80]   **8–017**

Re CM (EM Country Guidance: Disclosure: Zimbabwe) [2013] EWCA Civ 1303; [2014] Imm. A.R. 326.

[Add to end of n.82]   **8–019**

See also *R. (on the application of the Immigration Law Practitioners' Association) v Tribunal Procedure Committee* [2016] EWHC 218 (Admin); [2016] 1 W.L.R. 3519 (referring to the *Roberts* guidance on the minimum requirement of a fair hearing in the context of rules of the First-tier Tribunal).

[Add new para.8–019A after para.8–019]   **8–019A**

Detailed consideration has also been given recently to the extent to which the Secretary of State had to provide disclosure of closed material to special advocates appointed to represent the interests of claimants in proceedings before the Special Immigration Appeals Commission.[82a] It was held that a complete understanding of the issues involved was required by the commission and a recognition that the inability of the special advocates to take instructions from the interested parties on the closed-procedure material heightened the obligation to review that material with care.[82b] That limitation on the ability to have a complete understanding of the position from the interested parties' perspective, to contrast with the Secretary of State's arguments, was regarded as equally important in respect of the issue of the material which should be available.[82c] The Court held, however, that to require disclosure of all the material the summary writer could have accessed, took the investigation far beyond a review. The disclosure had to be sufficient to permit challenge, if appropriate, to the underlying rationality of any part of the decision and its reasoning. Therefore, the Secretary of State should disclose the underlying material relied on by the summary writer in identifying facts or reaching a conclusion. That was consistent with the obligation to ensure that the material enabled a proper determination of the proceedings as required under r.4(3).[82d] It was also observed that this level of disclosure was in addition to, and had to be distinguished from, the Secretary of State's duty of candour and as a matter of practice, the Secretary of State should require the material used to establish the facts to be annexed to, or identified by, the summary so that appropriate disclosure to the special advocates could proceed without difficulty.[82e]

[82a] *Secretary of State for the Home Department v Special Immigration Appeals Commission* [2015] EWHC 681 (Admin).

[82b] *Secretary of State for the Home Department v Special Immigration Appeals Commission* [2015] EWHC 681 (Admin) at [28].

[82c] *Secretary of State for the Home Department v Special Immigration Appeals Commission* [2015] EWHC 681 (Admin) at [29].

[82d] *Secretary of State for the Home Department v Special Immigration Appeals Commission* [2015] EWHC 681 (Admin) at [34].

[82e] *Secretary of State for the Home Department v Special Immigration Appeals Commission* [2015] EWHC 681 (Admin) at [34].

Other public interests

8–020 *[Add to n.84 after (". . . gaming club consents).")]*

R. (on the application of X) v Chief Constable of Y [2015] EWHC 484 (Admin) at [24] (referring to the "well established public interest in protecting the identity of policy informants")]

[Add to end of n.84]

See also *R. (on the application of X) v Chief Constable of Y* [2015] EWHC 484 (Admin) (while there was no pre-determination that the balance favoured non-disclosure in civil cases, the public interest in the protection of informants carried considerable weight).

[Add to end of n.87]

See also *R. (on the application of Bourgass) v Secretary of State for Justice* [2015] UKSC 54; [2015] 3 W.L.R. 457 at [103] (in the context of prison segregation decisions, fairness does not require the disclosure of information which could compromise the safety of an informant, the integrity of prison security or other overriding interests. It will be sufficient to inform the prisoner in more or less general terms of the gist of the reasons for seeking the authority of the Secretary of State; *Da Costa v Sargaco* [2016] EWCA Civ 764; [2016] C.P. Rep. 40 at [51] (the decision in *Al-Rawi v Security Service* [2011] UKSC 34; [2012] 1 A.C. 531 was not authority for the proposition that, in order to a party to have a fair trial, there was an absolute requirement that he or she had to have the opportunity to be present throughout the hearing).

FAIR PROCEDURES WOULD HINDER PROMPT ACTION

Statutory relaxation of procedural propriety

[Add after ". . . the court is effective.[94]*"]*   8–022

Similarly, where investors had participated in tax avoidance measures which were subsequently disputed in the First-tier Tribunal, HMRC was entitled to issue notices to those investors requiring accelerated payment of tax which it considered would be due after the resolution of that substantive dispute.[94a]

[94a] *R. (on the application of Rowe) v Revenue and Customs Commissioners* [2015] EWHC 2293 (Admin) at [62] (the accelerated payment required did not involve any determination of final liability, but rather addressed where the tax should be held pending resolution of the dispute and any hardship suffered by the taxpayer was always a risk that might materialise when entering a tax avoidance scheme without making provision for payment of tax if the scheme failed).

[Add to end of n.94]

See also *R. (on the application of the Howard League for Penal Reform, Prisoners' Advice Service) v Lord Chancellor* [2015] EWCA Civ 819 at [20] (applying the *Medical Justice* test of whether a system, removing certain categories of decisions affecting prisoners from the scope of criminal legal aid, considered in the round carried an unacceptable risk of unfairness.

SUBSEQUENT FAIR HEARING OR APPEAL

Common law and subsequent hearings

8–034 *[Add to end of n.147]*

See also *R. (on the application of Rowe) v Revenue and Customs Commissioners* [2015] EWHC 2293 (no breach of procedural fairness where accelerated payment notices where tax avoidance measures were in dispute did not give rise to determination of final liability).

ECHR art.6 and subsequent hearings

8–036 *[Add to end of n.159]*

See also *Re CS's Application for Judicial Review* [2015] NIQB 36 at [14] (holding that the art.6 compliance of a decision by a university's review panel required considering the hearing before the Board of Visitors and the right to such a hearing being reviewed by the High Court on certain limited, but defined grounds).

[Add to end of n.161]

R. (on the application of Derrin Bros Properties Ltd) v First-tier Tribunal [2016] EWCA Civ 15; [2016] 1 W.L.R. 2423 (judicial review was an adequate remedy to ensure that third party information notices had been validly issued) and Finance Act 2008 powers proportionately applied in connection with an offshore tax avoidance investigation).

8–037 *[In n.164, delete "[2012] EWCA Civ 376; [2012] 1 WLR 3602 (if ECHR art.6 was engaged, notwithstanding the absence of independence and impartiality in a prison in the context of decisions on segregation and cellular confinement, due do the availability of judicial review, the procedure as a whole was ECHR art.6 compliant) and insert]*

[2015] UKSC 54; [2015] 3 W.L.R. 457 at [123] (while a decision to authorise continued segregation does not fall within the ambit of art.6.1, in any event, the availability of judicial review would meet the requirements of art.6.1, in particular, given that such a decision is unlikely to turn on the determination of disputed questions of fact).

[Add to n.164 after ". . . [2011] A.C.D. 86"]

R. (on the application of Ali) v Secretary of State for Justice [2013] EWHC 72 (Admin); [2013] 1 W.L.R. 3536 at [66]–[72].

[Add to end of n.164]

. See also App No 47315/13 *Adorisio v Netherlands* (2015) 61 E.H.R.R. SE1.

[Add to end of n.165]

; *R. (on the application of Ali) v Secretary of State for Justice* [2013] EWHC 72 (Admin); [2013] 1 W.L.R. 3536 at [66]–[72].

PRELIMINARY DECISIONS

Proximity between investigation and act or decision

[Add to n.196 after (". . . satisfied by statutory procedure)"]   8–042

See also *R. (on the application of Rowe) v Revenue and Customs Commissioners* [2015] EWHC 2293 (Admin) (no breach of fair procedures where an accelerated payment notice was issued prior to determination of dispute regarding tax avoidance measures).

[Add to end of n.201]   8–043

See also *NXB v Crown Prosecution Service* [2015] EWHC 631 (QB).

Preliminary investigations subject to procedural fairness

Public inquiries

[Add to end of para.8–045]   8–045

It may also be the case that confidentiality is required in the conduct of the inquiry and such confidentiality will not mean that the right to fair procedures have been violated.[203a] It has been held in respect of an inquiry that while ultimately the question of fairness is one of law for the court, nonetheless, the court would give great weight to the tribunal's own view of what was fair and would not lightly decide that the tribunal had adopted an unfair procedure.[203b]

203a *Re LP's Application for Judicial Review* [2014] NICA 67 (holding that the Historical Institutional Abuse Inquiry was entitled to refuse to give a witness who had given evidence a recording of here statement; the forum was intended as a confidential service where victims and survivors could recount their experience with total confidence in the confidentiality of that stage of the inquiry, and witnesses had been informed at the outset that no recordings would be made available).

203b *Re LP's Application for Judicial Review* [2014] NICA 67 at [31].

[Add to end of n.208]

This does not, however, extend to giving rights of representation to those who might be linked to findings made by the decision-maker as a result of speculation or material put into the public domain: see *The Financial Conduct Authority v Macris* [2015] EWCA Civ 490 at [27].

[Add to end of n.221]

See also *Traveller Movement v Ofcom* [2015] EWHC 406 (Admin).

LACK OF FAIR PROCEDURE MADE NO DIFFERENCE OR CAUSED NO HARM

8–053 *[Add to end of n.226]*

See also A. Mills, "The 'Makes no Difference' Controversy" [2013] J.R. 124; D. Feldman, "Error of Law and Flawed Administrative Acts" [2014] C.L.J. 275.

Statutory applications to quash

8–055 *[Add to after ". . . should scrutinise the facts.236"]*

It has been held that it is not necessary for the claimant to show that the decision would inevitably have been different.236a

236a *R. (on the application of Gopikrishna) v Office of the Independent Adjudicator for Higher Education* [2015] EWHC 207 at [209].

Caution required in relation to the "no difference" argument

8–057 *[Add to end of n.242]*

San Vicente v Secretary of State for Communities and Local Government
[2013] EWHC 2713 (Admin); [2014] J.P.L. 217 at [29]–[31] (although over-
ruled on whether or not there had actually been unfairness on appeal, [2014]
EWCA Civ 1555; [2015] J.P.L. 562).

Illustrations

[Add to end of n.245]   8–059

See also *R. (on the application of Wilson) v Office of the Independent
Adjudicator for Higher Education* [2014] EWHC 558 (Admin); [2014]
E.L.R. 273 (lack of mathematical reasoning in arriving at a compensation
figure was not an error of law if the ultimate conclusion was within the
bracket of reasonable figures which could be arrived at). Contrast *R. (on the
application of Gopikrishna) v Office of the Independent Adjudicator for
Higher Education* [2015] EWHC 207 (Admin) at [209] (letters from the
personal and clinical tutors were inconsistent with the panel's view that the
student had been a weak student and it was not possible to be satisfied that
the adjudicator would necessarily have come to the same conclusion if it had
known the true situation). However, there was no real possibility that a
letter from the University confirming that it did not have formal procedures
for re-opening appeals and a response from the claimant would have materially affected the decision: [217].

[Add to end of n.249]

See also *Burger v Office of the Independent Adjudicator for Higher Education*
[2013] EWHC 172 (Admin); [2013] E.L.R. 331 (assessment criteria should
have been disclosed to students in advance of an examination; however,
non-publication would not have made any difference to complainant's
examination performance and would not gain from decision being quashed).

CHAPTER 9

PROCEDURAL FAIRNESS: FETTERING OF DISCRETION

FETTERING OF DISCRETION BY SELF-CREATED RULES OR POLICY

[Add after ". . . the ground of 'illegality' in Chapter 5.³"]   9–003

The non-fettering principle has also been described as a "general principle of the common law", which is critical to lawful public decision-making, since without it, decisions would be liable to be unfair, through failing to have regard to what affected persons had to say or unreasonable, through failing to have regard to relevant factors, or both.[3a]

[3a] *R. (on the application of West Berkshire District Council v Secretary of State for Communities and Local Government* [2016] EWCA Civ 441; [2016] P.T.S.R. 982 at [19] (adding that in the law of planning, the principle is reflected in the description of planning policy as not a rule, but a guide).

[Add to end of n.5]   9–004

There have also been a number of recent challenges in which decisions have been held to be unlawful for failure to follow policy: *R. (on the application of O) v Secretary of State for the Home Department* [2016] UKSC 19; *Onos v Secretary of State for the Home Department* [2016] EWHC 59 (Admin) at [62] (requiring good reason to depart from policy); *R. (on the application of FK) v Secretary of State for the Home Department* [2016] EWHC 56 (Admin); *Mandalia v Secretary of State for the Home Department* [2015] UKSC 59; [2015] 1 W.L.R. 4546.

[Add to end of n.7]

; [2014] UKSC 42 (CAT decision upheld, although the fettering point was not discussed).

[Add to end of n.8]

See also *R (on the application of St Mary Magdalene Academy) v Secretary of State for the Home Department* [2015] EWHC 725 (Admin) at [48] and [52] (finding that a policy of not granting sponsor licences to state schools seeking to admit foreign students, while lawful itself, had been applied too rigidly and that no consideration had been given to the individual circumstances with the *"flexibility, fairness and good sense that the law requires"*). A similar result was reached in *R. (on the application of Robson) v Crown Prosecution Service* [2016] EWHC 2191 (Admin) at [45] (a guidance on conditional cautions for offences was not unlawful, but the decision-maker had interpreted the guidance as possessing no flexibility at all and as permitting no exceptions). By contrast, in *R. (on the application of Project Management Institute) v Minister for the Cabinet Office* [2016] EWCA Civ 21; [2016] 1 W.L.R. 1737, the policy was found to allow a considerable degree of flexibility in its application (at [42]).

[Add to end of n.9]

It has also been observed that "the exercise of public discretionary power requires the decision-maker to bring his mind to bear on the very case; he cannot blindly follow a pre-existing policy without considering anything said to persuade him that the case in hand is an exception": *R. (on the application of West Berkshire District Council v Secretary of State for Communities and Local Government* [2016] EWCA Civ 441; [2016] P.T.S.R. 982.

[Add to end of para.9–004]

It is important to add that the non-fettering principle will not render mandatory rules unlawful in every statutory context, and a distinction has been drawn between statutes which expressly permit rules to be made and those which do not.[10a] For example, it has been held that the Immigration Rules were not statements of policy subject to all the public law constraints on policies and discretionary powers including the non-fettering principle, since they were expressly contemplated by the Immigration Act 1971.[10b]

[10a] *R. (on the application of Sayaniya) v Upper Tribunal* [2016] EWCA Civ 85; [2016] 4 W.L.R. 58 at [15].

[10b] The Court added that, to the extent that the non-fettering principle applied to Immigration Rules, a rule expressed in mandatory terms did not fall foul of it since the Secretary of State had discretion outside the rules which he could exercise in favour of those who did not qualify under them: *R. (on the application of Sayaniya) v Upper Tribunal* [2016] EWCA Civ 85; [2016] 4 W.L.R. 58 at [21].

Underlying rationale

9–005 *[Add after ". . . in the individual case.[12]"]*

As has been observed, there is a tension in public law decision-making between flexibility in the decision-making process and predictability of its outcome. The more there is of one, the less room there is for the other, and getting the balance right is often difficult.[12a]

[12a] *R. (on the application of Sayaniya) v Upper Tribunal* [2016] EWCA Civ 85; [2016] 4 W.L.R. 58 at [16] (citing from Lord Walker in *R. (on the application of Alvi) v Secretary of State for the Home Department (Joint Council for the Welfare of Immigrants intervening)* [2012] UKSC 33; [2012] 1 W.L.R. 2208 at [111]).

[Add after ". . . of equal treatment in fact.[13]"]

In this regard, the duty to follow policy has been described as subordinate to the duty to exercise statutory power lawfully, and it has been held to be wrong to allow policy to fetter discretion if there was good reason not to follow it.[13a]

[13a] *Gage v Scottish Ministers* [2015] CSOH 174 at [20]; see also *Mandalia v Secretary of State for the Home Department* [2015] UKSC 59; [2015] 1 W.L.R. 4546.

[Add to end of para.9–005]

It has also been observed that the principle against fettering ensures that decisions taken represent "a true and proper exercise of the discretion conferred by Parliament".[11a]

[11a] *R. (on the application of Hillsden) v Epping Forest* [2015] EWHC 98 (Admin) at [29].

Application of the no-fettering principle

Illustrations

[Add after "a failure to exercise discretion[46]"]   9–007

- By contrast, there was no fettering where a policy guidance explained that a regulatory discretion to waive fees for applicants seeking a visa to enter the United Kingdom would only be exercised where there were the most exceptional, compelling and compassionate circumstances, as the policy was consistent with expectations underlying the statutory scheme, relevant to the exercise of the relevant powers, consistent with the purpose of the enabling legislation and not arbitrary, capricious or unjust.[46a]

- In the context of an application for citizenship, it was held that the Secretary of State had fettered her discretion in refusing to register as a British citizen a 17-year-old South African national who had pleaded guilty to possessing cannabis and had been given a six-month conditional discharge.[46b]

[46a] *In the matter of An Application by Fowsiya Salad for Leave to Apply for Judicial Review* [2015] NIQB 32 at [22].

[46b] *R. (on the application of SA) v Secretary of State for the Home Department* [2015] EWHC 1611 (Admin).

[Add to end of n.14]

By contrast, in *St Albans City and District Council v Secretary of State for Communities and Local Government* [2015] EWHC 655 (Admin), the Secretary of State had not fettered his discretion when determining a second planning appeal by requiring a very good reason to be shown for departing from the conclusion reached in the first appeal, where the "very good reason" has been applied as a matter of judgment rather than as a legal test.

[Add to end of n.19]

Blanket policies may also create human rights challenges, see, e.g., *R. (on the application of Tigere) v Secretary of State for Business, Innovation and Skills* [2015] UKSC 57; [2015] 1 W.L.R. 3820.

[Add to end of n.30]

See also, *R (on the application of Hardy) v Sandwell Metropolitan Borough Council* [2015] EWHC 890 (Admin) at [43] (a council's policy of always taking into account the care component of disability living allowance when assessing the amount of a discretionary housing payment was an unlawful fetter).

[Add to end of n.46]

See also *R. (on the application of SA) v Secretary of State for the Home Department* [2015] EWHC 1611 at [36] and [42] (holding that the Defendant was entitled to adopt a policy on the way in which criminal convictions will normally be considered by her caseworkers, but it should not be applied mechanistically and inflexibly; there had to be a comprehensive assessment of each applicant's character, as an individual, which involves an exercise of judgment, not just ticking boxes on a form; the official did not properly weigh in the balance the strong countervailing evidence of the Claimant's good character against the fact of his conviction).

Power to articulate rules or policy

[Add to end of n.58] 9–010

See also *R. (on the application of SA) v Secretary of State for the Home Department* [2015] EWHC 1611 (Admin) at [31] (observing that the Defendant was entitled to adopt a policy "provided that she exercised her statutory function lawfully").

Do exceptions have to be specified in the rule or policy?

[Add new n.75a after ". . . in the words of the policy itself."] 9–013

[75a] This statement of principle was recently endorsed by the Court of Appeal in *R. (on the application of West Berkshire District Council v Secretary of State for Communities and Local Government* [2016] EWCA Civ 441; [2016] P.T.S.R. 982 at [17] (overturning the ruling of the lower court on the basis that it had conflated what the policy said with how it could lawfully be deployed).

[Add after ". . . in the words of the policy itself."]

It has also been held that this principle—and indeed the rule against fettering discretion—apply whether or not the policy-maker and the decision-maker are the same or different persons, since, if it were otherwise, neither would have any integrity as a principle.[75b] It was also observed that a policy-maker is entitled to express his policy in qualified terms, as it would be idle, and most likely confusing, to require every policy statement to include a health warning in the shape of a reminder that the policy must be applied consistently with the rule against fettering.[75c]

[75b] *R. (on the application of West Berkshire District Council v Secretary of State for Communities and Local Government* [2016] EWCA Civ 441; [2016] P.T.S.R. 982 at [18].

[75c] *R. (on the application of West Berkshire District Council v Secretary of State for Communities and Local Government* [2016] EWCA Civ 441; [2016] P.T.S.R. 982 at [21].

Evidence of a fetter on discretion

Conduct of the decision-maker

9–018 *[Add to end of n.92]*

; R. *(on the application of Sandiford) v The Secretary of State for Foreign and Commonwealth Affairs* [2014] UKSC 44; *The Times*, July 25, 2014 at [65] (blanket policy under prerogative powers to refuse funding of foreign litigation due to domestic policy and funding considerations not unacceptable).

UNDERTAKING NOT TO EXERCISE A DISCRETION

Discretion and contract

9–025 *[Add to end of n. 117]*

For an example of a case in which no fettering was found where there was an express term in the contract that the authority would not be constrained in acting in any other capacity as a result of being a contracting party: see R. *(on the application of Khan) v Sutton* [2014] EWHC 3663 (Admin).

9–028 *[Add to end of n.126]*

See also *Credit Suisse International v Stichting Vestia Groep* [2014] EWHC 3103 (Comm); [2015] Bus. L.R. D5.

Common law discretionary powers

9–029 *[Add to end of para.9–029]*

Similarly, the doctrine does not apply to prerogative powers.[132a]

[132a] R. *(on the Application of Sandiford) v Secretary of State for Foreign and Commonwealth Affairs* [2014] UKSC 44 at [54], [62] (referring to the reasoning in R. *(on the application of Elias) v Secretary of State for Defence* [2006] EWCA Civ 1293; [2006] 1 W.L.R. 3213, in which it had been held that it is within the power of the decision-maker to decide on the extent to which to exercise a power such as setting up a scheme, it was held that prerogative powers have to be approached on a different basis from statutory powers as there is no necessary implication, from their mere existence, that the State as their holder must keep open the possibility of their exercise in more than one sense). For comment, see K Costello "The scope of application of the rule against fettering in administrative law" (2015) 131 L.Q.R. 354.

CHAPTER 10

PROCEDURAL FAIRNESS: BIAS AND CONFLICT OF INTEREST

SCOPE

Introduction

[Add to end of n.1]   10–002

See also *R. (on the application of DM Digital Television Ltd) v Office of Communications* [2014] EWHC 961 (Admin) at [36].

[Add to end of n.6]   10–006

; *Thames Water Utilities Ltd v Newbound* [2015] EWCA Civ 677 at [91] (Lady Justice King observing that "[u]nderlying both of them is the fundamental consideration that justice should not only be done but should manifestly and undoubtedly be seen to be done").

[Add to end of n.10]   10–007

Resolution Chemicals Limited v H Lundbeck A/S [2013] EWCA Civ 1515; [2014] 1 W.L.R. 1943 at [35] ("underlying both article 6 of the Convention and the common law principles is the fundamental consideration that justice should not only be done but should manifestly and undoubtedly be seen to be done").

[Add new n.10a after ". . . and other decision-making bodies"]

10a In this respect, it is important to emphasise that if the fair-minded and informed observer would conclude that there is a real possibility that the tribunal will be biased, the judge is automatically disqualified from hearing the case. The decision to recuse in those circumstances is not a discretionary case management decision reached by weighing various relevant factors in the balance. Considerations of inconvenience, cost and delay are irrelevant: *Resolution Chemicals Limited v H Lundbeck A/S* [2013] EWCA Civ 1515; [2014] 1 W.L.R. 1943 at [35]. A "pragmatic precautionary approach" is required: [40].

Later developments

10–011 *[Add to end of n.31]*

See also R. *(on the application of Evans) v Attorney General* [2015] UKSC 21; [2015] 2 W.L.R. 813 (Lord Neuberger observing (at [52]) that "it is a basic principle that a decision of a court is binding as between the parties, and cannot be ignored or set aside by anyone, including (indeed it may fairly be said, least of all) the executive. Secondly, it is also fundamental to the rule of law that decisions and actions of the executive are, subject to necessary well established exceptions (such as declarations of war), and jealously scrutinised statutory exceptions, reviewable by the court at the suit of an interested citizen").

THE TEST OF BIAS

10–012 *[Add after ". . . investigate evidence of actual bias".]*

and there is authority to the effect that submissions of actual bias should not be made.[36a] There are a number of reasons why the courts have seldom embarked on such inquiries. Actual bias has been described as rare and difficult to prove.[36b]

[36a] *Jackson v Thompsons Solicitors* [2015] EWHC 218 (QB) at [16].

[36b] *Broadview Energy Developments Ltd v Secretary of State for Communities and Local Government* [2015] EWHC 1743 at [47].

[Add after ". . . in its effect.[38]"]

There are also obvious difficulties in exploring the actual state of mind of a judge (for example, a judge is not compellable as a witness in relation to his own decision) and it may be very difficult to establish.[36c]

[36c] *Jackson v Thompsons Solicitors* [2015] EWHC 218 (QB) at [16].

[Add after ". . . an appearance of bias.[39]"]

Of course, even allegation of apparent bias should only be made on a proper basis; it is open to submit that certain findings of a panel may be characterised as wrong or lacking any proper basis or even perverse, but that is quite a different thing from making a serious allegation of bias against a panel of this sort, whether actual or apparent.[39a]

[39a] *R. (on the application of Allen) v Parole Board of England and Wales* [2015] EWHC 2069 (Admin) at [43].

[Add to end of n.38]

See also *Jackson v Thompsons Solicitors* [2015] EWHC 218 (QB) at [16].
[Add to end of n.39]
See also *Jackson v Thompsons Solicitors* [2015] EWHC 218 (QB) at [17].

HISTORICAL DEVELOPMENT

Gough adjusted: "real possibility"

[Add to end of para.10–017]   10–017

This point was emphasised recently when the Court of Appeal observed that "the opinion of the notional informed and fair-minded observer is not to be confused with the opinion of the litigant".[56a] Indeed, the litigant has been noted to be not the fair-minded observer, lacking the objectivity which is the hallmark of the fair-minded observer, being "far from dispassionate"; since litigation is a stressful and expensive business, most litigants "are likely to oppose anything that they perceive might imperil their prospects of success, even if, when viewed objectively, their perception is not well-founded".[56b]

[56a] *Harb v Aziz* [2016] EWCA Civ 556 at [69] (adding that the test "ensures that there is a measure of detachment in the assessment of whether there is a real possibility of bias"). For comment, see C. Hollander "Apparent bias against an entire barristers' chambers? *Harb v HRH Prince Abdul Aziz* [2016] EWCA Civ 556" (2016) 35 C.J.Q. 287; K. Anderson "Lost luggage and judicial baggage: *Harb v HRH Prince Abdul Aziz* [2016] EWCA Civ 556" (2016) 35 C.J.Q. 290.

[56b] *Harb v Aziz* [2016] EWCA Civ 556 at [69].

[Add to para.10–018 after ". . . before the court."]   10–018

The notional observer has been described as "something of a paragon. Not only is he fair-minded and impartial, but he has diligently educated himself about the circumstances of the case".[57a]

[57a] *Dar Al Arkan Real Estate Development Company v Majid Al-Sayed Bader Hashim Refai* [2014] EWHC 1055 (COMM) at [37].

[Add to end of n.60]

; see also *Congregation of the Poor Sisters of Nazareth v Scottish Ministers* [2015] CSOH 87; 2015 S.L.T. 445 at [31] (applied in *Beggs, Petitioner* [2016] CSOH 61); *R. (on the application of Forge Field Society v Sevenoaks DC* [2014] EWHC 1895 (Admin) at [25] ("[t]he fair-minded observer is neither complacent nor unduly sensitive or suspicious. He views the relevant facts in an objective and dispassionate way"); *Ecovision Systems Limited v Vinci Construction UK Limited* [2015] EWHC 587 (TCC) at [95]. For reliance on *Helow* for the proposition that it could be assumed that a judge would be able to discount material which he or she had read and reach an impartial decision according to the law, see: *Rasool v General Pharmaceutical Council* [2015] EWHC 217.

[Add to end of n.61]

; *O'Neill v HM Advocate (No.2)* [2013] UKSC 36; [2013] 1 W.L.R. 1992 at [53] (the fair-minded and informed observer would be aware that a judge who had made negative comments about two convicted defendants in the context of trial for sexual offences was a professional judge who had taken the judicial oath and had years of relevant training and experience and who would hear and understand the context in which the remarks had been made—namely, in open court, from the bench, while performing his duty as judge and would also appreciate that when the judge was presiding over a second trial against the defendants for murder, he would be doing so in the performance of his duty to preside over that case). In the planning context, it has been held that the fair-minded and informed observer would appreciate, inter alia that an inspector's role had a strong inquisitorial dimension, such that it was fair and appropriate for him to perform robust case management and to focus debate by making interventions and giving indications; an inspector has to manage efficiently the conduct of the inquiry within a limited time-frame; an inspector is entitled to expect focused questioning, and the inspector is expected to have done a good deal of preparation before the inquiry and is entitled to focus debate on particular issues. Moreover, a lapse in courtesy or patience will not in itself give an appearance of bias: *Turner v Secretary of State for Communities and Local Government* [2015] EWCA Civ 582 at [18]. See also *Broadview Energy Developments Ltd v Secretary of State for Communities and Local Government* [2015] EWHC 1743 (Admin) at [45] (fair-minded observers would know that when recommending the grant of planning permission the planning inspector considered that the matter was finely balanced and that an MP was lobbying assiduously, and openly, against the proposal on behalf of her constituents; consequently they would antici-pate: (1) that she would be writing to Ministers, forwarding her constituents' correspondence against the proposal; (2) that when the issues had been extensively canvassed in this case at two public inquiries it was unlikely that there would be anything new to say; (3) that so long as the decision was outstanding, she would need to continue the lobbying, and be seen to be doing that by her constituents; and (4) that she would use every opportunity, including the inevitable encounter with Ministers on the Parliamentary estate, to advance the case. They would also know: (1) that Ministers are constantly lobbied by MPs; (2) that Planning Ministers are bound by the Ministerial Code and receive specific guidance on propriety requirements; and (3) that Ministers receive a briefing from officials as to how they should decide a matter of this nature). Similarly, it was held in *Rasool v General Pharmaceutical Council* [2015] EWHC 217 that the fair-minded observer would have regard to the fact that the chairman of a fitness to practice committee was an experienced QC, who could be assumed to be well aware of his duties and obligations to try hearings fairly and by reference only to the evidence and materials before him and who could be assumed to be capable of discounting anything that had been asserted by the pharmacist's colleague. In *Broadview Energy Developments Limited v Secretary of State for Communities and Local Government* [2016] EWCA Civ 562 at [36], it was held that where a local MP had lobbied the Minister against a proposed wind farm, the well-informed observer would know that it was the responsibility of the relevant Minister to make difficult decisions about controversial projects such as on-shore wind farms; he would also know that sometimes such decisions are, as this one was, finely balanced. He would not think that a Minister's decision in favour of a vocal body of local objectors supported by their local MP showed any bias against the promoter of the wind farm project; he would accept that the Minister had to make a decision one way or the other and think that the parties should accept the outcome. The fair-minded observer would know that a barrister was in independent practice, such that there was no basis for the suggestion that a local authority was paying him for favourable advice: *Somerford PC v Cheshire East BC* [2016] EWHC 619 (Admin). It has also been held that the fair-minded observer would understand that a member of staff was present at an internal complaints committee hearing as an employee, taking notes in an administrative capacity and not the decision-maker: *Beggs, Petitioner* [2016] CSOH 61, at [141]–[142].

[Add to end of n.65]

This was confirmed in *Harb v Aziz* [2016] EWCA Civ 556 at [72].

[Add to para.10–018 after ". . . in the public domain.[65]"]

In addition, it has been held that the court must look at all the circumstances as they appear from the material before it, not just at the facts known to the objectors or available to the hypothetical observer at the time of the decision;[65a] what is required is an examination of all the relevant facts.[65b] In other words, the position is to be judged at the time the matter comes before the court.[65c] The courts will also not readily make assumptions from the facts that indicate bias.[65d]

[65a] *Paice v Harding (t/a MJ Harding Contractors)* [2016] EWHC B22 (TCC) at [41].

[65b] *Harb v Aziz* [2016] EWCA Civ 556 at [75].

[65c] *Sisk & Son Ltd v Duro Felguera UK Ltd* [2016] EWHC 81 (TCC) at [37] (and will include consideration of the manner in which a decision or judgment has been reached).

[65d] *W Ltd v M Sdn Bhd* [2016] EWHC 422 (Comm) at [23] (where a conflict check did not alert an arbitrator to the relationship between the respondent and the parent company of his firm, or to the fact that the latter was the firm's client, the fair-minded observer would therefore conclude that the arbitrator did not know the relationship between the two companies, rather than being someone who "must have known" and whose credibility was therefore to be doubted).

[Add to end of n.66]

For a less onerous, albeit obiter, statement of the position, see *Thames Water Utilities Ltd v Newbound* [2015] EWCA Civ 677 at [91]–[94].

[Add to end of para.10–018]

In similar vein, the courts will also have regard to admissible evidence about what actually happened in the course of the deliberations of the tribunal against which apparent bias is alleged,[66a] and it has been observed that it is important to consider "all of the facts when considering whether apparent bias is established".[66b] Overall, the courts have been keen to emphasise that "[t]he test is not one of 'any possibility' but of a 'real' possibility of bias" and that each case turns on an intense focus on the essential facts of the case.[66c]

[66a] *R. (on the application of DM Digital Television Ltd) v Office of Communications* [2014] EWHC 961 (Admin) at [38], [45]–[47] (observing that, where it is available, it would be wrong in principle to reach a conclusion that there has been apparent bias without having regard to such admissible evidence and holding that the conclusion of a disciplinary panel was supported by the thoroughness of the final decision letters and the notes of the deliberations, which showed that the panel was at pains to address all relevant matters and that no new matters had been introduced in deliberations which the claimant had not had every opportunity to address).

[66b] *R. (on the application of DM Digital Television Ltd) v Office of Communications* [2014] EWHC 961 (Admin) at [37].

[66c] *Resolution Chemicals Ltd v H Hundbeck A/S* [2013] EWCA Civ 1515; [2014] 1 W.L.R. 1943 at [35]–[36] (also noting that a "pragmatic precautionary approach" should guide the approach of the court to applications for recusal: [40]). For commentary on recusals generally, see A.A. Olowofoyeku "Inappropriate recusals" (2016) 132 L.Q.R. 318.

AUTOMATIC DISQUALIFICATION FOR BIAS

Direct pecuniary or proprietary interest

[Add to end of n.80]   10–021

Contrast *Kelton v Wiltshire Council* [2015] EWHC 2853 (Admin) (apparent rather than actual bias found). For comment, see "Kelton v Wiltshire Council: disclosable pecuniary interests – apparent bias" [2016] Journal of Planning & Environment Law 273.

Exceptions to automatic disqualification

Trivial interests

[Add to end of n.91]   10–028

See also *Kelton v Wiltshire Council* [2015] EWHC 2853 (Admin) at [42] (no automatic disqualification where one of the councillors who had voted in favour of a grant of planning permission for a residential development including affordable housing was a director of the housing association likely to be awarded the contract to provide the affordable housing, since the decision of the committee did not lead to the councillor obtaining any benefit) (although apparent bias was found)).

Great degree of flexibility in application of automatic disqualification

[Add to para.10–031 after ". . . eight years previously did not amount to 10–031
bias.[100]"]

In a later case, the fact that a judge was a former pupil of an expert witness who had supervised his university thesis some 30 years previously was not enough to constitute bias in the absence of a continuing link.[100a]

[100a] *Resolution Chemicals Ltd v H Hundbeck A/S* [2013] EWCA Civ 1515; [2014] 1 W.L.R. 1943 at [45]–[49].

[In para.10–031 delete "In a later case" and substitute]

Similarly,

[Add to end of n.101]

; *Resolution Chemicals Limited v H Lundbeck A/S* [2013] EWCA Civ 1515; [2014] 1 W.L.R. 1943 at [46] (the fair-minded and informed observer would not discount the matters of judicial training, experience and ethos).

Can automatic disqualification be justified?

10–032 *[Add to end of n.104]*

; *Resolution Chemicals Limited v H Lundbeck A/S* [2013] EWCA Civ 1515; [2014] 1 W.L.R. 1943 at [42].

10–035 *[Add to end of n.113]*

However, see *R. (on the application of Shaw) v HM Coroner for Leicester City and South Leicestershire* [2013] EWHC 386 (Admin) (the fully informed independent observer would not have been troubled by a friend-ship between an assistant deputy coroner and a member of the management of the hospital in which the deceased had died, where the member of management had left the hospital before the deceased's procedure and death).

[Add to end of n.114]

Contrast *R. (on the application of Shaw) v HM Coroner for Leicester City and South Leicestershire* [2013] EWHC 386 (Admin) (no bias arose from the personal friendship between an assistant deputy coroner and the former chief executive of an NHS trust involved in an inquest where the executive had left the post before the incident giving rise to the inquest). In *Shaw*, guidance was provided (at [105]) to coroners where they have an interest which could create apparent bias: disclosure of the interest should be put in writing or otherwise recorded in a permanent record. The coroner should then usually advise any interested person affected of the options: (i) consent to the hearing going ahead and losing the right to object later (waiver); (ii) apply to the coroner to recuse himself (which the coroner will not take amiss), and, if he recuses himself, what effect recusal would have on the timing of the inquest. Any person affected should have adequate time to reflect and, if necessary, take legal or other advice before making a free and informed decision.

OTHER SITUATIONS IN WHICH BIAS MAY OCCUR

Participation in subsequent decision

[Add to end of n.116]   10–038

Of course, in almost every case, the judge who heard the substantial application will be the right judge to deal with consequential issues as to costs: *Mengiste v Endowment Fund for the Rehabilitation of Tigray* [2013] EWCA Civ 1003; [2014] P.N.L.R. 4 at [58].

[Add to n.117 after ". . . [2010] PTSR 1527"]

; *O'Neill v HM Advocate (No.2)* [2013] UKSC 36; [2013] 1 W.L.R. 1992 at [53] (the fair-minded observer would appreciate that a judge's comments, although condemning, were made separately in each context, and did not carry over to new decisions. It would only be where the judge had expressed entirely gratuitous opinions that expression of a prior opinion in the judicial context could demonstrate bias).

[Add to end of n.117]

; *Dar Al Arkan Real Estate Development Company v Majid Al-Sayed Bader Hashim Refai* [2014] EWHC 1055 (COMM) [37] (recusal appropriate where the facts informing an earlier and separate decision remained similar).

Illustrations

[In para. 10–039 insert two new bullet points after "continue to hold an oper-   10–039
ator's license.[125]*" as follows]*

- The fact that a trial judge made adverse comments about defendants at the conclusion of a sexual offences trial would not lead the fair-minded observer to doubt the professional judge's ability to preside over the defendant's subsequent murder trial, unless those comments consisted of entirely gratuitous opinions.[125a]
- A judge who had made two orders against a father for failing to cause the return of his son to the jurisdiction, and had made adverse comments about him and his likely imprisonment, should have recused herself from a committal application.[125b]

[125a] *O'Neill v HM Advocate (No.2)* [2013] UKSC 36; [2013] 1 W.L.R. 1992 at [53]. Contrast *Dar Al Arkan Real Estate Development Co v Majid Al-Sayed Bader Hashim Al Refa* [2014] EWHC 1055 (COMM) at [36]. Smith J. decided to recuse himself from subsequent application where initial decision contained detailed and specific views about the credibility of the witnesses and other crucial issues likely to arise on hearing of the subsequent application, observing as follows: "But it is one thing for the fair-minded and impartial observer to have faith that a judge will reassess his views with an open mind when presented with new evidence and argument. It is asking more of the observer's faith when similar evidence and arguments are presented to assess the same issues. There comes a point when he is entitled to think that, though 'o' independent mind', a judge is 'a man for a' that'. In this case the claimants and Sheikh Abdullatif are entitled to have another judge decide the contempt application." This case has been distinguished in *Butt v Commissioners for Her Majesty's Revenue and Customs* [2015] UKFTT 0510 (TC) at [563]. While in *Dar*, evidence had been called and robust findings of fact made, here, in an application for summary judgment, no evidence had been called, no findings of fact made and the judge had been cautious not to pre-judge the issues which fell to be determined in the context of the substantive appeal.

[125b] *K (A Child)* [2014] EWCA Civ 905 at [56]–[57] (while comments made at earlier hearings were no doubt made to emphasise the importance to the father of complying with court orders and a deep concern for the child's welfare, a fair-minded observer would have been minded to conclude that by April 3, 2014, the judge had made up her mind or was at least strongly disposed to find that the father was in clear breach of the orders requiring him to return or secure the return of the child to the jurisdiction, that those breaches were deliberate and that the father should be given a substantial custodial sentence).

Superior courts

10–040 *[Add after ". . . oral application for permission to appeal.*[128]*"]*

It has also been held that the general rule is that a judge hearing an application which relies on his own previous findings should not recuse himself, unless he either considers that he genuinely cannot give one or other party a fair hearing, or that a fair-minded and informed observer would conclude that there was a real possibility that he would not do so.[128a] Furthermore, it has been held that judges ought not to recuse themselves too readily in long and complex cases.[128b] It is obviously convenient in a case of any complexity that a single judge should deal with all relevant matters, actual bias or a real possibility of bias must conclude the matter in favour of the applicant; nevertheless there must be substantial evidence of actual or imputed bias before the general rule can be overcome. All the cases, moreover, emphasise that the issue of recusal is extremely fact-sensitive.[128c] The mere fact that allegations of actual bias are made does not alter the approach that ought to be adopted.[128d] This approach may, however, be less important in less complex cases.[128e] However, it may be that a judge will be concerned that an informed observer could not have the necessary confident proceedings where a judge had already considered the essential evidence that would be deployed on the committal application and had come to the conclusion that the witnesses giving it were lying.[128f] Moreover, strident and concluded comments in the interim report of a Commission of Inquiry about an individual's criminal conduct created a perception that the Commissioner's mind was closed to further evidence;[128g] a judge's comments during and conduct of a case management hearing created the impression that he had formed a final and adverse view of one of the parties,[128h] while a judge's threats of imprisonment with a heavy sentence for failure to comply with court orders created a similar apprehension of bias.[128i]

Overall, the decision for a judge whether or not to recuse himself involves a "delicate jurisdiction", and in summary, if the judge himself feels embarrassed to continue, he should not do so, and if he does not so feel, he should.[128j] In general, it seems that the stronger the terms in which an interim or provisional finding is expressed, the stronger the likelihood of there being apparent bias. Conversely, where interim findings are expressed with greater caution or expressly said to be provisional and subject to further evidence at the time they are made, it is seems unlikely that apparent bias will arise. The centrality of the issue arising for determination at the interim stage for the subsequent decision will also be of relevance.[128k]

[128a] *Otkritie International Investment Management Ltd v Urumov* [2014] EWCA Civ 1315; [2015] C.P. Rep. 6 at [13] and [22]. See also A.A. Olowofoyeku "Inappropriate recusals" (2016) 132 L.Q.R. 318.

[128b] *Otkritie International Investment Management Ltd v Urumov* [2014] EWCA Civ 1315; [2015] C.P. Rep. 6 at [32] (holding that a judge who had conducted a trial had been wrong to recuse himself from hearing a subsequent committal application).

[128c] *Otkritie International Investment Management Ltd v Urumov* [2014] EWCA Civ 1315; [2015] C.P. Rep. 6 at [13].

[128d] *Otkritie International Investment Management Ltd v Urumov* [2014] EWCA Civ 1315; [2015] C.P. Rep. 6 at [23] ("the mere fact that a litigant decides to raise the stakes in that way cannot give rise to any difference of legal principle").

[128e] *Otkritie International Investment Management Ltd v Urumov* [2014] EWCA Civ 1315; [2015] C.P. Rep. 6 at [33]. See also *Re K* [2014] EWCA Civ 905.

[128f] *Dar Al Arkan Real Estate Development Company v Al Refai* [2014] EWHC 1055.

[128g] *Mitchell v Georges* [2014] UKPC 43.

[128h] *Re Q (Children)* [2014] EWCA Civ 918; [2014] 3 F.C.R. 517 (CA (Civ Div)).

[128i] *Re K* [2014] EWCA Civ 905.

[128j] *Otkritie International Investment Management Ltd v Urumov* [2014] EWCA Civ 1315; [2015] C.P. Rep. 6 at [32].

[128k] D Heaton "Bias and previous determinations: four recent decisions in the Court of Appeal and Privy Council" (2015) 34 CJQ 138, 149.

Sub-committees

10–042 *[Add to end of para.10–042]*

In general, the mere fact that a tribunal has previously decided an issue would not in itself be sufficient to justify a conclusion of apparent bias if there were to be a second adjudication.[132a]

[132a] *Ecovision Systems Limited v Vinci Construction UK Limited* [2015] EWHC 587 (TCC) at [99].

10–042A *[Add new para.10–042A after 10–042]*

A similar issue has arisen where persons other than the decision-makers are present during the decision-making process.[132b] In this context, a finding of bias can arise where the identity or status of the outsider either does influence the tribunal or would lead a fair-minded person who knows the facts to conclude that there is a real possibility that the tribunal will be influenced.[132c] It seems, however, that a pragmatic approach may be taken to the assistance of outsiders; in *R. (on the application of DM Digital Television Ltd) v Office of Communications*, it was held that it was inevitable that the Board of Ofcom should be assisted by others in the discharge of its regulatory function, as otherwise, the sheer volume of work could not be managed.[132d]

[132b] *R. (on the application of DM Digital Television Ltd) v Office of Communications* [2014] EWHC 961 (Admin) at [32]–[36].

[132c] *R. (on the application of DM Digital Television Ltd) v Office of Communications* [2014] EWHC 961 (Admin) at [36].

[132d] *R. (on the application of DM Digital Television Ltd) v Office of Communications* [2014] EWHC 961 (Admin) at [44].

Relationships

Friendship

[Add to para.10–044 after ". . . have been indicative of bias"]   10–044

Similarly, the friendship of an assistant deputy coroner with the former chief executive of an NHS trust involved in an inquest was not indicative of bias where the executive had left the post before the matter giving rise to the inquest arose, and the inquest concerned the hospital's specialist medical team, rather than management.[137a]

[137a] *R. (on the application of Shaw) v HM Coroner for Leicester City and South Leicestershire* [2013] EWHC 386 (Admin).

Professional and vocational relationships

[Add to end of n.146]   10–046

See also *R. (on the application of Project Management Institute) v Minister for the Cabinet Office* [2016] EWCA Civ 21; [2016] 1 W.L.R. 1737 (a decision of the Privy Council to recommend the grant of a Royal Charter to a professional project management association was not invalidated on the basis of apparent bias where steps had been taken to subject the application to an independent assessment by the Cabinet Office and an opportunity had been given to the claimant to make representations).

[Add to end of n.147]

See also *Peter Sanders, Brian Ross v Airports Commission, Secretary of State for Transport* [2013] EWHC 3754 (Admin) at [121], [138], [150], [164], [165] (no real possibility of bias where a Commissioner was appointed to a Commission set up to report on airport expansion where the Commissioner had worked as chief executive with a potential purchaser for the airport for 16 years and been involved at the highest level with the potential purchaser for some 22 years, given that the fair-minded and informed observer would be aware that the Commissioner had been retired for almost two years, had been absent from the purchaser's core business and long terms for what would be a lengthy period of time in a dynamic industry; even after the purchaser had announced its intention to purchase, there was nothing to suggest the Commissioner would have been given undue deference and the fair-minded and informed observer would conclude that the Commissioners were a group of people of substance and experience who would regard each other as equals; moreover, the fair-minded and informed observer would have viewed sift criteria as generic criteria developed through an iterative process; however, once proposals were received, the Commissioner was then placed in the position of carrying out a quasi-judicial function of assessing the proposals against sift criteria and the fair-minded and informed observer would have expected him to step down).

[Add after first sentence]

For example, an arbitrator was removed on the ground of apparent bias where 18 per cent of his appointments and 25 per cent of his arbitrator income over the previous three years derived from cases involving the defendant.[147a]

[147a] *Cofely Ltd v Bingham* [2016] EWHC 240 (Comm).

[Add to n.149 after ". . . husband's trade union)"]

; *Resolution Chemicals Limited v H Lundbeck A/S* [2013] EWCA Civ 1515; [2014] 1 W.L.R. 1943 at [46] (the fact that an expert witness in the trial of a complex patent action had supervised the doctoral thesis of the specialist High Court judge 30 years previously, where there was no continuing link, did not give rise to apparent bias).

[Add to end of n.150]

See also *R. (on the application of Leathley) v Visitors to the Inns of Court* [2014] EWCA Civ 1630 (no apparent bias where a member of the Tribunal Appointments Board was one of four individuals who selected the pool of members of the Inns of Court Council).

10–048 *[Add to n.158 after "[1894] 1 Q.B. 750."]*

See also *Congregation of the Poor Sisters of Nazareth v Scottish Ministers* [2015] CSOH 87; 2015 S.L.T. 445 at [23] (advocate did not have close relationship with an interested party to an inquiry and had no involvement "away from the ordinary receipt of instructions").

[Add after ". . . against the judge.[158]"]

Similarly, the argument that a scheme pursuant to which judges assessed barristers' competence would affect the independence of the judge in his conduct of the trial, due to the possibility of the judge being sued for giving an unfavourable assessment, was rejected. While a concern about being sued might cause the judge to refuse to complete the assessment, or to give a more favourable assessment than he otherwise would have done, it would not have an impact on the conduct of the proceedings.[159a] It has also been held that a barrister sitting as a deputy High Court judge had been correct in not recusing herself from a probate action on the ground of appearance of bias where she was leading the claimant's barrister in another unrelated matter,[159b] while apparent bias also did not arise where a judge presiding over the trial of a wildlife campaigner for offences committed against a terrierman because the judge had previously represented the terrierman when acting as a solicitor.[159c]

[159a] *R. (on the application of Lumsdon) v Legal Services Board* [2014] EWCA Civ 1276; [2014] H.R.L.R. 29 at [63].

[159b] *Watts v Watts* [2015] EWCA Civ 1297.

[159c] *R. (on the application of Hewitt) v Denbighshire Magistrates' Court* [2015] EWHC 2956 (Admin). For comment, see "Judge: R. (on the application of Hewitt) v Denbighshire Magistrates' Court" [2016] Crim. L.R. 209.

[Add to end of n.159]   10–049

See also *R. v Connors (Josie)* [2013] EWCA Crim 368; [2013] Crim. L.R. 854 at [34]–[35].

[Add to end of n.161]

; cf. *R. v Puladian-Kari (Ramin)* [2013] EWCA Crim 158; [2013] Crim. L.R. 510 at [80]–[85] (a fair-minded and informed observer would have concluded that there was a real possibility of bias where a juror passed a note to the judge stating that, in his professional experience, the alleged transaction of the defendant would entail automatic rejection at his institution, and found it difficult to forget details of the case which would be "red signals" in his professional environment).

[Add to end of n.173]   10–052

See also *Galojan v Estonia* [2014] EWHC 3942, in which an interesting argument was made unsuccessfully that because of the relationship between the appellant and two individuals who held the office of Minister of Justice in Estonia, from whose Ministry a European Arrest Warrant issued, the Ministry was precluded from being a judicial authority for the purpose of s.2 of the Extradition Act 2003.

10–053A *[Add new para.10–053A after para.10–053]*

Judicial tenure

Useful consideration has also been given recently to the impact of judicial tenure on independence. In *Misick v The Queen*,[176a] at issue was whether a retired judge, appointed ad hoc to preside over a high profile criminal trial, had sufficient security of tenure to demonstrate judicial independence. The Privy Council observed that temporary or ad hoc appointments are not uncommon and need not necessarily involve any lack of independence.[176b] If the judge has genuinely accepted appointment for a specific task, at least in the absence of some special factor, he will have no expectation of renewal or of further appointment. No objective observer would therefore fear that he would be unable independently to discharge his duty as a judge because he was in place for a limited period; indeed, his ad hoc position often strengthens his independence.[176c]

[176a] [2015] UKPC 31; [2015] 1 W.L.R. 325.

[176b] [2015] UKPC 31; [2015] 1 W.L.R. 325 at [25].

[176c] [2015] UKPC 31; [2015] 1 W.L.R. 325 at [26] (it was also relevant that the judge had been asked to take on his appointment outside his home territory and in his retirement, such that his temporary appointment, far from carrying a danger of lack of independence had very clearly been made in order to bring to locally highly controversial cases an independent outsider).

10–053B *[Add new para.10–053B after para.10–053A]*

Communications between the decision-maker and one of the parties

Decision-makers are required to be very open regarding communications with parties. A deliberate failure to disclose communications between the decision-maker and one of the parties may in itself give rise to apparent bias. Thus, where the adjudicator determining a contract dispute failed to disclose a lengthy telephone conversation between one of the parties and his office manager (who was his wife) about the dispute, this failure to disclose, in itself, gave rise to apparent bias.[176d] A denial by the adjudicator that any contact took place was misleading, where no contact had taken place with the adjudicator personally, but it had taken place with his office manager and also gave rise to apparent bias.[176e] The explanations provided for any communications will also be relevant, and where the adjudicator's explanations were aggressive and unapologetic, this too gave rise to apparent bias.[176f]

[176d] *Paice v Harding (t/a MJ Harding Contractors)* [2015] EWHC 661 (TCC); [2015] B.L.R. 345 at [38].

[176e] *Paice v Harding (t/a MJ Harding Contractors)* [2015] EWHC 661 (TCC); [2015] B.L.R. 345 at [45].

[176f] *Paice v Harding (t/a MJ Harding Contractors)* [2015] EWHC 661 (TCC); [2015] B.L.R. 345 at [51].

Personal hostility

[Add to beginning of n.180]   10–054

O'Neill v HM Advocate (No.2) [2013] UKSC 36; [2013] 1 W.L.R. 1992 at [53] (the fair-minded observer would understand the context in which judicial comments were made, and would appreciate that the judge could differentiate his decision in one case from his duty to be impartial in another).

[Add to n.187 after ". . . of either party held to be vitiating bias);"]

Mengiste v Endowment Fund for the Rehabilitation of Tigray [2013] EWCA Civ 1003; [2014] P.N.L.R. 4 at [58]–[64] (judge who had made trenchant criticisms of the appellant's solicitors should have recused himself as he had expressed his criticisms in absolute terms, failing to leave room for any explanation and had made criticisms at a time when there had been no need to make them to anticipate an application for wasted costs that had not been made).

[Add to end of para.10–054]

Furthermore, it is important to distinguish between hostility to an advocate, and hostility to the parties. It has been observed that even if a judge is irritated by or shows hostility towards an advocate, it does not follow that there is a real possibility that it will affects his approach to the parties and jeopardise the fairness of the proceedings, since, "[f]rom time to time, the patience of judges can be sorely tested by the behaviour of advocates".[192a] Thus, where a barrister had written to Heads of Chambers, complaining about an article written about a member of that Chambers, it could not be concluded without more that bias would affect a determination of case in which other members of the Chambers were appearing, in particular, given that the judge had given an indication of his conclusions before reading the article.[192b]

[192a] *Harb v Aziz* [2016] EWCA Civ 556 at [71].

192b *Harb v Aziz* [2016] EWCA Civ 556 at [76] (in this situation, it was regarded as "fanciful" to suppose that the judge made major changes to the judgment as a reaction to the article).

Partisan views on a particular issue

10–057 *[Add after ". . . may taint the consultation process.202"]*

However, directing questions to counsel with scepticism will not be demonstrative of apparent bias or predetermination.202a

202a *Worldspreads v Foley* [2015] EWCA Civ 697 at [11]–[15].

[Add to end of n.202]

On the role of advisers, contrast *Dr Kofi Adu v General Medical Council* [2014] EWHC 4080 (Admin) (an unrelated experience nine years earlier had no real or apparent bearing upon any advice given to the Panel).

Pre-determination

10–058 *[Add after ". . . with what has in fact happened.205"]*

The importance of observing the distinction has recently been confirmed, given that administrative decision-makers, unlike judicial decision-makers, are often quite properly influenced by policy considerations and may, in some cases, slip silently from predisposition to predetermination.205a There is, however, a distinction between a predisposition and a predetermination.205b For example, a decision-maker may consult upon an issue that he has a firm view about. Indeed, if the decision-maker's cards are laid squarely upon the table consultees are fully informed as to that predisposition and have the clearest possible target at which to aim their submissions. A strong predisposition is not, therefore, inimical to a fair consultation assuming, of course, that the decision-maker is prepared to keep an open mind and be willing to change his or her views if the evidence and submissions tendered are properly persuasive.

205a *Michael v Official Receiver* [2014] EWCA Civ 1590 at [15].

205b *R. (on the application of British Academy of Songwriters, Composers and Authors v Secretary of State for Business, Innovation and Skills* [2015] EWHC 1723 (Admin) at [277].

[Add to n.206 after ". . . Eu. L.R. 615"]   10–059

; *R. (on the application of Forge Field Society v Sevenoaks DC* [2014] EWHC 1895 (Admin). In *R. (on the application of T) v West Berkshire Council* [2016] EWHC 1876 (Admin), predetermination did arise where a local authority's initial decision to cut funding to voluntary sector organisations which provided short breaks for disabled children was unlawful, as the authority had failed to take into account mandatory relevant considerations and a subsequent decision affirming the initial decision was vitiated by apparent predetermination.

[Add to end of n.207]

Neither the fact that an ombudsman expressed views in an initial assessment, nor her unwillingness to accept that the doctors discharged certain duties as a matter of practice without recording that they had done them, were evidence of predetermination: *Miller v Parliamentary and Health Service Ombudsman* [2015] EWHC 2981 (Admin). There is also a distinction between a predisposition and a predetermination: *In the Matter of an Application by JR 65 for Judicial Review* [2016] NICA 20 at [82].

[Add after ". . . views is insufficient.²⁰⁷"]

This is because it has been observed that it is a human characteristic that people have predilections, beliefs and sympathies, and judges and tribunals are no exception. The fact that a Judge or tribunal may hold certain pre-conceived views does not by itself constitute actual bias unless it is such as to render them immune to contrary argument; "the crucial distinction is between a predisposition towards a particular outcome and a predetermina-tion of the outcome".[207a] Furthermore, it has been held that disclosure of a judge of his current thinking may positively assist the advocate or litigant in knowing where particular efforts may need to be pointed, so that, in general terms, there need be no bar on robust expression by a judge, so long as it is not indicative of a closed mind.[207b] It is also necessary to consider the proceedings as a whole in engaging in the objective assessment of whether there was a real possibility that the tribunal was biased.[207c] In addition, a lengthy period of deliberations has no bearing on the issue of bias.[207d] Similarly, the provision of an incomplete draft judgment, although unusual, was intended to help the parties and did not Indicate any real possibility of bias.[207e]

[207a] *Jackson v Thompsons Solicitors* [2015] EWHC 218 (QB) at [15]. For the distinction between predisposition and predetermination, see *R. (on the application of British Academy of Songwriters, Composers and Authors v Secretary of State for Business, Innovation and Skills* [2015] EWHC 1723

(Admin) at [277]. See also *R. (on the application of Mackaill) v Independent Police Complaints Commission* [2014] EWHC 3170 (the decision of the Independent Police Complaints Commission to redetermine the mode of an investigation into police officers' conduct had vitiated by apparent bias, since it had been taken by the Commission's deputy chair, who had publicly and repeatedly made plain her disagreement with the conclusions of the investigation).

[207b] *Singh v Secretary of State for the Home Department* [2016] EWCA Civ 492 at [35]. See also *Gulf Agencies Ltd v Ahmed* [2016] EWCA Civ 44 at [47]–[60] (the fact that a judge had challenged whether a landlord was in fact a solicitor at the start of a trial, and subsequently explained that his experience in other cases prompted the question, did not provide a legitimate ground for suggesting that the judge had formed an adverse view of the landlord and his credibility). See similarly *R. v Bush* [2015] EWCA Crim 2313; see also *R. v Uddin* [2015] EWCA Crim 1918; [2016] 4 W.L.R. 24 at [35] (no apparent bias arising where the judge did not require the prosecution to make submissions about why ASBOs were necessary).

[207c] *Singh v Secretary of State for the Home Department* [2016] EWCA Civ 492 at [36]. The Court in this case also set out general guidance as to the approach to be taken by the Upper Tribunal in cases where allegations of bias or misconduct had been made: (a) any intended appeal should be closely scrutinised at the permission stage and allegations meriting the grant of permission to appeal should be properly particularised and appropriately evidenced; (b) if an allegation of bias or misconduct was deemed sufficient to merit the grant of permission to appeal, the Upper Tribunal should normally obtain the written comments of the judge concerned; (c) any such written comments should be provided to the parties for the purposes of the appeal hearing in the Upper Tribunal and retained on file pending any further appeal to the Court of Appeal; (d) since proceedings in the First-tier Tribunal were not ordinarily recorded, it might be necessary to obtain the tribunal judge's own notes of the hearing; (e) it would normally assist the Upper Tribunal to obtain a statement from the respondent's advocate as to his recollection of the events before the First-tier Tribunal; (f) consideration should be given to whether oral evidence was needed at the appeal hearing; (g) the file should be reviewed and any directions given by the Upper Tribunal in good time before the substantive appeal hearing ([53]–[54]).

[207d] *R. (on the application of Gopalakrishnan) v General Medical Council* [2016] EWHC 1247 (Admin) at [110].

[207e] *Marsh v Ministry of Justice* [2015] EWHC 3767 (QB) at [33].

[Add to end of n.210]

See also *Michael v Official Receiver* [2014] EWCA Civ 1590 at [22]–[26] (the test was also not satisfied where the Chief Registrar had frequently interrupted a litigant who had produced prolix written submissions and who would not focus on the real issues in either evidence or oral submissions and who had commented that the litigant's answers were not always regarded as honest).

SITUATIONS WHERE BIAS WILL NOT APPLY

Waiver

[Add to end of n.214]   10–061

O'Neill v HM Advocate (No.2) [2013] UKSC 36; [2013] 1 W.L.R. 1992 at [56] (failure to object may also indicate to the fair-minded observer that the parties did not consider that there was indeed an existence of bias); *R. (on the application of DM Digital Television Ltd) v Office of Communications* [2014] EWHC 961 (Admin) at [41]. It was also held in this case that waiver can be inferred from conduct or even silence, provided that the conduct or silence is voluntary, informed and unequivocal: at [43]. See also *R. (on the application of Shaw) v HM Coroner for Leicester City and South Leicestershire* [2013] EWHC 386 (Admin) at [101]. See also *Bhardwaj v FDA* [2016] EWCA Civ 800 at [75] (employment tribunal had informed the applicant during the hearing that one of the respondents was a lay member in the same region as the panel such that her waiver of her right to object to the tribunal continuing was valid and irrevocable).

[Add to end of n.215]

Paice v Harding (t/a MJ Harding Contractors) [2015] EWHC 661 (TCC); [2015] B.L.R. 345 at [54]–[57] (where a defendant was aware that calls had taken place between the adjudicator and the claimant, but not the content of the calls or between whom exactly the calls had taken place, the defendant could not have waived his right to allege apparent bias).

[Add after "right to object at the time.[217]*"]*

Where an explanation for the circumstances that may give rise to apparent bias is accepted by the applicant, it may be treated as accurate. Where the explanation is not treated as accurate by the applicant, it becomes one further matter to be considered from the viewpoint of a fair-minded observer, and the court does not have to rule on whether the explanation should be accepted or rejected.[217a] In order for waiver to arise, there must be both awareness of the right to challenge the adjudicator's decision and a clear and unequivocal act, which, with the required knowledge, amounts to waiver of the right.[217b]

[217a] *Paice v Harding (t/a MJ Harding Contractors)* [2015] EWHC 661 (TCC); [2015] B.L.R. 345 at [17] (endorsing the comments of Lord Phillips in *In re Medicaments and Related Classes of Goods (No 2)* [2001] 1 W.L.R. 700).

[217b] *Paice v Harding (t/a MJ Harding Contractors)* [2015] EWHC 661 (TCC); [2015] B.L.R. 345 at [55] (endorsing *Farrelly (M&E) Building Services Ltd v Byrne Brothers (Formwork) Ltd* [2013] EWHC 1186 (TCC)).

10–064 *[Add after ". . . consent of the parties.*[223]*"]*

A distinction has also been drawn between an objection to the judge based on facts discovered during the course of, or only at the end of, the hearing and a situation where the objection is taken before the hearing has begun. In the latter situation, there is scope for the sensible application of the precautionary principle, and prudence naturally leans on the side of being safe rather than sorry.[223a]

[223a] *Thames Water Utilities Ltd v Newbound* [2015] EWCA Civ 677 at [92].

ECHR Art.6

10–086 *[Add to end of para.10–086]*

That "full jurisdiction" requires "sufficient jurisdiction" has also recently been confirmed by the ECtHR.[279a]

[279a] App. No. 40378/10 *Ali v United Kingdom* [2015] H.L.R. 46 at [76] (requirement of a fair hearing before an impartial tribunal was satisfied by the local authority's internal review process and the availability of a subsequent appeal to the county court, even though such an appeal was by way of review rather than rehearing).

10–089 *[Add to end of n.290]*

See also *R. (on the application of XH) v Secretary of State for the Home Department* [2016] EWHC 1898 (Admin) at [106] (while the Secretary of State's decision would involve a consideration of facts, it essentially involved a risk assessment being made in the light of a policy set out in a written ministerial statement; the Court added (at [107]) that "judicial review is a flexible process and the court can examine facts in an appropriate case"); *R. (on the application of Derrin Brother Properties Ltd) v Revenue and*

Customs Commissioners [2016] EWCA Civ 15; [2016] 1 W.L.R. 2423 at [112] (judicial review was adequate to ensure compliance with statutory pre-conditions for judicial approval of third party information notices).

[Add to end of n.291]   10–090

; see also *Resolution Chemicals Limited v H Lundbeck A/S* [2013] EWCA Civ 1515; [2014] 1 W.L.R. 1943 at [35] ("underlying both article 6 of the Convention and the common law principles is the fundamental consideration that justice should not only be done but should manifestly and undoubtedly be seen to be done").

[Add new para 10–091A after para.10–091]   10–091A

Recently, the ECtHR has stressed that it is not the function of art.6 to ensure review by a body that could substitute its opinion for that of the administrative authority, since respect had to be accorded to decisions taken by administrative authorities. Thus, in assessing the sufficiency of a judicial review, it is necessary to consider: the powers of the judicial body; whether the decision concerned a specialist issue requiring professional knowledge; the extent to which the decision involved the exercise of administrative discretion; the manner in which the decision had been reached; the procedural guarantees available before the adjudicatory body; and the content of the dispute; and the legislative scheme as a whole.[297a]

[297a] App No 40378/10 *Ali v United Kingdom* [2015] H.L.R. 46 at [78]–[79].

[Add new para 10–091B after para.10–091A]   10–091B

The obligation in ECHR art.6 to ensure access to independent and impartial courts for the resolution of "civil rights and obligations" imposes an obligation on states to respect the court process and to comply with judgments delivered by the courts. This means that contracting states cannot legislate in a manner which affects the judicial determination of a dispute involving the State or private parties. Thus, in *R. (on the application of Reilly) (No 2) v Secretary of State for Work and Pensions*,[297b] the Jobseekers (Back to Work Scheme) Act 2013 was declared incompatible with ECHR art.6 insofar as it purported to validate sanctions retrospectively for those claimants who had already appealed against their sanctions..

[297b] [2016] EWCA Civ 413.

CHAPTER 11

SUBSTANTIVE REVIEW AND JUSTIFICATION

INTRODUCTION

Overlap between unreasonableness and proportionality

[Add to n.23 after ". . . 'Problems and Proportionality' [2010] N.Z.L.R. **11–010**
303;"]

See also J. Goodwin, "The Last Defence of Wednesbury" [2012] P.L. 445.

Constitutional and institutional limitations on the court's role

[Add to end of n.35] **11–014**

; *R. (Hurley) v Secretary of State for Work and Pensions* (Equality and Human
Rights Commission intervening) [2015] EWHC 3382 (Admin); [2016]
P.T.S.R. 636 (Collins J: "public finance is a particularly . . . inapt subject for
judicial scrutiny, albeit such scrutiny is not ruled out.").

[Add to end of n.39] **11–014**

*R. (on the application of Lord Carlile of Berriew) v Secretary of State for the
Home Department* [2014] UKSC 60; [2015] A.C. 945 (refusal to allow the
entry of a dissident Iranian politician into the United Kingdom) at [105] per
Baroness Hale D.P.S.C.: "The court has a particular expertise in assessing the
importance of fundamental rights and protecting individuals against the
over-mighty power of the state or the majority. The Government has much
greater expertise in assessing risks to national security or the safety of people
for whom we are responsible." In *Bank Mellat v HM Treasury* [2013] UKSC
39; [2014] A.C. 700 (Order in Council prohibiting transactions or business
relationships with Iranian Bank to prevent development of nuclear weapons
in Iran) at [21] Lord Sumption cautioned against the court taking over the
functions of the executive, least of all in the area of foreign policy and
national security "which would once have been regarded as unsuitable for
judicial scrutiny"; the question whether a measure was apt to limit the risk
posed for the national interest by nuclear proliferation was "pre-eminently a
matter for the executive". He endorsed the view of Lord Reed J.S.C. that

"the making of government and legislative policy cannot be turned into a judicial process". Lord Sumption J.S.C., in a majority of five to four, nevertheless allowed the Bank's appeal on the ground, inter alia, that the Order in Council was not a rational or proportionate response to the aim of hindering Iran's nuclear ambitions.

Courts' secondary function of testing the quality of reasoning and justification

11–016 *[Add new n.43a after ". . . the situation in immigration policy where those elements were not present"]*

43a But see *R. (on the application of MM (Lebanon)) v Secretary of State for the Home Department* [2014] EWCA Civ 985 (where the Court of Appeal was persuaded as to the Secretary of State's proposed "Minimum Income Requirement" for a UK partner to sponsor the entry of a nonEEA partner) at [148] per Aikens L.J.: ". . . appropriate weight has to be given to the judgment of the Secretary of State, particularly where, as here, she has acted on the results of independent research and wide consultations".

THE WEDNESBURY FORMULATION AND ITS SUBSEQUENT DEVELOPMENT

Wednesbury is tautological

11–020 *[Add new n.56a after ". . . in the minds of reasonable men."]*

56a Lord Russell's formulation was approved by Aikens L.J.in the context of a challenge to immigration rules in *R. (on the application of MM (Lebanon)) v Secretary of State for the Home Department* [2014] EWCA Civ 985 at [94]–[95].

Categories of unreasonableness

11–028 *[Add new note 81a after "We believe that both the accessibility of the principles of judicial review and its coherence are best served by extrapolating those distinct tenets and principles rather than hiding them under the general and much more vague concept of unreasonableness, however defined."]*

81a This approach received judicial endorsement from Lord Mance J.S.C. in *Kennedy v Charity Commission (Secretary of State for Justice intervening)* [2014] UKSC 20; [2015] A.C. 455 at [55]: "But the right approach is now surely to recognise, as *de Smith's Judicial Review*, 7th ed (2013), para.11–028 suggests, that it is inappropriate to treat all cases of judicial review together under a general but vague principle of reasonableness, and preferable to look for the underlying tenet or principle which indicates the basis on which the court should approach any administrative law challenge in a particular situation. Among the categories of situation identified in *de Smith* are those where a common law right or constitutional principle is in issue". See also J. Jowell, Ch. 4 ("Proportionality and Unreasonableness: Neither Merger Nor Takeover") in M. Elliott and H. Wiberg (eds), *The Scope and Intensity of Substantive Review* (Hart Publishing, 2015).

UNREASONABLE PROCESS

Balance of relevant considerations

[Add to end of n.95]   11–035

; *R. (on the application of Rahman) v Secretary of State for the Home Department* [2015] EWHC 1146 (Admin); [2015] A.C.D. 107 (irrational for the Home Secretary to ignore findings of fact made by the Asylum and Immigration Tribunal when refusing to renew a passport).

Rationality: logic and reasoning

[Add to end of n.99]   11–036

Also, *R. (on the application of Demetrio) v Independent Police Complaints Commission* [2015] EWHC 593 (Admin); [2015] A.C.D. 98 at [65]: "Whether the lack of ostensible logic is sufficient to render the decision irrational . . .".

Inadequate evidence and mistake of fact

Decisions unsupported by substantial evidence

[Add to end of n.145]   11–052

R. (on the application of Trafford) v Blackpool BC [2014] EWHC 85; [2014] 2 All E.R. 947 (see n.259 below) (no evidence that the nature of a solicitor's business whose lease the defendant council refused to renew was "wholly contrary to the stated aims and objectives" of the council).

[Add to end of n.147]

In *R. (on the application of Mott) v Environment Agency* [2015] EWHC 314 (Admin); [2015] Env.L.R. 27 the imposition of conditions upon a licence to fish was held irrational where the decision-maker had failed to consider whether the evidence upon which it based its decision was credible and capable of supporting the conclusions drawn from it.

VIOLATION OF COMMON LAW RIGHTS OR CONSTITUTIONAL PRINCIPLE

The rule of law

[Add to end of para.11–061]

11–061 Retrospective legislation also violates the rule of law in the absence of very strong justification.[180a]

[180a] *R. (on the application of Reilly (No.2) and Hewstone) v Secretary of State for Work and Pensions* [2014] EWHC 2182 (Admin); [2015] Q.B. 573(the Jobseeker's (Back to Work Schemes) Act 2013 sought to retrospectively validate the 2011 Jobseeker's Allowance (Employment, Skills and Enterprise Scheme) Regulations, notification letters that had failed to comply with those regulations and sanctions which had been imposed pursuant to the regulations; the court granted a declaration of incompatibility) at [82] per Lang J.: "The constitutional principle of the rule of law was expressly recognised in section 1, Constitutional Reform Act 2005. It requires, *inter alia*, that Parliament and the Executive recognise and respect the separation of powers and abide by the principle of legality. Although the Crown in Parliament is the sovereign legislative power, the Courts have the constitutional role of determining and enforcing legality. Thus, Parliament's undoubted power to legislate to overrule the effect of court judgments generally ought not to take the form of retrospective legislation designed to favour the Executive in ongoing litigation in the courts brought against it by one of its citizens, unless there are compelling reasons to do so. Otherwise it is likely to offend a citizen's sense of fair play." See also para.1–033 nn.94 and 105.

Substantive equality

11–067 *[Add to end of n.202]*

The UK government has not signed ECHR Protocol 12, which contains a freestanding prohibition of discrimination. See para.13–030 below.

OPPRESSIVE DECISIONS

Illustrations of oppressive decisions

[Add to end of n.259]   11–072

See also *R. (on the application of Trafford) v Blackpool BC* [2014] EWHC 85; [2014] 2 All E.R. 947 (decision not to renew solicitor's business tenancy because the solicitor had acted for a number of clients who had brought personal injury claims against the council held to be unlawful) at [71] per H.H. Judge Stephen Davies: "The exercise of a power with the sole or the dominant intention of punishing the claimant . . . in circumstances where there was no evidence that the claimant was actually doing anything at all unlawful or improper, was . . . the intentionally improper exercise of the power . . . and the exercise of that power for unauthorised purposes."

[Add to end of n.262]

See also *R. (on the application of MM (Lebanon)) v Secretary of State for the Home Department* [2014] EWCA Civ 985, [150] (reversing [2013] EWHC 1900 (Admin); [2014] 1 W.L.R 2306) (challenge to a "Minimum Income Requirement" for a UK partner to sponsor the entry of a non-EEA partner) at [147]–[148] per Aikens L.J.: "Essentially the debate is about figures and what should be the minimum necessary income figure and what other possible sources of income should or should not be taken into account to see if that minimum can be reached . . . the key question is: to what extent should the court substitute its own view of what, as a matter of general policy, is the appropriate level of income for that rationally chosen as a matter of policy by the executive, which is headed by ministers who are democratically accountable? . . . Individuals will have different views on what constitutes the minimum income requirements needed to accomplish the stated policy aims . . . it is not the court's job to impose its own views unless, objectively judged, the levels chosen are . . . irrational, or inherently unjust or inherently unfair."

THE PLACE OF PROPORTIONALITY

[Add after "Yet it has been said that the adoption of proportionality 11–073 *into domestic law would lower the threshold of judicial intervention and involve the courts in considering the merits and facts of administrative decisions".]*

This understanding has, however, come more recently to be questioned.[264a]

264a See, e.g. *Kennedy v Charity Commission (Secretary of State for Justice intervening)* [2014] UKSC 20; [2015] A.C. 455, [54] (Lord Mance J.S.C.: "As Professor Paul Craig has shown (see e.g. "The Nature of Reasonableness" (2013) 66 C.L.P. 131), both reasonableness review and proportionality involve considerations of weight and balance, with the intensity of the scrutiny and the weight to be given to any primary decision maker's view depending on the context. The advantage of the terminology of proportionality is that it introduces an element of structure into the exercise, by directing attention to factors such as suitability or appropriateness, necessity and the balance or imbalance of benefits and disadvantages. There seems no reason why such factors should not be relevant in judicial review even outside the scope of Convention and EU law. Whatever the context, the court deploying them must be aware that they overlap potentially and that the intensity with which they are applied is heavily dependent on the context").

11–074 *[Add after ". . . without the sanction of the House of Lords, yet to "perform its [unreasonableness'] burial rights.*271"*]*

Since then, in the UK Supreme Court, Lord Mance J.S.C. has expressed clear preference for the advantages of proportionality over the vagueness of irrationality.271a Nonetheless, the prevailing orthodoxy is that (in the words of Lord Sumption J.S.C.) "although English law has not adopted the principle of proportionality generally, it has stumbled towards a concept which is in significant respects similar" – namely, variable intensity rationality review."271b

271a See *Kennedy v Charity Commission (Secretary of State for Justice intervening)* [2014] UKSC 20; [2015] A.C. 455 at [54] (Lord Mance J.S.C., with whom Lord Neuberger of Abbotsbury P.S.C. And Lord Clarke Of Stone-Cum-Ebony J.S.C. agreed), discussed above at para.11–073; *Pham v Secretary of State for the Home Department (Open Society Justice Initiative intervening)* [2015] UKSC 19; [2015] 1 W.L.R. 1591, [98] ("Removal of British citizenship under a power by provided by s.40(2) of the British Nationality Act 1981 is, on any view, a radical step . . . A correspondingly strict standard of judicial review must apply to any exercise of the power contained in s.40(2), and the tool of proportionality is one which would, in my view and for the reasons explained in [*Kennedy*], be both available and valuable for the purposes of such a review"); *R. (Keyu) v Secretary of State for Foreign and Commonwealth Affaris* [2015] UKSC 69; [2015] 3 W.L.R. 1665 (in which Lord Neuberger, Lord Mance and Lord Hughes indicated that the move from irrationality to to proportionality was a decision which ought to be taken by a panel of nine justices rather than the five in the instant case).

[271b] *Pham v Secretary of State for the Home Department (Open Society Justice Initiative intervening)* [2015] UKSC 19; [2015] 1 W.L.R. 1591, [105] (Lord Neuberger of Abbotsbury P.S.C., Baroness Hale of Richmond D.P.S.C. and Lord Wilson J.S.C. agreed). In *R. (Youssef) v Secretary of State for Foreign and Commonwealth Affairs* [2016] UKSC 3; [2016] 2 W.L.R. 509, the Supreme Court considered the standard of review applicable to a challenge to the Foreign Secretary's decision to no longer to support the removal of the claimant from an official list of people associated with Islamic terrorism. Counsel for the Foreign Secretary accepted "that the court is likely to take the approach signalled in *Kennedy* and *Pham* as its starting point, and that the facts of the case make it one in which the review to be conducted will be towards 'the intense end of the scale', conducted 'in accordance with common law principles, incorporating notions of proportionality'" (at [54]). Lord Carnwath JSC (with whom the other Justices agreed) noted the need for the consideration by the Supreme Court of "a general move from the traditional judicial review tests to one of proportionality" and "[s]uch a review might aim for rather more structured guidance for the lower courts than such imprecise concepts as 'anxious scrutiny' and 'sliding scales'" (at [55]).

[Add to end of n.271]

See Lord Neuberger P.S.C., "The Role of Judges in Human Rights Jurisprudence: A Comparison of the Australian and UK Experience" (conference speech given at the Supreme Court of Victoria, Melbourne, August 8, 2014, available at *http://www.supremecourt.uk/docs/speech-140808.pdf* para.31): ". . . we now have new ideas to grapple with and to apply to our domestic law, such as the concept of proportionality. But we are also wondering whether . . . it makes sense to have such different approaches between a traditional JR challenge to an executive decision on the merits, and a Convention challenge to an administrative decision. On that issue, the judgment in *Kennedy (Kennedy v Charity Commission* [2014] UKSC 20; [2015] A.C. UKSC 455) has something to offer."

Proportionality as a structured test of justifiability

Structured proportionality in European Union law

[Add to end of n.281]   11–078

For detailed consideration of proportionality in domestic courts where European Union law is engaged see the decision of the Supreme Court in *R.(on the application of Lumsdon) v Legal Services Board* [2015] UKSC 41; [2015] 3 W.L.R. 121.

Structured proportionality in Convention rights

11–079 *[Add to end of n.287]*

In *Bank Mellat v HM Treasury* [2013] UKSC 39; [2014] A.C. 700 at [70], [72] Lord Reed commented that the European Court of Human Rights often approached striking a fair balance "in a relatively broad-brush way . . . The intensity of review varies considerably according to the right in issue and the context in which the question arises. Unsurprisingly . . . its approach to proportionality does not correspond precisely to the various approaches adopted in contracting states". Further, on the approach to proportionality adopted in the UK domestic courts under the Human Rights Act, he continued: "In accordance with the analytical approach to legal reasoning characteristic of the common law, a more clearly structured approach has generally been adopted."

Structured proportionality in English law

11–081 *[Add to end of n.294]*

In *Bank Mellat v HM Treasury* [2013] UKSC 39; [2014] A.C. 700 at [74] Lord Reed, in a statement approved by the whole court, said that the approach in *Oakes* could be summarised by saying that it is necessary to determine: "(1) whether the objective of the measure is sufficiently important to justify the limitation of a protected right, (2) whether the measure is rationally connected to the objective, (3) whether a less intrusive measure could have been used without unacceptably compromising the achievement of the objective, and (4) whether, balancing the severity of the measure's effects on the rights of the persons to whom it applies against the importance of the objective, to the extent that the measure will contribute to its achievement, the former outweighs the latter." Further, ". . . there is a meaningful distinction to be drawn . . . between the question whether a particular objective is in principle sufficiently important to justify limiting a particular right (step one), and the question whether, having determined that no less drastic means of achieving the objective are available, the impact of the rights infringement is disproportionate to the likely benefits of the impugned measure (step four)" (at [76]). Lord Sumption also acknowledged the fourth step in his leading judgment as requiring "a fair balance . . . between the rights of the individual and the interests of the community" (at [20]). In *R. (on the application of Miranda) v Secretary of State for the Home Department* [2014] EWHC 255 (Admin); [2014] 1 W.L.R. 3140 at [40] Laws L.J. said of the *Oakes* fourth step: "I think it needs to be approached with some care. It requires the court . . . to decide whether the measure, though it has a justified purpose and is no more intrusive than necessary, is nevertheless offensive because it fails to strike the right balance between private right and

public interest; and the court is the judge of where that balance should lie
. . . there is real difficulty in distinguishing this from a political question to
be decided by the elected arm of government. If it is properly within the
judicial sphere, it must be on the footing that there is a plain case." On the
facts of that case, however, the balance was to be struck between two aspects
of the public interest—press freedom and national security—and, on the
facts, the balance clearly favoured national security.

[Add to end of para.11–083]   11–083

The application of a common law test of proportionality was considered by
the Supreme Court in *Pham v Secretary of State for the Home Department.*[302a]
While the case did not turn upon proportionality, all seven justices gave
support to the "flexible approach to principles of judicial review" (*per* Lord
Carnworth at [60]) endorsed by the Supreme Court in *Kennedy v Information
a Commissioner (Secretary of State for Justice intervening).*[302b] Moreover, the
majority of the Court explicitly endorsed the possibility of a common law
standard of proportionality review. As Lord Mance observed at [98]:
"Removal of British citizenship under the power provided by section 40(2)
of the British Nationality Act 1981 is, on any view, a radical step, particularly
if the person affected has little real attachment to the country of any other
nationality that he possesses and is unlikely to be able to return there. A
correspondingly strict standard of judicial review must apply to any exercise
of the power contained in section 40(2), and the tool of proportionality is
one which would, in my view and for the reasons explained in *Kennedy v
Information Comr* . . . be both available and valuable for the purposes of
such a review." Similarly, Lord Sumption at [105]: ". . . although English law
has not adopted the principle of proportionality generally, it has for many
years stumbled towards a concept which is in significant respects similar, and
over the last three decades has been influenced by European jurisprudence
even in areas of law lying beyond the domains of EU and international
human rights law. Starting with the decision of the House of Lords in *R v
Secretary of State for the Home Department, Ex p Bugdaycay* [1987] A.C.
514 it has recognised the need, even in the context of rights arising wholly
from domestic law, to differentiate between rights of greater or lesser importance and interference with them of greater or lesser degree. This is essentially the same problem as the one to which proportionality analysis is
directed. The solution adopted, albeit sometimes without acknowledgment,
was to expand the scope of rationality review so as to incorporate at common
law significant elements of the principle of proportionality."[302c]

[302a] [2015] UKSC 19; [2015] 1 W.L.R. 1591.

[302b] [2014] UKSC 20; [2015] A.C. 455

302c See also *R. (Keyu) v Secretary of State for Foreign and Commonwealth Affairs* [2015] UKSC 69; [2015] 3 W.L.R. 1665, in which the majority in the Supreme Court emphasised the close relationship between rationality and proportionality, indicating that they would produce identical outcomes in the instant case; *R. (Youssef) v Secretary of State for Foreign and Commonwealth Affairs* [2016] UKSC 3; [2016] 2 W.L.R. 509, to similar effect.

Intensity of Review

11–086 *[Add to n.310 after ". . . the minimum interference test, counselled its "cautious deployment");"]*

The Court of Appeal's decision was reversed by the Supreme Court [2013] UKSC 39; [2014] A.C. 700. In his leading judgment, however, Lord Sumption stated at [20] that he agreed with the view expressed in the court below by Maurice Kay L.J. that "this debate [on minimum interference] is sterile in the normal case where the effectiveness of the measure and the degree of interference are not absolute values but a question of degree, inversely related to each other. The question is whether a less intrusive measure could have been used without unacceptably compromising the objective". Lord Reed commented at [75]: "In relation to (the minimum interference test) Dickson CJ made clear in *R v Edwards Books and Art Ltd* [1986] . . . that the limitation of the protected right must be one that "it was reasonable for the legislature to impose", and that the courts were "not called on to substitute judicial opinions for legislative ones as to the place at which to draw a precise line." This approach is unavoidable, if there is to be any real prospect of a limitation on rights being justified: as Blackmun J once observed, "a judge would be unimaginative indeed if he could not come up with something a little less drastic or a little less restrictive in almost any situation, and thereby enable himself to vote to strike legislation down".

[Add to end of n.314]

See also *SS (Nigeria) v Secretary of State for the Home Department* [2013] EWCA Civ 550; [2014] 1 W.L.R. 998 at [41]–[42] per Laws L.J.: "But the principle [of minimal interference] does *not* tell us that . . . the court must always be the primary judge of the principle's fulfilment or otherwise. The court insists that the decisionmaker respect the principle; but this is perfectly consonant with the decisionmaker's enjoyment of a margin of discretion as to what constitutes minimal interference . . . . the breadth of this margin is conditioned by context, and in particular driven by two factors: (1) the nature of the public decision, and (2) its source . . . The principle . . . can never . . . be treated as a token or ritual. But the margin of discretionary judgment enjoyed by the primary decisionmaker, though variable, means that the court's role is kept in balance with that of the elected arms of government." See A. Vaughan, "Minimum Interference Versus Rationality: The New Battleground in HRA Proportionality?" [2013] J.R. 416. In *Pham v Secretary of State for the Home Department (Open Society Justice Initiative intervening)* [2015] UKSC 19; [2015] 1 W.L.R. 1591, [107] Lord Sumption J.S.C. questioned whether the distinctions drawn by Lord Steyn in *Daly* between proportionality and rationality review were "as simple as this", stating that "It is for the court to assess how broad the range of rational decisions is in the circumstances of any given case. That must necessarily depend on the significance of the right interfered with, the degree of interference involved, and notably the extent to which, even on a statutory appeal, the court is competent to reassess the balance which the decision-maker was called on to make given the subject-matter. The differences pointed out by Lord Steyn may in practice be more or less significant depending on the answers to these questions. In some cases, the range of rational decisions is so narrow as to determine the outcome".)

Variable intensity unreasonableness review

[Add to end of n.332]   11–092

And see *Kennedy v Information Commissioner (Secretary of State for Justice intervening)* [2014] UKSC 20; [2015] A.C. 455, [51] (Lord Mance: "The common law no longer insists on the uniform application of a rigid test of irrationality once thought applicable under the so-called *Wednesbury* principle . . . The nature of judicial review in every case depends on the context").

Heightened scrutiny unreasonableness review

[Add new n.337a after "This notion of 'anxious' or 'heightened' scrutiny is 11–094 *difficult to define with any precision, but it does indicate that the full rigour of* Wednesbury *is softened."]*

[337a] See generally P. Craig, "Judicial Review and Anxious Scrutiny: Foundations, Evolution and Application" [2015] P.L. 60.

[Add to end of para.11–096]   11–096

Nevertheless, some role for anxious scrutiny remains. In *R. (on the application of Lumsdon) v Legal Services Board* the Court of Appeal approved the use of a heightened form of *Wednesbury* when reviewing the Quality Assurance Scheme for Advocates, citing the court's "high level of institutional competence and constitutional legitimacy when addressing challenges to the criminal justice process."[345a] "Rigorous" scrutiny was also adopted in

R. (SF(St Lucia)) v Secretary of State for the Home Department when the challenge was to a decision whether a child was a victim of human trafficking for the purposes of the Convention on Action against Trafficking in Human Beings, with the Administrative Court emphasising both that a fundamental right was engaged and that the claim arose in an area "in which a court has the requisite knowledge."[345b] Different intensities of review may apply to a chain of decisions: the Home Secretary's determination that a person had been trafficked involved fundamental rights to which anxious scrutiny review should be applied; whereas a consequential decision about the person's eligibility for a residence permit would be subject to the ordinary standard.[345c]

By contrast, an attempt to apply a heightened scrutiny approach in reviewing the Lord Chancellor's proposals to make significant changes to the provision of criminal legal aid services by solicitors was rejected in *R. (on the application of London Criminal Courts Solicitors' Association) v Lord Chancellor*,[345d] despite the criminal justice dimension to the case.

[345a] [2014] EWCA Civ 1276; [2014] H.R.L.R. 29.

[345b] [2015] EWHC 2705 (Admin); [2016] 1 W.L.R. 1439.

[345c] *R. (K) v Secretary of State for the Home Department* [2015] EWHC 3668 (Admin); [2016] 4 W.L.R. 25.

[345d] [2015] EWHC 295 (Admin); [2015] A.C.D. 95.

Wednesbury, light-touch review and non-justiciability

11–097 *[Add to end of n.350]*

In *R. (on the application of Woods) v Chief Constable of Merseyside* [2014] EWHC 2784 (Admin); [2015] 1 W.L.R. 539, the Administrative Court considered the appropriate approach to *Wednesbury* review where the reason for a decision had been subject to a successful public interest immunity claim such that a reasoned justification for the decision could not be provided. In such circumstances, it was held at [36] *per* Stewart J "there would have to be clear evidence of dishonesty or bias or caprice" to justify intervention; that threshold was not reached on the facts.

CHAPTER 12

LEGITIMATE EXPECTATIONS

INTRODUCTION

Legitimate expectations of procedural fairness

Secondary procedural legitimate expectation

[Add to n.20 after "[2008] EWCA Civ 755;"]   12–011

(2008) 152(29) S.J.L.B. 29;

Illustrations

[Add to end of n.35]   12–015

In *R. (on the application of LH) v Shropshire Council* [2014] EWCA Civ
404; (2014) 17 C.C.L. Rep. 216, the *Baker* principle was applied in the
context of the closure of adult day care centres. In *LH* the council had
engaged in a general consultation process on reorganisation of day centres
across the county but the issue was whether there should have been specific
consultation about the closure of Hartleys Day Centre, used by LH. Informed
by that general consultation, the council then decided which particular day
centres to close. The Court of Appeal, reversing the Administrative Court
decision [2013] EWHC 4222 (Admin), concluded that the fairness of the
procedure was for the court to decide and although the council had initially
undertaken wideranging consultation it should have mounted a fresh consultation in relation to any individual day centre it then sought to close; *R. (on
the application of Save our Surgery Ltd* [2013] EWHC 439 (Admin); [2013]
Med. L.R. 150 (consultation process for identification of seven specialist
centres in England for the future performance of paediatric cardiac surgery
declared unfair; in the subsequent determination of what relief to grant the
claimant, the court granted a quashing order but declined to dictate what
steps should be taken because it had neither the requisite knowledge or
expertise: [2013] EWHC 1011 (Admin); [2013] Med. L.R. 172).

[Add additional bullet point at end of para.12–015]

- A person qualifying as a doctor could rely on clear, unequivocal and unqualified assurances from the GMC that if he completed his proposed distance learning course of study in a reasonable time his qualification would be recognised even though the registration criteria had been changed before completion.[40a]

[40a] *R. (on the application of Patel) v General Medical Council* [2013] EWCA Civ 327; [2013] 1 W.L.R. 2801, reversing [2012] EWHC 2120 (Admin); (2012) 128 B.M.L.R. 146.

THE SOURCE OF A LEGITIMATE EXPECTATION

12–016 *[Add new n.41a after "The representations which induce a legitimate expectation can thus be express or implied"]*

[41a] See F. Ahmed and A. Perry, "The Coherence of the Doctrine of Legitimate Expectations" [2014] C.L.J. 61 for a rulebased account of why certain promises, practices and policies give rise to legitimate expectations whereas others do not.

LEGITIMACY

12–030 *[Add new n.88a after ". . . must possess the following qualities"]*

[88a] In *United Kingdom Association of Fish Producer Organisations v Secretary of State for the Environment, Food and Rural Affairs* [2013] EWHC 1959 (Admin) at [92] Cranston J. said:

"[T]he threads of the English doctrine of substantive legitimate expectation can be drawn together in the following propositions: 1. The undertaking must be clear, unambiguous and without relevant qualification: *Bancoult*, [60]. 2. On ordinary principles an undertaking can derive from a representation or a course of conduct. However, the mere existence of a scheme is inadequate in itself to generate a substantive legitimate expectation: *Bhatt Murphy*, [63]. 3. Whether there is such an undertaking is ascertained by asking how, on a fair reading, the representation or course of conduct would reasonably have been understood by those to whom it was made: *Patel*, [44]–[45], applying *Paponette*, [30]. 4. Although in theory the defined class being large is no bar to their having a substantive legitimate expectation, in reality it is likely to be small if the expectation is to be made good: *Bhatt Murphy*, [46]. In *Paponette* the successful class to whom a collective promise had been made was some 2,000. 5. Detrimental reliance is not an essential requirement. However, it may be necessary where the issue is in the macropolitical field or a personspecific under- taking is alleged: *Bancoult*, [60]; *Begbie*, 1124 BC, 1133 DF. 6. To justify frustration of a substantive legitimate expectation, the decision maker must have taken into account as a relevant consideration the undertaking and the fact that it will be frustrated: *Paponette*, [45]–[46]. 7. Legitimate expectation is concerned with exceptional situations: *Bhatt Murphy*, [41]. 8. Justification turns on issues of fairness and good administration, whether frustrating the substantive legitimate expectation can be objectively justi- fied in the public interest and as a proportionate response. Abuse of power is not an adequate guide: *Nadarajah*, [70]. 9. The intensity of review depends on the character of the decision. There will be a more rigorous standard than *Wednesbury* review, with a decision being judged by the court's own view of fairness. A public body will not often be held bound to maintain a policy which on reasonable grounds it has chosen to change. There will be less intrusive review in the macropolitical field. As well, respect will be accorded to the relative expertise of a decisionmaker: *Bhatt Murphy*, [35], [41]; *Patel*, [60]–[62], [83]. 10. Transitional arrangements, and whether there has been a warning of possible change, are not essential but may be relevant to the court's assessment of justification: *Bhatt Murphy* [18]–[20], [56]–[57], [60]–[61], [65]–[70]; *Patel*, [77], [83]."

Clear, unambiguous and devoid of relevant qualification

[Add to end of n.89]   12–031

R. (on the application of Lewisham LBC v Assessment and Qualifications Alliance (AQA) [2013] EWHC 211 (Admin); [2013] E.L.R. 281 (assurance relied upon not sufficiently unequivocal to create a legitimate expectation that GCSE grade boundaries would not change from one assessment point to the next); *United Kingdom Association of Fish Producer Organisations v Secretary of State for the Environment, Food and Rural Affairs* [2013] EWHC 1959 (Admin) (no clear, unambiguous and without qualification undertaking by the Secretary of State that the fishing fixed quota allocation system adopted for the past 13 years would continue in its existing form; the repre- sentations amounted to no more than an explanation as to how the system operated); *R. (on the application of Enfield LBC) v Secretary of State for Transport* [2016] EWCA Civ 480 (while emails stating that train service tender would require a four train per hour service were clear and unambig- uous, they had not been sent to the local authority directly and moreover, the local authority knew that a four train per hour service was "inherently unlikely").

When is the Disappointment of a Substantive Legitimate Expectation Unlawful?

12–046 *[Add to end of n.145]*

R. *(on the application of Alansi) v Newham LBC* [2013] EWHC 3722; [2014] B.L.G.R. 138 (a change of housing policy resulting in A losing her status as a priority home seeker was a proportionate response to a pressing and widespread social problem despite a prior clear and unequivocal assurance that A would retain her priority status if she took up a private rented tenancy which the new policy then excluded from priority status); R. *(on the application of Birks) v Commissioner of Police of the Metropolis* [2014] EWHC 3041 (Admin); [2015] I.C.R 204 (rescinding acceptance of the claimant's resignation from the police was proportionate, despite clear prior representations to the contrary, due to the public interest in facilitating the investigation of a death in custody); R. *(Project Management Institute) v Minister for the Cabinet Office* [2016] EWCA Civ 21; [2016] 1 W.L.R. 1737 (the policy of the Privy Council in deciding whether or not to grant a Royal Charter was to be given a broad construction and to allow for a degree of flexibility, such that a compelling public interest in favour of the grant outweighed any failure to meet the main criteria of the policy in full).

12–047 *[Add to end of para.12–047]*

In *Patel*, the Court of Appeal held that the GMC had to honour a clear, unequivocal and unqualified assurance given to P that if he completed his distancelearning course of study in a reasonable time, his qualification would be recognised. This was not outweighed by any prevailing public interest; transitional arrangements should have been put in place.[147a]

[147a] R. *(on the application of Patel) v General Medical Council* [2013] EWCA Civ 327; [2013] 1 W.L.R. 2801.

The Standard of Judicial Review

12–052 *[Add to end of n.160]*

In R. *(on the application of Patel) v General Medical Council* [2013] EWCA Civ 327; [2013] 1 W.L.R. 2801 at [83], Lloyd Jones L.J. held: "When the court considers the fairness of overriding a substantive legitimate expectation, the standard of review is a sliding scale . . . Normally, the court would accord a considerable degree of respect to a specialist body such as the GMC which is required by Parliament to decide what qualifications should be recognised." But: (i) there was no reason to conclude that distance learning was such a problem as to demand immediate withdrawal of recognition without any steps to mitigate the impact of such a decision; (ii) the expectation was founded upon an express statement rather than a former policy or course of conduct; (iii) the representation was made to an individual personally; (iv) the expectation was of high importance to P; (v) detrimental reliance was present in abundance; and (vi) the decision of the GMC was not in the macropolitical field.

The subject matter of the representation

[Add to end of n.176]   12–055

Cf. R. *(on the application of Patel) v General Medical Council* [2013] EWCA Civ 327; [2013] 1 W.L.R. 2801 (expectation that undertaking an existing distance learning course would lead to recognition of the qualification awarded in the future).

Degree of reassurance

[Add new n.179a after ". . . as much weight as an oral or written 12–057
representation"]

[179a] R. *(on the application of Patel) v General Medical Council* [2013] EWCA Civ 327; [2013] 1 W.L.R. 2801.

Nature of the decision

[Add to end of n.182]   12–058

See also R. *(on the application of Patel) v General Medical Council* [2013] EWCA Civ 327; [2013] 1 W.L.R. 2801; *Re Finucane's Application for Judicial Review* [2015] NIQB 57; and *United Policyholders Group v Attorney General of Trinidad and Tobago* [2016] UKPC 17; Times, July 26, 2016, in which the Privy Council took the same approach to macro-economic decisions.

Detrimental reliance

[Add to end of n.185]   12–059

R. (on the application of Patel) v General Medical Council [2013] EWCA Civ 327; [2013] 1 W.L.R. 2801 (course undertaken in expectation that it would lead to a recognised qualification was extremely demanding in terms of time and effort with a total financial cost of some US$40,000).

CHAPTER 13

CONVENTION RIGHTS AS GROUNDS FOR JUDICIAL REVIEW

PROTECTION OF FUNDAMENTAL RIGHTS IN DOMESTIC AND INTERNATIONAL LAW

The Council of Europe

[Add to end of n.14]   13–006

The total number of pending applications on December 31, 2015 was 64,850, a decrease of 19% in relation to the same date the previous year (79,900). On June 30, 2016, it had risen to 71,050 (see *http://www.echr.coe.int/Documents/ Stats_pending_2016_BIL.pdf*). Two further Protocols have been adopted but not yet entered into force. Protocol 15 would give effect to the proposed reduction in the time limit for bringing proceedings in art.35 of the ECHR from six months to four and would introduce references in the Preamble to the ECHR to the principles of subsidiarity and the margin of appreciation (on which, see A. Tickell, "More 'efficient' justice at the European Court of Human Rights: but at whose expense?" [2015] P.L. 206). Protocol 16 would permit the highest courts of state parties to request an advisory opinion relating to the interpretation or application of Convention rights (on which, see K. Dzehtsiarou and N. O'Meara, "Advisory Jurisdiction and the European Court of Human Rights: A Magic Bullet for Dialogue and Docket Control?" (2014) 34 L.S. 444). The Joint Committee on Human Rights in *Protocol 15 to the European Convention on Human Rights* (HL Paper 71); (HC Paper 837) (2014–2015) recommended that the UK should ratify Protocol 15 after its having been debated in both Houses. The same report noted that the Government has no intention of signing or ratifying Protocol 16, on the basis that it is "unconvinced" of the value of advisory opinions.

[In n.19 delete final sentence and substitute]   13–007

Nine such Guides have so far been published: on arts 4, 5, 6 (civil and criminal), 7 (French only) and 9; arts 2 and 3 of the First Protocol; and art.4 of the Fourth Protocol. Of the applications pending before the ECtHR in June 2015, 24.4 per cent were against Ukraine, 12.8 per cent were against Russia, 11.6 per cent were against Turkey and 10.1 per cent were against Hungary. In the first six months of 2016, some 18,630 applications were decided, a fall of 28 per cent from the same period in 2015. For up-to-date statistics, see *http://www.echr.coe.int/Pages/home.aspx?p=reports*.

13–008 *[In n.23 delete "5ᵗʰ edn (2010)" and substitute]*

6ᵗʰ edn (2014)

THE EUROPEAN CONVENTION ON HUMAN RIGHTS

13–010 *[Add to end of n.25]*

In *Poghosyan v Armenia* (2015) 61 E.H.R.R. 2 at [43]–[48], the ECtHR held that there had been a breach of art.13 where under domestic law the applicant was unable to apply for compensation for the non-pecuniary damage he had suffered as a result of his ill-treatment in detention. See further A. Lee, "Focus on Article 13 ECHR" [2015] J.R. 33.

13–011 *[Add to end of n.26]*

See also *Nada v Switzerland* (2013) 56 E.H.R.R. 18. Mr Nada was added to the UN Security Council sanctions list as a suspected funder and supporter of al-Qaeda and the Taliban. This required states to impose a travel ban, implemented in Switzerland by way of its domestic "Taliban Ordinance". Although Mr Nada could apply to the national authorities to have his name deleted from the list annexed to the Taliban Ordinance, the national courts held that Switzerland was bound by the UN Security Council resolution such that it did not have the power to do so. The ECtHR held that Mr Nada had been deprived of an effective remedy, but did not rule determinatively on the question of how to resolve such conflicts between a requirement of a UN Security Resolution and of the ECHR (on which, see S. Hollenberg, "The diverging approaches of the European Court of Human Rights in the cases of Nada and Al-Dulimi" [2015] I.C.L.Q. 445).

13–019 *[Add to end of n.40]*

In *HADEP v Turkey* (2013) 56 E.H.R.R. 5 at [61], the ECtHR stated that a political party whose leaders incite others to violence or put forward a policy which does not comply with one or more of the rules of democracy or which is aimed at the destruction of democracy and the flouting of the rights and freedoms recognised in a democracy cannot lay claim to the Convention's protection against penalties imposed on those grounds (although the dissolution of HADEP was held to have breached art.11 on the grounds that it was disproportionate). In *Paksas v Lithuania* (2014) 59 E.H.R.R. 30 at [87]–[88], the ECtHR reiterated that "since the general purpose of art.17 is

. . . to prevent individuals or groups with totalitarian aims from exploiting in their own interests the principles enunciated in the Convention, this article is applicable only on an exceptional basis and in extreme cases." *Perinçek v Switzerland* (2016) 63 E.H.R.R. 6 at [114]–[115] concerned public statements made by the applicant denying the Armenian genocide. The ECtHR held that in cases concerning art.10, art.17 applies to preclude consideration of the substantive right only where it is "immediately clear that the impugned statements sought to deflect [art.10] from its real purpose by employing the right to freedom of expression for ends clearly contrary to the values of the Convention". Absent that clarity, the art.17 question fell to be joined to the merits of the complaint under art.10. See further, A. Buyse, "Dangerous expressions: the ECHR, violence and free speech" [2014] I.C.L.Q. 491.

[Add to end of n.42]

Similarly, in *Ould Dah v France* (2013) 56 E.H.R.R. SE17 at [35]–[36], the ECtHR rejected the argument that an application brought on the basis of a breach of art.7 was an abuse of rights within the meaning of art.17 because the applicant had committed acts in breach of art.3.

[Add to end of n.43] 13–020

In *Khodorkovskiy v Russia* (2014) 59 E.H.R.R. 7 at [644], the ECtHR affirmed that there was no restriction on an individual waiving his rights under art.6 so long as any such a waiver is established in an unequivocal manner and is attended by minimum safeguards commensurate with its importance. In addition, it must not run counter to any important public interest. Waiver has also arisen in relation to art.8. In *M v Chief Constable of Hampshire* [2014] EWCA Civ 1651; [2015] 1 W.L.R. 1176 at [18], the CA held that where a sex offender allowed the police to enter his home without objection he would in almost all cases have waived his right, both at common law and under art.8, to refuse entry.

[Add to end of n.45] 13–022

As to the limitations imposed on the right of access to a court by virtue of an assertion of state immunity, see P. Luckhurst, "State Immunity in Employment Disputes and the Fundamental Right of Access to a Court" [2015] J.R. 90.

Derogations

[Add to end of n.47] 13–023

Article 15 must be read as applying to the extraterritorial jurisdiction of the Convention: *Mohammed v Ministry of Defence* [2014] EWHC 1369 (QB) at

[155]–[157] (doubting the dictum in *Al-Jedda v Secretary of State for Defence* [2007] UKHL 58; [2008] 1 A.C. 332 at [38]). *Mohammed* concerned a successful claim for a violation of art.5 by an Afghan national detained for over 100 days by British forces in Afghanistan without any lawful authority (beyond the first 96 hours). On appeal to the Court of Appeal (*Mohammed v Secretary of State for Defence* [2015] EWCA Civ 843; [2016] 2 W.L.R. 247), this finding was not overturned.

13–025   *[Add to end of n.49]*

The decision of the ECtHR in *Al-Skeini* was applied in the UK by the SC in *Smith v Ministry of Defence* [2013] UKSC 41; [2014] A.C. 52, in which it was held that the requirement of "exceptionality" does not set an especially high threshold [46] and that the jurisdiction of the United Kingdom extends to securing the protection of art.2 to members of the armed forces when they are serving outside its territory [55]. *Al-Skeini* was also applied in *R. (on the application of Sandiford) v Secretary of State for Foreign and Commonwealth Affairs* [2014] UKSC 44; [2014] 1 W.L.R. 2697, in which it was held that the applicant was not within the jurisdiction of the UK for the purposes of art.1 in relation to the policy of refusing to fund legal representation for those facing capital charges overseas. The decisions in *Al-Skeini* and *Smith* are heavily criticised in the context of military operations by the CA in *Mohammed v Secretary of State for Defence* [2015] EWCA Civ 843; [2016] 2 W.L.R. 247 at [93]–[97] on the basis that they involve a substantial extension of the scope of the ECHR to all cases where the state exercises control over an individual as opposed to a territorial area. See also *Jaloud v Netherlands* (2015) 60 E.H.R.R. 29 at [152], where jurisdiction was established in respect of the Netherlands in circumstances where Mr Jaloud died when a vehicle in which he was a passenger was fired upon while passing through a checkpoint manned by personnel under the command and direct supervision of a Netherlands Royal Army officer. In *R (Keyu & Ors) v Secretary of State for Foreign and Commonwealth Affairs & Secretary of State for Defence* [2015] UKSC 69; [2015] 3 W.L.R. 1665 at [64]–[65], the SC (while rejecting the claim on time grounds) accepted that under the constitutional arrangements then in force, the United Kingdom was in complete control of the State of Malaya and hence the relatives of victims of the 1948 massacre of 24 civilians by members of the British Army in the State of Selangor could potentially rely on art. 2.

13–026   *[Add to end of n.51]*

In *Michael v Chief Constable of South Wales* [2015] UKSC 2; [2015] A.C. 1732 at [139], the applicant's art.2 claim was permitted to proceed to trial. The case concerned an emergency call handler's failure to prioritise the police response to a call stating that the victim's former partner had threatened to kill her. See also *O'Keeffe v Ireland* (2014) 59 E.H.R.R.15 (Ireland's failure to implement an adequate legal or regulatory framework to protect children in primary education against the risk of sexual abuse by teachers constituted a breach of art.3).

[Add to end of n.54]

The ECtHR in *O'Keeffe v Ireland* (2014) 59 E.H.R.R.15 at [144] indicated that more is required by way of positive obligation in relation to children and vulnerable persons.

Interpreting the ECHR

[Add to end of n.60]   13–029

In *Vallianatos v Greece* (2014) 59 E.H.R.R. 12 at [91], the ECtHR acknowledged the trend emerging in the legal systems of the Council of Europe (which has yet to reach consensus) to recognise same-sex relation-ships. A 2008 Greek law which excluded same-sex couples from forming civil unions was a breach of art.8 read with art.14. See further *Oliari and Others v. Italy* (App. Nos. 18766/11 and 36030/11) (21 July, 2015) at [178]. In contrast, in *Jones v United Kingdom* (2014) 59 E.H.R.R. 1 at [213]–[215], the ECtHR held that, despite some emerging support in favour of a special rule or exception in public international law cases concerning civil claims for torture lodged against foreign state officials, it was still the case that a grant of immunity to state officials reflected generally recognised rules of public international law, such that there had been no violation of art.6(1).

[Delete first sentence of para.13–030 and substitute]   13–030

The Council of Europe has adopted a total of 16 Protocols.

The Human Rights Act 1998

[In n.66 delete "C. Brown" and substitute]   13–031

R. Desai

[In n.66 delete "6th edn (2011) and substitute]

7th edn (2015)

The omission of arts 1 and 13

13–034 *[Add to end of n.76]*

Section 6 was held to fulfil the same role in relation to art.1 in *DSD v Commissioner of Police of the Metropolis* [2015] EWCA Civ 646; [2016] Q.B. 161 at [17].

The authority of Strasbourg decisions

13–035 *[Add to end of n.80]*

In *R. (on the application of Nicklinson) v Ministry of Justice* [2014] UKSC 38; [2015] A.C. 657 at [70], Lord Kerr suggested that Lord Bingham's dictum was not on point in cases to which a wide margin of appreciation applied.

[Add to end of n.81]

See also N. Ferreira, "The Supreme Court in a final push to go beyond Strasbourg" [2015] P.L. 367, commenting on the decisions in *Ullah* and *Nicklinson,* and P. Mahoney, "The relationship between the Strasbourg court and the national courts" (2014) 130 L.Q.R. 568.

13–036 *[Add to end of n.82]*

Lines of Strasbourg authority may become less clear over time. However, the fact that there may be a "direction of travel" in Strasbourg jurisprudence which appears to depart from a formerly stated principle will not allow for that principle to be replaced with a "new interpretation" without "a clear, high level exegesis of the salient principle and its essential components": *Kennedy v Charity Commission* [2014] UKSC 20; [2015] A.C. 455 at [145]–[148]. In *Kennedy,* the SC held that there was no art.10 right to receive information from public authorities: see para.13–090. In *Moohan v Lord Advocate* [2014] UKSC 67; [2015] A.C. 901 at [104]–[105], Lord Hodge chronicled the SC's substantial modification of the *Ullah* principle, holding that "where there is no directly relevant decision of the ECtHR with which it would be possible (even if appropriate) to keep pace, we can and must do more. We must determine for ourselves the existence or otherwise of an alleged Convention right." That principle was reflected in the judgment of Lord Kerr in *R (Keyu & Ors) v Secretary of State for Foreign and Commonwealth Affairs & Secretary of State for Defence* [2015] UKSC 69; [2015] 3 W.L.R. at [234]–[235]. His Lordship postulated that while a domestic court should exercise "caution" in determining what the ECtHR would decide absent relevant jurisprudence, it should not be deterred from that duty.

[Add to end of n.83]

In *Rabone and another v Pennine Care NHS Trust* [2012] UKSC 2; [2012] 2 A.C. 72 at [112], Lord Brown (agreeing with the leading judgment of Lord Dyson) made clear that the absence of Strasbourg authority does not prevent a domestic court from addressing a question of the interpretation of the ECHR. Rather, Lord Brown stated that a domestic court should not unwillingly decide a case against a public authority (which would have no right to seek to have that decision overturned in Strasbourg) unless the existing authorities compel that result.

[Add to end of n.85]

The CA has summarised the above authorities and the more recent SC cases of *R. (on the application of Osborn) v Parole Board* [2013] UKSC 61; [2014] A.C. 1115 at [56]–[57] and *R. (on the application of Chester) v Secretary of State for Justice* [2013] UKSC 63; [2014] A.C. 271 at [27], [120]–[124] in the following principles: (1) it is the duty of the national courts to enforce domestically enacted Convention rights; (2) the ECtHR is the court that, ultimately, must interpret the meaning of the Convention; (3) the UK courts will be bound to follow an interpretation of a provision of the Convention if given by the Grand Chamber as authoritative, unless it is apparent that it has misunderstood or overlooked some significant feature of English law or practice which, properly explained, would lead to that interpretation being reviewed by the ECtHR when its interpretation was being applied to English circumstances; (4) the same principle and qualification applies to a "clear and constant" line of decisions of the ECtHR other than one of the Grand Chamber; (5) Convention rights have to be given effect in the light of the domestic law which implements in detail the "high level" rights set out in the Convention; and (6) where there are "mixed messages" in the existing Strasbourg case law, a "real judicial choice" will have to be made about the scope and application of the relevant provision of the Convention (*R. (on the application of Hicks) v Commissioner of Police of the Metropolis* [2014] EWCA Civ 3; [2014] 1 W.L.R. 2152 at [80]). In *Hicks*, the CA declined to follow the recent decision of the ECtHR in *Ostendorf v Germany* 34 B.H.R.C. 738 on the basis that it was not consistent with the ECtHR's earlier case law. See further n.170.

[Add to end of n.86]   13–037

The CA granted permission to appeal to the SC in *R. (on the application of Kaiyam) v Secretary of State for Justice* [2013] EWCA Civ 1587; [2014] 1 W.L.R. 1208 rather than follow the ECtHR's decision in *James, Wells and Lee v UK* (2013) 56 E.H.R.R. 12 (see n.191). The CA's decision was reversed in part. The SC decision is *R. (on the application of Kaiyam) v Secretary of*

State for Justice [2014] UKSC 66; [2015] A.C. 1344. The circumstances in which the domestic court may depart from Strasbourg authority were considered at [18]–[21]. The SC held that the degree of constraint imposed or freedom allowed by the phrase "must take into account" is context specific (at [21]). The SC declined to follow the ECtHR's interpretation of the term "unlawful" in art.5(4) (at [35]).

Public authorities

13–040 *[Add to end of n.95]*

See also C. Gearty, "On Fantasy Island: British politics, English judges and the European Convention on Human Rights" [2015] E.H.R.L.R. 1.

The duty to interpret legislation compatibly with Convention rights

13–042 *[Delete the last sentence of n.101 and substitute]*

In *R. (on the application of T) v Chief Constable of Greater Manchester* [2014] UKSC 35; [2015] A.C. 49 at [53], the SC held it was impossible to read and give effect to the domestic provisions on the disclosure of convictions and cautions (however old and minor) of the Police Act 1997 in a way which was compatible with art.8. Recent cases in which it was held not possible to "read down" the relevant legislation in order to give effect to the applicants' Convention rights include *R. (on the application of Tigere) v Secretary of State for Business, Innovation and Skills* [2015] UKSC 57; [2015] 1 W.L.R. 3820 at [48]–[49] (concerning student loans and immigration status); *Lawrence and another v Fen Tigers Ltd and others (No 3)* [2015] UKSC 50; [2015] 1 W.L.R. 3485 at [88] (concerning success fee up-lifts in litigation); *Benkharbouche v Embassy of Sudan* [2015] EWCA Civ 33; [2015] 3 W.L.R. 301 (concerning the State Immunity Act 1978 in relation to which a declaration of incompatibility was granted) and *McDonald v McDonald* [2016] UKSC 28; [2016] 3 W.L.R. 45 at [70] (concerning mandatory possession orders in favour of private landlords, although the court found no incompatibility). In *Re. X (A Child) (Parental Order: Time Limit)* [2014] EWHC 3135 (Fam); [2015] Fam. 186 at [68], the court read down s.54 of the Human Fertilisation and Embryology Act 2008 (which imposes a six-month time limit on applications for a parental order) to achieve compatibility with art.8. In *Re Z (A Child) (Surrogate Father: Parental Order)* [2015] EWFC 73; [2015] 1 W.L.R. 4993 at [35]–[40], however, while the court affirmed previous cases in which s.54 was read down, it was not possible to read down that legislative provision in order to bring a single parent within the statutory requirements for the grant of a parental order. The Secretary of

State conceded that the legislation was incompatible with art.8 read with art.14 and a declaration of incompatibility was granted ([2016] EWHC 1191 (Fam); [2016] HRLR 15).

[Add to end of n.109]   13–045

See also *Lawrence and another v Fen Tigers Ltd and others (No 3)* [2015] UKSC 50; [2015] 1 W.L.R. 3485 at [89]–[94].

Declaration of incompatibility

[Delete all text in n.112 and substitute]   13–047

See Table 1 at the end of this Chapter for a summary of the declarations of incompatibility made up to the end of July 2016. Section 4 of the Joint Committee on Human Rights' *Human Rights Judgments* (HL Paper 130); (HC Paper 1088) (March, 4 2015) notes that during the 2010–2015 Parliament, there was a significant downward trend in the numbers of declarations of incompatibility made.

[Add to end of n.115]   13–048

In *R. (on the application of Nicklinson) v Ministry of Justice* [2014] UKSC 38; [2015] A.C. 657, the majority of the nine-member SC held that it would not have been outside the court's institutional power to declare the Suicide Act 1961 s.2 to be incompatible with the ECHR even though the question was one within the UK's margin of appreciation as far as the ECtHR was concerned. However, in a "controversial area raising difficult moral and ethical issues", the court should adopt a "light touch" when reviewing the proportionality of primary legislation (at [112]–[113]). The majority stated that a declaration of incompatibility would not have the effect of forcing Parliament to act, but declined to grant one on the facts. See J. Finnis, "A British 'Convention right' to assistance in suicide?" (2015) 131 L.Q.R. 1.

Special regard to the freedoms of expression and of thought, conscience and religion

[Add to end of n. 144]   13–057

In *PJS v News Group Newspapers Ltd* [2016] UKSC 26; [2016] 2 W.L.R. 1253 at [33]–[35], the SC granted an injunction and held that the court should have regard to the qualitative difference between the availability of material on the internet and its widespread dissemination in hard copy (and on newspaper websites) by the English media.

Territorial and temporal scope of the HRA

13-059 *[Add to end of n.151]*

In *R. (on the application of Barclay) v Secretary of State for Justice* [2014] UKSC 54; [2015] A.C. 276 at [36], the SC held that it was not for a UK court to read down Channel Island legislation to make it compatible with Convention rights. The HRA does not apply to the Channel Islands. An Order in Council made in exercise of the royal prerogative did not fall within the definition of primary legislation in s.2(1) of the HRA.

[Add to end of n.153]

See also *Smith v Carillion (JM) Ltd* [2015] EWCA Civ 209; [2015] I.R.L.R. 467 at [43]. There, all the impugned acts occurred prior to the coming into force of the HRA. An argument that the acts were "continuing" was rejected on the facts. In *R (Keyu & Ors) v Secretary of State for Foreign and Commonwealth Affairs & Secretary of State for Defence* [2015] UKSC 69; [2015] 3 W.L.R. 1665 at [246]–[249], the SC considered that *Re McKerr* [2004] UKHL 12; [2004] 1 W.L.R. 807 remained good law, as such the HRA did not have retrospective effect. However, the impact of the ECtHR's decision in *Silih v Slovenia* (2009) 49 EHRR 996 on art.2 is significant. In *In re McCaughey & Or* [2011] UKSC 20; [2012] 1 A.C. 725 at [61]–[63], the SC held that *Silih* had extended the scope of the free-standing and autonomous procedural obligation in art.2 where death occurred before the court's assumption of jurisdiction and if significant procedural steps required by art.2 took place after that date. In *McCaughey*, therefore, although the deaths took place in 1990, an inquest in 2009 was required to comply with the requirements of art.2.

The content of Convention rights under the HRA

Absolute rights

The right to life

13-062 *[In n.156 delete "(Evans . . .). In Evans" and substitute]*

(Evans v UK (2006) 43 E.H.R.R. 21 at [45]–[46]). In *Evans v UK* (2008) 46 E.H.R.R. 34 at [54]–[56]

[Delete all text in n.157 and substitute]

In *Pretty v UK* (2002) 35 E.H.R.R. 1 at [38]–[40], the ECtHR followed the reasoning of the HL in rejecting a challenge by the victim of a degenerative disease to the Director of Public Prosecution's decision not to offer an assurance not to prosecute the victim's husband if he assisted her suicide. The HL decision is *R. (on the application of Pretty) v DPP* [2001] UKHL 61; [2002] 1 A.C. 800. The HL subsequently departed from its position in *Pretty* and required the Director of Public Prosecutions to clarify prosecution policy on assisted suicide on the grounds that the uncertainty in the current policy did not satisfy the requirements of art.8(2) (see *Purdy* at [54]–[56], n.86 above). The CPS published its new policy on assisted suicide in February 2010 (*http://www.cps.gov.uk/publications/prosecution/assisted_suicide_policy. html*), updated in October 2014. In *R. (on the application of Nicklinson) v Ministry of Justice* [2014] UKSC 38; [2015] A.C. 657 at [141], [145], [249], [278], the SC declined to go further and tell the Director of Public Prosecutions what her policy should actually contain. An application to the ECtHR (*Nicklinson and Lamb v the United Kingdom* (App. nos. 2478/15 and 1787/15) was declared inadmissible on the basis that art.8 did not impose procedural obligations requiring domestic courts to examine the merits of a challenge brought in respect of primary legislation; to do so would deny the domestic court the opportunity to conclude, as did the SC, that Parliament is best placed to take a decision on certain issues. In any case, the ECtHR held that the SC had considered the substance of Ms Nicklinson's claim. Lord Falconer's (private members') Assisted Dying Bill [HL] 2014–2015 reached the second reading stage before running out of time. The second reading of Lord Falconer's re-tabled Assisted Dying Bill [HL] 2015–2016 is yet to be scheduled. Robert Marris MP's (private members') Assisted Dying (No. 2) Bill 2015–16 was rejected by the House of Commons at the second reading debate on September 11, 2015 by 330 votes to 112. See also *Lambert v France* (46043/14) (2015) 38 B.H.R.C. 709; (2015) 145 B.M.L.R. 28.

[Add to end of n.158]   13–063

There is no requirement that there should be a risk to the life of an identified or identifiable individual; it is sufficient, for example, that individuals were known to be in the vicinity of the street where disorder was being caused (*Sarjantson v Chief Constable of Humberside Police* [2013] EWCA Civ 1252; [2014] Q.B. 411 at [22]–[36]).

[Add to end of n.160]

In *Smith v Ministry of Defence* [2013] UKSC 41; [2014] A.C. 41, the SC permitted claims of a breach of the positive substantive obligation in art.2 to proceed to trial. The claims related to the deaths of British servicemen in

Iraq from improvised explosive devices while they were travelling in modified Land Rover vehicles.

[Add to end of n.162]

See also *Jaloud v Netherlands* (2015) 60 E.H.R.R. 29 (concerning the failure effectively to investigate the shooting of an Iraqi civilian potentially caused by troops from the Netherlands). In *Al-Saadoon v Secretary of State for Defence* [2015] EWHC 715 (Admin); [2015] 3 W.L.R. 503 at [281]–[285] and [294(10)], the Court held that no investigative obligation under art.2 can arise in circumstances where there is no arguable breach of a substantive obligation. In *Al-Saadoon & Ors v Secretary of State for Defence* [2016] EWCA Civ 811 at [69], the CA (overturning the decision at first instance) held that the use of lethal or potentially lethal force was not sufficient to establish extra-territorial jurisdiction in the absence of an element of control over the individual prior to the use of force. Further, the CA held that the investigative duty under art.3 is triggered by an arguable claim that the individual has suffered treatment infringing art.3, not merely a breach of the *Soering* obligation not to send an individual to another state where there are substantial grounds for believing that he would face a real risk of being subject to torture or other prohibited treatment (at [124]–[125]).

[Add to end of n.163]

In *R (Keyu & Ors) v Secretary of State for Foreign and Commonwealth Affairs & Secretary of State for Defence* [2015] UKSC 69; [2015] 3 W.L.R. 1665 at [71] –[89], the SC rejected the application for judicial review of the Minister's decision not to order an inquiry into the deaths in 1948 of 24 civilians at the hands of British troops in what was then the State of Malaya. However, the SC held that while the Convention did not generally have retrospective effect, the European court's jurisprudence (in particular, *Janowiec v Russia* (2013) 58 EHRR 792) obliged a state to investigate a death which had occurred before the critical date, namely the date of entry into force of the Convention with respect to that state, where (i) there existed relevant acts or omissions after the critical date; and (ii) there was a genuine connection between the death, as the triggering event, and the critical date, so long as the period between the two did not exceed ten years. The first criterion was fulfilled as there had been no full or public investigation prior to 1970 (and the critical date was 1966 when the UK had first recognised the right of individual petition), but more than ten years had passed between the deaths and 1966. In *R. (on the application of Litvinenko) v Secretary of State for the Home Department* [2014] EWHC 194 (Admin); [2014] H.R.L.R. 6 at [50]–[54], the DC found that the extensive police investigation into Mr Litvinenko's death was sufficient to fulfil art.2. In *Mocanu v Romania* (2015) 60 E.H.R.R. 19, an investigation into civilian deaths following a state crackdown on demonstrations was held to be inadequate where it had been entrusted to military prosecutors, who lacked objectivity and impartiality.

[Add to end of n.166]

See also *Al-Saadoon v Secretary of State for Defence* [2015] EWHC 715 (Admin); [2015] 3 W.L.R. 503 at [111] which holds that a killing may be lawful under art.2 even if it is not strictly necessary for the purposes of art.2(2)(a)–(c) if it is authorised under international humanitarian law.

The right to be free from torture, inhuman and degrading treatment or punishment

[Add to end of n.167]   13–065

Rape can also amount to torture: *Aydin (Sukran) v Turkey* (1998) 25 E.H.R.R. 251. In *Cestaro v Italy* (App. No. 6884/11) (April 7, 2015), the ECtHR found that repeated kicks and beatings with a baton, causing multiple fractures and a permanent impediment in the applicant's right arm and right leg amounted to torture. In *Bataliny v Russia* (App. No. 10060/07) (July 23, 2015), forced psychiatric treatment in the absence of an established medical need and being included in scientific research into a new antipsychotic drug (without consent) amounted to inhuman and degrading treatment. In *NXB v Crown Prosecution Service* [2015] EWHC 631 (QB) at [79], the court entertained the possibility of a breach of art.3 occasioned by a decision to withdraw a prosecution for sexual assault against a minor, although on the facts no breach was found. In *Blokhin v. Russia* (App. No. 47152/06) (March 23, 2016), inadequacy of medical assessment and treatment in juvenile detention amounted to inhuman and degrading treatment.

[Add to end of n.169]

In *DD v Secretary of State for the Home Department* [2015] EWHC 1681 (Admin), it was held that the requirement to wear an electronic monitoring tag pursuant to a terrorism prevention and investigation measure had become a violation of the subject's art.3 rights given a deterioration in his mental health and paranoid belief that the tag contained a bomb. The ECtHR has also held that particular importance should be attached to the increased vulnerability of asylum seekers. In *V.M. and others v Belgium* (App. No. 60125/11) (July 7, 2015), it was held that conditions of extreme poverty faced by a family of asylum seekers constituted a violation of art.3 (inhuman or degrading treatment). In *Razzakov v Russia* (App. No. 57519/09) (February 5, 2015), it was held that the applicant's vulnerability had been exacerbated by the fact that he was a foreigner who understood little Russian. In *Korneykova and Korneykov v Ukraine* (App. No. 56660/12) (March 24, 2016), it was held that unjustified restraint of a prisoner who had just given birth and was therefore "particularly sensitive" amounted to inhuman and degrading treatment, and that having regard to her son's young age, the failure to ensure his medical monitoring also amounted to a breach of art.3 in his case.

[In n.170 delete "Sentences of life . . . [25]–[30])" and substitute]

A number of judgments of the ECtHR in 2015 found overcrowded detention conditions to amount to a breach of art.3, *inter alia*, *Martzaklis and Others v Greece* (App. No. 20378/13) (July 9, 2015) and *Gégény v Hungary* (App. No. 44753/12) (July 16, 2015). In *Vinter v UK* (2016) 63 E.H.R.R. 1 at [110]–[115], the ECtHR held that it was a breach of art.3 to impose whole life sentences on prisoners which only permitted release on compassionate grounds at the discretion of the Secretary of State. In *Re Attorney General's Reference (No. 69 of 2013)* [2014] EWCA Crim 188; [2014] 1 W.L.R. 3964 at [25]–[36], a five-person CA held that, despite *Vinter*, such sentences were still permitted in exceptional cases and that the circumstances in which continued detention could be reviewed were sufficiently clear and had to be read consistently with art.3. In *Hutchinson v United Kingdom* (2015) 61 E.H.R.R. 13 at [24]–[25], the ECtHR considered itself bound to recognise the CA's interpretation of national law as definitive and accepted that the UK's system of reviewing whole-life sentences complied with art.3. In *Elashmawy v Italy* [2015] EWHC 28 (Admin), the court set out the principles applicable to an alleged violation of art.3 deriving from prison conditions in another contracting state. In *Murray v the Netherlands* (App. No. 10511/10) (April 26, 2016) at [125]–[127], the applicant's life sentence was found to be *de facto* irreducible, and therefore in breach of art.3, where a lack of any kind of treatment or assessment of treatment needs rendered his rehabilitation impossible.

[Add to end of n.171]

In a possible extension of this principle, in *Identoba v Georgia* (App. No. 73235/12) (May 12, 2015) at [65], the ECtHR held, citing *East African Asians* in the context of homophobic, rather than racist, remarks, that "Discriminatory remarks and insults must in any event be considered as an aggravating factor when considering a given instance of ill-treatment in the light of Article 3."

13–066 *[Add to end of n.173]*

If the conditions under which an asylum seeker would be required to live if returned to another state under the Dublin II Regulation (in this case Italy) created a real risk that art.3 would be violated (even if not as a result of systemic failings), this would violate the ECHR (*R. (on the application of EM (Eritrea)) v Secretary of State for the Home Department* [2014] UKSC 12; [2014] A.C. 1321 at [58]–[64], [68]–[69]). The case was remitted to the

Administrative Court to determine on the facts whether such a risk arose. Such returns were considered by the ECtHR in the recent case of *Tarakhel v Switzerland* (2015) 60 E.H.R.R. 28. It was held that the Swiss authorities would be in breach of art.3 if they returned a family of asylum seekers to Italy without first obtaining assurances that they would be received in facilities and in conditions adapted to the age of the children, and that the family would be kept together. In *FG v Sweden* (App. No. 43611/11) (March 23, 2016), the ECtHR held that there was a duty on the returning state to assess individual risk factors of which it became aware, even if they were not relied on by the applicant in support of a claim against expulsion on the grounds of arts 2 or 3.

[Add to end of n.176]

The relevant principles are summarised in *DSD v Commissioner of Police for the Metropolis* [2015] EWCA Civ 646; [2016] Q.B. 161 at [59]–[69], in which the CA held that the police investigations relating to the so-called "Black cab rapist" did not fulfil art.3. Laws LJ rejected the concept that the investigative duty was "ancillary" or "adjectival" to a substantive breach. Rather, at [45] he held that "there is perhaps a sliding scale: from deliberate torture by State officials to the consequences of negligence by non-State agents . . . The margin of appreciation enjoyed by the State as to the means of compliance with Article 3 widens at the bottom of the scale but narrows at the top". In *Al-Saadoon & Ors v Secretary of State for Defence* [2016] EWCA Civ 811 at [124]–[125], the CA held that the investigative duty under art.3 is triggered by an arguable claim that the individual has suffered treatment infringing art.3, not merely a breach of the *Soering* obligation not to send an individual to another state where there are substantial grounds for believing that he would face a real risk of being subject to torture or other prohibited treatment.

The prohibition on slavery and forced labour

[Add to end of n.179] 13–068

On the application of art.4 to instances of child labour, see S. Egan, "Tackling the rise of child labour in Europe: homework for the European Court of Human Rights" [2015] 64 I.C.L.Q. 601.

[Add to end of n.181]

The SC in *Reilly* affirmed the CA's decision with regard to art.4: "Jobseeker's allowance, as its name suggests, is a benefit designed for a person seeking work, and the purpose of the condition is directly linked to the purpose of the benefit. The provision of a conditional benefit of that kind comes nowhere close to the type of exploitative conduct at which article 4 is aimed" ([2013] UKSC 68; [2014] A.C. 453 at [83]). The provisions were found to be ultra vires on other grounds. The claimant's art.4 submissions were not revisited in *R. (on the application of Reilly (No.2)) v Secretary of State for Work and Pensions* [2014] EWHC 2182 (Admin); [2015] Q.B. 573 which concerned the attempt to retrospectively validate the Regulations.

[In n.182 delete the final sentence and substitute]

In *R. (on the application of H) v Secretary of State for the Home Department* [2016] EWCA Civ 565 at [35], the Secretary of State was found not to have breached her positive obligation to identify and support victims of trafficking under ECHR art.4. The Competent Authority's failure to follow policy guidance did not amount to a breach of art.4; the application of the guidance not being the mechanism by which the UK satisfied its procedural obligations under the Convention. In *Al-Malki v Reyes* [2015] EWCA Civ 32; [2016] 1 W.L.R. 1785, the appellants, who were victims of trafficking, were domestic workers for Saudi Arabian diplomats. They brought claims against the diplomats for racial discrimination and harassment and failure to pay the national minimum wage. The employers claimed diplomatic immunity. The CA held that granting immunity in such circumstances did not breach arts 4 or 6 ECHR which had to be read in light of general principles of international law, including diplomatic immunity. The Modern Slavery Act 2015 received Royal Assent on March 26, 2015 and entered into force on July 31, 2015. Section 1(1) provides for an offence of slavery, servitude and forced or compulsory labour. It replaces the existing offence in s.71 of the Coroners and Justice Act 2009. Subsection (2) requires subsection (1) to be interpreted in accordance with art.4 of the ECHR. Section 2 provides for a single offence of human trafficking covering sexual and non-sexual exploitation.

The ban on punishment without lawful authority

13–069 *[Add to end of n.183]*

In *Contrada v Italy (no. 3)* (App. No. 66655/13) (April 14, 2015), a conviction for "aiding and abetting a mafia-type organisation from the outside" was held to breach art.7. The applicant's actions took place in 1979–1988 and the relevant offence had resulted from a development in case law which had begun toward the end of the 1980s and was consolidated in 1994. It was not therefore sufficiently clear and foreseeable at the time of the events in question. In *Vasiliauskas v. Lithuania* (2016) 62 E.H.R.R. 31 at [183]–[184], the ECtHR held that the applicant's conviction in 2004 for genocide had no basis in law in 1953. While genocide was a crime in international law in 1953, it was unclear and therefore not foreseeable that political groups came under the definition of protected groups at that point, or that the Lithuanian partisans killed constituted part of the protected groups of "ethnic" Lithuanians or Lithuanian "nationals", rather than a separate group.

[Add to end of n.186]   **13–070**

Nor is art.7 engaged when the Parole Board conducts a review under s.28(6) of the Crime (Sentences) Act 1997 (*Hall, Koselka v Parole Board of England & Wales* [2015] EWHC 252 (Admin) at [46]).

[Add to end of n.188]

In *Rohlena v Czech Republic* (App. No. 59552/08) (January 27, 2015) at [70]–[73], the Grand Chamber found art.7 not to have been breached. The applicant had been convicted for a continuous criminal offence of abusing a person living under the same roof. The applicant complained that his conviction encompassed his conduct before that offence had been introduced into the law on June 1, 2004. The Court ruled that the fact of finding the applicant guilty under a later version of the Code in respect of acts committed before, as well as after, that date, did not constitute a retroactive application of the law. The offence had had a basis in national law at the time it was committed and the law had defined the offence sufficiently clearly to meet the requirement of foreseeability.

[Add to end of n.189]

Scoppola did not prevent a judge from imposing a sentence of imprisonment for public protection just before such sentences were abolished (see n.191) as life imprisonment was plainly a sentencing option in light of the nature of the offences (*R. v Docherty (Shaun Kevin)* [2014] EWCA Crim 1197; [2014] 2 Cr. App. R. (S.) 76 at [46]–[60]). That point of law has been appealed to the SC, judgment pending.

Limited rights

The right to liberty and security of the person

[Add to end of n.191]   **13–072**

In *R. (on the application of Sturnham) v Parole Board* [2013] UKSC 47; [2013] 2 A.C. 254 at [18]–[23], the SC confirmed that a breach of art.5(4) does not necessarily lead to a finding that art.5(1) has been violated, distinguishing *James*. A violation of art.5(1) will only follow if the detention has become arbitrary. In *Bayliss v Parole Board for England and Wales* [2014] EWCA Civ 1631, the applicant had sought to appeal, over six years out of time, against his sentence of imprisonment for public protection. The Court of Appeal allowed his appeal, quashed the order of imprisonment and imposed a determinate sentence of four years, resulting in his immediate release. The applicant argued that the Court of Appeal's decision rendered his detention from April 2008 unlawful; alternatively, his detention was arbitrary for the purposes of ECHR art.5(1). The CA held that an appeal decision quashing a sentence did not render detention pursuant to that sentence unlawful. In *Mozer v Republic of Moldova and Russia* (App. No. 11138/10) (February 23, 2016) at [147]–[150], the ECtHR held that detention ordered by the courts of the "Moldavian Republic of Transdniestria" ("MRT") could not be considered "lawful" for the purposes of art.5. Russia (which controlled the MRT courts) had failed to demonstrate, and it could not be assumed, that the MRT court system reflected a judicial tradition compatible with the Convention.

[Add to end of n.192]

The decision in *Hicks* was affirmed in the CA on modified grounds: [2014] EWCA Civ 3; [2014] 1 W.L.R. 2152 at [85]–[88] and required that those responsible for the arrest should have intended to bring the detainee before a competent legal authority at the time of the arrest even if this did not subsequently take place. On the inter-relation of art.5(1)(b) and (c), see *Ostendorf v Germany* 34 B.H.R.C. 738 at [66]–[68], [82]–[86], [93]–[95] and the CA's criticisms of it in *Hicks*, above.

13–073 *[Add to end of n.196]*

See further, *Hassan v UK* 38 B.H.R.C. 358 which holds that art.5 must be interpreted and applied in a way which takes account of international humanitarian law and this may supplement the grounds in art.5(1)(a)–(f).

[Add to end of n.197]

See *Mohammed v Secretary of State for Defence* [2015] EWCA Civ 843 (discussed at para.13–023).

[In n.198 delete final sentence and substitute]

In *Surrey County Council v P* [2014] UKSC 19; [2014] A.C. 896 at [45]–[50], the majority of the SC held that a deprivation of liberty must be assessed objectively: living arrangements that would amount to a deprivation of liberty in the case of a non-disabled person would also be a deprivation of liberty in the case of a disabled person (irrespective of the reasons for the deprivation or whether the person consented). In *R. (on the application of Roberts) v Commissioner of Police of the Metropolis* [2014] EWCA Civ 69; [2014] 2 Cr. App. R. 6 at [10]–[13], the CA held that there was no deprivation of liberty under art.5 where the claimant was detained (at one point in handcuffs) in order for a police officer to search her under a stop and search authority granted under the Criminal Justice and Public Order Act 1994 s.60. The appellant unsuccessfully appealed to the SC in *R. (on the application of Roberts) v Commissioner of Police of the Metropolis* [2015] UKSC 79; [2016] 1 W.L.R. 210, not on the basis of art.5. Control orders were replaced with orders under the Terrorism Prevention and Investigation Measures Act 2011; on which, see *Mohamed v Secretary of State for the Home Department* [2014] EWCA Civ 559; [2014] 1 W.L.R. 4240. Further amendments to this regime were made by Part 2 of the Counter-Terrorism and Security Act 2015.

[Add to end of n.202]   13–075

In *R. (on the application of Osborn) v Parole Board* [2013] UKSC 61; [2014] A.C. 1115 at [81]–[96], the SC indicated that an oral hearing before the Parole Board as a matter of common law fairness and compliance with art.5(4) was likely to be necessary where: important facts or issues of mitigation were in dispute; the Board could not otherwise make an independent assessment of risk; face-to-face encounter with the Board was necessary to enable the prisoner's case to be put or tested effectively; or where, in light of the prisoner's representations, it would be unfair for the matter to be determined on paper. In *Sher and others v UK* (App. No. 5201/11) (October 20, 2015), the ECtHR found no breach of art.5 where the applicants, Pakistani nationals, had been arrested and detained for 13 days without charge in connection with an anti-terrorism operation. The applicants complained of failure to disclose evidence in their detention review hearings, some of which were also held in private session. The ECtHR held that the threat of an imminent terrorist attack at the time of their detention justified the restrictions on the applicants' art.5 rights.

[Add to end of n.203]

In *Betteridge v UK* (2013) 57 E.H.R.R. 7, the ECtHR held that a delay in the applicant's Parole Board review breached art.5(4) and awarded £750 for nonpecuniary damage arising from feelings of frustration at the delay of just over a year.

[Add to end of n.205]

In *R. (on the application of Kaiyam) v Secretary of State for Justice* [2014] UKSC 66; [2015] 2 W.L.R. 76 (discussed at para.13–037) at [38], the SC identified an implied ancillary obligation under art.5, namely the duty to facilitate the progress of indeterminate sentence prisoners towards release by appropriate courses and facilities. This duty does not affect the lawfulness of the detention itself, but will sound in damages if breached. The state has an investigative duty in relation to detainees who have disappeared, but not more generally (*Al-Saadoon v Secretary of State for Defence* [2016] EWCA Civ 811 at [162]–[170]).

The right to marry and found a family

13–078 *[Add to end of n.209]*

See further, *Vallianatos v Greece* (2014) 59 E.H.R.R. 12 (discussed at para.13–029). The position in *Schalk* was re-stated in *Hämäläinen v Finland* [2015] 1 F.C.R. 379 at [71] and in *Aldeguer Tomás v Spain* (App. No. 35214/09) (June 14, 2016) at [90].

The right to education

13–079 *[Add to end of n.213]*

In *Mansur Yalçın and Others v Turkey* (App. No. 21163/11) (September 6, 2014) (French text) the ECtHR held, in response to an application by members of the Alevi faith, that the Turkish education system did not provide adequate means by which the convictions of parents of children holding a faith other than Sunni Islam might be respected.

[Add to end of n.216]

In *R. (on the application of Tigere) v Secretary of State for Business, Innovation and Skills* [2015] UKSC 57; [2015] 1 W.L.R. 3820 at [47]–[49], the SC found a breach of art.2 of the First Protocol, read with art.14 ECHR, in the context of funding for higher education. The applicant was a Zambian national who had been educated in the UK since her arrival in 2012, and who held discretionary leave. She was unable to obtain a student loan due to the requirement that an applicant for a student loan has to be "settled" in the UK (i.e. having indefinite leave to remain).

13–080 *[Add to end of n.217]*

In *R. (on the application of Fox) v Secretary of State for Education* [2015] EWHC 3404 (Admin); [2016] P.T.S.R. 405 at [74]–[75], the HC reviewed the ECtHR jurisprudence on religious instruction, acknowledging that the state's duties of impartiality and plurality do not require equal emphasis to be given to all shades of belief or conviction. However, the "complete exclusion of any study of non-religious belief", as mandated by the impugned syllabus, was incompatible with art.2. The state's assertion that such a syllabus would fulfil its religious education duties failed to ensure pluralism and as such amounted to a breach of the right to education.

[Add to end of n.218]

In *R. (on the application of Diocese of Menevia) v Swansea City and County Council* [2015] EWHC 1436 (Admin) at [87]–[89], it was held that the obligation to respect a parent's rights did not extend to subsidising or paying for transportation to school. The applicants had challenged the local authority's decision to alter its free transport policy for budgetary reasons, such that children attending faith schools would only be given free transport if there were no other alternative schools, including non-faith schools, located within two or three miles of their homes. Although there was no breach of art.2 of the First Protocol, the effect was indirectly discriminatory against black and minority ethnic children.

Qualified rights

Prescribed by law

[Add to end of n.219]   13–082

In *R. (on the application of Catt) v Association of Chief Police Officers of England, Wales and Northern Ireland* [2015] UKSC 9; [2015] A.C. 1065 at [11]–[13], the SC held that retaining information on a "domestic extremism" database maintained by the National Public Order Intelligence Unit and supervised by the first defendant was in accordance with the law for the purposes of art.8 although it lacked any statutory basis as it was subject to the provisions of the Data Protection Act 1998 and administrative codes issued under the Police Act 1996. In *R. (on the application of Roberts) v Commissioner of Police of the Metropolis* [2015] UKSC 79; [2016] 1 W.L.R. 210 at [42]–[48], the SC held that the power of stop and search under the Criminal Justice and Public Order Act 1994, s.60, was in accordance with the law for the purposes of art.8. The power had to be exercised lawfully and in accordance with s.6(1) HRA, the Equality Act 2010, the Police and Criminal Evidence Act 1984 and the Force's Standard Operating Procedures, all of which provided safeguards enabling the proportionality of the interference to be adequately examined. In contrast, in *Christian Institute v Lord Advocate* [2016] UKSC 51; 2016 S.L.T. 805 at [79]–[85], the provisions of Part 4 of the Children and Young People (Scotland) Act 2014 which created the "named person scheme" for all children was not in accordance with the law. In *Cumhuriyet Halk Partisi v Turkey* (App. No. 19920/13) (July 26, 2016) at [106]–[107], the ECtHR found that the imposition of financial sanctions on the applicant, the largest opposition party in Turkey, was an interference with its rights under art.11. A lack of foreseeability of the applicable law on political expenditure and absence of guidance on sanctions meant that the interference was not prescribed by law.

[Add to end of n.220]

The same result was reached in *Elberte v Latvia* (2015) 61 E.H.R.R. 7 (concerning the removal of tissue from the applicant's deceased husband's body without her consent). A violation of art.3 was also found.

Necessary in a democratic society: proportionality

13–084 *[Add to end of n.223]*

For a recent discussion of proportionality under the HRA, see *R. (on the application of MM (Lebanon)) v Secretary of State for the Home Department* [2014] EWCA Civ 985; [2015] 1 W.L.R. 1073 at [139]–[153]. On proportionality more generally, see *Bank Mellat v HM Treasury (No.2)* [2013] UKSC 38; [2014] A.C. 700 at [20]–[21], [68]–[76], [93]. In particular, Lord Reed identified four questions (at [72]) for the court to answer: (1) is the legislative objective sufficiently important to justify limiting a fundamental right; (2) are the measures which have been designed to meet it rationally connected to it; (3) are they no more than are necessary to accomplish it; and (4) do they strike a fair balance between the rights of the individual and the interests of the community? In *R. (Lord Carlile of Berriew and others) v Secretary of State for the Home Department* [2014] UKSC 60; [2015] A.C. 945 at [34] the SC gave guidance on the quality of the judicial scrutiny called for when considering the proportionality of an interference with a Convention right. The principle of proportionality in EU law is neither expressed nor applied in the same way as the principle of proportionality under the European Convention on Human Rights: see *R. (on the application of Lumsdon) v Legal Services Board* [2015] UKSC 41 at [22]–[82], in which Lord Reed comprehensively summarised the principles of proportionality under EU law. On the potential for a proportionality approach to supplant the common law ground of rationality in claims for judicial review, particularly those which engage fundamental rights, see *Youssef v Secretary of State for Foreign and Commonwealth Affairs* [2016] UKSC 3; [2016] 2 W.L.R. 509 at [55]–[57].

[In n.225 delete "433" and substitute]

439

The right to respect for private and family life

13–085 *[In n.230, delete the final sentence and substitute]*

The Defamation Act 2013 came into force on April 25, 2013.

[Delete all text in n.231 and substitute]

Pretty v United Kingdom (2002) 35 E.H.R.R. 1 at [61]. A majority of the SC (Baroness Hale and Lord Kerr dissenting) rejected a challenge to the blanket ban on assisted suicide on the basis of art.8 in *R. (Nicklinson) v Ministry of Justice* [2014] UKSC 38; [2015] A.C. 657. An application to the ECtHR by the same individuals was ruled inadmissible: [2015] ECHR 709 (July 16, 2015).

[In n.232 add after ". . . houses)."   **13–086**

See also *Dubetska v Ukraine* (2015) 61 E.H.R.R.11 (a factory and mine causing subsidence).

[Add to end of n.232]

The SC agreed that the latter was unlawful (reversing the CA's decision) but decided the case on the basis that the segregation had not been authorised by the relevant legislation. The SC decision is *R. (on the application of King) v Secretary of State for Justice* [2015] UKSC 54; [2016] A.C. 384. Further examples of situations in which art.8 may be engaged include: long-lasting and severe restrictions on a prisoner's ability to receive prison visits (*Khoroshenko v Russia* (App. No. 41418/04) (June 30, 2015) at [148]); the manner in which criminal proceedings are conducted (*Y. v. Slovenia* (App. No. 41107/10) (May 28, 2015), in which during criminal proceedings for sexual assault the alleged victim was subjected to lengthy and traumatic cross-examination by the alleged perpetrator); the requirement for an individual wishing to undergo sex reassignment surgery to first obtain a court authorisation which would only be granted where the individual had undergone sterilisation (*Y.Y. v Turkey* (App. No. 14793/08) (March 10, 2015)); the failure of the state to provide information about the fate of a baby who died in a state-run medical centre (*Jovanovic v Serbia* (2015) 61 EHRR 3 at [74]–[75]); the failure to provide legal aid in certain immigration cases (*R. (on the application of Gudanaviciene) v Director of Legal Aid Casework* [2014] EWCA Civ 1622; [2015] 1 W.L.R. 2247); the failure of the state properly to investigate allegations of racially motivated abuse (*R.B. v Hungary* (App. No. 64602/12) (April 12, 2016)); and a prison policy implementing an absolute prohibition on growing a beard where the state failed to demonstrate a pressing social need or any justification based on hygiene or the need to identify prisoners (*Biržietis v. Lithuania* (App. No. 49304/09) (June 14, 2016)). In *R. (on the application of JK) v Registrar General for England and Wales* [2015] EWHC 990 (Admin), it was held that the UK's birth registration scheme did not breach arts 8 or 14 by requiring men who had changed gender from male to female to be listed as the "father" on the birth certificates of their biological children.

[Add to end of n.233]

In *Re. JR38's Application for Judicial Review* [2015] UKSC 42; [2015] 3 W.L.R. 155, the SC found that publication by the police of images of a 14-year-old boy committing public order offences did not violate his art.8 rights as he could not have had a reasonable expectation that photographs of him committing the offences would not be published. Opinion was divided as to whether art.8(1) was engaged at all. Participation in politics has been held to be a matter of public life, to which art.8 can have only limited application: *Misick v United Kingdom* (2013) 56 E.H.R.R. SE13 at [29]. There, the applicant claimed his removal as the elected representative of the North Caicos East constituency violated his art.8 right to respect for his private life. The application was declared inadmissible in the absence of any evidence of an encroachment on the applicant's private life or privacy. In *Weller v Associated Newspapers Ltd* [2015] EWCA Civ 1176; [2016] 1 W.L.R. 1541, the CA found that publication of photographs taken in California of the children of a British celebrity by an English newspaper breached the children's art.8 rights, and that the family had a reasonable expectation of privacy notwithstanding that publication of the photographs would have been lawful under Californian law (appeal outstanding).

[Add to end of n.234]

See *Vallianatos v Greece* (2014) 59 E.H.R.R. 12 and *Oliari and others v Italy* (App. Nos. 18766/11 and 36030/11) 21 July 2015 at [178] and [185]–[187] on the ECtHR's developing recognition of same-sex relationships. In *R. (on the application of Bright) v Secretary of State for Justice* [2014] EWCA Civ 1628; [2015] 1 W.L.R. 723, the CA held that the decision to separate prisoners who were in long-term, same-sex relationships with fellow prisoners had not breached their art.8 rights. In *R. (on the application of MM (Lebanon)) v Secretary of State for the Home Department* [2014] EWCA Civ 985; [2015] 1 W.L.R. 1073 at [139]–[153], the CA rejected a challenge to the requirements of the Immigration Rules which imposed minimum income requirements on those with the right to live in the United Kingdom who wished to bring their spouses who were non-EEA citizens to this country. An appeal to the SC has been heard, and judgment reserved. The positive obligations imposed on a state by art.8 are also frequently cited in cases concerning the Hague Convention on the Civil Aspects of International Child Abduction. In an important decision, the HC of Northern Ireland held that the criminal prohibition on abortion violated art.8 in relation to fatal foetal abnormalities at any time and pregnancies resulting from rape and sexual assault up to the date of viability, and issued a declaration of incompatibility (*In the Matter of an Application for Judicial Review by the Northern Ireland Human Rights Commission* [2015] NIQB 96 at [160]–[166]).

[Add to end of n.235]

See also *R. (on the application of N) v Lewisham LBC* [2014] UKSC 62; [2014] 3 W.L.R. 1548 (eviction from temporary accommodation under the Housing Act 1996 s.188 did not breach art.8) and *R. (on the application of SG) v Secretary of State for Work and Pensions* [2015] UKSC 16; [2015] 1 W.L.R. 1449 at [139] (in which Lord Hughes held that the art.8 rights of children were not infringed by the benefit cap scheme introduced by the Benefit Cap (Housing Benefit) Regulations 2012: "elastic as that article has undoubtedly proved, it does not extend to requiring the state to provide benefits, still less benefits calculated simply according to need, nor does it require the state to provide a home". Nor was there a violation of art.14 read with art.1 of the First Protocol).

[In n.236 delete final sentence and substitute]

In R. *(on the application of T) v Chief Constable of Greater Manchester Police* [2014] UKSC 35; [2015] A.C. 49, the SC held that provisions in Pt V of the Police Act 1997 concerning the disclosure of enhanced criminal record certificates, including records of privately issued police cautions, constitute an aspect of the private life of the recipient and so engage art.8. The SC held that the provisions breached the requirements in art.8(2) since the cumulative effect of the failure to draw distinctions based on: the nature of the offence; the disposal of the case; the time elapsed since the offence took place; the relevance of the offence to the employment sought; and the absence of any independent review of the decision to disclose was that the provisions were not in accordance with the law (at [119], [158]). The SC also held that the provisions bore no rational connection to the assessment of the risks posed by those wishing to work with children or the elderly and were therefore not necessary in a democratic society (at [121], [158]). The SC held that the powers to detain and question those suspected of involvement in terrorism contained in Sch.7 to the Terrorism Act 2000 do not violate art.8 as it contained sufficient safeguards to avoid arbitrary application *(Beghal v Director of Public Prosecutions* [2015] UKSC 49; [2015] 3 W.L.R. 344 at [52]–[56]). In *Re Gaughran's Application for Judicial Review* [2015] UKSC 29; [2015] 2 W.L.R. 1303 at [44]–[49,] the SC held that the indefinite retention of the DNA profiles (not samples) of those who had been convicted of recordable offences was proportionate and justified under art.8(2). The case was distinguished from *S v Marper*. In R. *(on the application of Catt) v Association of Chief Police Officers of England, Wales and Northern Ireland* [2015] UKSC 9; [2015] A.C. 1065 at [33]–35], the retention of records of an elderly man's non-violent participation in demonstrations organised by an extremist protest group was held to be proportionate. See *Secretary of State for the Home Department v Davis and others* [2015] EWCA Civ 1185; [2016] 1 C.M.L.R. 48 at [110] for consideration of data retention under EU law and the "more extensive protection" provided by the Charter of Fundamental Rights of European Union arts 7 and 8 compared to art.8 of the Convention.

[Add to end of n.237]

Norway's failure to provide information about the damaging effects of decompression on divers amounted to a breach of art.8 *(Vilnes v Norway* 36 B.H.R.C. 297 at [233]–[245]).

13–087 *[Add to end of n.239]*

In *X (A Child) v Dartford & Gravesham NHS Trust* [2015] EWCA Civ 96; [2015] 1 W.L.R. 3647, the CA gave guidance as to the granting of anonymity orders where the court approves the settlement of personal injury damages. Unless it is judged unnecessary, an order should normally be made without the need for a formal application (though the press should first be permitted to make submissions). In *McDonald v UK* (2015) 60 E.H.R.R. 1 at [53]–[58], the ECtHR found that the decision to reduce the amount allocated for Ms McDonald's care did interfere with her art.8 rights since it required her to wear incontinence pads at night when she was not incontinent and had previously been assisted to use the lavatory by a night-time carer. However, the ECtHR found the interference to be necessary in the field of allocating scarce welfare resources and to have appropriately balanced her needs against the interests of the wider community.

[Add to end of n.240]

In *Jeunesse v Netherlands* (2015) 60 E.H.R.R. 17, the Grand Chamber noted that where family life is created in the knowledge of precarious immigration status, only in exceptional circumstances will removal of a non-national family member violate art.8. However, such exceptional circumstances did, on the facts, exist: all members of the applicant's family with the exception of herself were Netherlands nationals; the applicant had been in the Netherlands for more than 16 years and had no criminal record; although there would apparently be no insurmountable obstacles for the family to settle in Suriname, it was likely that the applicant and her family would experience a degree of hardship if they were forced to do so; and the best interests of the children were of paramount importance and were not served by disrupting their present circumstances. In the UK, "Appendix FM" to the Immigration Rules purports to establish a "complete code" for the court's assessment of art.8 claims under the Rules. *MF (Nigeria) v Secretary of State for the Home Department* [2013] EWCA Civ 1192; [2014] 1 W.L.R. 544 at [38]–[49] sets out the correct approach to be adopted in such cases. In *R. (MA (Pakistan)) v Upper Tribunal (Immigration and Asylum Chamber)* [2016] EWCA Civ 705, the CA held that when assessing the best interests of a child in the context of an art.8 evaluation, the court is not obliged to start by considering the child's best interests, but must nevertheless treat them as a primary consideration.

Freedom of thought, conscience and religion

13–088 *[Add to end of n.242]*

See further, J. Dingemans, C. Yeginsu, T. Cross and H. Masood, *The Protections for Religious Rights: Law and Practice* (2013).

[Add to end of n.243]

In *R. (on the application of Hodkin) v Registrar of Births, Deaths and Marriages* [2013] UKSC 77; [2014] A.C. 610, the SC held that a chapel of the Church of Scientology was a "place of meeting for religious worship" for the purposes of the Places of Worship Registration Act 1855. In *İzzettin Doğan and Others v Turkey* (App. No. 62649/10) (April 26, 2016), the GC found a violation of art.9 taken alone and in conjunction with art.14. The Turkish authorities' failure to recognise the Alevi faith amounted to denying its members their right to "effectively enjoy" their religious freedom. The GC reiterated (at [107]) that while states may assess objective elements of a belief (seriousness, cohesion etc.), that role excluded "any discretion on its part to determine whether religious beliefs or the means used to express such beliefs are legitimate".

[Add to end of n.244]

Article 9 also protects the negative right not to manifest one's faith: In *Isik v Turkey* (2015) 61 EHRR 6 at [42]–[53], it was held, on this basis, that the art.9 rights of the Alevi applicant had been violated by the mandatory requirement to display his faith on an identity card (though it was not violated by the refusal of the authorities to indicate Alevi, rather than Islam).

[Add to n.245 after "manifesting their religion"]   13–089

The ECtHR found no violation of art.9 in *Church of Jesus Christ of Latter-Day Saints v UK* (2014) 59 E.H.R.R. 18.

[Add to n.246 after "Debate in Europe (2006)"]

In *SAS v France* (2015) 60 E.H.R.R. 11 at [106]–[159], the Grand Chamber held that the interference with the art.9 rights of the applicant, who wore a niqab (full face veil) occasioned by Law No.2010–1192, which prohibited concealment of the face in public places, was proportionate to the aim pursued: namely the preservation of the conditions of "living together".

[Add to n.246 after "Rafferty L.J.))"]

The SC affirmed the CA's decision in *Preddy v Bull* [2013] UKSC 73; [2013] 1 W.L.R. 3741 at [38]–[39] and [51]–[55]. For helpful discussion of the relationship between the state's duties under art.9 and art.11, see *Sindicatul "Pʿstorul Cel Bun" v Romania* (2014) 58 E.H.R.R. 10, discussed in the updated n.263 below. On the interrelation of arts 9 and 11 see also *Karaahmed v Bulgaria* (App. No. 30587/13) (February 24, 2015). There was a violation of the art.9 rights of worshippers in a Bulgarian mosque on the basis that the state had failed to strike a proper balance in the steps they took to ensure the effective and peaceful exercise of rights of demonstrators from the Ataka political party and the rights of the applicant and the other worshippers to pray together. See also *Church of Scientology of St Petersburg and others v Russia* (App. No. 47191/06) (October 2, 2014) at [37]–[48], in which the ECtHR held that Russia's refusal to grant legal-entity status to the applicant amounted to a breach of art.9 interpreted in the light of art.11.

[Add to end of n.246]

The CA upheld a requirement that a carer should work on Sundays despite her Christian faith since there was no other viable and practicable way of running a care home (*Mba v Merton LBC* [2013] EWCA Civ 1562; [2014] 1 W.L.R. 1501 at [34]–[37]). In *Doogan v Greater Glasgow and Clyde Health Board* [2014] UKSC 68; [2015] A.C. 640, the "conscience clause" in s. 4(1) of the Abortion Act 1967 was held not to exempt the midwife applicants from various managerial and supervisory tasks in a labour ward in which abortions were carried out. At [23]–[24] Baroness Hale, while describing art.9 as a "distraction", observed: "a state employer has also to respect his employees' Convention rights . . . even if not protected by the conscience clause in section 4, the petitioners may still claim that, either under the Human Rights Act 1998 or under the Equality Act 2010, their employers should have made reasonable adjustments to the requirements of the job in order to cater for their religious beliefs". In *Lee v Ashers Baking Co Ltd* [2016] NICA 39, the refusal of a bakery owned by two Christians to bake a cake which had printed on it a picture of "Bert and Ernie" and the caption "Support Gay Marriage" was held to be unlawful direct discrimination on grounds of sexual orientation. In *Süveges v Hungary* (App. No. 50255/12) (January 5, 2016) at [151]–[157], the ECtHR held that the art.9 right of an applicant held under house arrest pre-trial had not been violated, the interference with his ability to attend Mass being proportionate to the state's legitimate aim. In *Ebrahumian v France* (App. No. 64846/11) (February 26, 2016) (French text), the ECtHR found no violation of art.9 where a public hospital had refused to renew the contract of a social assistant who refused to remove her headscarf, a symbol of her Muslim faith.

Freedom of expression

13–090 *[Add to n.248 after "highest level of protection"]*

In *Rubins v Latvia* [2015] I.R.L.R 319 at [80]–[93], the ECtHR held that the state had violated art.10 by upholding the dismissal of a university professor who had, in an email, criticised the management of his university following changes to his employment contract, in part on the basis that the email covered matters of public interest. In contrast, in *R. (on the application of Lord Carlile of Berriew QC) v Secretary of State for the Home Department* [2014] UKSC 60; [2015] A.C. 945, the SC upheld the Secretary of State's decision to maintain a ban on a dissident Iranian politician entering the United Kingdom to address the House of Lords (on the basis that Iran would see any lifting of the exclusion as a political move against it and would be likely to engage in reprisals). In *Karácsony and Others v Hungary* (App. No. 42461/13) (May 17, 2016), the GC found a violation of art.10 where opposition members of parliament were subject to disciplinary measures and fined for displaying banners and using a megaphone during a parliamentary session.

[Add to end of n.248]

The ECtHR distinguished *Financial Times* and similar authorities in a case where the "source" in question was the perpetrator of a bomb attack whose disclosure was "not motivated by the desire to provide information which the public were entitled to know", but rather who "was claiming responsibility for crimes which he had himself committed . . . to don the veil of anonymity with a view to evading his own criminal accountability" (*Stichting Ostade Blade v Netherlands* (2014) 59 E.H.R.R. SE9 at [65]). Where the identity of the source is not secret, the issue does not arise as was the case with material appropriated by Edward Snowden: *R. (on the application of Miranda) v Secretary of State for the Home Department* [2016] EWCA Civ 6; [2016] 1 W.L.R. 1505 at [102]. In *Miranda*, the CA found that the stopping and detention of David Miranda at Heathrow airport for nine hours under Sch.7 of the Terrorism Act 2000 was lawful. However, due to the absence of adequate safeguards against its arbitrary exercise, the CA declared that the stop power conferred by para.2(1) of Sch.7 was incompatible with art.10 in relation to journalistic material (at [113]–[115]). In *Morice v France* (2015) 39 B.H.R.C. 1, the conviction of a lawyer for complicity in defamation following publication of comments in the press was held to be in breach of art.10, those comments comprising value judgments with a sufficient factual basis. The ECtHR acknowledged the special role of lawyers in the administration of justice and held that they may comment in public on the administration of justice, provided that their criticism does not overstep certain bounds (at [132]–[139]). However, lawyers, as protagonists in the justice system, cannot be equated with journalists, who are external witnesses whose task it is to inform the public (at [148]). In *Bédat v Switzerland* (2016) 63 E.H.R.R. 15, the GC considered the art.10 rights of a journalist versus the art.6 rights of a person accused in pending criminal proceedings. The GC determined that the same balancing exercise should be applied as in cases where arts 8 and 10 were engaged (at [52]–[53]). In the present case, there was no art.10 violation by the state where a journalist was convicted and fined for publishing information covered by secrecy of the on-going criminal investigation. In *C (A Child)* [2016] EWCA Civ 798 at [24]–[34], the CA considered the balancing of arts 6 and 10, where a judge had refused to allow publication of care proceedings because the child's father, convicted of her murder, had indicated an intention to appeal. The CA held that the risk of art.6 violation was minimal and was outweighed by the principle of open justice and the art.10 rights of the media organisations seeking publication of the judgment.

[Add to end of n.249]

In *Gough v United Kingdom* (2015) 61 E.H.R.R. 8 at [150], the ECtHR held that the applicant's public nudity, in order to give expression to his opinion as to the inoffensive nature of the human body, fell within the ambit of art.10 (though no breach of art.10 was found).

[Add to end of n.250]

In the GC judgment of *Delfi AS v Estonia* [2015] E.M.L.R. 26, the ECtHR for the first time considered the duties and responsibilities of internet news portals, such as Delfi, under art.10(2). Following Delfi's news articles was a facility for readers to add comments. There was also a facility for readers to mark comments as obscene or insulting (upon which they were removed). Victims of defamatory comments were, in addition, able to notify Delfi directly and Delfi would then immediately remove the comment. Delfi explained this system, along with a statement that the comments did not reflect its own opinion and that the authors of comments were responsible for their content, in its "Rules of Comment". Nevertheless, the Grand Chamber found that the domestic courts' imposition of liability on Delfi for certain offensive and threatening comments posted by readers did not constitute a breach of art.10.

[Add to n.251 after "degenerated into gratuitous abuse."]

An application to Strasbourg was declared inadmissible in *Gaunt v United Kingdom* (App No. 26448/12) (September 6, 2016).

[Add to end of n.251]

In *R. (on the application of Core Issues Trust) v Transport for London* [2014] EWCA Civ 34; [2014] P.T.S.R. 785 at [63]–[70], [83]–[89], the CA upheld the defendant's decision to refuse to carry advertisements on its buses on behalf of a Christian organisation ("Not gay! Ex-gay, post-gay and proud. Get over it!"), which responded to a campaign that it had carried by Stonewall ("Some people are gay. Get over it."). Despite this preference for one viewpoint over another, the CA upheld the decision on the grounds that the Christian organisation's message may be offensive to homosexuals. In *Maguire v United Kingdom* (2015) 60 E.H.R.R. SE12, the applicant claimed his art.10 rights had been breached by his sentence and conviction for breach of the peace deriving from his clothing (a black top which, in bright green letters displayed on the front the letters "INLA" (the Irish National Liberation Army), and on the back of which was the slogan "FXCK YOUR POPPY REMEMBER DERRY"). The application was declared inadmissible. In *James Rhodes v OPO*

[2015] UKSC 32, a mother sought to prevent a father from publishing a book about his life containing descriptions of his subjection to sexual abuse which she considered risked causing psychological harm to their son relying on the tort of intentionally causing of physical or psychological harm. The SC held that the tort was not made out. Brief reference was made to art.10 at [120], in stating that the common law should be "generally consistent" with the Convention. In *M'Bala M'Bala v France* (App. No. 25239/13) (October 20, 2015) at [34]–[42], the ECtHR considered a well-known comedian's challenge to sanctions imposed by the state following a public performance of an anti-Semitic nature. The ECtHR was "unable to accept that the expression of an ideology which is at odds with the basic values of the Convention, [. . .] can be assimilated to a form of entertainment [. . .] which would be afforded protection" by art.10, and therefore held that the application was inadmissible *ratione materiae*. In *Perinçek v Switzerland* (see n.40 above), the GC found a violation of art.10 where the applicant had been convicted of a crime for statements made denying the existence of an Armenian genocide.

[In n.253 delete final sentence and substitute]

In *Kennedy v Charity Commission* [2014] UKSC 20; [2015] A.C. 455 at [57]–[89], Lord Mance undertook an extensive review of the Strasbourg authorities concerning whether art.10 contained a positive right to receive information from the state. While acknowledging the ECtHR's apparent inconsistency on the point, the SC concluded that no such right could be said to exist on the present state of the authorities (at [93]–[96], [144]–[148], [154]). See further, K. O'Byrne, "Freedom of Information under Article 10 ECHR and the Common Law" (2014) E.H.R.L.R. 284. In *Kalda v Estonia* (App. No. 1742/10) (January 19, 2016) at [48]–[54], the ECtHR considered restrictions places by the state on a prisoner's access to certain internet sites. While the court did not assert that states were required to give prisoners access to the internet, where access was available, restrictions and limitations must be lawful and justified. In the present case, restrictions on access to sites containing legal information on fundamental and prisoners' rights were unnecessary in a democratic society and thus a violation of art.10.

[Add to n.254 after "Autotronic . . . at [49]–[52]"]   13–091

In *R. v Dryzner (Ewa)* [2014] EWCA Crim 2438; (2015) 179 J.P. 29, the applicants applied for permission to appeal against convictions for supplying video recordings without classification contrary to the Video Recordings Act 1984 s.9 and a declaration that that provision was incompatible with art.10. The applicant had affixed his own labels to the DVDs choosing their age classification himself. He submitted that the inflexible classification regime was disproportionate when applied to innocuous material and infringed the right to freedom of expression. It was held that the classification requirements that the Act imposed were lawful, necessary and justified for the protection of public health and morals.

[Add to n.254 after ". . . [2009] P.L. 89"]

By the narrowest majority (of nine votes to eight), the ECtHR upheld the ban as proportionate on the basis of the widespread debate which preceded it and the impact of the broadcast media (*Animal Defenders International v UK* (2013) 57 E.H.R.R. 21 at [106]–[125]). See J. Rowbottom, "Animal Defenders International: Speech, Spending, and a Change of Direction in Strasbourg" (2013) 5 J.M.L. 1.

Freedom of peaceful assembly and association

13–092 *[Add to end of n.257]*

In *Karpyuk v Ukraine* (App. No. 30582/04) (October 6, 2015) at [222]–[238], the ECtHR held that in relation to three of the seven applicants, the imposition of long prison sentences for organising an initially peaceful although disruptive protest was a violation of art.11. While a sanction for organising an obstructive gathering and inciting violence might be warranted, the severe sanctions imposed "must have had a chilling effect" on others organising protests and were disproportionate.

13–094 *[Add to n.262 after ". . . (Richards L.J.)"]*

See now [2014] EWCA Civ 3; [2014] 1 W.L.R. 2152.

[Add to end of n.263]

The ECtHR held that a statutory ban on secondary industrial action did not breach art.11 in *National Union of Rail, Maritime and Transport Workers v UK* (App. No.31045/2010) (April 8, 2014) at [78]–[105]. In *Sindicatul "P storul Cel Bun" v Romania* (2014) 58 E.H.R.R. 10 at [143]–[145], [157], [159]–[173], the ECtHR held, by a majority of 11 to six, that a decision of a Romanian Court to revoke registration of a trade union comprised of members of the Orthodox clergy did not amount to a violation of art.11. While the duties performed by the clergy in question did have many of the characteristic features of an employment relationship (which had been denied by the Romanian Government), the ECtHR found that the decision was prescribed by law and not disproportionate (particularly in light of the state's duties under art.9 of the Convention).

13–095 *[Add to end of n.265]*

In *ADEFDROMIL v France* (App. No. 32191/09) (October 2, 2014) and *Matelly v France* (App. No. 10609/10) (October 2, 2014), the ECtHR held, unanimously, that the blanket ban on trade unions within the French armed forces contravened art.11.

The right to the enjoyment of possessions

[Add to end of n.267]   **13–096**

New London College Ltd was decided by the SC on other grounds: [2013] UKSC 51; [2013] 1 W.L.R. 2358. See further on this issue, *R. (on the application of Guildhall College) v Secretary of State for Business, Innovation and Skills* [2014] EWCA Civ 986 at [72]–[75]. *Salvesen v Riddell* [2013] UKSC 22; [2013] H.R.L.R. 23 at [40]–[45] held that provisions of the Agricultural Holdings (Scotland) Act 2003 breached the art.1 rights of landlords. In *Breyer Group Plc v Department of Energy and Climate Change* [2015] EWCA Civ 408 at [23] and [47]–[49], the CA held that goodwill was (and loss of future income was not) a possession: a distinction that may require analysing the marketability of the goodwill and the accounting arrangements of the alleged victim. In *R. (on the application of APVCO 19 Ltd) v HM Treasury* [2015] EWCA Civ 648 at [46], the CA held that money impressed with an arguable claim by HMRC is not a possession where legislation retrospectively removed loopholes relating to the payment of stamp duty. In *Parrillo v Italy* (App. No. 46470/11) (August 27, 2015) at [214]–[216], the GC held that human embryos cannot be considered a possession for the purposes of art.1, "[h]aving regard to the economic and pecuniary scope of that Article". In *Bank Mellat v HM Treasury* [2016] EWCA Civ 452 at [28]–[30], the CA held that the general principle is that the company and not its shareholders have the status of victim in relation to claims under art.1. There may be exceptional circumstances where, for example, the sole shareholder is sufficiently linked to the business as to be in effect the owner.

[Add to end of n.268]

See also *AM v Secretary of State for Work and Pensions* [2015] UKSC 47; [2015] 1 W.L.R. 3250 at [24]–[26], in which it was held that the withdrawal of disability living allowance falling within the ambit of art.1 of the First Protocol from a child who was hospitalised for more than 84 days violated his human rights under art.14. In *Béláné Nagy v Hungary* (App. No. 53080/13) (February 10, 2015), the majority found that the applicant's loss of entitlement to a disability pension due to newly introduced eligibility criteria resulted in a violation of art.1 of the First Protocol. The dissenting judges criticised this for going further than existing ECHR jurisprudence. The GC heard this case on December 16, 2015, and judgment is pending.

[Add to end of n.269]

The state's positive obligations may be engaged in cases concerning the property and housing rights of persons displaced as a result of international or internal armed conflict. In *Sargsyan v. Azerbaijan* (App. No. 40167/06) (June 16, 2015), the Armenian applicant had been unable to return to his land and home in the disputed territory of Nagorno-Karabakh since 1992. The ECtHR held that the situation concerned a restriction of the applicant's right to the peaceful enjoyment of his possessions (at [218]) and that Azerbaijan's failure to take any alternative measures to restore his property rights or to provide him with compensation resulted in a continuing breach of art.1 of the First Protocol (at [241]–[242]). The case also addresses jurisdictional issues under art.1 at [121]–[151].

13–098 *[Add to end of n.274]*

Nor, when the state seeks to control the use of property, and could do so using different provisions with different consequences in terms of compensation, is there any requirement that it invoke the provision carrying some (or greater) compensation: *Cusack v Harrow LBC* [2013] UKSC 40; [2013] 1 W.L.R. 2022 at [45]–[49], [69]. In *Re. Recovery of Medical Costs for Asbestos Diseases (Wales) Bill* [2015] UKSC 3; [2015] A.C. 1016 at [35]–[69], although decided on other grounds, the SC held that the Recovery of Medical Costs for Asbestos Diseases (Wales) Bill had the potential to deprive both compensators and their liability insurers of their possessions by retrospectively altering their existing legal liabilities. Article 1 of the First Protocol was engaged and special justification was required before the court would accept that a fair balance had been struck between the demands of the general interest of the community and the requirement to protect individual rights. None had been shown.

The right to free elections

13–099 *[Add to end of n.278]*

In *Grosaru v Romania* (2015) 61 EHRR 1 at [54]–[57], there was held to have been a violation of art.3 of the First Protocol read with art.13. The applicant stood as a candidate in parliamentary elections and secured 5,624 votes in 19 constituencies. The parliamentary seat was allocated instead to a candidate who had secured 2,943 votes in a single constituency. The breach was found on the basis of a lack of clarity of the electoral law and a lack of sufficient guarantees of impartiality on the part of those examining the applicant's challenges. That art.3 of the First Protocol is inapplicable to referenda was confirmed in *Moohan, Petitioner* [2014] UKSC 67; [2015] A.C. 901 which at [7]–[18] considered the Strasbourg case law in the context of the Scottish referendum on independence. In *Paunović and Milivojević v Serbia* (App. No. 41683/06) (May 24, 2016), the ECtHR found a violation of art.3 of the First Protocol read with art.13. The applicants, elected to parliament in 2003, had been required to sign undated resignation letters which were then held by the party. In 2006, following internal trouble, the MPs declared their intention to retain their seats. The party leader nevertheless tendered their resignations, which the parliamentary committee accepted as genuine. The ECtHR reaffirmed that art.3 guarantees not only a right to stand for election, but to sit as MP once elected (at [58]), and held that the impugned measure was not compliant with the domestic framework which required resignations to be submitted in person (at [63]–[66]).

The prohibition on discrimination

[Add to end of n.281]   13-101

In *R. (on the application of Hardy) v Sandwell MBC* [2015] EWHC 890 (Admin); [2015] B.L.G.R. 283, a local authority's policy of taking into account the care component of disability living allowance when assessing the amount of a discretionary housing payment breached art.14.

[Add to end of n.282]

Poverty has been held not to constitute "other status": *R. (on the application of Williams) v Secretary of State for the Home Department* [2015] EWHC 1268 (Admin) at [96] (rejecting the argument that *RJM* supported this wider proposition) (appeal outstanding).

[Add to end of n.283]

Article 14 prohibits a third form of discrimination described in the case of *Thlimmenos v Greece* (2001) 31 E.H.R.R. 411 at [44]: where the state fails to treat differently persons whose situations are significantly distinct without objective and reasonable justification.

[Add to end of n.284]

In *Boyraz v Turkey* [2015] I.R.L.R. 164; (2015) 60 E.H.R.R. 30 at [56], the ECtHR held no legitimate aim had been shown, where the applicant was dismissed from her post as a security guard for not being a man.

[Add to end of n.285]

The benefit cap introduced in the Welfare Reform Act 2012 was held to discriminate indirectly against women, but its discriminatory effect was not manifestly without reasonable foundation and so not unlawful. There was thus no violation of art.14 read with art.1 of the First Protocol: *R. (on the application of JS) v Secretary of State for Work and Pensions* [2015] UKSC 16; [2015] 1 W.L.R. 1449 at [63]–[77]. The reduction in the eligible rent used to calculate housing benefit based on the number of bedrooms in the property discriminated against disabled people, but was justified in the circumstances (*R. (on the application of MA) v Secretary of State for Work and Pensions* [2014] EWCA Civ 13; [2014] P.T.S.R. 584 at [48]–[60]). The "manifestly without reasonable foundation" test was applied (and was not met) in *R. (Cushnie) v Secretary of State for Health* [2014] EWHC 3626 (Admin); [2015] P.T.S.R. 384. This case concerned an unsuccessful asylum seeker who could not be removed from the UK because he was unfit to fly. Being disabled he received support from his local authority under s.21 of the National Assistance Act 1948, rather than from the Home Office. He required non-urgent medical treatment, which he could not pay for, but was not entitled to free NHS treatment, whereas an able-bodied destitute failed asylum seeker receiving Home Office support was so entitled. In *Sanneh v Secretary of State for Work and Pensions* [2015] EWCA Civ 49; [2016] Q.B. 455 at [28]–[29], the CA held that "Zambrano carers" (non-EU citizens responsible for the care of an EU citizen child) were not entitled to social assistance on the same basis as lawfully resident EU citizens. Article 14 was not breached as the Government's policy reasons for differentiating the two categories of carers were not "clearly without foundation".

The impact of the HRA

13–104 *[Add to n.290 after ". . . could be implemented"]*

The Commission on a Bill of Rights appointed by the Coalition Government reported in two volumes in 2012: *A UK Bill of Rights? The Choice Before Us.* The majority of the Commission was in favour of a UK Bill of Rights in order to promote a sense of "ownership" by the public. The Commission expressed support for the inclusion in such a Bill of a right to equality and non-discrimination, perhaps with additional protections in the administrative and criminal justice fields. The majority opposed including socio-economic and environmental rights. The enforcement mechanisms would remain largely as under the HRA. The proposals are convincingly criticised by F. Klug and A. Williams, "The Choice Before Us? The Report of the Commission on a Bill of Rights" [2013] P.L. 459. The manifesto of the current Conservative government in 2015 pledged that they will repeal the Human Rights Act, curtail the powers of the ECtHR (reducing it to giving advisory opinions) and enact a British Bill of Rights (S. Greer and R. Slowe, "The Conservatives' Proposals for a British Bill of Rights: Mired in Muddle, Misconception and Misrepresentation?" [2015] E.H.R.L.R. 372 and L. Blom-Cooper, "The Road to Rome and Strasbourg via San Francisco: Human Rights in Charters and Declarations" [2015] P.L. 571); see also D. Grieve QC MP "Can a Bill of Rights do better than the Human Rights Act?" [2016] P.L. 223, and A. Williams and G. Williams, "The British Bill of Rights Debate: Lessons from Australia" [2016] P.L. 471.

[Delete existing heading of Table 1 and substitute]

Table 1: Declarations of incompatibility under HRA s.4—updated to September 2016

[Add to end of Table 1]

	Judgment	Right	Legislation	Response
20	R. (on the application of Reilly (No. 2)) v Secretary of State for Work and Pensions [2014] EWHC 2182 (Admin); [2015] Q.B. 573	Art.6.1	Jobseekers (Back to Work Schemes) Act 2013; retroactive effect not justified by compelling grounds of the general interest	The Secretary of State unsuccessfully appealed the grant of a declaration of incompatibility: [2016] EWCA Civ 413. No remedial action has been taken
21	R. (on the application of T) v Chief Constable of Greater Manchester Police [2014] UKSC 35; [2015] A.C. 49	Art.8	Police Act 1997	Repealed by the Serious Organised Crime and Police Act 2005
22	Benkharbouche v Embassy of Sudan [2015] EWCA Civ 33; [2015] 3 W.L.R. 301	Art.6, art.14	State Immunity Act 1978 s.16(1)(a)	No remedial action has been taken
23	Re Northern Ireland Human Rights Commission's Application for Judicial Review [2015] NIQB 102	Art.8	Offences against the Person Act 1861 ss. 58 and 59; Criminal Justice Act (NI) 1945 s. 25	The Department of Justice and the Attorney General were granted permission to appeal. No remedial action has been taken

24	*R. (Miranda) v Secretary of State for the Home Department and another* [2016] EWCA Civ 6; [2016] 1 W.L.R. 1505	Art.10	Terrorism Act 2000 Sch. 7 para. 2(1) insofar as it relates to journalistic material	No remedial action has been taken
25	*Re Z (A Child) (No 2)* [2016] EWHC 1191 (Fam); [2016] HRLR 15	Art.8 read with art.14	Human Fertilisation and Embryology Act 2008 s.54	No remedial action has been taken

CHAPTER 14

REVIEW UNDER EUROPEAN UNION LAW

INTRODUCTION

[Add after ". . . and the UK constitution.[11]]　　　　　　　14–002

However, on June 23, 2016, the United Kingdom voted in the "Brexit" referendum, by a margin of 52% to 48%, to leave the European Union. This referendum was conducted pursuant to the European Union Referendum Act 2015. Unsurprisingly, the outcome of this historic vote sent shockwaves across Europe and worldwide, and has been the subject of much debate, analysis and commentary since. The terms on which the United Kingdom will leave the European Union are unknown at present. As for the timing of the United Kingdom's withdrawal, it is currently anticipated that the United Kingdom will formally notify its intention to withdraw pursuant to Article 50 of the Treaty on European Union before April 2017. Article 50 states that the Treaties shall cease to apply to a Member State which has invoked Article 50 from the date of entry into force of a withdrawal agreement negotiated between that State and the Union, or failing that, two years after notification of an intention to withdraw pursuant to Article 50. This suggests that, by April 2019, the United Kingdom will have withdrawn from the Union. However, a challenge to the status and validity of the referendum is currently under consideration by the courts, and that will have to be resolved before Article 50 is engaged.

It is clear though that the status of all of the legal principles and laws in this Chapter will be open for question and reconsideration in the coming years, and the relationship between the United Kingdom and the European Union will be entering a new and uncertain phase. At the time of writing, the Prime Minister had just announced that the European Communities Act 1972 will be repealed, but that the body of law emanating from the EU will, through a savings clause, continue to operate until the final Brexit agreement comes into effect.[11a] This should assure some degree of stability. However, there will still be uncertainty as to which of the UK's myriad of "rights, powers, liabilities, obligations and restrictions from time to time created or arising by under the Treaties" will have legal effect, or the same legal effect, when the savings provision lapses. This is because the rights, powers, and so on, have become part of UK law in so many different ways: through UK regulations implementing EU directives; through directly effective EU regulations; through rulings of the ECJ, or even by way of non-enforcement of a UK statute which has been held to be in breach of EU law.[11b] Reciprocal "passporting" arrangements, for products as wide-ranging as electrical appliances and financial instruments, will also require attention. In the area of human rights, the UK will no longer be bound (insofar as it is now) by the requirements of the Charter of Fundamental Rights of the European Union or, presumably, the EU's "fundamental principles".[11c] New treaty arrangements may or may not also need to be in conformity with the EHCR.[11d] For now, Union law continues in full force, but the impact of the "Brexit" vote, which will take time to fully emerge, can be expected to be far-reaching.

[11a] European Communities Act 1972, Section 2(1).

[11b] See, e.g. *HSBC Holdings plc and Vidacos Nominees Ltd v Commissioners of Her Majesty's Revenue & Customs* (C–569/07) EU:C:2009:594.

[11c] See below 14–030—14–035.

[11d] House of Commons Library, "Brexit: Impact Across Policy Areas", August 26, 2016.

[Delete "This Chapter" and insert]

Thankfully, this Chapter

[In n.11 delete "10th edn (2012)" and substitute]

11th edn (2014)

[In n.11 delete "7th edn (2010)" and substitute]

8th edn (2014)

Overview of the EU Legal System

14–005 *[Add new n.22a after ". . . enhanced cooperation"]*

[22a] For recent consideration, see *Spain and Italy v Council* (Cases C–274/11 and C–295/11) EU:C:2013:240.

14–007 *[Add to end of n.30]*

See Opinion 2/13 (December 18, 2014) at [172] (noting that TEU 3 sets out provisions which "are part of the framework of a system that is specific to the EU, are structured in such a way as to contribute – each within its specific field and with its own particular characteristics – to the implementation of the process of integration that is the *raison d'être* of the EU itself ").

Policy areas within the field of the European Union

[In para.14–010 delete "or decentralised"]   14–010

[In n.33 delete "Regulation (EC) 1605/2002 on the Financial Regulation Applicable to the General Budget of the European Communities [2002] OJ L248/1 art 53(b)" and substitute]

Regulation (EU, Euratom) No 966/2012 of the European Parliament and of the Council of October 25, 2012 on the financial rules applicable to the general budget of the Union and repealing Council Regulation (EC, Euratom) No 1605/2002 art.58(1)(b);

[In para.14–010 delete " 'centralised' management" and substitute]

"direct" or "indirect" management

[In n.34 delete "Regulation (EC) 1605/2002 on the Financial Regulation Applicable to the General Budget of the European Communities [2002] OJ L248/1 arts 53(a), 53a, and 54–57" and substitute]

Regulation (EU, EURATOM) 966/2012 on the financial rules applicable to the general budget of the Union and repealing Council Regulation (EC, Euratom) No 1605/2002 [2012] OJ L298/1 arts 58(1)(a), 58(1)(b), 60–63.

[Add to end of n.35]

For recent consideration of competence by the ECJ, see *Philip Morris Brands SARL v Secretary of State for Health* (C-547/14) EU:C:2016:325; *Commission v Council* (C–137/12) EU:C:2013:675 and *Daiichi Sankyo and Sanofi-Aventis Deutschland* (C–414/11) EU:C:2013:520, applied in *R. (on the application of British American Tobacco Ltd) v Secretary of State for Health* [2016] EWHC 1169 (Admin); and *United Kingdom v Council* (C–431/11) EU:C:2013:589.

[Add to end of n.36]   14–011

See also: Opinion 2/13 (December 18, 2014) at [157] (noting that "the founding treaties of the EU, unlike ordinary international treaties, established a new legal order, possessing its own institutions, for the benefit of which the Member States thereof have limited their sovereign rights, in ever wider fields, and the subjects of which comprise not only those States but also their nationals" and holding that the accession of the EU to the ECHR as envisaged by the draft agreement was liable adversely to affect the specific characteristics of EU law and its autonomy).

[Add after ". . . national law of Member States."]

A critical review of the characteristics of this new legal order can be found in Opinion 2/13, which considered the draft agreement for accession of the Union to the ECHR.[36a] The ECJ observed that Union law was characterised by the fact that it stems from an independent source of law, the Treaties, by its primacy over the laws of the Member States, and by the direct effect of a whole series of provisions which are applicable to their nationals and to the Member States themselves.[36b] These essential characteristics of Union law have given rise to a structured network of principles, rules and mutually interdependent legal relations linking the Union and its Member States, and its Member States with each other, which are now engaged, as is recalled in the second paragraph of Article 1 TEU, in a "process of creating an ever closer union among the peoples of Europe".[36c] It was also observed that the Union was, under international law, precluded by its very nature from being considered a State.[36d] This legal structure is based on the fundamental premiss that each Member State shares with all the other Member States, and recognises that they share with it, a set of common values on which the Union is founded, as stated in TEU art.2, which premise implies and justifies the existence of mutual trust between the Member States that those values will be recognised and, therefore, that the law of the EU that implements them will be respected.[36e] Moreover, the principle of mutual trust between the Member States is of fundamental importance in EU law, given that it allows an area without internal borders to be created and maintained. That principle requires, particularly with regard to the area of freedom, security and justice, each of those States, save in exceptional circumstances, to consider all the other Member States to be complying with EU law and particularly with the fundamental rights recognised by EU law.[36f]

[36a] Opinion 2/13 (December 18, 2014).

[36b] Opinion 2/13 (December 18, 2014) at [166].

[36c] Opinion 2/13 (December 18, 2014) at [167].

[36d] Opinion 2/13 (December 18, 2014) at [156].

[36e] Opinion 2/13 (December 18, 2014) at [168].

[36f] Opinion 2/13 (December 18, 2014) at [191]–[192].

Primacy of Union law

[Add to end of n.38]   **14–012**

See also Opinion 2/13 (December 18, 2014) at [166].

[Add to end of n.39]

See also even in the criminal context, *Criminal Proceedings against Taricco* (C-105/14) EU:C:2015:55.

[Add new para.14–012A after para.14–012]   **14–012A**

There may, however, be limits to the primacy of EU law. In *R. on the application of Buckinghamshire v Secretary of State for Transport*.[42a] In this case, requirements laid down in Directive 2011/92/EU concerning the way in which Member States take certain decisions were at issue, including the decision in respect of the construction of the proposed "HS2" high-speed rail network. The decision was taken through the enactment of a "hybrid Bill", which was described as effectively a public bill, which affects a particular private interest in a manner different from the private interests of other persons or bodies of the same category or class.[42b] The difficulty with scrutinising the decision-making process therefore was that it might impinge "upon long-established constitutional principles governing the relationship between Parliament and the courts, as reflected for example in article 9 of the Bill of Rights 1689".[42c] It was decided that the Directive did not require review that was constitutionally problematic, but considered briefly what would have happened had the Directive called for such scrutiny and commented as follows:

> "resolved simply by applying the doctrine developed by the Court of Justice of the supremacy of EU law, since the application of that doctrine in our law itself depends upon the [European Communities Act 1972]. If there is a conflict between a constitutional principle, such as that embodied in article 9 of the Bill of Rights, and EU law, that conflict has to be resolved by our courts as an issue arising under the constitutional law of the United Kingdom. Nor can the issue be resolved, as was also suggested, by following the decision in *R v Secretary of State for Transport, Ex p Factortame Ltd (No 2)* [1991] 1 AC 603, since that case was not concerned with the compatibility with EU law of the process by which legislation is enacted in Parliament."[42d]

[42a] [2014] UKSC 3; [2014] 1 W.L.R. 324.

[42b] [2014] UKSC 3; [2014] 1 W.L.R. 324 at [57].

[42c] [2014] UKSC 3; [2014] 1 W.L.R. 324 at [78].

[42d] [2014] UKSC 3; [2014] 1 W.L.R. 324 at [79].

Direct effect of Union law measures

14–013 *[Add to end of n.44]*

; *Association de médiation sociale v Union locale des syndicats CGT* (C–176/12) EU:C:2014:2 at [31].

[Add to end of n.47]

; *Association de médiation sociale v Union locale des syndicats CGT* (C–176/12) EU:C:2014:2 at [44]–[45] (Charter art.27 must be given more specific expression in European Union or national law). Contrast *Benkharbouche v Embassy of the Republic of Sudan* [2015] EWCA Civ 33; [2015] 3 W.L.R. 301 at [80] (Charter art.47 is capable of vertical and horizontal direct effect).

[Add to n.51 after ". . . I-5939 at [41]–[46]"]

; *Fra.bo Spa v Deutsche Vereinigung des Gas-und Wasserfaches eV* (C–171/11) EU:C:2012:453 at [31]–[32] (holding that TFEU art.34 applied to a private standardisation and certification body where the body "in reality [held] the power to regulate the entry into the German market of products such as the copper fittings at issue in the main proceedings").

SECONDARY LEGISLATION

Directives

Direct Effect of Directives

14–022 *[Add to end of n.71]*

; *Association de médiation sociale v Union locale des syndicats CGT* (C–176/12) EU:C:2014:2 at [36].

14–023 *[Add to end of n.74]*

For recent confirmation that Directives do not, in themselves, create obligations on the part of individuals and cannot be relied upon against those individuals, see: *Papasavvas v O Fileleftheros Dimosia Etairia Ltd* (C–291/13) EU:C:2014:2209 [2015] 1 C.M.L.R. 24 at [54].

[Add to end of n.83]   14–024

See also *Fish Legal v Information Commissioner* (C–279/12) EU:C:2013:853 [2014] Q.B. 521 at [64]–[73] (in the context of art.2 of Directive 2003/4/EC of the European Parliament and of the Council of January 28, 2003 on public access to environmental information and repealing Council Directive 90/313/EEC, to determine whether an entity is a legal person which performs "public administrative functions", it is necessary to examine whether those entities are vested, under national law, with special powers beyond those which result from the normal rules applicable in relations between persons governed by private law and a body will be under the "control" of such an entity where it does not determine in a genuinely autonomous manner the way in which it provides those services since a public authority is in a position to exert decisive influence on its action in the environmental field).

[Add to end of para.14–028]   14–028

However, in *Dansk Industri (DI), acting on behalf of Ajos A/S v Estate of Karsten Eigil Rasmussen,* the ECJ rejected an objection raised on grounds of legal certainty and protection of legitimate expectations, and held that the principle of non-discrimination on grounds of age is a general principle of Union law, such that it precluded—including in disputes between private persons—national legislation that deprived an employee of entitlement to a severance allowance where the employee was entitled to claim an old-age pension from the employer under a pension scheme which the employee had joined before reaching the age of 50, regardless of whether the employee chose to remain on the employment market or take his retirement.[100a]

[100a] (C-441/14) EU:C:2016:278.

[Add after ". . . refer to the Charter provisions.[118]]   14–030

In this regard, the ECJ has emphasised that the ECHR "does not constitute, as long as the European Union has acceded to it, a legal instrument which has been formally incorporated into EU law".[118a]

[118a] *Inuit Tapiriit Kanatami v Commission, Parliament and Council* (T–526/10) EU:T:2013:215 at [105] (the ECJ concluding that it was appropriate for the General Court to examine the legislation under challenge solely by reference to provisions of the Charter). However, contrast *Deutsche Bahn AG v Commission* (C–583/13 P) EU:C:2015:404 at [32]–[36] and [46]–[48] (reaching a determination by reference to ECHR case law before considering the Charter).

[Add to end of n.103]

; K. O'Brien and B. Kolterman, "The Charter of Fundamental Rights of the EU in Practice" (2013) 14 ERA Forum 457.

[Add to end of n.112]

See also *R. (on the application of AB) v Secretary of State for the Home Department* [2013] EWHC 3453 (Admin); [2014] 2 C.M.L.R. 22 at [12]–[16] (obiter, noting that the Charter "enunciates a host of new rights" not expressly incorporated into EU law under the Human Rights Act 1998).

[Add to end of n.114]

The distinction between rights and principles may have an impact on whether a Charter provision may have horizontal direct effect: *Association de médiation sociale v Union locale des syndicats CGT* (C–176/12) (Opinion of AG Villalón) EU:C:2013:491 [2014] I.C.R. 411 at [49]–[60] (differing from the Advocate General and considering that rights may have such effects, but principles may not); and (C–176/12) EU:C:2014:2 at [43]–[48] (finding that some Charter provisions, such as art.21(1), are capable of horizontal direct effect, but others, such as art.27, are not). See also N. Lazzerini, "(Some of) the Fundamental Rights Granted by the Charter may be a Source of Obligations for Private Parties" [2014] 51(3) C.M.L. Rev. 907; H. Hofmann and B. Mihaescu, "The Relation between the Charter's Fundamental Rights and the Unwritten General Principles of EU Law: Good Administration as the Test Case" [2013] 9(1) E.C.L. Review 73.

[Add to end of n.117]

; cf. *R. (on the application of EM (Eritrea)) v Secretary of State for the Home Department* [2014] UKSC 12; [2014] 2 W.L.R. 409 at [44]–[62] (the Supreme Court, when faced with an ECJ interpretation of a Charter right which would involve incompatibility with ECHR art.3, considered that the ECJ "did not intend" to alter the meaning of art.3).

[In n.119 delete "(art.53) does not mean national rights override EU law)" and substitute]

[60] (holding that, while art.53 confirms that national courts remain free to apply national standards of protection of fundamental rights, this is "provided that the level of protection provided for by the Charter, as interpreted by the Court, and the primacy, unity and effectiveness of EU law are not thereby compromised"). On the facts of the case, this meant that the Spanish courts could not make the surrender, pursuant to Framework Decision 2002/584, of

a person convicted in absentia conditional upon the conviction being open to review in the issuing Member State, in order to avoid an adverse effect on the right to a fair trial and the rights of defence guaranteed by the national constitution: [64]. The Spanish Constitutional Court reacted by lowering the degree of protection afforded by the Spanish Constitution in line with Union law: STC 26/2014. See also *Cruciano Siragusa v Regione Sicilia – Soprintendenza Beni Culturali e Ambientali di Palermo* (C–206/13) EU:C:2014:126 at [32]. For discussion of *Melloni*, see, eg A. Torres Perez, "*Melloni* in Three Acts: From Dialogue to Monologue" (2014) 10 E.C.L. Review 308; L.F.M. Besselink, "The Parameters of Constitutional Conflict after *Melloni*" (2014) 39 E.L. Rev. 531. See also Opinion 2/13 (December 18, 2014) at [188] (noting that in *Melloni*, the Court of Justice had interpreted Charter art.53 as meaning that the application of national standards of protection of fundamental rights must not compromise the level of protection provided by the Charter or the primary, unity and effectiveness of Union law). In Opinion 2/13, the Court of Justice also observed (at [192]) that when implementing Union law, the Member States may, under Union law, be required to presume that fundamental rights have been observed by the other Member States, so that not only may they not demand a higher level of national protection of fundamental rights from another Member State than that provided by EU law, but, save in exceptional cases, they may not check whether that other Member State has actually, in a specific case, observed the fundamental rights guaranteed by the EU.

[Add to end of n.125]   14–031

See also *Digital Rights Ireland v Minister for Communications, Marine and Natural Resources* (C–293, 594/12) EU:C:2014:238 at [45]–[70] (holding that the Data Retention Directive violated art.7 of the Charter due to a lack of proportionality); *Google Inc v Agencia Española de Protección de Datos (AEPD)* (C–131/12) EU:C:2014:317 at [97]–[99] (finding that the right to private life and the production of personal data overrode the economic interests of the operator of a search engine and the interests of the general public, unless the data in question played a role in public life). For an example in the national context, see *Vidal-Hall v Google Inc* [2015] EWCA Civ 311; [2015] 3 W.L.R. 409 at [70]–[79] (observing that it was important that data subjects had an effective remedy for a distressing invasion of privacy rights falling short of pecuniary damages, especially as art.7 and art.8 of the Charter made specific provision for the protection of personal data); see also *Tele2 Sverige AB v Post-och telestyrelsen* (C-203/15) Opinion of the Court of Justice, July 19, 2016; *Secretary of State for the Home Department v Davis and others* [2015] EWCA Civ 1185 (reference sought on the implications of the *Digital Rights Ireland* case).

[Add to para.14–031 after ". . . novel aspects of the Charter, such as"]

workers' rights to information and consultation in art.27,[126a]

[126a] *Association de médiation sociale v Union locale des syndicats CGT* (C–176/12) EU:C:2014:2.

[Add to end of n.128]

; *Užsienio reikalų ministerija v Vladimir Peftiev* (C–314/13) EU:C:2014:1645 (freezing of funds should not prevent access to legal representation); *Inuit Tapiriit Kanatami v Parliament and Council* (C–583/11) EU:C:2013:625 [2014] Q.B. 648; [2014] 1 C.M.L.R. 54 at [105] (art.47 does not require that an individual should have an unconditional entitlement to bring an action for annulment of Union legislative acts directly before the courts of the European Union); *Commission v Kadi (Bulgaria intervening)* (C–584/10P, C–593/10P, C–595/10P) EU:C:2013:518 [2014] 1 C.M.L.R. 24; *ZZ v Secretary of State for the Home Department* (C–300/11) EU:C:2013:363 at [57] (where a national authority opposes disclosure of documents submitted to a court for reasons of state security, the court with jurisdiction in the Member State concerned must have at its disposal and apply techniques and rules of procedural law which accommodate, on the one hand, legitimate State security considerations and on the other hand, the need to ensure sufficient compliance with the person's procedural rights); *R. (on the application of Edwards and Pallikaropoulos) v Environment Agency* (C–260/11) EU:C:2013:221 at [35] (the requirement in art.10a of Council Directive 85/337/EEC of 27 June 1985 on the assessment of the effects of certain public and private projects on the environment [1985] OJ L175/40 meant that proceedings should not be prohibitively expensive means that persons concerned should not be prevented from seeking, or pursuing a claim for, a review by the courts that falls within the scope of the relevant provisions of EU law by reason of the financial burden that might arise as a result). See also *Commission v United Kingdom of Great Britain and Northern Ireland* (C–530/11) EU:C:2014:67. For an interpretation of art.47 in the domestic courts, see *R. (on the application of AZ) v Secretary of State for the Home Department* [2015] EWHC 3695 (Admin); [2016] 4 W.L.R. 12 (the court refusing to grant permission to apply for judicial review under art.47 on the basis of an obligation to disclose the reasons and the essentials of the national security case against the applicant); *R. (on the application of XH) v Secretary of State for the Home Department* [2016] EWHC 1898 (Admin) at [97] (the second paragraph of art.47 corresponds with ECHR art.6, which means that regard can be had to the art.6 case law in interpreting art.47); *S1, T1, U1, V1 v Secretary of State for the Home Department* [2016] EWCA Civ 560 at [34] (although ultimately EU law did not apply to the decisions to deprive British citizenship, if it had, art.47 and the obligations under *ZZ v Secretary of State for the Home Department,* cited above, would have been correctly adhered to); and *Yanukovych v Council* (Case T–346/14) EU:T:2016:497 (duty to give reasons).

[Add after ". . . of art.47"]

; see also *Schindler Holding v Commission* (C–501/11) EU:C:2013:522 at [33]–[34].

[Add to end of n.131]   14–032

; *Ministero dell'Interno v Fastweb SpA* (C–19/13) EU:C:2014:2194 [2015] P.T.S.R. 111 (review of Directive 89/665 art.2d(4) for compatibility with Charter art.47). See also *Ledra Advertising and others v Commission and European Central Bank* (C–8/15 P to C–10/15 P), where it was held in this case that, even where the Commission is acting outside the scope of Union law and in the context of a Memorandum of Understanding within the framework of the European Stability Mechanism, it is bound by the Charter. It was added that the Commission, in "its role of guardian of the Treaties", should "refrain from signing a memorandum of understanding whose consistency with EU law it doubts" (including consistency with the Charter) (see [59]). The ECJ also held that the Charter is addressed to EU institutions when they act outside the EU legal framework (see [67]).

[Add to end of n.132]

For a recent application of the Charter to national measures, see *R. (on the application of British American Tobacco Ltd) v Secretary of State for Health* [2016] EWHC 1169 (Admin); and *United Kingdom v Council* (C–431/11) EU:C:2013:589.

[Add new para.14–032A after para.14–032]   14–032A

Following *Åklagaren*, the ECJ has also explained, in *Cruciano Siragusa*, that the concept of "implementing Union law" requires a certain degree of connection with Union law above and beyond the matters covered being closely related or one of those matters having an indirect impact on the other. When determining whether national legislation involves the implementation of Union law, some of the points to be considered are whether that legislation is intended to implement a provision of Union law; the nature of that legislation and whether it pursues objectives other than those covered by Union law, even if it is capable of indirectly affecting Union law; and also whether there are specific rules of EU law on the matter or capable of affecting it. Furthermore, the fact that national legislation could have an indirect effect on a system established by Union law could not constitute a sufficient connection to bring such legislation within the scope of Union law. This meant that an order requiring a property owner to restore property within a landscape conservation area to its original state did not engage art.17 of the Charter where EU law did not impose any obligations to protect the specific landscape; there was only an indirect connection between the facts and Union law which was not sufficient to attract the application of the Charter.[138a] It is also apparent that the Charter is not unlimited in its scope of application, and, for example, where a Member State stores and uses fingerprint data, originally collected in compliance with a Union Regulation, but which the Member State then uses for purposes other than those stipulated in the Regulation, the Member State is not acting within the scope of Union law and therefore is not bound by the Charter.[138b]

[138a] *Cruciano Siragusa v Region Sicilia – Soprintendenza Beni Culturali e Ambientali di Palermo* (C–206/13) EU:C:2014:126 at [24]–[27]. The ECJ also observed (at [22]) that Member States were only bound by EU fundamental rights in respect of matters "covered by EU law". See also *Érsekcsanádi Mezogazdasági Zrt v Bács-Kiskun Megyei Kormányhivatal* (C–56/13) EU:C:2014:352 (parts of a national implementing measure providing for compensation to affected parties could not be challenged under the Charter because the compensation provisions themselves were not part of the original directive; this was so despite the fact that the national measure implemented EU law, and that the court had previously held that the EU may consider full or partial compensation for owners of farms whose animals have been destroyed); *Pelckmans Turnhout NV v Walter Van Gastel Balen NV* (C–483/12) EU:C:2014:304 at [20] (prohibition on seven-day trading outside the scope of Union law and could not be considered for compatibility with the Charter). See also Opinion 2/13 (December 18, 2014) at [171].

[138b] *Willems v Burgemeester van Nuth* (C–446/12) EU:C:2015:238 ([2015] 3 C.M.L.R 26). See also *Fag og Arbejde v Kommunernes Landsforening (KL)* (C–354/13) EU:C:2014:2463 [2015] 2 C.M.L.R 19 (holding that the Charter was inapplicable to a complaint of discrimination on grounds of obesity because obesity discrimination does not fall within the scope of Union law (albeit that the ECJ proceeded to rule that in certain circumstances, obesity may give rise to a disability engaging the duty not to discriminate on grounds of disability)).

14–032B *[Add new para.14–032B after 14–032A]*

It has been held that certain provisions of the Charter are capable of horizontal direct effect, although there is a lack of clarity on which provisions are capable of such effect.[138c]

[138c] *Association de médiation sociale v Union locale des syndicats CGT* (C–176/12) EU:C:2014:2 at [43]–[48] (see also *Dansk Industri (DI), acting on behalf of Ajos A/S v Estate of Karsten Eigil Rasmussen* (C–441/14) EU:C:2016:278 at [36]).

[Add to end of n.139]   14–033

See *Digital Rights Ireland v Minister for Communications, Marine and Natural Resources* (C–293, 594/12) EU:C:2014:238 at [45]–[71] for an example of a case in which legislation, the Data Retention Directive, was found incompatible with the Charter due to a lack of proportionality. See also *The Queen on the application of British American Tobacco (UK) Ltd and others v Secretary of State for Health* [2016] EWHC 1169 (Admin) at [825] (the court did not accept the argument of the applicants that a measure, although proportionate, may still be unlawful if impairing the essence of the claimant's interest).

[Add to end of para.14–034]   14–034

The ECJ's approach was considered in *R. (on the application of AB) v Secretary of State for the Home Department* by Mostyn J., who regarded it as "absolutely clear that the contracting parties agreed that the Charter did not create one single further justiciable right in our domestic courts" but that this view was not shared by the ECJ.[141a] The Supreme Court has also observed recently that the UK, as an EU Member State, is obliged to observe and promote the application of the Charter whenever implementing an instrument of EU law.[141b]

[141a] [2013] EWHC 3453 (Admin); [2014] 2 C.M.L.R. 22 at [12]–[13].

[141b] *R. (on the application of EM (Eritrea)) v Secretary of State for the Home Department* [2014] UKSC 12; [2014] 2 W.L.R. 409 at [62].

GENERAL PRINCIPLES OF LAW

[Add new n.143a after ". . . [ex EC art.288(2)]."]   14–035

[143a] See, e.g. *Commission v Systran and Systran Luxembourg* (C–103/11) EU:C:2013:245.

[Add to n.146 after ". . . was reaffirmed in Kücükdeveci"]

Likewise, in *Association de médiation sociale v Union locale des syndicats CGT* (C–176/12) EU:C:2014:2 at [41], the ECJ endorsed *Kücükdeveci*, albeit in passing and albeit distinguishing it from the circumstances at issue. Both cases were applied in *Dansk Industri (DI), acting on behalf of Ajos A/S v Estate of Karsten Eigil Rasmussen* (C–441/14) EU:C:2016:278 at [50], in which the ECJ held that if national legislation cannot be interpreted compatibly with a Directive due to constraints of legal certainty, the court should proceed to interpret the general principle of law which the provision of secondary law is intended to put into specific terms; in the event of a conflict between the principle and national law, the general principle can be invoked in a dispute between individuals in order to preclude the application of the national provision which is contrary to EU law. It is not clear how far or when the principles of *Kücükdeveci* apply in cases not involving age discrimination: see *United States v Nolan* [2015] UKSC 63; [2016] A.C. 463 at [43].

[Add to end of n.146]

; C. Murphy, "Using the EU Charter of Fundamental Rights against Private Parties after Association de Mediation Sociale" [2014] E.H.R.L.R. 170.

EUROPEAN COMMUNITES ACT 1972 AND THE EUROPEAN UNION ACT 2011

14–036 *[Add to end of n.147]*

; *R. (on the application of Buckinghamshire County Council) v Secretary of State for Transport* [2014] UKSC 3; [2014] P.T.S.R. 182 at [207] (describing it as a "constitutional instrument").

14–041 *[Add to end of n.160]*

; S. Peers, "European Integration and the European Union Act 2011: An Irresistible Force Meets an Immovable Object" [2013] P.L. 119.

CHALLENGING A NATIONAL MEASURE IN A NATIONAL COURT

14–042 *[Add to end of n.162]*

Vidal-Hall v Google Inc [2015] EWCA Civ 311 [2015] 3 W.L.R. 409.

INTERPRETATION BY NATIONAL COURTS

14–047 *[Add after ". . . ensuring the effectiveness of directives.[188]"]*

It is worth noting that when interpreting the provision of Union law itself, account should be taken not only of the wording of that provision and the objectives which it pursues, but also of its context and the provisions of Union law as a whole.[188a]

[188a] See, Advocate General Opinion, *Council of the European Union v Vereniging Milieudefensie* (C–401/12 P) EU:C:2014:310 [2015] 2 C.M.L.R. 32 at [116] (adding that the context to a provision of Union law may also contain elements relevant to its interpretation: see Case C–370/12 *Pringle v Ireland* [2013] 2 C.M.L.R. 2 at [135]).

[Add to end of n.185]   14–048

For a useful discussion of the use of recitals in interpretation of EU secondary legislation, see *Recall Support Services Ltd v Secretary of State for Culture, Media and Sport* [2013] EWHC 3091 (Ch); [2014] 2 C.M.L.R. 2 at [50] (not overturned on appeal: [2014] EWCA Civ 1370; [2015] 1 C.M.L.R. 38).

[Add to end of n.187]

The ECJ has recently explained that a provision of Union law itself will be interpreted in light of its wording and objectives, its context and the provisions of Union law as a whole, as well as its origins: *Inuit Tapiriit Kanatami v Parliament and Council* (Case C–583/11) EU:C:2013:625 [2014] Q.B. 648; [2014] 1 C.M.L.R. 54 at [50]. In this case, the ECJ placed particular emphasis on the *travaux préparatoires*: [59], [60], [70].

[Add to end of n.190]   14–049

See also *R. (on the application of Nutricia Limited) v The Secretary of State for Health* [2015] EWHC 2285 (Admin) at [115].

[In para.14–051 delete "in the past"]   14–051

[In para.14–051 after " 'cardinal principles' " delete "or"]

[In para.14–051, insert after ". . . of the legislation",[200]]

or "alter a fundamental feature" of the legislation.[200a] As it has also been put, "it is not possible to construe a national measure to mean 'black' (the requirement in the Directive) when it explicitly states that it means 'blue' ".[200b] There are number of techniques of which courts may avail themselves in order to comply with the principle of conforming interpretation, including reading words into a national measure (to expand its potential field of application) or by reading the national provision down (to narrow its potential field of application), and even by disapplying or striking down part of it in order to make it compatible with a Directive; "[v]arious interpretative techniques may be deployed in order to eliminate an incompatibility".[200c]

[200a] *Vidal-Hall v Google Inc (Information Commissioner intervening)* [2015] EWCA Civ 311; [2015] 3 W.L.R. 409 at [91]–[92] (holding that s.13(2) of

the Data Protection Act 1998 enacted limits on the right to compensation for breaches of the right to privacy of individuals with respect to the processing of their personal data which were a fundamental feature of the legislation, such that s.13(2) could not be interpreted compatibly with art.23 of Parliament and Council Directive 95/46/EC and had to be disapplied). It was also observed in *Vidal-Hall* (at [86]) that if a national court is unable to rely on the *Marleasing* principle to interpret the national legislation so as to conform with the Directive, the appropriate remedy for an aggrieved person is to claim Francovich damages against the state). See also *R. (on the application of Chester) v Secretary of State for Justice* [2013] UKSC 63; [2014] A.C. 271 at [74]–[75]; *Littlewoods Retail Ltd v Revenue and Customs Commissioners* [2015] EWCA Civ 515.

200b *R. (on the application of Nutricia Limited) v The Secretary of State for Health* [2015] EWHC 2285 (Admin) at [120] (adding that "[t]he principle of purposive [construction] is not therefore, a rule which requires national courts to do permanent and irrevocable damage to the language of domestic implementing legislation, or other legislation existing within the field and scope of the directive, in order to achieve the object of the Directive").

200c *Vidal-Hall v Google Inc (Information Commissioner intervening)* [2015] EWCA Civ 311; [2015] 3 W.L.R. 409 at [89]–[90].

[Add to end of n.196]

See also *Swift (trading as A Swift Move) v Robertson* [2014] UKSC 50; [2014] 1 W.L.R. 3438 at [22] (the court must not only keep faith with the wording of Union law but "must have closely in mind its purpose").

[Add to end of n.199]

See, for example, *Vidal-Hall v Google Inc (Information Commissioner intervening)* [2015] EWCA Civ 311; [2015] 3 W.L.R. 409 at [87] (Lord Dyson MR observing that "our courts have noticed a close parallel between the Marleasing principle and section 3 of the Human Rights Act 1998").

[Add to end of n.201]

Association de médiation sociale v Union locale des syndicats CGT (C–176/12) EU:C:2014:2 at [39]; *Dansk Industri (DI), acting on behalf of Ajos A/S v Estate of Karsten Eigil Rasmussen* (C-441/14) EU:C:2016:278 at [32], [43], *Klausner Holz Niedersachsen GmbH v Land Nordrhein-Westfalen* (C–505/14) at [32]; *Dansk Industri (DI), acting on behalf of Ajos A/S v Estate of Karsten Eigil Rasmussen* (C-441/14) EU:C:2016:278.

[Add to end of n.205]   14–052

; *Association de médiation sociale v Union locale des syndicats CGT* (C–176/12) EU:C:2014:2 at [39]. See also *Dansk Industri (DI), acting on behalf of Ajos A/S v Estate of Karsten Eigil Rasmussen* (C-441/14) EU:C:2016:278 at [21]–[42].

[Add to end of n.206]

; *Prudential Assurance Co. Ltd. v Revenue and Customs Commissioners* [2013] EWHC 3249 (Ch); [2014] 2 C.M.L.R 10 at [102], [105] (*Marleasing* implies a "highly muscular" approach to conforming interpretation).

EFFECTIVE PROCEDURES AND REMEDIES

[Add after ". . . in the fields covered by Union law" "]   14–055

National courts and tribunals and the ECJ must ensure the full application of Union law in all Member States and ensure judicial protection of an individual's rights under that law.[214a]

[214a] Opinion 2/13 (December 18, 2014) at [175].

Principle of national procedural autonomy

[Add to end of n.217]

For recent consideration of the principle of effectiveness, in the context of the fee regime for bringing and continuing claims in employment tribunals and the Employment Appeal Tribunal, see *R. (on the application of Unison) v Lord Chancellor* [2014] EWHC 4198 (Admin); [2015] 2 C.M.L.R. 4 (noting that the principle of effectiveness was closely related to the common law principle that access to a court was a fundamental right and to ECHR art.6).

Principle of effective judicial protection

[Add after ". . . conferred on him by EU law.[228]"]   14–057

It has also been held that the "piggyback argument"—that wherever a domestic statutory provision infringes the EU rights of one person, then anyone else who is a national of a Member State may claim relief for the adverse consequence for him of the existence or enforcement of that provision—is assessed by reference to the principle of effectiveness. In short, if the protection intended to be conferred by a particular EU right or freedom upon nationals of EU Member States will not be effective if only those whose rights are thereby infringed can take proceedings in relation to that infringement, then the right of action may be extended to a wider class of persons adversely affected by the infringement.[228a]

[228a] *The Trustees of the BT Pension Scheme v The Commissioners for Her Majesty's Revenue and Customs* [2015] EWCA Civ 713 at [51] (holding that the question of whether the non-availability of tax credits to a tax-exempt shareholder upon receipt of foreign income dividends from UK-resident companies breached the shareholder's right to free movement of capital was not acte clair and would be referred to the ECJ).

[Add to end of n.221]

See also *The Trustees of the BT Pension Scheme v The Commissioners for Her Majesty's Revenue and Customs* [2015] EWCA Civ 713 at [117] (describing the decision in *Emmott* as "highly fact-specific").

[In n.223 delete "Commission Draft Guidance Paper on quantifying harm in actions for damages based on breaches of the EU antitrust rules (2011), available at http://ec.europa.eu/competition/consultations/2011_actions_damages/ draft_guidance_paper_en.pdf (accessed March 25, 2013)" and substitute]

Communication from the Commission on quantifying harm in actions for damages based on breaches of Article 101 or 102 [TFEU] [2012] OJ C167/07; and see now Directive 2014/104/EU of the European Parliament and of the Council of November 26, 2014 on certain rules governing actions for damages under national law for infringements of the competition law provisions of the Member States and of the European Union. For discussion of the principle of national procedural autonomy in the competition law context, see: SB Volcker "Ignorantia legis non excusat and the demise of national procedural autonomy in the application of the EU competition rules" (2014) 51 C.M.L. Rev. 1497; N Dunne "Courage and compromise: the Directive on Antitrust Damages" (2015) 40 E.L.Rev. 581.

[Add to end of n.226]

See also *Centre public d'action sociale d'Ottignies-Louvain-la-Neuve v Abdida* (C–562/13) EU:C:2014:2453 [2015] 1 W.L.R. 3109; [2015] 2 C.M.L.R. 15 (holding that Directive 2008/115, arts 5 and 13, taken in conjunction with Charter arts 19(2) and 47, must be interpreted as precluding national legislation which does not make provision for a remedy with suspensive effect in respect of a return decision whose enforcement may expose a third country national to a serious risk of grave and irreversible deterioration in his state of health).

Limitation Periods

[Add to end of ". . . must also be sufficiently foreseeable.²⁶²"]   **14–063**

However, there is no general principle that ignorance or uncertainty about the state of the law is sufficient to prevent time running on grounds of effectiveness.²⁶²ᵃ

²⁶²ᵃ *The Trustees of the BT Pension Scheme v The Commissioners for Her Majesty's Revenue and Customs* [2015] EWCA Civ 713 at [117].

[Add to end of n.261]

See also: *Investment Trust Companies (In Liquidation) v Revenue and Customs Commissioners* [2015] EWCA Civ 82; [2015] S.T.C. 1280; *European Commission v United Kingdom* (C–640/13) EU:C:2014:2457 [2015] Ch. 476; [2015] 2 W.L.R. 1555 (the United Kingdom failed to comply with its obligations under TEU art.4(3) given that s.107 of the Finance Act 2007 curtailed retroactively and without notice or transitional arrangements, the right of taxpayers to recover taxes levied in breach of Union law).

[Add to n.271 after ". . . Levez [1998] ECR I–7835 at [20], [27]–[34]"]   **14–066**

See also *Birmingham Hippodrome Theatre Trust Ltd v Commissioners for HM Revenue and Customs* [2014] EWCA Civ 684; [2014] B.V.C. 27 at [46]–[49] (noting that "certainty is not a trump card" such that it did not breach the principles of effectiveness, equality or legal certainty for Revenue and Customs to be entitled to set off a repayment of input tax which should not have been made against a taxpayer's claim for repayment of output tax, despite being out of time to claim repayment of the wrongly repaid input tax).

[Add after ". . . known of the alleged infringement.²⁷⁴"]   **14–067**

Union law does not however require that a time limit in the field of environmental law should be subject to the court's discretionary power to extend it.²⁷⁴ᵃ

²⁷⁴ᵃ *R. (on the application of Williams) v Secretary of State for Energy and Climate Change* [2015] EWHC 1202.

Effective judicial review

14–068 *[Add after ". . . with the basic constitutional charter, the Treaty".".]*

275a See also Advocate General Opinion, *Council v Vereniging Milieudefensie and Stichting Stop Lucthverontreiniging Utrecht (C–401–403/12 P) EU:C:2015:4* [2015] 2 C.M.L.R. 32 at [70].

[Add to end of n.276]

For a recent consideration of the rule of law and institutional balance, see: *Council of the European Union v European Commission* (C–409/13) EU:C:2015:217 [2015] 3 C.M.L.R. 21 (consideration of the Commission's power to withdraw legislative proposals).

*[Add to ". . . for breach of Convention rights).*277a*"]*

277a See also Opinion 2/13 (December 18, 2014) at [175].

Repayment

14–071 *[Add to end of n.286]*

For recent applications of *San Giorgio*, see *Investment Trust Companies (In Liquidation) v Revenue and Customs Commissioners* [2015] EWCA Civ 82; [2015] S.T.C. 1280 and *Littlewoods Retail Ltd v Revenue and Customs Commissioners* [2015] EWCA Civ 515. See also *Test Claimants in the FII Group Litigation v Revenue and Customs Commissioners* [2014] EWHC 4302; [2015] S.T.C. 1471 (holding that the remedy in Union law in respect of tax unlawfully levied based on *San Giorgio* was wider than the recovery which would be provided for unjust enrichment in English law). See also *Coin-a-Drink Ltd v Revenue and Customs Commissioners* [2015] UKFTT 495 (TC).

State liability in damages for breach of Union law

14–075 *[Add new n.304a after ". . . for which they are held responsible"]*

304a The High Court has recently affirmed that a person adversely affected by a breach of EU law is not required to challenge the legality of the measure in proceedings before the national court before bringing a claim for *Francovich* damages: see *Recall Support Services Ltd v Secretary of State for Culture, Media and Sport* [2013] EWHC 3091 (Ch); [2014] 2 C.M.L.R. 2 at

[220] (following *Metallgesellschaft Ltd v Inland Revenue Commissioners* (C–397/98) [2001] E.C.R. I–1727 (see now: [2014] EWCA Civ 1370; [2015] 1 C.M.L.R. 38)).

Sufficiently serious breach

[Add after "contrary to Union law."] 14–078

[325a] These factors were endorsed recently in *Delaney v Secretary of State for Transport* [2015] EWCA Civ 172; [2015] 3 All E.R. 329 at [36].

[Add to end of para.14–078]

However, where the Commission considers whether to bring an infringement and decides against it, that will be a "pointer" against a finding of sufficiently serious breach.[336a]

[336a] *Recall Support Services Ltd v Secretary of State for Culture Media and Sport* [2014] EWCA Civ 1370; [2015] 1 C.M.L.R. 38 at [87].

[Add to end of n.322]

; *Recall Support Services Ltd v Secretary of State for Culture, Media and Sport* [2013] EWHC 3091 (Ch); [2014] 2 C.M.L.R. 2 at [165] (see now: [2014] EWCA Civ 1370; [2015] 1 C.M.L.R. 38).

[Add to end of n.323]

; *Specht v Land Berlin* (C–501/12–C–506/12) EU:C:2014:2005 at [105] (legislation which is not clear and precise may become so from the date upon which the court gives clarity and definition to a rule of EU law); *R. (on the application of Chester) v Secretary of State for Justice* [2013] UKSC 63; [2014] A.C. 271 at [79].

[Add to end of n.324]

R. (on the application of Chester) v Secretary of State for Justice [2013] UKSC 63; [2014] A.C. 271 at [76] ("[a]n important factor in determining whether liability in damages may exist under European law is the width of the discretion available to the legislator"). See also *Delaney v Secretary of State for Transport* [2015] EWCA Civ 172; [2015] 3 All E.R. 329 (where the natural reading of an article of a Directive only permitted exclusions which were set out in the article itself; a reference in the recitals to the Directive to "certain limited exclusions" was not a sound basis for adding additional exclusions and there was no discretion to adopt additional exclusions, resulting in a sufficiently serious breach in *Francovich* damages). See also *Angus Growers Ltd v Scottish Ministers* [2016] CSOH 26 at [40] (confirming that where there is a lack of discretion, it may not be sufficient to merely prove that there has been a breach of EU law—more may be required).

[Add to end of n.325]

See also *Angus Growers Ltd v Scottish Ministers* [2016] CSOH 26 at [43]–[45].

[Add to end of n.330]

Hogan v Minister for Social and Family Affairs (C–398/11) EU:C:2013:272 [2013] 3 C.M.L.R. 27 at [51]–[52] (the requirements of art.8 of Directive 80/987 as amended were clear and specific from the date of a prior judgment, as such, Ireland's failure to transpose the Directive correctly gave rise to a sufficiently serious breach of Union law); *Specht v Land Berlin* (C–501/12–C–506/12) EU:C:2014:2005 at [105] (legislation which is not clear and precise may become so from the date upon which the court gives clarity and definition to a rule of EU law).

The reach of the Francovich principles

14–085 *[Add to end of n.361]*

For recent consideration in the national context, see *Energy Solutions EU Ltd v Nuclear Decommissioning Authority* [2015] EWHC 73 (TCC); [2015] 2 C.M.L.R. 24.

PRELIMINARY RULINGS

Limitations to the jurisdiction of the court in a preliminary reference

14–088 *[Add to end of n.366]*

; see also *Érsekcsanádi Mezogazdasági Zrt v Bács–Kiskun Megyei Kormányhivatal* (C–56/13) EU:C:2014:352 at [48]–[57] (a national requirement to pay compensation subject to an exclusion of compensation for loss of profits in an implementing measure where the EU measure did not provide for any compensation could not be challenged under the Charter and the ECJ did not have jurisdiction to rule on it).

[Add after ". . . the interpretation of Union law^{367}"]

The preliminary ruling procedure has recently been described by the Grand Chamber as "keystone", which, by setting up dialogue between one court and another, specifically between the Court of Justice and the courts and tribunals of the Member States, has the object of securing uniform interpretation of EU law", which thereby serves "to ensure its consistency, its full effect and its autonomy as well as ultimately, the particular nature of the law established by the Treaties"[367a]

[367a] Opinion 2/13 (December 18, 2014) at [176].

[Add after ". . . in the wording of the question".[371]]

It has also been observed that, where a preliminary reference is made on a question of proportionality, for example, the court often effectively determines the proportionality of the national measure in issue, by reformulating the question referred so as to ask whether the relevant provision of EU legislation, or general principles of EU law, preclude a measure of that kind, or alternatively whether the measure in question is compatible with the relevant provision of EU legislation or general principles. As the Supreme Court has noted, that practice reflects the fact that it can be difficult to draw a clear dividing line between the inter-pretation of the law and its application in concrete circumstances, and an answer which explains how the law applies in the circumstances of the case before the referring court is likely to be helpful to it; this practice also avoids the risk that Member States may apply EU law differently in similar situations, or may be insufficiently stringent in their scrutiny of national measures.[367a]

[371] *R. (on the application of Lumsdon) v Legal Services Board* [2015] UKSC 41; [2016] A.C. 697 (it was added that this may give rise to difficulties if the ECJ's understanding of the measure, or of the relevant facts, is different from that of the referring court and reference was made to *Revenue and Customs Commissioners v Aimia Coalition Loyalty UK Ltd* [2013] UKSC 15; [2013] 2 C.M.L.R. 51) at [30].

[Add to end of n.368]

See also: *Raad van Bestuur van de Sociale Verzekeringsbank v Evans* (C–179/13) EU:C:2015:12 [2015] 2 C.M.L.R. 35 at [35].

[Add to end of n.374]   14–089

The ECJ has also emphasised recently that a national procedural rule pursuant to which legal rulings of a higher court bind the lower courts cannot call into question the discretion of the latter courts to request the court for a preliminary ruling where they have doubts as to the interpretation of European Union law: *Križan v Slovenská inšpekcia životného prostredia* (C–416/10) EU:C:2013:8 at [67].

[Add to end of n.377]

For a recent summary of the position, see *Fish Legal v Information Commissioner* (C–279/12) EU:C:2013:853 at [30].

[Add to end of n.378]

; *Fish Legal v Information Commissioner* (C–279/12) EU:C:2013:853 at [30]; *Maatschap T van Oosterom en A van Oosterom-Boelhouwer v Staatssecretaris van Economische Zaken* (C–485/12) EU:C:2014:250 at [31]–[32] (presumption cannot be rebutted by fact that the facts remain contested).

[Add to end of n.384]

; *Revenue and Customs Commissioners v Aimia Coalition Loyalty UK Ltd* [2013] UKSC 15; [2013] 2 C.M.L.R. 51 (declining to follow the ECJ's ruling in a preliminary reference, or make a further preliminary reference, where the ECJ had ruled on arguments not made by the parties, and due to the UK court's understanding of the established EU principle and greater understanding of the facts and arguments made).

[Add to end of n.389]

There has been some gentle criticism of the ECJ by the Supreme Court recently. In *Revenue and Customs Commissioners v Aimia Coalition Loyalty UK Ltd* [2013] UKSC 15; [2013] 2 C.M.L.R. 51 at [87], Lord Hope observed that a judgment, in respect of which the ECJ had not sought an opinion from the Advocate General before it proceeded to judgment, lacked the depth of reasoning which a judgment informed by an opinion would have provided, albeit that his Lordship noted that this was quite rare.

Referral obligation of national courts of last instance

14–090 *[Add to end of n.390]*

See also *Križan v Slovenská inšpekcia životného prostredia* (C–416/10) EU:C:2013:8 at [62] (the ECJ ruling that a national court is a court against whose decisions there is no judicial remedy under national law, within the meaning of TFEU art.267(3) and which is thus required to request a preliminary ruling, even where national law provides for the possibility of bringing before the constitutional court of the Member State concerned an action against is decisions limited to an examination of a potential infringement of the rights and freedoms guaranteed by the national constitution or by an international agreement).

[Add to end of n.393]

; *R. (on the application of Buckinghamshire County Council) v Secretary of State for Transport* [2014] UKSC 3; [2014] P.T.S.R. 182 at [53], [117], [128]; *Revenue and Customs Commissioners v Aimia Coalition Loyalty UK Ltd* [2013] UKSC 15; [2013] 2 C.M.L.R. 51.

[Add to end of n.395]

For a recent strict application of the *CILFIT* criteria, in which it was held that where a question of Union law had given rise to conflicting decisions in the lower courts of that Member State and the issue was one which frequently gave rise to issues of interpretation in Member States, the court of final instance had an obligation to make a reference, see *João Filipe Ferreira da Silva e Brito and Others v Portugal* (C–160/14) EU:C:2015:565. However, it does not necessarily suffice to trigger the obligation to make a reference if a lower court has made a reference to the ECJ in a similar case with the same legal issue, if the court of last instance regards the issue as acte clair: *X v Inspecteur van Rijksbelastingdienst* (C–72/14) EU:C:2015:564.

DIRECT ACTIONS IN THE ECJ AND GENERAL COURT

Enforcement

[Add to end of n.406]   14–093

For a recent example, see *Commission v Germany* (C–95/12) EU:C:2013: 676 (dismissal of an action brought by the Commission for a failure to comply with a previous judgment of the ECJ finding a failure to fulfil obligations).

Review of legality

[Add to end of n.407]   14–094

For recent examples of annulment actions, see *Inuit Tapiriit Kanatami v Parliament and Council* (C–583/11) EU:C:2013:625 ([2014] Q.B. 648) and *Telefónica v Commission* (C–274/12 P) EU:C:2013:852. See also *Mallis and Malli v Commission and ECB* (C–105/15 P to C-109/15P) EU:C:2016:702 (a statement of the Eurogroup, which remains a forum for discussion between ministers of the Member States whose currency is the euro, cannot be regarded as a measure intended to produce legal effects with respect to third parties, and can therefore not be annulled under TFEU art.263).

14–096 *[Add to end of n.412]*

; A. Kornezov, "Locus standi of Private Parties in Actions for Annulment: Has the Gap been Closed?" [2014] 73(1) C.L.J. 25.

[Add to end of n.414]

It was held in *Telefónica v Commission* (C–274/12 P) EU:C:2013:852 at [30]–[31] that the question of whether a regulatory act entails "implementing measures" must be assessed by reference to the position of the person pleading the right to bring proceedings and that it is irrelevant whether the act in question entails implementing measures with regard to other persons. Furthermore, reference should be made exclusively to the subject matter of the action, and where the applicant seeks only the partial annulment of an act, it is solely the implementing measures which that part of the act entails that must, as the case may be, be taken into consideration. For a recent example of the ECJ being quick to conclude that a measure entailed "implementing measures" which ought to be challenged at national level, see: *T & L Sugars Ltd v Sidul Açúcares, Unipessoal Lda* (C–456/13 P), EU:C:2015:284 (the Court disagreeing with the Advocate General and observing that the "allegedly mechanical nature of the measures taken at national level" did not undermine the conclusion that they were implementing measures: at [41]). Thus, even non-substantive, administrative implementing measures appear to be capable of falling within the scope of the concept of "implementing measure", a conclusion which the Advocate General in *T & L Sugars* argued against "if the objective of relaxing the admissibility conditions for natural and legal persons in connection with non-legislative regulatory acts is not to be wholly frustrated" (at [31]).

14–097 *[Delete "It is not yet clear to what extent the ECJ's approach will change in light of the revised test." and substitute]*

The impact of the revised test has been explored recently.

[Add to start of n.415]

Inuit Tapiriit Kanatami v Parliament and Council (Case C–583/11) EU:C:2013:625 [2014] Q.B. 648; [2014] 1 C.M.L.R. 54; *Telefónica v Commission* (C–274/12 P) EU:C:2013:852.

[Add to end of n.417]

and (Grand Chamber) [2014] Q.B. 648; [2014] 1 C.M.L.R. 54 at [59]. For an interesting example of the Union courts appearing to assume without deciding that a regulation was a "regulatory act", see *Inuit Tapiriit Kanatami v Commission, Parliament and Council,* (T–526/10) EU:T:2013:215 (the Court not deciding locus standi but proceeding to consider the merits).

[Add to para.14–097 after ". . . direct and individual concern.⁴¹⁷"]

This position has been endorsed by the ECJ which has accepted that the term "regulatory act" does not extend to legislative acts.⁴¹⁷ᵃ

⁴¹⁷ᵃ *Inuit Tapiriit Kanatami v Parliament and Council* (C–583/11) EU:C:2013:625 [2014] Q.B. 648; [2014] 1 C.M.L.R. 54 at [60]. The ECJ rejected an argument made in the case for the requirement for "direct and individual concern" to be replaced with a criterion of "substantial adverse effect": [69]–[71]. The case is also notable for its heavy reliance on the *travaux preparatoires* relating to Article III–365(4) of the proposed Treaty establishing a Constitution for Europe, the content of which was reproduced in identical terms in TFEU art.263(4).

[In n.421 delete "(pending appeal: C–267/11)" and substitute]   **14–099**

(the point was not raised on appeal: C–267/11 P EU:C:2013:624 at [46]).

[Add to end of n.422]

; *Commission v Kadi (Bulgaria intervening)* (C–584/10P, C–593/10P, C–595/10P) EU:C:2013:518 [2014] 1 C.M.L.R. 24 at [134].

[Add to end of n.423]

See, e.g. *Commission v Kadi* [2014] 1 C.M.L.R. 24 at [130] (finding that if the application of a contested asset-freezing measure has grounding in at least one valid reason, the decision will not be annulled, notwithstanding that the same cannot be said of other reasons).

GROUNDS FOR JUDICIAL REVIEW AGAINST UNION MEASURES: OVERVIEW

[Add after ". . . substantiating the conclusions drawn from it.⁴²⁷"]   **14–100**

The provisions of an international agreement to which the Union is a party may be relied upon in support of an action for annulment of an act of secondary Union legislation or an exception based on the illegality of such an act. However, this is only where the nature and the broad logic of that agreement do not preclude it and where the provisions appear, as to their content, to be unconditional and sufficiently precise.⁴²⁷ᵃ There are two very specific exceptions to this position: first, where the Union intended to implement a particular obligation assumed in the context of agreements concluded in the context of the World Trade Organisation or where the Union act sought to be annulled explicitly refers to the specific provisions of the international agreements, it is appropriate to review the legality of the act under challenge and the acts adopted for its implementation, in light of the rules of the international agreements.[427b]

[427a] *Council v Vereniging Milieudefensie and Stichting Stop Lucthverontreiniging Utrecht* (C–401—403/12 P) EU:C:2015:4 [2015] 2 C.M.L.R. 32 at [54] (holding that art.9(3) of the Aarhus Convention did not contain any unconstitutional and sufficiently precise obligation capable of directly regulating the legal position of individuals); see also *Council of the European Union v Stichting Natuur en Milieu* (C–404/12 P) EU:C:2015:5 [2015] 2 C.M.L.R. 31.

[427b] Cases (C–401—403/12 P) *Council v Vereniging Milieudefensie and Stichting Stop Lucthverontreiniging Utrecht* EU:C:2015:4 [2015] 2 C.M.L.R. 32 at [56]–[57] (Regulation 1367/2006, art.10(1) did not implement specific obligations of art.9(3) of the Aarhus Convention).

[Add to end of n.428]

; *Commission v Kadi* [2014] 1 C.M.L.R. 24 at [97].

Equal treatment and non-discrimination

14–103 *[Add to end of n.436]*

For a recent case on equality in the context of sexual orientation (in which TFEU art.19 was ignored), see *Leger v Ministre des Affaires sociales, de la Sante et des Droits des femmes* (C–528/13) EU:C:2015:288 [2015] All E.R. (EC) 755. For an interesting holding that obesity may, where it hinders the full and effective participation of some persons in professional life on a long-term basis, constitute a disability, see: *Fag og Arbejde v Kommunernes Landsforening* (KL) (C–354/13) EU:C:2014:2463 [2015] 2 C.M.L.R. 19.

Proportionality

14–105 *[Add after ". . . must not be disproportionate to the aims pursued.[448]"]*

It has recently been observed, in the context of review of national measures for compliance with the principle of proportionality, that "[p]roportionality is a test for assessing the lawfulness of a decision-maker's choice between some legal norm and a competing public interest. Baldly stated, the principle is that where the act of a public authority derogates from some legal standard in pursuit of a recognised but inconsistent public interest, the question arises whether the derogation is worth it."[448a]

[448a] *R. (on the application of Rotherham Metropolitan Borough Council) v Secretary of State for Business, Innovation and Skills* [2015] UKSC 6; [2015] 3 C.M.L.R. 20 at [47].

[Add to end of n.446]

, and has been described more recently by the Supreme Court as "open to criticism" and as not providing "reliable guidance" where at issue is a derogation from a Union right (see *R. (on the application of Lumsdon) v Legal Services Board* [2015] UKSC 41; [2016] A.C. 697 at [82] and [103]).

[Add to n.447 after ". . . and third test': p.139"]

More recently, in *Herbert Schaible v Land Baden-Württemberg* (C–101/12), Advocate General Wahl EU:C:2013:334 expressed the view at [40] that the court's jurisdiction also extends to evaluating whether the measure strikes a fair balance between the interests of those affected, i.e. proportionality *stricto sensu*).

[Add to end of n.447]

; *Herbert Schaible v Land Baden–Württemberg* (C–101/12) EU:C:2013:661 at [29]; *Digital Rights Ireland v Minister for Communications, Marine and Natural Resources* (C–293, 594/12) EU:C:2014:238 at [45]–[70]. That proportionality usually entails a two-part test has recently been endorsed by the Supreme Court: *R. (on the application of Lumsdon) v Legal Services Board* [2015] UKSC 41; [2016] A.C. 697 at [33] (adding that there is some debate as to whether there is a third question, sometimes referred to as proportionality *stricto sensu*: namely, whether the burden imposed by the measure is disproportionate to the benefits secured. In practice, the court usually omits this question from its formulation of the proportionality principle. It was added that where the question has been argued, however, the court has often included it in its formulation and addressed it separately, as in *R. v Minister for Agriculture, Fisheries and Food, Ex p Fedesa* (Case C–331/88) EU:C:1990:391 [1990] ECR I–4023).

Insert after ". . . common agricultural policy,[454]"]   14–107

distribution of European Structural Funds among regions of the United Kingdom,[454a]

454a R. *(on the application of Rotherham Metropolitan Borough Council) v Secretary of State for Business, Innovation and Skills* [2015] UKSC 6; [2015] 3 C.M.L.R. 20 at [167] (Lord Mance noting that he agreed with the Court of Appeal that the decisions "were concerned with matters of broad economic, social and political judgment, for which the objectives were widely defined").

14–108A *[Add new para.14–108A after para.14–108]*

As a general matter, proportionality as a ground of review of EU measures is concerned with the balancing of private interests adversely affected by such measures against the public interests which the measures are intended to promote. Proportionality functions in that context as a check on the exercise of public power of a kind traditionally found in public law, although cases in which measures adopted by the EU legislator or administration in the public interest are held by the EU judicature to be disproportionate interferences with private interests are likely to be relatively infrequent.461a

461a R. *(on the application of Lumsdon) v Legal Services Board* [2015] UKSC 41; [2016] A.C. 697 at [36]. See also R *(on the application of British American Tobacco Ltd) v Secretary of State for Health* [2016] EWHC 1169 (Admin).

Human rights

14–116 *[Add to end of n.511]*

See now *Gascogne Sack Deutschland GmbH v Commission* (C–40/12) EU:C:2013:768; *Kendrion NV v Commission* (C–50/12) EU:C:2013:771; *Groupe Gascogne SA v Commission* (C–58/12) EU:C:2013:770.

[Add to end of n.512]

; *Inuit Tapiriit Kanatami v Parliament and Council* (C–583/11) EU:C:2013:625 [2014] Q.B. 648; [2014] 1 C.M.L.R. 54 at [105] (art.47 does not require that an individual should have an unconditional entitlement to bring an action for annulment of Union legislative acts directly before the Courts of the European Union); *Abdulraihim v Council of the European Union and European Commission* (C–239/12 P) EU:C:2013:331 [2013] 3 C.M.L.R. 41 at [67]–[70] (effective judicial protection meant that an appellant still had an interest in annulling legislation which had already been repealed, since annulment was retrospective and not merely *ex nunc*).

[Add to para.14–116 after ". . . freedom of trade518"]

, freedom to conduct business.[518a]

[518a] See, e.g. *Herbert Schaible v Land Baden-Württemberg* (C–101/12) EU:C:2013:661.

Emerging principles

[Add to end of n.535]   14–118

In the environmental context, see *Križan v Slovenská inšpekcia životného prostredia* (C–416/10) EU:C:2013:8.

[Add to end of n.542]

In *Recall Support Services Ltd v Secretary of State for Culture, Media and Sport* [2013] EWHC 3091 (Ch); [2014] 2 C.M.L.R. 2, the principle was described (at [112]) as meaning that a Member State did not have to wait until some harm arose to the public before adopting measures to prevent a recurrence of that harm and which required authorities to take appropriate measures to prevent potential risks to public health, safety and the environment, by giving precedence to the requirements related to the protection of those interests over economic interests. Whether to have recourse to the precautionary principle depends on the level of protection chosen by the competent authority in the exercise of its discretion, taking account of the priorities that it defined in the light of the objectives it pursued in accordance with the relevant rules of the Treaty and of secondary law (see now [2014] EWCA Civ 1370; [2015] 1 C.M.L.R. 38).

The requirement to state reasons

[Add to para.14–120 after ". . . exercise its power of review.[546]"]   14–120

The reasons must be appropriate to the nature of the contested act and to the context in which it was adopted.[546a] For example, where provision of the reasons preclude the disclosure to the person concerned of information or evidence produced before the courts of the European Union due to security concerns, it is necessary to strike an appropriate balance between the requirements attached to the right to effective judicial protection and those flowing from the security of the Union or its Member States or the conduct of their international relations.[546b]

[546a] *Yanukovych v Council* (T-346/14) EU:T:2016:497 at [77]; *Ben Ali v Council* (T-200/14) EU:T:2016:216 at [94].

546b *Commission v Kadi* (C–584/10) [2014] 1 C.M.L.R. 24 at [128]; but see *R. (on the application of AZ) v Secretary of State for the Home Department* [2015] EWHC 3695 (Admin).

[Add to end of n.546]

; *Commission v Kadi* (C–584/10) EU:C:2013:518 [2014] 1 C.M.L.R. 24 at [116] (for the requirements for reasons where the reasons represent reasons stated by an international body where the Union is implementing international measures).

14–121 *[Add to end of n.553]*

The reasoning may be "implicit, on condition it enables the persons concerned to know why the measures in question were taken and provides the competent court with sufficient material for it to exercise its power of review": *Inuit Tapiriit Kanatami v Parliament and Council* (C–583/11) EU:C:2013:625 [2014] Q.B. 648; [2014] 1 C.M.L.R. 54 at [82].

14–124 *[Add to end of n.563]*

; *Commission v Kadi* [2014] 1 C.M.L.R. 24 at [116]–[117].

GROUNDS FOR JUDICIAL REVIEW OF NATIONAL MEASURES

14–126 *[Add to end of n.570]*

But see now: (see *R. (on the application of Lumsdon) v Legal Services Board* [2015] UKSC 41; [2016] A.C. 697 at [82] and [103]).

[Add to end of n.571]

Recall Support Services Ltd v Secretary of State for Culture, Media and Sport [2013] EWHC 3091 (Ch); [2014] 2 C.M.L.R. 2; *R. (on the application of Buckinghamshire CC) v Secretary of State for Transport* [2014] UKSC 3; [2014] 1 W.L.R. 324 (unsuccessful challenge to a Government Command Paper setting out parameters for a high speed rail project).

[Add to end of n.575]

But see now: *R. (on the application of Lumsdon) v Legal Services Board* [2015] UKSC 41; [2016] A.C. 697 at [82] and [103].

The requirement to state reasons

[Add to end of n.581]   14–130

; *Commission v Kadi* [2014] 1 C.M.L.R. 24 at [111].

Fundamental rights

Where the Member State is not directly implementing EU measures

[Add to end of n.594]   14–137

For recent parallel developments in the context of the Charter, see
para.14–032A.

[Add to n.597 after ". . . 394 at 437"]

(but see now *R. (on the application of Lumsdon) v Legal Services Board*
[2015] UKSC 41; [2015] 3 W.L.R. 121 at [82] and [103]).

Proportionality

[Add new para.14–138A after para.14–138]   14–138A

In a recent important judgment, the Supreme Court endeavoured to clarify
the principle of proportionality as it applies in the context of Union law,
while emphasising that the way in which the principle of proportionality is
applied in Union law depends to a significant extent upon the context.[597a]
The Supreme Court began by observing that the principle of proportionality
is a general principle of Union law, enshrined in TFEU art.5(4),[597b] and
reflected elsewhere in the Treaties, such as in TEU art.3(6).[597c] but that it had
been most obviously developed by the ECJ in its jurisprudence.[597d] The principle applies generally to legislative and administrative measures adopted by
EU institutions. It also applies to national measures falling within the scope of
EU law.[597e] The principle only applies to measures interfering with protected
interest, and is neither expressed nor applied in the same way as the principle
of proportionality under the ECHR.[597f] Where the proportionality principle
is applied by a national court, it must, as a principle of EU law, be applied in
a manner which is consistent with the jurisprudence of the court: "as is sometimes said, the national judge is also a European judge".[597g] The Court
endorsed the concept of proportionality as entailing two questions: first,
whether the measure in question is suitable or appropriate to achieve the
objective pursued; and secondly, whether the measure is necessary to achieve

that objective, or whether it could be attained by a less onerous method.[597h] The Court observed that the other critical aspect of the principle of proportionality is the intensity with which it is applied, and it drew a distinction between review of national measures relying upon derogations from general EU rights, and the review of national measures implementing Union law.[597i] As a ground of review of national measures, proportionality has been applied most frequently to measures interfering with the fundamental freedoms guaranteed by the EU Treaties. Although private interests may be engaged, the court is therefore concerned first and foremost with the question of whether a Member State can justify an interference with a freedom guaranteed in the interests of promoting the integration of the internal market, and the related social values, which lie at the heart of the EU project. In circumstances of that kind, the principle of proportionality generally functions as a means of preventing disguised discrimination and unnecessary barriers to market integration. In that context, the court, seeing itself as the guardian of the Treaties and of the uniform application of EU law, generally applies the principle more strictly.[597j] By contrast, where Member States adopt measures implementing EU legislation, they are generally contributing towards the integration of the internal market, rather than seeking to limit it in their national interests. In general, therefore, proportionality functions in that context as a conventional public law principle. On the other hand, where Member States rely on reservations or derogations in EU legislation in order to introduce measures restricting fundamental freedoms, proportionality is generally applied more strictly, subject to the qualifications which we have mentioned.[597k]

[597a] R. (on the application of Lumsdon) v Legal Services Board [2015] UKSC 41; [2016] A.C. 697. See also Scotch Whiskey Association v Lord Advocate (C–333/14) EU:C:2015:845 for consideration of proportionality.

[597b] TFEU art.5(4) provides as follows: "Under the principle of proportionality, the content and form of Union action shall not exceed what is necessary to achieve the objectives of the Treaties."

[597c] TEU art.3(6) provides as follows: "The Union shall pursue its objectives by appropriate means commensurate with the competences which are conferred upon it in the Treaties."

[597d] R. (on the application of Lumsdon) v Legal Services Board [2015] UKSC 41; [2016] A.C. 697 at [24].

[597e] R. (on the application of Lumsdon) v Legal Services Board [2015] UKSC 41; [2016] A.C. 697 at [25].

[597f] R. (on the application of Lumsdon) v Legal Services Board [2015] UKSC 41; [2016] A.C. 697 at [26].

[597g] *R. (on the application of Lumsdon) v Legal Services Board* [2015] UKSC 41; [2016] A.C. 697 at [31].

[597h] *R. (on the application of Lumsdon) v Legal Services Board* [2015] UKSC 41; [2016] A.C. 697 at [33] (see also n.447 above).

[597i] *R. (on the application of Lumsdon) v Legal Services Board* [2015] UKSC 41; [[2016] A.C. 697 at [34]–[35] (a third category, review of EU measures, has already been set out above at text to n.461a).

[597j] *R. (on the application of Lumsdon) v Legal Services Board* [2015] UKSC 41; [2016] A.C. 697 at [37] (for further detail see [51]–[72]).

[597k] *R. (on the application of Lumsdon) v Legal Services Board* [2015] UKSC 41; [2016] A.C. 697 at [38] (for further detail see [73]–[74].

[Delete "Many" at start of para.14–139 and substitute]   14–139

As just noted, many

Proportionality

[Add to end of n.608]   14–142

For an example of a structured application of proportionality, see *R. (on the application of British American Tobacco UK Ltd) v Secretary of State for Health* [2016] EWHC 1169 (Admin). Here it was held that the authorities "struck a fair balance between the competing interests and they were justified, proportionate and in the public interest".

Equality

[Add to end of n.612]   14–145

For an interesting example of anomalies in funding between different regions being such as to require explanation, which had not been given, thereby rendering the decisions manifestly inappropriate under EU (and domestic law), see: *R. (on the application of Rotherham MBC) v Secretary of State for Business, Innovation and Skills* [2015] UKSC 6; [2015] 3 All E.R. 1 (Lord Carnwath noting at [174] that issues of equal or unequal treatment and proportionality may play a part in the assessment of whether reasoning was affected by legal error or otherwise manifestly inappropriate).

Part III
PROCEDURES AND REMEDIES

CHAPTER 15

THE HISTORICAL DEVELOPMENT OF JUDICIAL REVIEW REMEDIES AND PROCEDURES

The importance of a historical perspective

[In n.7 after "Judicial Review" delete "3rd edn (2005)" and substitute]   15–004

5th edn (2014)

Statutory applications to quash

[Add to n.216 after "Airport Act 1986 s.49"]   15–078

(now repealed)

The creation of the rsc, Ord.53 application for judicial review

Recent reforms

[Add to end of n.262]   15–099

See also Ministry of Justice, Command Paper 8703, September 2013, in which proposals for further reform were put forward. Some of these have now been enacted and are discussed at para.16–002, n.9.

CHAPTER 16

CPR PT 54 CLAIMS FOR JUDICIAL REVIEW

SCOPE

[Add to end of n.1]   16–001

The Administrative Court has produced its own *Judicial Review Guide 2016* (July 2016).

[Add to end of final bullet point]

The Upper Tribunal also exercises its own judicial review jurisdiction in certain areas.

[In n.7 delete "4ᵗʰ edn (2008)" and substitute]   16–002

5ᵗʰ edn (2014)

[Add to n.9 after "31"]

, 31A

[Add to end of n.9]

The Government's proposals for extensive reforms to the judicial review procedure are described at paras 1–005 and 1–005A. Many of the proposals have now been enacted in the Criminal Justice and Courts Act 2015 (although not all have yet entered into force). They are set out at paras 16–049A (permission) and 16–082 (leapfrog appeals to the SC); and nn 268 (information on claimant's funding); 279 (intervener's costs); and 296 (costs capping orders). See further, A. Samuels, "Judicial review: the new law: the Criminal Justice and Courts Act 2015 Chapter 2" [2015] J.P.L. 754–758 and A. Mills, "Reforms to Judicial Review in the Criminal Justice and Courts Act 2015: Promoting Efficiency or Weakening the Rule of Law?" [2015] P.L. 583.

[In n.11 delete final two sentences and substitute]

Section 6(4) of the Justice and Security Act 2013 (which came into force on June 25, 2013) sets out the conditions under which the court (on the application of either of the parties or the Secretary of State, or of its own motion) may declare that a closed material application may be made; see para.8–009. The Bill which led to the 2013 Act was convincingly criticised by A. Peto and A. Tyrie, *Neither Just nor Secure* (2012).

[In n.12 delete "para.5" and substitute]

para.2

[In n.12 delete "May 2012" and substitute]

May 2015

[In n.13 delete "http://www.justice.gov.uk/downloads/courts/administrative-court" and substitute]

http://www.justice.gov.uk/courts/rcj-rolls-building/administrative-court/applying-for-judicial-review.

THE ADMINISTRATIVE COURT

16–003 *[Delete sentence "The following considerations are relevant to determining the appropriate venue for proceedings:" and substitute]*

The general expectation is that proceedings will be administered and determined in the region with which the claimant has the closest connection, subject to the following considerations:

[Add to para.16–003 after ". . . media interest in a particular area;"]

the time within which it is appropriate for the proceedings to be determined;

[Add to end of n.16]

See now S. Nason, "Justice Outside London? Five Years of 'Regional' Administrative Courts" [2014] J.R. 188.

16–004 *[In n.23 delete the final sentence]*

The overriding objective

16–011 *[In para. 16–011 add after "justly"]*

and at proportionate cost

[Add to end of n.42]   16–012

See also *San Vicente v Secretary of State for Communities and Local Government* [2013] EWCA Civ 817; [2014] 1 W.L.R. 966 at [52] on applications to amend claims under s.288 of the Town and Country Planning Act 1990. In relation to applying the new provisions on relief from sanctions in CPR r.3.9, see *Mitchell v News Group Newspapers Ltd* [2013] EWCA Civ 1537; [2014] 1 W.L.R. 795 at [40]–[41] and *Denton v TH White Ltd* [2014] EWCA Civ 906; [2014] 1 W.L.R. 3926 at [24]–[38]. In *Denton*, the CA restated the *Mitchell* principles and set out the three stages which should be addressed: to identify and assess the seriousness and significance of the failure to comply with any rule, practice direction or court order; then to consider why the default occurred; and finally to evaluate all the circumstances of the case in order to deal with the application justly. *Denton* (rather than *Mitchell*) was followed in *Michael Wilson & Partners, Limited v Thomas Ian Sinclair and others* [2015] EWCA Civ 774. Both were followed by the SC in *Thevarajah v Riordan* [2015] UKSC 78; [2016] 1 W.L.R. 76 at [13]–[15], in which Lord Neuberger described the CA in *Denton* as having "clarified some of the reasoning" in *Mitchell*.

[Add to end of n.44]

Tariq was followed in *Kiani v Secretary of State for the Home Department* [2015] EWCA Civ 776; *The Times*, August 19, 2015. *Al-Rawi* was distinguished in *R. (on the application of B) v Westminster Magistrates' Court* [2014] UKSC 59; [2015] A.C. 1195 (extradition proceedings do not justify or call for a further qualification of the principle of open justice, beyond any recognised in *Al Rawi*).

THE PROCEDURAL STAGES

Exhaustion of other remedies and ADR

[In n.45 delete "(May 2012) . . . exhausted")" and substitute]   16–014

(May 2015), para.5 ("Judicial review should only be used where no adequate alternative remedy, such as a right of appeal, is available")

[In n.45 delete "4ᵗʰ edn (2008), paras 11–042—11–074" and substitute]

5ᵗʰ edn (2014), paras 12–042—12–076

[Add to end of n.45]

See also *R. (on the application of Willford) v Financial Services Authority* [2013] EWCA Civ 677 at [36]–[38] (Upper Tribunal "can reconsider the whole matter afresh" and therefore provides a more appropriate alternative remedy).

[In n.46 delete "; R (on the application of C) v Financial Services Authority [2012] EWHC 1417 (Admin) at [83], [90]–[93] (Upper Tribunal had no power to order the Defendant to comply with its statutory duty to give reasons)"]

[Add to end of n.46]

See also *R. (on the application of Willford) v Financial Services Authority* [2013] EWCA Civ 677 at [36].

Avenues of appeal or review created by statute

16–018   *[Add to end of n.54]*

See further *R. (on the application of Watch Tower Bible & Tract Society of Britain) v Charity Commission* [2016] EWCA Civ 154; [2016] 1 W.L.R. 2625 at [19] (Lord Dyson MR): "It is only in a most exceptional case that a court will entertain an application for judicial review if other means of redress are conveniently and effectively available. This principle applies with particular force where Parliament has enacted a statutory scheme that enables persons against whom decisions are made and actions taken to refer the matter to a specialist tribunal". In *Watch Tower*, an appeal to the First-tier Tribunal provided an effective remedy in relation to the Charity Commission's decision to initiate the inquiry, but not the challenge to its production order which could proceed by way of judicial review. The principle has little relevance "where the alternative remedy which it is said that the claimant must pursue is a profoundly different claim from the judicial review claim which they seek to advance": *R. (on the application of Veolia ES Landfill Ltd) v Revenue and Customs Commissioners* [2015] EWCA Civ 747; [2015] B.T.C. 23 at [29].

16–019   *[Add to end of n.56]*

Section 64 of the Criminal Justice and Courts Act 2015 (in force from August 8, 2016) inserts new ss.14A–14C into the Tribunals, Courts and Enforcement Act 2007, allowing leapfrog appeals from the Upper Tribunal to the SC in certain circumstances: see paras 16–082, 17–005 and n.17 thereto.

[Add to end of n.61]   16–020

and *R. (on the application of Watch Tower Bible & Tract Society of Britain) v Charity Commission* [2016] EWCA Civ 154; [2016] 1 W.L.R. 2625 at [19].

Other avenues of legal challenge

[Add to end of n.68]   16–021

In *R. (on the application of Roche Registration Ltd) v Secretary of State for Health* [2015] EWCA Civ 1311; [2016] 4 W.L.R. 46 at [60]–[64], it was inappropriate for the domestic courts to grant relief in judicial review proceedings where the claimant would have the opportunity to challenge any penalty imposed pursuant to the EC Penalties Regulation in the appropriate EU courts "which will be able to give a determinative answer".

[In n.72 delete "applied by . . . [83]"]

Alternative Dispute Resolution (ADR)

[In para.16–022 delete "early neutral evaluation by an independent third   16–022
party" and substitute

using relevant public authority complaints or review procedures

[In para.16–022 delete "To this . . . decision-maker"]

[In n.77 delete "(d)" and substitute]

(e)

[In n.79 delete first two sentences and substitute]

Paras 9–12 (May 2015 issue). Para.11 refers to S.Blake, J. Browne and S.Sime, *The Jackson ADR Handbook* (2013); the Citizens Advice Bureaux website: http://www.ad viceguide.org.uk/england/law_e/law_legal_system_e/law_taking_legal_action_e/alternatives_to_court.htm (for information on ADR); and http://www.civilmediation.justice.gov.uk/ (to find a mediation provider).

[In n.82 delete the first sentence and substitute]

The Pre-Action Protocol for Judicial Review (May 2015) states only that "parties should consider whether some form of alternative dispute resolution . . . or complaints procedure would be more suitable than litigation, and if so, endeavour to agree which to adopt"; indeed, exploring ADR does not excuse non-compliance with the time limit and so it may be appropriate to issue a claim without having done so (para.9).

[Add to end of n.82]

In *PGF II SA v OMFS Co 1 Ltd* [2013] EWCA Civ 1288; [2014] 1 W.L.R. 1386 at [34]–[40], the CA extended the guidance given by the CA in *Halsey v Milton Keynes General NHS Trust* [2004] EWCA Civ 576; [2004] 1 W.L.R. 3002 to the effect that, in general, a party's silence in the face of an invitation to participate in ADR was itself unreasonable regardless of whether or not refusal to engage in ADR might have been reasonable. See also *Laporte v Commissioner of Police of the Metropolis* [2015] EWHC 371 (QB); [2015] 3 Costs L.R. 471 (QBD) at [9]–[14]; and the Pre-Action Protocol for Judicial Review (May 2015) at paras 9 and 12.

16–023 *[Add to end of n.83]*

In *R. (on the application of Wood) v Leeds City Council* [2014] EWHC 2598 (Admin) at [105]–[110], a case which involved issues of statutory construction, an application to the Local Government Ombudsman was held not to provide a suitable alternative remedy. See however, *R. (on the application of David Soar) v Secretary of State for Justice* [2015] EWHC 392 (Admin) at [47]–[49]: a case involving "fundamental points of procedure relating to natural justice" was granted permission on the basis that judicial review was arguably more suitable than the ombudsman procedure. The HC held that the ombudsman procedure may have been equally effective and appropriate; however, as proceedings had been commenced, the court granted the relief sought rather than remitting the claim to the ombudsman in light of the overriding objective.

Exchange of letters before claim

16–025 *[In para.16–025 after "establish whether" add]*

they can be narrowed or

[In n.87 delete "8" and substitute]

14

Gathering evidence and information

16–026 *[Add to end of n.92]*

In *HK (Bulgaria) v Secretary of State for the Home Department* [2016] EWHC 857 (Admin); [2016] A.C.D. 86 at [13]–[18], the Court reluctantly agreed to admit an expert report by Amnesty International on conditions for returned asylum seekers in Bulgaria, but emphasised that strict compliance with the conditions in CPR Part 35 was essential in relation to expert reports in judicial review proceedings.

The duty of candour

[In n.95, delete "Treasury Solicitor's Department" and substitute]   16–027

Government Legal Department

[In n.95, delete "http://www.tsol.gov.uk" and substitute]

https://www.gov.uk/government/organisations/government-legal-department

[Add to end of n.95]

In *R. (on the application of Midcounties Co-operative Ltd) v Forest of Dean DC* [2015] EWHC 1251 (Admin); [2015] P.T.S.R. D32 at [148]–[151], the defendant had taken no active part in proceedings for financial reasons, leaving the interested third party to defend its decision. It was observed that although a third party may be subject to the duty of candour, such an arrangement may not necessarily meet all the practical difficulties which may arise so as to properly discharge the defendant's own duty in this regard. In *Abraha v Secretary of State for the Home Department* [2015] EWHC 1980 (Admin) at [111] and [114], the duty was described as an aspect of, and essential to, the rule of law. In *R. (on the application of Mohammad Shazad Khan) v Secretary of State for the Home Department)* [2016] EWCA Civ 416 at [42]–[47], the claimant's duty of candour was held to extend beyond the furnishing of relevant documents and to include drawing to the attention of the court the significance of particular documents adverse to the claim. At the time of writing, the Lord Chief Justice is undertaking a consultation into the defendant's duty of candour and disclosure in judicial review proceedings.

[Add to end of n.97]

In *R. (on the application of Bancoult) v Secretary of State for Foreign and Commonwealth Affairs (No. 4)* [2016] UKSC 35; [2016] 3 W.L.R. 157 at [24], an omission to disclose documents casting into doubt the independence and reliability of a resettlement report relied on by the government amounted to a "highly regrettable" breach of the Secretary of State's duty of candour (which he accepted). Lord Kerr, dissenting on a slightly different issue, considered the breach "wholly unacceptable when such a fundamental right was at stake" ([183]–[187]). However, that failure was on its own insufficient to justify setting aside the decision of the HL in prior proceedings.

Freedom of Information Act 2000

16–028 *[In n.99, delete "7th edn (2011)" and substitute]*

8th edn (2015)

[In n.99 delete "3rd edn (2010)" and substitute]

4th edn (2014)

[Add to end of n.99]

A helpful and authoritative account of the Act is set out in *R. (on the application of Evans) v Attorney General* [2015] UKSC 21; [2015] A.C. 1787 at [8]–[18].

16–029 *[In n.104 delete "s.17" and substitute]*

s.12

16–030 *[Add to start of list of cases in n.105]*

Department for Work and Pensions v Information Commissioner [2016] EWCA Civ 758 (identities of organisations hosting placements under mandatory "workfare" schemes for unemployed people); *Information Commissioner v Colenso-Dunne* [2015] UKUT 471 (AAC) (list of 305 journalists' names seized by the ICO during a raid on the home of a private investigator); *Independent Parliamentary Standards Authority v Information Commissioner* [2015] EWCA Civ 388; [2015] 1 W.L.R. 2879 (on receipts for expense claims made by Members of Parliament); *Ranger v The House of Lords Appointments Commission* [2015] EWHC 45 (QB) (information relating to the conferring by the Crown of any honour or dignity); *Kennedy v Information Commissioner* [2014] UKSC 20; [2015] A.C. 455 (on documents created by, or provided to, a public body relating to an inquiry conducted by that body);

[In n.105 delete http://ico.gov.uk/ and substitute]

http://ico.org.uk

[Add to end of n.105]

In the first quarter of 2016, this figure was 12,791 (Freedom of Information Statistics: Implementation in Central Government, January – March 2016,

June 16, 2016). The SC overturned the exercise of the Attorney General's veto in relation to correspondence between the Prince of Wales and government departments on the ground that mere disagreement with the conclusions of the Upper Tribunal was not a sufficient basis for the exercise of the veto (*R. (on the application of Evans) v Attorney General* [2015] UKSC 21; [2015] A.C. 1787). On the use of a closed material procedure under the 2000 Act, see *Browning v Information Commissioner* [2014] EWCA Civ 1050; [2014] 1 W.L.R. 3848 at [31]–[36].

Environmental Information Regulations 2004

[Add to end of n.106] 16–031

The power to veto a decision to disclose information under the 2000 Act must be exercised compatibly with EU law (see the discussion in *R. (on the application of Evans) v Attorney General* [2015] UKSC 21; [2015] A.C. 1787 at [98]–[108]).

Access requests under the Data Protection Act 1998

[In para.16–032 delete "working days" and substitute] 16–032

calendar days

[In nn.108–111 and 113–114 delete "Freedom of Information Act 2000" 16–033
and substitute]

Data Protection Act 1998

Preparing the Claim Form

[In n.116 delete the final sentence and substitute] 16–036

The fee is £140: Civil Proceedings Fees (Amendment) Order (2014/874), Sch.1.

[Add to end of n.121] 16–037

In *R. (on the application of Gul) v Secretary of State for Justice* [2014] EWHC 373 (Admin); [2014] A.C.D. 106 at [41]–[44], the DC made two important observations on the obligations of claimants: to give full and frank disclosure of matters which may undermine their case (failure to do so may lead to relief being refused); and to reconsider the merits of the claim on receipt of the defendant's evidence (which may have costs consequences). See *R. (on the application of Mohammad Shazad Khan) v Secretary of State for the Home Department)* [2016] EWCA Civ 416 at [42]–[47], n.95 above.

16–037 *[Add to end of n.124]*

The statement of truth is "not an irrelevant mantra or mere verbiage": *R. (on the application of Akram) v Secretary of State for the Home Department* [2015] EWHC 1359 (Admin) at [25].

Urgent cases

16–042 *[Add to end of n.135]*

See further *R. (on the application of Butt) v Secretary of State for the Home Department* [2014] EWHC 264 (Admin), citing *Hamid* in speaking of the "vigorous action" taken by the courts against legal representatives who fail to comply with the rules (not specifically relating to urgent cases), in turn cited in *R. (on the application of Akram) v Secretary of State for the Home Department* [2015] EWHC 1359 (Admin) (see n.124).

Permission

The purpose of the permission stage

16–048 *[Add to end of n.147]*

The refusal rate reached its peak in 2013, during which permission was granted in only nine per cent of applications. In that year, immigration and asylum cases accounted for 84 per cent of all judicial reviews. From November 2013, the majority of immigration and asylum judicial review cases were transferred from the Administrative Court to the Upper Tribunal (Immigration and Asylum Chamber) (UTIAC), resulting in a decreased number of applications received by the Administrative Court. Leaving aside such transferred immigration and asylum cases in 2014, 4,062 applications were received and 16 per cent of these were granted permission to proceed. In the first quarter of 2016, 1,176 applications were made to the Administrative Court, 4 per cent of which had in that quarter been granted permission. For more detailed information, see Ministry of Justice, Civil Justice Statistics Quarterly, England and Wales (Incorporating The Royal Courts of Justice 2015) January to March 2016 (June 2, 2016); and Ministry of Justice, Tribunals and Gender Recognition Certificate Statistics Quarterly January to March 2016 and annual statistics 2015/16 (June 9, 2016).

Criteria on which permission is granted or refused

[Add to end of n.154]   16–049

In *R. (on the application of Wasif) v Secretary of State for the Home Department (Practice Note)* [2016] EWCA Civ 82; [2016] 1 W.L.R. 2793 at [13], the CA identified *Sharma v Brown-Antoine* [2007] 1 W.L.R. 780 as the "locus classicus" on permission.

[Add new para.16–049A after 16–049]   16–049A

The Criminal Justice and Courts Act 2015 has introduced a new criterion at the permission stage. If the court considers it "highly likely" that "the outcome for the applicant" would not "have been substantially different if the conduct complained of had not occurred" then it must refuse permission.[154a] The court may consider this question of its own motion, but it must do so if the defendant requests that it does.[154b] The Court has a limited discretion to grant permission even if the "no difference" test is made out where it "considers that it is appropriate to do so for reasons of exceptional public interest".[154c] If the court grants permission on grounds of exceptional public interest, it must certify that this condition is satisfied.[154d] The court may direct a hearing on the issue of "no difference" and the exception to it on at least two days' notice to those who have filed an Acknowledgement of Service.[154e] The senior judiciary's response to the Government's consultation warned of "Dress rehearsal permission hearings" involving "detailed consideration of the facts".[154f]

[154a] Criminal Justice and Courts Act 2015 s.84(1)–(3), in force from April 13, 2015, inserting new subs. (3C)–(3F) into Senior Courts Act 1981 s.31. See para.18–049A.

[154b] Senior Courts Act 1981 s.31(3C).

[154c] Senior Courts Act 1981 s.31(3E). CPR Pt 54.8(4)(a)(ia) requires a defendant to include in their Acknowledgement of Service a summary of their case for inviting the court to refuse permission on the "no difference" basis.

[154d] Senior Courts Act 1981 s.31(3F).

[154e] CPR Pt 54.11A.

[154f] "Response of the Senior Judiciary to the Ministry of Justice's Consultation entitled 'Judicial Review: Proposals for Further Reform'" (November 1, 2013) at [22].

16–049B *[Add new para 16–049B after 16–049A]*

Amendments to the Senior Courts Act 1981 (not yet in force) will also prevent the court from granting permission unless the claimant has provided the court with such information about the financing of the claim as is specified in rules of court.[154g]

[154g] Senior Courts Act 1981 s.31(3)(b) and (3A) inserted by the Criminal Justice and Courts Act 2015 s.85. For the information required, see n.268. Equivalent provisions will apply to the Upper Tribunal (Tribunals, Courts and Enforcement Act 2007 s.16(3) and (3A)).

The timing of the application for permission

16–053 *[In n.167 delete "CPR r.54.4" and substitute]*

CPR r.54.5(2)

16–054 *[Add to end of n.172]*

The views of the Compliance Committee have no direct legal consequences in domestic law (*R. (on the application of Evans) v Secretary of State for Communities and Local Government* [2013] EWCA Civ 114; [2013] J.P.L. 1027 at [37]–[38])

16–055 *[Add to end of n.174]*

In *R. (on the application of Nash) v Barnet LBC* [2013] EWCA Civ 1004; [2013] P.T.S.R. 1457 at [54]–[65], the CA distinguished *Burkett* and held that the crucial question was not when the decision was finally or irrevocably made, but when the relevant duty (in this case to consult) properly arose. The decisions in the present case were not provisional and each stage might have significant consequences.

[Add to end of n.177]

Uniplex was distinguished in *R. (on the application of Williams) v Secretary of State for Energy and Climate Change* [2015] EWHC 1202 (Admin) in which the court held it had no jurisdiction to hear a claim for judicial review of a development consent order where the claim had been issued one day after the expiry of the time limit in the Planning Act 2008 s.118: "The court has no discretion to vary a time limit of this kind. And the judgment of the Court of Justice of the European Union in *Uniplex* does not decide that it should" (at [59]).

[Add to end of n.178]   **16–056**

In *Mulvenna v Secretary of State for Communities and Local Government*
[2015] EWHC 3494 (Admin); [2016] J.P.L. 487 at [46]–[49], the HC refused
to extend time for judicial review where the claimants failed to challenge a
planning decision until judgment was given in a similar claim, at which point
they became aware that the Secretary of State had acted unlawfully. An
existing claim may be stayed pending a test case, but claimants "cannot
wait until others show that the way is clear". The HC also held that the time
limit did not deny the claimants, an Irish Traveller and a Roma Gypsy, an
effective remedy regarding their EU right not to be discriminated against
(at [52]–[56]) (appeal pending).

See paras 16–061A and 17–028, and Appendix HA, on the new Planning
Court.

[Add to n.189 after "330"]   **16–058**

(overruling *R. v Tavistock General Commissioners Ex p. Worth* [1985] S.T.C.
564 (see n.186) on different grounds).

[Add new para.16–061A after para.16–061]   **16–061A**

In claims for judicial review where the grounds arose after July 1, 2013: (1) a
claim for judicial review of a planning decision by the Secretary of State or the
local planning authority under the planning Acts (as defined) must be brought
within six weeks of the date when the application first arose; and (2) a claim for
judicial review of a decision to award a contract to which the Public Contracts
Regulations 2015 (SI 2015/102) apply must be brought within 30 days beginning with the date when the claimant first knew or ought to have known that
grounds for challenging the decision had arisen.[198a]

[198a] CPR r.54.5 (as amended by Public Contracts Regulations 2015/102
Sch.6(2) para.11(3))). Schedule 16 to the Criminal Justice and Courts Act
2015 makes a number of amendments to planning legislation concerning
permission to bring challenges and costs. R. Harwood, "The Planning Court
comes into being" [2014] J.P.L. 699. See Practice Direction 54E for timescales and designation in Planning Court claims.

Challenging the refusal of permission

[Add to para.16–063 after ". . . at a hearing.[202]"]   **16–063**

Where a claim is filed on or after July 2013 and the court refuses permission
to proceed and records the fact that the application is totally without merit
in accordance with CPR r.23.12, the claimant cannot request that the

decision be reconsidered at an oral hearing (CPR r.54.12(7)). In *R. (on the application of Wasif) v Secretary of State for the Home Department (Practice Note)* [2016] EWCA Civ 82; [2016] 1 W.L.R. 2793 at [13]–[21], the CA stated that an application is totally without merit where it is bound to fail in the sense that the judge can see no rational basis upon which it could succeed. In such cases, judges should feel no inhibition in so certifying. However, if the judge considers that the claimant has a rational argument, but the judge is confident that the argument is wrong, the proper course is simply to refuse permission. Where a judge does certify a claim as totally without merit, it is particularly important that the reasons for so doing are fully recorded.

[Delete all text in n.202 and substitute]

CPR r.54.12(3)–(5) and (7); *R. (on the application of MD (Afghanistan) v Secretary of State for the Home Department* [2012] EWCA Civ 194; [2012] 1 W.L.R. 2422 at [19]–[23]. The fee for a request for reconsideration is £350. On the meaning of "totally without merit" see J. Maurici, " 'Totally Without Merit' and Judicial Review" [2014] J.R. 258 and *R (Wasif) v Secretary of State for the Home Department* [2016] EWCA Civ 82; [2016] 1 W.L.R. 2793 at [17].

16–065 *[In n.207 delete "PD 52, para.4.13" and substitute]*

PD 52C, para.15(2)

[In n.209 delete "CPR r.52.15(3)" and substitute]

CPR r. 52.15(4)

Interlocutory Stage

16–067 *[Delete all text in n.213 and substitute]*

£770 (from July 2016), Civil Proceedings, First-tier Tribunal, Upper Tribunal and Employment Tribunals Fees (Amendment) Order 2016, Sch.1. If the claimant has already paid the fee of £385 for an oral hearing, the fee is a further £385.

Applications by interveners

16–068 *[In n. 216 delete " "If the applicant . . . grounds" "]*

[Add to end of n.216]

Section 87 of the Criminal Justice and Courts Act 2015 now provides that interveners may not seek their costs from the parties and should pay any costs caused by their intervention (see n.279).

Disclosure

[Add to end of para.16–069]   16–069

The court may order pre-action disclosure in judicial review proceedings pursuant to CPR r.31.16(3), although such applications will "rarely" be successful.[218a]

[218a] See *British Union for the Abolition of Vivisection (BUAV) v Secretary of State for the Home Department* [2014] EWHC 43 (Admin); [2014] A.C.D. 69 at [32]–[34], [54]–[67]. Applications for further information under CPR Pt 18 in judicial review cases were discouraged in *R. (on the application of Bredenkamp) v Secretary of State for Foreign and Commonwealth Affairs* [2013] EWHC 2480 (Admin) at [20].

[Add to end of n.219]   16–070

At the time of writing, the Lord Chief Justice is undertaking a consultation exercise into disclosure in judicial review (see n.95), and has suggested a procedure be adopted by which a party could apply for specific directions for disclosure. Such a procedure would apply only to the "small minority" of cases in which such directions are required.

[In n.220 delete final sentence and substitute]

Section 17 of the Justice and Security Act 2013 provides that the court may not exercise its *Norwich Pharmacal* jurisdiction in relation to "sensitive information", which is information: (a) held by an intelligence service; (b) obtained from, or held on behalf of, an intelligence service; (c) derived in whole or part from information obtained from, or held on behalf of, an intelligence service; (d) relating to an intelligence service; or (e) specified or described in a certificate issued by the Secretary of State in relation to the proceedings as information which the disclosing party should not be ordered to disclose. The Secretary of State may issue such a certificate if she considers that it would be contrary to the public interest to disclose: (i) the information; (ii) whether the information exists; or (iii) whether the disclosing party has the information. A disclosure is contrary to the public interest if it would cause damage to the interests of national security or to the interests of the international relations of the United Kingdom.

Preparation of skeleton arguments

16–073 *[Add to end of n.234]*

See also *Standard Bank v Via Mat International* [2013] EWCA Civ 490; [2013] 2 All E.R. (Comm) 1222 at [26]–[27] and in *Inplayer Limited v Thorogood* [2014] EWCA Civ 1511 at [52]–[57], where a successful appellant was refused costs for preparation of a skeleton argument which failed to comply with Practice Direction 52.

The full hearing

16–075 *[Delete current text of n.238 and substitute]*

In 2015, 4,679 applications were lodged: of these, 16 per cent were granted permission. Only 198 have reached a decision: Ministry of Justice, Civil Justice Statistics Quarterly, England and Wales (Incorporating The Royal Courts of Justice 2015) January to March 2016 (June 2, 2015).

16–077 *[Add to end of n.242]*

Cross-examination was refused, applying these principles, in *R. v Criminal Injuries Compensation Board Ex p. A* [1999] 2 A.C. 330; [1999] 2 W.L.R. 974, but permitted in *Jedwell v Denbighshire CC* [2015] EWCA Civ 1232 (to determine whether the reasons given for a decision were genuine or part of an attempt to justify the decision retrospectively). In *R. (on the application of Bourgass) v Secretary of State for Justice* [2015] UKSC 54; [2016] A.C. 384 at [126], Lord Reed emphasised the flexibility of the judicial review procedure to resolve disputed questions of fact and to allow cross-examination where appropriate. In *R. (on the application of Radha Naran Patel) v Secretary of State for the Home Department* [2015] EWCA Civ 645 at [64], Underhill LJ strongly encouraged the parties to give careful consideration to whether a case started under CPR Part 54 which "throws up substantial issues of primary fact" should be resolved on the papers or whether it requires oral evidence to be given.

16–078 *[Add to end of n.243]*

See further *HCA International Ltd v Competition and Markets Authority* [2014] CAT 10; [2015] Comp. A.R. 9 at [2]–[4] (in relation to expert evidence); and J. Tomlinson, "Adducing Fresh Expert Evidence in Section 179 Review Proceedings in the CAT" [2014] J.R. 253. See *HK (Bulgaria) v Secretary of State for the Home Department* [2016] EWHC 857 (Admin); [2016] A.C.D. 86 at [13]–[18], n.92 above.

[Add to end of n.244]

Ermakov was followed and treated as an important statement of principle by the CA in *R. (on the application of Lanner Parish Council) v Cornwall Council* [2013] EWCA Civ 1290; [2013] 45 E.G. 75 (C.S.) at [59]–[66].

Appeals after the full hearing

Appeals in civil judicial review claims

[In para. 16–082 delete from "For this to happen" to "previous proceedings" and substitute"]   **16–082**

The Criminal Justice and Courts Act 2015 has expanded the circumstances in which an appeal may "leapfrog" to the SC (Supreme Court) by removing the requirement that all parties should consent to it (s.63(2)(b)) and setting out alternative conditions. These are that there is a point of law of general public importance which either relates to a fully-argued matter of statutory construction or is one in respect of which the judge is bound by a decision of the Court of Appeal, the House of Lords or the SC or that there is a point of law of general public importance and: either the proceedings relate to a matter of national importance; or the proceedings are so significant that the judge considers a hearing by the SC is justified; or the judge considers that the benefit of the matter being considered by the SC outweighs those of it being heard by the Court of Appeal.

[In n.252 delete the second sentence and substitute]

In 2015, there were 240 appeals from the Admin Ct to the CA (Ministry of Justice, "Civil Justice Statistics Quarterly, England and Wales (Incorporating The Royal Courts of Justice 2015) January to March 2016" (June 2, 2015).)

[In n.253 add after "s.12(3)"]

and (3A)

[Add to end of n.253]

Section 64 of the Criminal Justice and Courts Act 2015 (in force from August 8, 2016) permits appeals to "leapfrog" to the SC from the Upper Tribunal in similar circumstances.

Funding judicial review

16–083 *[In n.254 delete "CPR r.44.3(2)" and substitute]*

CPR r.44.2(2)

[Delete all text in n.256 and substitute]

As of July 25, 2016, the application fee for permission to apply for judicial review is £154. There is a fee of £385 for a request for oral renewal of an application for permission. For judicial review after permission is granted, the fee is £770, or £385 if permission was granted after oral renewal of the application (Civil Proceedings Fees Order 2008/1053 (as amended)).

[In n.257 delete "Multiplying these figures by 1.3 would provide the 2013 values" and substitute]

Multiplying these figures by 1.4 would provide the 2016 values.

16–084 *[Delete all text in para.16–084, but retain all footnotes, and substitute]*

For most claimants, this expense is prohibitive and judicial review litigation cannot be pursued without some form of public funding. The provision of public funding for judicial review has undergone profound change. The old system was based on the Community Legal Service (CLS) Fund administered by the Legal Services Commission (LSC).[258] Since April 1, 2013, the new system has operated under the Legal Aid, Sentencing and Punishment of Offenders Act 2012.[259]

The functions previously discharged by the LSC are now within the remit of the Lord Chancellor, and individual decisions to award legal aid are taken by the Director of Legal Aid Casework as part of the Legal Aid Agency (an executive agency of the Ministry of Justice).[260] Civil legal aid is available for legal services which fall within Pt 1 of Sch.1 to the 2012 Act and where the Director has determined that the individual qualifies for the relevant services: s.9 of the 2012 Act.

Schedule 1 includes "judicial review of an enactment, decision, act or omission", habeas corpus, deliberate or dishonest abuse by a public authority of its position or powers which results in reasonably foreseeable harm to a person or property and a significant breach of Convention rights.[261] However, this is subject to the specific exclusion of services provided to an individual which do not have the potential to produce a benefit for the individual, a member of his family or the environment.[262] The requirement of benefit has the obvious potential to reduce the availability of legal aid for public interest challenges. It is also questionable whether a claimant whose only remedy would be a declaration of incompatibility under the HRA is likely to qualify. If a claimant falls outside of these provisions, he must rely on the Director's discretion to make an exceptional case determination where the legal services are necessary to avoid a breach of the individual's Convention rights or enforceable EU law rights.[263]

Section 11 of the 2012 Act provides that the Director's determination that an individual qualifies for the legal services described above is governed by (a) the financial resources of the individual and (b) criteria set out by the Lord Chancellor in regulations to reflect: the likely cost of providing the services and the benefit which may be thus obtained; the availability of resources; the appropriateness of applying those resources, having regard to present and likely future demands; the importance of the matter for the individual; the nature and seriousness of the act, omission, circumstances or other matter in question; other means of resolving the dispute; the individual's prospects of success; the conduct of the individual; and the public interest.[264] Regulations now provide for appeals to an adjudicator against the Director's Determinations.[265]

[Add to end of n.259]

The Public Law Project has produced a useful guide, *How to Apply for Legal Aid Funding for Judicial Review* (Short Guide 05, 2016).

[Add to end of n.263]

In *Gudanaviciene v Director of Legal Aid* [2014] EWCA Civ 1622; [2015] 1 W.L.R. 2247, the court overturned a number of decisions of the Director in cases involving art.8 of the ECHR on the basis that they were too restrictive. The Lord Chancellor's guidance on exceptional funding was held to be incompatible with the requirements of art.6 ECHR and art.47 of the EU Charter of Fundamental Rights because it sent a signal that refusal of legal aid would breach these provisions only in rare and extreme cases (at [45] and [59]). Appeal to SC outstanding. Amended guidance can be found at https://www.gov.uk/government/publications/legal-aid-exceptional-case-funding-form-and-guidance. Further resources relating to exceptional funding are available at http://www.publiclawproject.org.uk/exceptional-funding-project. The CA in *IS v Director of Legal Aid Casework* [2016] EWCA Civ 464; [2016] 3 Costs L.R. 569 overturned declarations made by the HC in *IS v Director of Legal Aid Casework* [2015] EWHC 1965 (Admin); [2015] 1 W.L.R. 5283. The HC had found that the Defendants' guidance on Exceptional Case Funding was too restrictive and too unclear (especially in light of those to whom they were addressed) to be compatible with ECHR arts 6 and 8 and required substantial change. While acknowledging the "many difficulties" with the regime, the CA found that it fell within the range of lawful choices in the administration of the Legal Aid, Sentencing and Punishment of Offenders Act 2012. See also H. Mountfield QC, "Judicial

Review and Human Rights: Challenges to Court Fees and Legal Aid Changes which Limit or Effectively Exclude Right of Access to Court" [2014] J.R. 217.

[Delete all text in n.264 and substitute]

The criteria reflecting the above factors are contained in the Civil Legal Aid (Merits Criteria) Regulations 2013/104 as amended. The "general merits criteria", set out in regulation 39, are that the applicant does not have access to other potential sources of funding other than a conditional fee agreement; the case is unsuitable for a CFA; there is no person other than the individual who can reasonably be expected to bring the proceedings; all reasonable alternatives have been exhausted (including any complaints system, ombudsman scheme or other form of ADR); there is a need for representation in all the circumstances of the case (including the nature and complexity of the issues; the existence of other proceedings; and the interests of other parties to the proceedings); and the proceedings are not likely to be allocated to the small claims track.

In addition, Regulations 53–56 make special provision for public law cases. Regulation 53 (standard criteria for determinations for legal representation) requires that Regulation 39 is met; that the relevant act, omission or other matter is susceptible to challenge; and that no alternative proceedings before a court or tribunal are available (unless they are considered to be ineffective). Regulations 54 and 55 relate to investigative representation. Regulation 56 (criteria for determinations for full representation) provides that as well as satisfying the general criteria in Regulation 39, and the standard criteria in Regulation 53, the proportionality test set out in Regulation 8 must be met (the likely benefits of the proceedings to the individual and others must justify the likely costs, having regard to the prospects of success and all the other circumstances of the case) and the prospects of success are above 50 per cent, or, if they are either above 45 per cent ("marginal") or "unclear", only if the case is of significant wider public interest; one with overwhelming importance to the individual; or if the substance of the case relates to a breach of Convention rights. The attempt to introduce a residence test for legal aid by delegated legislation was found to be unlawful in R. *(on the application of the Public Law Project) v Secretary of State for Justice* [2016] UKSC 39; [2016] 3 W.L.R. 387.

The Civil Legal Aid (Remuneration) Regulations 2013 govern remuneration. Amendments to the provisions relating to judicial review were made by the Civil Legal Aid (Remuneration) (Amendment) (No. 3) Regulations 2014, restricting payment for work conducted to cases in which permission was granted. This was successfully challenged in R. *(on the application of Ben Hoare Bell and Others) v the Lord Chancellor* [2015] EWHC 523 (Admin), following which the 2014 Amendment Regulations were quashed.

The current position under regulation 2 of the Civil Legal Aid (Remuneration) (Amendment) Regulations 2015, in force from March 27, 2015, inserting new regulation 5A into the 2013 Regulations, is as follows. Public funding for work conducted is available in five situations where: (i) the court gives permission to bring judicial review proceedings; (ii) the court neither gives nor refuses permission and the Legal Aid Agency considers payment is reasonable in the circumstances; (iii) the defendant withdraws the decision to which the application for judicial review relates and the withdrawal results in the court (a) refusing permission to bring judicial review proceedings, or (b) neither refusing nor giving permission; (iv) the court orders an oral hearing to consider whether to give permission to bring judicial review proceedings; or (v) the court orders a rolled-up hearing. For a useful summary of the legislative changes in this area see *R. (on the application of Ben Hoare Bell and Others)* at [8]–[16], above.

[Delete all text in n.265 and substitute]

Civil Legal Aid (Procedure) Regulations (2012/3098) regs 28, 45–48, 53, 59.

Costs

[In n.267 add after "(96/61/EC)"   16–085

The EIA Directive is now consolidated in Directive 2011/92/EU and has been subsequently amended by Directive 2014/52/EU. The IPPC Directive, consolidated as Directive 2008/1/EC, has now been recast as the Industrial Emissions Directive 2010/75/EU.

[Add to n.267 before "The Civil Procedure Rules . . ."]

The SC considered the CJEU's response and decided that the following factors were relevant to the ultimate level of recovery by the defendant: (i) whether the claim had a reasonable prospect of success; (ii) the importance of what is at stake for the claimant; (iii) the importance of what is at stake for the protection of the environment; (iv) the complexity of the relevant law and procedure (in that greater complexity is likely to require higher expenditure by the defendants); and the potentially frivolous nature of the claim at its various stages: *R. (on the application of Edwards) v Environment Agency (No.2)* [2013] UKSC 78; [2014] 1 W.L.R. 55 at [28].

[Add to end of n.267]

In *Venn v Secretary of State for Communities and Local Government* [2014] EWCA Civ 1539; [2015] 1 W.L.R. 2328 at [34], Sullivan LJ stated: "it is now clear that the costs protection regime introduced by CPR r.45.41 is not Aarhus-compliant in so far as it is confined to applications for judicial review, and excludes statutory appeals and applications. A costs regime . . . under which costs protection depends not on the nature of the environmental decision or the legal principles on which it may be challenged, but on the identity of the decision-taker, is systemically flawed in terms of Aarhus compliance". In *R. (HS2 AA Ltd) v Transport Secretary (Nos 1&2)* [2014] EWCA Civ 1578 and [2015] EWCA Civ 203; [2015] P.T.S.R. 1025 at [12], the CA held that once it had been determined that a claim for judicial review was an "Aarhus Convention claim", costs liability was dealt with in CPR r.45.43 and Practice Direction 45, no further reference to the Aarhus Convention being necessary.

16–086 *[Delete final sentence of para.16–086 and substitute]*

Since April 2013, the success fee under such an agreement is no longer recoverable from the losing party.

[In n.268 delete "CPR r.44.3" and substitute]

CPR r.44.2

[Add to end of n.268]

The Criminal Justice and Courts Act 2015 ss. 85 and 86 (not in force at the time of writing) will require an applicant to provide information as to the source, nature and extent of the financial resources available. Section 85 amends s.31(3) of the Senior Courts Act 1981 and s.16(3) of the Tribunals, Courts and Enforcement Act 2007, both of which deal with the grant of permission. By s.86, when the High Court, the Upper Tribunal or the Court of Appeal is determining by whom and to what extent costs of or incidental to judicial review proceedings are to be paid, it must have regard to the information required by s.85. The Government's stated purpose in legislating is to obtain greater transparency about how judicial reviews are funded and to limit the potential for third-party funders to avoid their appropriate liability for litigation costs. These concerns were partly based on the judicial review surrounding the burial of the remains of Richard III in which the Government incurred £90,000 of costs in successfully defending proceedings in which the claimant had the benefit of a protective costs order (*R. (on the application of the Plantagenet Alliance) v Secretary of State for Justice* [2014] EWHC 1662 (Admin)). A consultation as to the implementation of these provisions was undertaken in 2015. At the time of writing, the Government is seeking further views on one aspect of the proposals: the provision to other parties of financial information provided under s.85 (see Ministry of Justice Command Paper 9303, "Reform of Judicial Review: Proposals for the provision and use of financial information"). Following the main consultation, the Government remains committed to implementing the planned reforms, with some amendments to the information certain claimant corporate bodies must provide, the suggested threshold amount and the court's ability to make a costs capping order in the absence of full financial information. On the limits to the court's discretion to pay the costs of legal representation, see *K (Children) (Unrepresented Father: Cross-Examination of Child), Re* [2015] EWCA Civ 543; [2015] 1 W.L.R. 3801, in which it was held that the Family Court had no power, outside the legal aid scheme established by the Legal Aid, Sentencing and Punishment of Offenders Act 2012, to order that the court service pay the costs of legal representation for a father for the cross-examination of a child (declining to follow *Q v Q* [2014] EWFC 31; [2015] 1 W.L.R. 2040). There were other means available to avoid a breach of ECHR arts 6 or 8. However, at [62] it was held that this might not always be the case and that consideration should be given to legislating for the payment from central funds for legal representation to conduct such cross-examination.

[In n.269 delete "CPR r.44.3(1)" and substitute]

CPR r.44.2(2)

[Add to end of n.270]

In *R. (on the application of Sino) v Secretary of State for the Home Department* [2016] EWHC 803 (Admin), Hayden J took account of the fact that lawyers taking on publicly-funded work may not be able to recover remuneration at inter partes rates where the claim is successful and this gave rise to a real risk that such practices would become unsustainable which would pose a threat to access to justice.

[In n.273 delete "CPR r.44.3(5)" and substitute]

CPR r.44.2(5)

[Add to end of n.275]

See also CPR r.46.2 and, for a survey of the authorities, *Weatherford Global Products Ltd v Hydropath Holdings Ltd* [2014] EWHC 3243 (TCC) at [4]–[12] and *Deutsche Bank AG v Sebastian Holdings Inc* [2016] EWCA Civ 23; [2016] 4 W.L.R. 17 at [41]–[21] and [62].

[In n.279 delete "s.44" and substitute]

ss. 44 and 46

[Add to end of n.279]

By s.87 of the Criminal Justice and Courts Act 2015, a party to judicial review proceedings may not be required to pay an intervener's costs unless there are exceptional circumstances (so far undefined). The court must order an intervener to pay a party's costs if they have been incurred as a result of the intervener's involvement in the proceedings, and one of four further conditions is made out (s.87(5)). The conditions are (s.87(6)): (a) the intervener has acted, in substance, as the sole or principal applicant, defendant, appellant or respondent; (b) the intervener's evidence and representations, taken as a whole, have not been of significant assistance to the court; (c) a significant part of the intervener's evidence and representations relates to matters that it is not necessary for the court to consider in order to resolve the issues that are the subject of the stage in the proceedings; or (d) the intervener has behaved unreasonably. (in both cases unless there are exceptional circumstances that make it inappropriate to do so).

Protective costs orders in public interest cases

16–087 *[In para. 16–087 delete from "A protective costs order (PCO)" to "have developed this mechanism" but retain all footnotes and substitute]*

A costs capping order[280] fixes in advance the maximum sum in costs that may be awarded to a party, or determines that whatever the outcome of the claim there should be no order as to costs (with the consequence that the claimant bears only its own costs).[281] The court's power to make such an order has now been placed on an exclusive statutory footing by the s.88 of the Criminal Justice and Courts Act 2015 (see further para.16–090A). Claims for judicial review where the claim form was filed in the High Court before August 8, 2016 continue to be governed by the protective costs orders ("PCO") mechanism developed by the courts.

16–089 *[Add to end of n.289]*

See further *R. (on the application of Litvinenko) v Secretary of State for the Home Department* [2013] EWHC 3135 (Admin); [2014] A.C.D. 25 at [18]–[26]. Note that the Divisional Court in *Litvinenko* appeared to consider that the *Corner House* principles only apply to "exceptional cases" (at [32]). As the Administrative Court observed in *R. (on the application of the Plantagenet Alliance) v Secretary of State for Justice* [2013] EWHC 3164 (Admin); [2014] A.C.D. 26 at [28], any "exceptionality" requirement would be contrary to the approach in the CA in *Buglife* and *Morgan*. In *Begg v HM Treasury* [2016] EWCA Civ 568 at [19]–[21], the CA accepted that PCOs were not limited to public interest litigation and could be made in terrorism cases where the use of the closed material procedure made it impossible for the accused to determine the merits of the claim.

[Add to end of n.290]

The Criminal Justice and Courts Act 2015 s.89(1)(d) requires the court to have regard to whether the applicant's legal representatives are acting free of charge.

[In n.291 delete "CPO" and substitute]

PCO

[Add to end of n.291]

The Criminal Justice and Courts Act 2015 s.88(6) reintroduces this requirement, see para.16–090A.

[Delete all text in n.296 and substitute]   16–090

See para.16–090A.

[Add new para.16–090A after 16–090]   16–090A

The Government has legislated to place PCOs on an exclusive statutory footing in s.88 of the Criminal Justice and Courts Act 2015 (in force from August 8, 2016). They are now called "costs capping orders" and are only available if permission to apply for judicial review has been granted (s.88(3)). This is a major change which is likely drastically to limit the usefulness of such orders since defendants often incur very substantial costs before permission is granted and claimants would be exposed to these costs in full. The list of factors relevant to the grant of a costs capping order which are set out in the Act substantially reflect the current law, but the statutory test is stricter than the common law in requiring that the applicant for the order would withdraw their application for judicial review or cease to participate in the proceedings if the order were not made (and it would be reasonable for them to do so) (s.88(6)). The Act also requires that in order to qualify as public interest proceedings, they are an appropriate means of resolving the issue of general public importance (s.88(7)). The Lord Chancellor is empowered by s.90 to make regulations excluding environmental cases from the statutory rules.

Costs before and at the permission stage

[Add to end of n.303]   16–092

In *R. (on the application of Smoke Club Ltd) v Network Rail Infrastructure Ltd* [2013] EWHC 3830 (Admin); [2014] 2 Costs L.O. 123, the Administrative Court declined to follow the usual rules on costs after discontinuance in CPR r.38.6(1) on the basis that special considerations apply to judicial review cases. The court awarded the defendant a proportion of their costs after the

Acknowledgement of Service to reflect the fact that the claimant had renewed a hopeless claim and produced fresh evidence which put the defendant to additional expense before the claim was withdrawn.

[Add to end of n.304]

The Government proposes to invite the Civil Procedure Rule Committee to introduce a principle that the defendant's costs of attending an oral permission hearing should usually be recoverable from the claimant (see para.1–005A).

Costs when a claim is discontinued after permission

16–095 *[In n.310 before the final sentence add]*

R. (on the application of M) was applied in *R. (on the application of E) v Croydon LBC* [2015] EWHC 2016 (Admin) (a compromise agreement was reached at the substantive hearing; the LBC was ordered to pay half the claimant's costs, taking into account that the claimant had a "very strong moral claim but a much less strong legal claim") and in *R. (on the application of Baxter) v Lincolnshire County Council* [2015] EWCA Civ 1290; [2016] 1 Costs L.O. 37 at [40]–[45] (a claimant failed to establish a clear enough link between the relief sought in the claim and the consent order to be treated as the successful party for the purpose of costs, the claim falling within the third type of case identified by Lord Neuberger MR in *M* at [7], i.e. "a case where there has been some compromise which does not actually reflect the claimant's claims"). *R. (on the application of Bahta)* and *R. (on the application of M)* were distinguished in *R. (on the application of Abraha) v Secretary of State for the Home Department (Costs)* [2014] EWHC 3372 (Admin) (judicial review of allegedly unlawful detention in which the claimant was released on the day of his substantive hearing; costs were refused on the basis that there had been no trial or similar substantive determination by a court of law, nor a consent order or settlement). In *R. (on the application of Tesfay) v Secretary of State for the Home Department* [2016] EWCA Civ 415 at [56]–[64] (a case regarding the Secretary of State's withdrawal of human rights certification decisions and settlement of related claims), the CA held that the judge below should have approached the matter by asking two questions: (a) whether the effect of the settlement was that the appellants should be regarded as having succeeded so that they should normally receive their costs; and (b) if so, whether there was a good reason for making a different order. It was appropriate to consider why the Secretary of State withdrew the decisions.

[Add to end of n.311]

See further *R. (on the application of E) v Croydon LBC* [2015] EWHC 2016 (Admin) (n.310). There is new Guidance for judicial review cases in which the parties have agreed to settle the claim but are unable to agree liability for costs and have submitted that issue for determination by the court: https://www.justice.gov.uk/downloads/courts/administrative-court/aco-costs-guidance-dec-13.pdf.

[Add to end of n.314]   **16–096**

See also *R. (on the application of Henderson) v Secretary of State for Justice* [2015] EWHC 130 (Admin); [2015] 1 Cr. App. R. 29 at [35]–[38].

CHAPTER 17

OTHER JUDICIAL REVIEW PROCEEDINGS

SCOPE

[In para.17–001 delete second bullet point, retaining footnote, and **17–001**
substitute]

Applications for the writ of habeas corpus for release under CPR Pt. 87;

[In n.2 delete "4ᵗʰ edn . . . applications)." and substitute]

5ᵗʰ edn (2014), Ch.13 (habeas corpus) (although published prior to the introduction of CPR Pt. 87) and Ch.14 (appeals and statutory applications).

[Add to end of n.3]

CPR Pt. 87 replaces RSC, Ord. 54, part of the old Rules of the Supreme
Court which had been preserved in Sch.1 to the CPR (revoked by the Civil
Procedure (Amendment No. 8) Rules 2014/3299). Although the term
"habeas corpus" is retained, its three forms are renamed "for release", "to
give evidence", and "to answer a charge" (formerly *ad subjiciendum, ad
testificandum* and *ad respondendum* respectively). Applications for habeas
corpus heard since the introduction of Pt. 87 include *Tague v Governor of
HM Prison Full Sutton and National Crime Agency* [2015] EWHC 3576
(Admin); [2016] 1 Cr. App. R. 15, *Harkins v United States* [2015] EWHC
2336 (Admin) and *R. (on the application of Freeman) v Director of Thameside
Prison* [2015] EWHC 1569 (Admin).

JUDICIAL REVIEW AND TRIBUNALS

[In n.14 delete "In 2011 . . . Table 7.12)" and substitute]   **17–004**

In 2012, 85 per cent of applications for permission to apply for judicial
review concerned immigration or asylum matters: over 10,000 applications
were received, 31 per cent of which were found to be totally without merit
(Ministry of Justice, *Court Statistics Quarterly July to September 2013*,
pp.29–34). In November 2013, the Upper Tribunal (Immigration and

Asylum Chamber) took responsibility for the majority of civil asylum and immigration judicial reviews, reducing the number of total applications received by the Administrative Court considerably: see 16–048 and n.147 thereto. R. Thomas, "Mapping Immigration Judicial Review Litigation: An Empirical Legal Analysis" [2015] P.L. 652.

[In n.14 delete "(2010)" and substitute]

9th edn (2014)

17–005 *[Add to end of n.16]*

The list of "excluded decisions" has also been expanded by s.48(4), Sch 2, para. 5 of the Crime and Security Act 2010, and s.116 of the Tax Collection and Management (Wales) Act 2016 (not yet in force).

[Add to end of n.17]

The Upper Tribunal cannot review its own decision to refuse permission to appeal and the only remedy in such cases is for the party aggrieved to seek judicial review of the Upper Tribunal's refusal (*Samuda v Secretary of State for Work and Pensions* [2014] EWCA Civ 1; [2014] 3 All E.R. 201 at [13]). Section 64 of the Criminal Justice and Courts Act 2015 (in force from August 8, 2016) inserts new ss.14A–14C into the Tribunals, Courts and Enforcement Act 2007, with the effect of allowing leapfrog appeals to the SC to be initiated in the Upper Tribunal under the same conditions as appeals from the High Court. See the Explanatory Note to the Criminal Justice and Courts Act 2015, paras 520–524.

Judicial review in the Upper Tribunal

17–006 *[Add to end of n.18]*

On appeal from decisions of the Upper Tribunal in cases involving judicial review of First-tier Tribunal decisions, the appellate court should exercise restraint and permit flexibility to the Upper Tribunal to develop guidance on the specialised area of law concerned in order to promote consistency (*R. (on the application of Jones) v First-tier Tribunal* [2013] UKSC 19; [2013] 2 A.C. 48 at [26], [41]–[43], followed in *Criminal Injuries Compensation Authority v First-tier Tribunal (Social Entitlement Chamber)* [2014] EWCA Civ 1554; [2015] Q.B. 459. See also the comments of Lord Carnwath in *Pendragon Plc v Revenue and Customs Commissioners* [2015] UKSC 37; [2015] 1 W.L.R. 2838 at [44]–[51], a case in which the First-tier Tribunal had failed to ask itself the critical question (which was whether certain of the steps in a series of transactions had any purpose save to produce a tax advantage) and hence had made an error of law which should be corrected on appeal.

[In n.19 delete final sentence and substitute]

Where permission to bring judicial review proceedings has been refused by the Upper Tribunal and permission to appeal has been refused by the Upper Tribunal, an application for permission to appeal may be made to the Court of Appeal. The appellant's notice must be filed within 28 days of the date on which notice of the Upper Tribunal's decision on permission to appeal is sent to the appellant: CPR r.52.15A, added by Civil Procedure (Amendment No.6) Rules 2014 (SI 2014/2044) with effect from October 1, 2014, and Practice Direction 52D para.3.3. In considering out of time applications for reconsideration of a refusal of permission to seek judicial review by the Upper Tribunal, the court should adopt the approach in relief from sanctions cases and consider: (i) the seriousness and significance of the failure; (ii) why the default occurred; and (iii) all the circumstances of the case (*R. (on the application of Kigen) v Secretary of State for the Home Department (Practice Note)* [2015] EWCA Civ 1286; [2016] 1 W.L.R.723 at [20]). The Upper Tribunal has produced its own Judicial Review standard forms for statements of case (and guidance on them), which are available at *http://www. justice.gov.uk/tribunals/immigration-asylum-upper/application-for-judicial-review*. The Upper Tribunal has also produced guideline judgments on, for example, how it will deal with immigration judicial reviews where the Secretary of State has failed to submit an Acknowledgement of Service within the time limit required by the Tribunal Procedure (Upper Tribunal) Rules 2008 (*R. (on the application of Kumar) v Secretary of State for the Home Department* [2014] UKUT 00104). See the additional guideline judgments on the claimant's continuing duty to re-assess the claim in light of developments (*R. (on the application of Mahmood) v Secretary of State for the Home Department* [2014] UKUT 00439 (IAC); [2015] Imm. A.R. 193), on the generally unjustifiable incorporation of a claim for costs in an Acknowledgment of Service which contains a concession (*Muwonge v Secretary of State for the Home Department* [2014] UKUT 514 (IAC); [2015] Imm. A.R. 341), and on appealing costs orders of the Upper Tribunal made in immigration judicial review proceedings (*R. (on the application of Soreefan and others) v Secretary of State for the Home Department* [2015] UKUT 594 (IAC)).

[Delete all text in n.20 and substitute]

In outline, they are: the application does not seek relief beyond the ordinary judicial review remedies; does not question anything done by the Crown Court; and falls within a class specified by the Lord Chief Justice. Section 31A of the Senior Courts Act 1981 provides for mandatory transfer if all three conditions are met. The Lord Chief Justice has so far identified the following such classes of case: decisions of the First-tier Tribunal on an appeal under the Criminal Injuries Compensation Scheme; where the First-tier Tribunal has declined to review one of its decisions and there is no right of appeal (Practice Direction (Upper Tribunal: Judicial Review Jurisdiction) [2009] 1 W.L.R. 327); and, as of 1 November 2013, any decision made under the Immigration Acts or otherwise relating to leave to enter or remain in the UK outside the immigration rules and a decision of the Immigration and Asylum Chamber of the First-tier Tribunal from which no appeal lies to the Upper Tribunal (except where the application includes: a challenge to the validity of primary or subordinate legislation; a challenge to the lawfulness of detention; a challenge to a decision on citizenship; a challenge to a decision of the Upper Tribunal; an application for a declaration of incompatibility under the HRA (and certain other matters specified in the Direction)) (Direction given in accordance with Pt 1 of Sch.2 to the Constitutional Reform Act 2005 and s.18 of the Tribunals, Courts and Enforcement Act 2007, August 21, 2013). In *Ashraf v Secretary of State for the Home Department* [2013] EWHC 4028 (Admin) at [2], the court indicated that it may well be treated as an abuse of process to issue judicial review proceedings challenging removal in the Administrative Court on the basis of an unmeritorious claim of unlawful detention.

[In n.21 delete internet address and substitute]

http://judiciary.gov.uk/publications

HABEAS CORPUS

17–007 *[In para.17–007 delete "It is therefore surprising . . . CPR" and note 27, and substitute]*

Until the recent introduction of new Pt. 87 into the CPR in April 2015, the procedure for obtaining habeas corpus had been left to languish in the backwater of Sch.1 to the CPR.

[Add to end of n.24]

There was a violation of art.5(4) in a case where the detained individual lacked capacity to instruct a lawyer to seek a remedy and where her nearest relative was barred from doing so (*MH v UK* (2014) 58 E.H.R.R. 35).

[In n.25 delete "2008" and substitute]

2011

[Add to end of n.34] 17–008

See also *K v Kingswood Centre Hospital Manager* [2014] EWCA Civ 1332; [2015] P.T.S.R. 287.

[In n.35 delete "RSC Ord.54 r.11" and substitute] 17–009

SCA 1981, Sch.1, para.3

[Add to end of n.37]

This outcome is unaffected by the decision of the ECtHR in *James, Lee and Wells v UK* (2013) 56 E.H.R.R. 12. In *Thomas v Secretary of State for Justice* (unreported, August 8, 2016), the CA upheld the HC's refusal of an application for habeas corpus by an individual detained and refused bail pending his trial, holding that the magistrates' decision to detain should be challenged by way of judicial review.

[Add new sentence to end of para.17–010] 17–010

However, although habeas corpus still forms no part of CPR Pt. 54, it has now been incorporated into the CPR proper. CPR Pt. 87 was inserted by the Civil Procedure (Amendment No. 8) Rules 2014 (SI 2014/3299), in force April 6, 2015, replacing RSC Ord. 54, as "part of the ongoing work of the CPR Committee to transfer the remaining Rules of the Supreme Court into the CPR."[42a]

[42a] Explanatory Memorandum to the Civil Procedure (Amendment No.8) Rules 2014/3299 (L. 36)). The associated Practice Direction – RSC 54 (Application for Writ of Habeas Corpus) was not replicated; there is presently no Practice Direction supplementing CPR Pt 87. Since, according to CPR Update 78 (April 25, 2015, accessible at: https://www.justice.gov.uk/courts/procedure-rules/civil), the intention in modifying the rules was "to update the language and to reflect the process in the Administrative Court which deals with such applications"; it is suggested that the existing authorities will still apply in the context of the new rules.

Procedure: RSC, Ord.54

[Delete all text in para.17–015, including heading and footnotes and substitute] 17–015

Procedure: CPR Pt. 87

Applications for habeas corpus for release are made under CPR Pt. 87. This is quite separate from the procedure for claims for judicial review made under CPR Pt. 54, although, where no claim for judicial review is made, the High Court judge considering the application for habeas corpus may order it to continue as an application for permission to apply for judicial review.[63] In principle, claimants may commence both forms of proceedings simultaneously though there will normally be no practical need to do so and this should be avoided if it will increase costs unnecessarily. Where a CPR Pt. 54 claim and an application for habeas corpus are commenced, "every effort should be made to harmonise the proceedings".[64] In practice this means that the same affidavit and witness statement should be used for both proceedings, both cases should come before a court for interlocutory and full hearings, and in the event of an appeal, the same notice of appeal should suffice. Applications for habeas corpus involve a two-stage procedure: an application which may be made without notice to the other party (formerly called "ex parte"); and a hearing on notice.

[63] CPR r. 87.4(1)(d) (where the application is considered under r.87.2 on paper) and r.87.5(d) (where the application is considered at a hearing).

[64] *R. v BHB Community Healthcare NHS Trust Ex p. B* [1999] 1 F.L.R. 106 at 117 (Lord Woolf M.R.).

Applications without notice

17–016 *[Delete all text in para.17–016, including footnotes, and substitute]*

Applications must be made by filing a Pt. 8 claim form in the Administrative Court, supported by a witness statement or affidavit.[65] The witness statement or affidavit must: state that the application is made "at the instance of the person being detained"; must set out the nature of the detention; and must be made by the detained person. If the detained person is unable to make the witness statement or affidavit, it may be made by another on his or her behalf, stating the reasons why the detainee is unable to do so.[66] The application may be made without notice.[67] If the case is urgent, the judge may dispense with the requirement that a claim form be filed and must give directions for the conduct of the application.[68] Applications for habeas corpus have priority over all other court business.

A single judge of the High Court may give initial consideration to an application on paper. Where this is not done, initial consideration must be by a judge sitting in court, or otherwise than in court.[68a] Where consideration is given on the papers, the judge has power to make an order for the issue of the writ; to adjourn the application to a hearing (in which case two days' notice must be given to both parties); to direct that the application be considered by a Divisional Court of the Queen's Bench Division; to direct that the application continues as an application for judicial review; to give other directions; or to dismiss the application.[68b] Where the application is dismissed on the papers, the applicant may request the decision to be reconsidered at a hearing; this must be filed within seven days after service of the order.[68c] Modern practice to date has almost invariably dictated an adjournment, except perhaps in cases where there is no possible defence to the application.

[65] CPR r.87.2(1). Forms 87 (Claim form for writ of *habeas corpus ad subjiciendum*), 88 and 90 have now been deleted. Applications made on behalf of a minor must be made to the Family Court; see n.35 above and the High Court (Distribution of Business) Order 2014 (SI 2014/3257).

[66] CPR r.87.2(2)–(3). On third party applications see also *Justice for Families Ltd v Secretary of State for Justice* [2014] EWCA Civ 1477; [2015] 2 F.L.R. 321 at [19]–[23].

[67] CPR r.87.2(5).

[68] CPR r.87.2(6).

[68a] CPR r.87.3. Any application made on behalf of a protected party must initially be considered by a judge otherwise than in court: CPR r.87.7.

[68b] CPR r.87.4(1).

[68c] CPR r.87.4(2)–(3). There is no statement that the applicant may not appeal this decision; nor that where applications dismissed on the papers are certified as "totally without merit" pursuant to CPR r.23.12, reconsideration is unavailable, as appear in the comparable provisions relating to judicial review, CPR r.54.12.

On notice hearing

[Delete all text in para.17–018 and footnotes and substitute]   **17–018**

Where the application is considered at a hearing (including where, following initial consideration on the papers, the application is adjourned to a hearing or where a reconsideration hearing is requested following the dismissal of the application on the papers), the judge has the same powers as are available at the paper stage with the additional power to "order that the detained person be released". This is sufficient authorisation for the detainee's release.[71] At the hearing, oral argument takes place, although disputed questions of fact are normally dealt with on the basis of witness statements or affidavits upon which deponents are only exceptionally subject to cross-examination.[72] Occasionally, as a formality, the court will order the writ to issue – somewhat incongruously after the release of the claimant. CPR rr.87.8—87.11 apply where the court makes an order for the issue of a writ.

[71] CPR rr.87.5; 87.6.

[72] R. v Secretary of State for the Home Department ex p. Khawaja [1984] A.C.74, 124–125.

APPLICATIONS TO QUASH CERTAIN ORDERS, ETC.

17–022 *[Correction to n.84]*

Delete "Clean Neighbourhoods . . . gating orders");".

Procedure

17–025 *[Add to end of n.89]*

See further R. *(on the application of Blue Green London Plan) v Secretary of State for the Environment, Food and Rural Affairs* [2015] EWHC 495 (Admin) at [43] (no discretion to extend time limit imposed by Planning Act 2008 s.118), *Nottingham CC v Calverton Parish Council* [2015] EWHC 503 (Admin); [2015] A.C.D. 97 at [33]–[34],[46] (relating to the Planning and Compulsory Purchase Act 2004 s.113, where a statutory provision provides that proceedings must be brought no later than the end of a specified period, the bringing of proceedings requires that the court office be functioning and the last day of the prescribed period falls on a day when the court office is closed, then proceedings may be brought on the next day when the court office is open), and R. *(on the application of Williams) v Secretary of State for Energy and Climate Change* [2015] EWHC 1202 (Admin); [2015] J.P.L. 1257 at [44]–[45] (the date on which an order was published online and a link was emailed to the claimant started the time period under s.118 Planning Act 2008, notwithstanding that the order was later published in a different way). Time began to run regardless of the claimant's actual knowledge (at [58–60]), and the fact that decision letters gave misleading guidance on the time limit in s.118 had no effect (at [63])).

17–028 *[Add to end of n.95]*

This is an area of recent development: Criminal Justice and Courts Act 2015 s.91 (in force from October 26, 2015) "introduces Sch.16, which contains amendments to provide that challenges to a range of planning related decisions and actions may only be brought with the leave of the High Court", within a six-week time limit: see the Explanatory Memorandum to the 2015 Act at [674]–[675].The amendments affect ss.287 and 288 of the Town and Country Planning Act 1990; s.63 of the Planning (Listed Buildings and Conservation Areas) Act 1990; s.22 of the Planning (Hazardous Substances) Act 1990; and s.113 of the Planning and Compulsory Purchase Act 2004. The amendments do not apply to proceedings where the publication date of the relevant document is earlier than October 26, 2015.

[Add new para.17–028A after para.17–028]   17–028A

The Administrative Court now has a specialist list called the Planning Court governed by CPR Pt 54.21–24 and Practice Direction 54E.[96a] The Planning Court hears all claims lodged after April 6, 2014 (or transferred to it after that date) which involve a judicial review or statutory challenge to planning and some environmental decisions.[96b] Significant Planning Court claims are dealt with according to the target time scales set out in the Practice Direction.[96c]

[96a] The proposal to establish the Planning Court appeared in Ch.3 of Ministry of Justice, *Judicial Review: Proposals for Further Reform*, Cm 8703 (September 2013). The Government's aim was stated to be to streamline the legal process for determining challenges in order to reduce the extent to which such challenges unduly hinder economic development and regeneration. Section 91 of the Criminal Justice and Courts Act 2015 (not in force at the time of writing) contains Sch.16, which introduces a permission stage for certain planning challenges. When s.91 enters into force, a new Practice Direction 8C – Alternative Procedure for Statutory Review of Certain Planning Matters will also be introduced to support its implementation, along with related amendments to Pt. 52, Practice Direction 8A – Alternative Procedure for Claims, and PD54E – Judicial and Statutory Review. See n.95.

[96b] A Planning Court claim includes a judicial review or statutory challenge to: planning permission or other development consents; the enforcement of planning control and the enforcement of other statutory schemes; applications under the Transport and Works Act 1992; wayleaves; highways and other rights of way; compulsory purchase orders; village greens; European Union environmental legislation and domestic transpositions, including assessments for development consents, habitats, waste and pollution control; national, regional or other planning policy documents; and any other matter which the Planning Liaison Judge considers appropriate. The Planning Liaison Judge will be nominated by the President of the Queen's Bench Division who will also nominate specialist planning judges to deal with significant Planning Court claims.

[96c] Significant Planning Court claims are defined in Practice Direction 54EPD3.2 as those: relating to developments with significant economic impact either locally or more broadly; which raise important points of law; which generate significant public interest; or, by virtue of the volume or nature of the technical material, are best dealt with by judges with significant experience of handling such matters. It is for the Planning Liaison Judge to designate claims as significant. See further I. Dove and F. Patterson, "The Planning Court: future directions" [2015] J.P.L. 1118.

Grounds of review

17–029 *[Add to end of n.100]*

See further *Holywell Property (St Albans) Ltd v Dacorum BC* [2014] EWHC 32 (Admin) at [14]–[15] and *R. (on the application of Brown) v Welsh Ministers* [2016] EWHC 750 (Admin) at [24]–[25].

17–030 *[Add to end of n.104]*

The language of the "fairly and reasonably" requirement has been adopted in the Community Infrastructure Levy Regulations 2010 (SI 2010/948), Regulation 122. See *Smyth v Secretary of State for Communities and Local Government* [2015] EWCA Civ 174; [2015] P.T.S.R 1417 at [19] (the Regulations require that conservation contributions fairly and reasonably relate to the scale and kind of a proposed development).

17–032 *[Add to end of n.109]*

The *Bolton* principles were recently approved in e.g. *R. (on the application of Watson) v Richmond upon Thames LBC* [2013] EWCA Civ 513 at [26], *Hiam v Secretary of State for Communities and Local Government* [2014] EWHC 4112 (Admin) at [40] and *R. (on the application of Manchester City Council) v Secretary of State for Local Government* [2016] EWHC (Admin) 4209 at [11].

CORONERS

17–034 *[In para.17–034 add after "hold an inquest"]*

or investigation

[In para.17–034 add after "where an inquest"]

or an investigation

[In para. 17–034 after "interests of justice that" delete "another inquest" and substitute]

an investigation (or, as the case may be, another investigation)

[Delete "inquisition" in n.116 and substitute]

Record of Inquest

[Add to end of n.117]

See also e.g. *HM Coroner for Isle of Wight v Prison Service* [2015] EWHC 1360 (Admin) at [5]. In *HM Coroner for the District of Avon v Elam* [2014] EWHC 3013 (Admin), a further inquest was ordered in the interests of justice as a result of new facts and evidence as to the identity of a previously unidentified person in respect of whom an inquest had already been conducted.

[In para.17–035 delete "inquisition" and substitute]   17–035

Record of Inquest

[Add to end of n.119]

Judicial review will remain available for those decisions which cannot be challenged under s.13 of the 1998 Act such as those made in advance of the hearing and those relating to the actual conduct of the proceedings.

[Add to end of n.120]

On the relevant costs principles, see *R. (on the application of Davies) v Birmingham Deputy Coroner* [2004] EWCA Civ 207; [2004] 1 W.L.R. 2739 at [47], *R. (on the application of Medihani) v HM Coroner for Inner South District of Greater London* [2012] EWHC 1104 (Admin); [2012] A.C.D. 63 at [59]–[64] and *R. (on the application of Joseph) v Director of Legal Aid Casework* [2015] EWHC 2749 (Admin). In *R. (on the application of Letts) v Lord Chancellor* [2015] EWHC 402 (Admin); [2015] 2 Costs L.R. 217, the criteria applied by the Legal Aid Agency to the grant of legal aid for representation at an inquest to the relatives of a deceased where the death may engage art.2 of the ECHR were found to be materially in error in lacking detail and creating a misleading impression as to what the law was. In *R. (on the application of RJ) v Director of Legal Aid Casework* [2016] EWHC 645 (Admin); [2016] A.C.D. 90 at [24]–[29], the refusal of legal aid for representation at an inquest to an "interested person" as designated by the Coroners and Justice Act 2009 s.47(2)(f) (a person who might by any act or omission have caused or contributed to a death), was not a breach of art.6 as the individual was not a person "charged with a criminal offence" and the inquest was not a criminal proceeding.

17–036 *[Delete all text in para.17–036, but retain all footnotes, and substitute]*

With effect from July 25, 2013 (and subject to the exception described below), the Coroners Act 1988 has been repealed by the Coroners and Justices Act 2009. Under the 2009 Act, a new post of Chief Coroner of England and Wales has been created.[121] The main responsibilities of the Chief Coroner include: to set national standards for all coroners (including new inquest rules); to oversee the implementation of the 2009 Act; to maintain a register of coroner investigations which last more than 12 months; to take steps to reduce unnecessary delays; and monitor investigations into the death of service personnel. As originally enacted in the 2009 Act, s.13 of the 1988 Act was to be replaced by a statutory right of appeal to the new post of Chief Coroner. However, the provisions of the 2009 Act creating the new right of appeal have now themselves been repealed on grounds of cost and s.13 of the 1988 Act and judicial review remain the mechanisms for challenge.

HOMELESS APPEALS

17–037 *[Add to end of n.123]*

Puhlhofer was cited in *Sharif v Camden London Borough Council* [2013] UKSC 10; [2013] 2 All E.R. 309 in which, on appeal (rather than an application for judicial review), a similarly restrictive approach was adopted (the word "accommodation" did not equate to "unit of accommodation", such that the duty imposed by s.193(2) of the Housing Act 1996 could be discharged by housing members of the same family in separate units).

[Add to end of n.125]

See s.204 of the Housing Act 1996 and *Johnston v City of Westminster* [2015] EWCA Civ 554 at [38].

[Add to end of n.126]

See also *Hines v Lambeth LBC* [2014] EWCA Civ 660; [2014] 1 W.L.R. 4112 at [13]–[15], at which *Tower Hamlets* was cited as authority for the proposition that an appeal under s.204 of the 1996 Act is to be scrutinised on judicial review principles; no greater intensity of review is to be applied. In *Nzolameso v Westminster City Council* [2015] UKSC 22; [2015] 2 All

E.R. 942 at [38]–[41], guidance was provided as to the desirability of the local authority maintaining a procurement policy for "out of borough" housing. If publicly available, this would "enable a general challenge to those policies to be brought by way of judicial review. In some ways this might be preferable to a challenge by way of an individual appeal to a county court. But it may not always be practicable to mount a judicial review of an authority's policy, and an individual must be able to rely on any point of law arising from the decision under appeal, including the legality of the policy which has been applied in her case". However, despite the "substantial overlap" between judicial review claims and appeals on points of law, it does not follow that every judicial body with jurisdiction limited to points of law is required to apply judicial review principles in every case: *Bhatia Best Ltd v Lord Chancellor* [2014] EWHC 746 (QB); [2014] 1 W.L.R. 3487 at [30]–[33], [40] and [43]. There, the question before the court was whether s.204 was an enactment which required the county court "to make a decision applying the principles that are applied by the court on an application for judicial review". If so, then s.204 appeals would, for the purposes of legal aid funding, fall within the "public law" category created by para.19(10) of Sch.1 of the Legal Aid, Sentencing and Punishment of Offenders Act 2012. It was held that the absence of reference to judicial review principles in s.204 showed that it was not intended that judicial review principles would be applied, and that this conclusion was unaffected by *Tower Hamlets*: the latter did not develop the jurisprudence beyond *Nipa Begum v Tower Hamlets London Borough Council* [2000] 1 W.L.R. 306, which simply established that s.204 gives rise to a right "akin to" judicial review. In *Ali v United Kingdom* [2015] H.L.R. 46 at [82]–[86], the ECtHR held that the legislative scheme for challenging homelessness decision-making pursuant to the Housing Act 1996, including the County Court's powers under s.204, was compatible with art.6. The ECtHR stated at [13] (without reference to the decision of the HC in *Bhatia Best*) that the "jurisdiction exercised by the county court under s.204 was that of judicial review."

EVALUATION OF JUDICIAL REVIEW PROCEDURES

The role of the court in judicial review

Questions of law

[Add to end of n.134]   17–040

The courts have adopted a functional, rather than principled, approach to defining what constitutes a question of law for the purposes of the powers of the Upper Tribunal; with the aims of allowing the Upper Tribunal scope to provide guidance in the interests of consistency while retaining a sufficient level of scrutiny by the ordinary courts to protect the rule of law (*R. (on the application of Cart) v Upper Tribunal* [2011] UKSC 28; [2012] 1 A.C. 663 and *R. (on the application of Jones) v First-tier Tribunal* [2013] UKSC 19; [2013] 2 A.C. 48 at [41]–[46] in which Lord Carnwath describes the distinction between law and fact as a matter of policy or expediency). See D. Feldman, "Error of Law and Flawed Administrative Acts" [2014] C.L.J. 275.

Questions of fact

17–042 *[Add to end of n.141]*

R. (on the application of Wright) v Secretary of State for Health [2009] UKHL 3 at [23] and *Ali v United Kingdom* [2015] H.L.R. 46 at [75]–[76].

The different interests of those affected by judicial review

17–049 *[Add to end of n.147]*

See para.1–005 and Ch.16 for the latest Government proposals.

CHAPTER 18

JUDICIAL REVIEW REMEDIES

INTERIM REMEDIES

Stay of proceedings

[Add to end of n.47]   18–017

and R. *(on the application of Yousuf) v Secretary of State for Foreign and Commonwealth Affairs* [2016] EWHC 663 (Admin) (stay of a judicial review claim inappropriate where the decision-maker had agreed to reconsider the decision with a fresh and open mind).

[In n.54 delete "4ᵗʰ edn (2008)" and substitute]   18–018

5ᵗʰ edn (2014),

Bail

[Add to end of n.63]   18–022

The court may also permit judicial review where the decisionmaker took into account a legally irrelevant factor: R. *(on the application of U) v Northampton Crown Court* [2013] EWHC 4519 (Admin) at [12]. A defendant on trial on indictment in the Crown Court may not challenge a decision to revoke bail made in the midst of a trial: R. *(on the application of Uddin) v Crown Court at Leeds* [2013] EWHC 2752 (Admin); [2014] 1 W.L.R. 1742 at [35].

FINAL REMEDIAL ORDERS

[Add to end of n.71]   18–023

Amendments introduced by the Criminal Justice and Courts Act 2015 to the Senior Courts Act 1981 s.31(2A) (which entered into force on April 13, 2015) require the Administrative Court to refuse to grant relief where "it appears to the court to be highly likely that the outcome for the applicant would not have been substantially different if the conduct complained of had not occurred". The court has a limited discretion to award a remedy even if the "no difference" test is made out where it "considers that it is appropriate to do so for reasons of exceptional public interest". If the court awards a remedy on grounds of exceptional public interest, it must certify that this condition is satisfied. This introduces a lower threshold than the previous law which required that the same result would almost inevitably have been reached and very much reduces the court's discretion (see para.18–049A).

Mandatory orders

[Add to end of n.73]

In *R. (on the application of ClientEarth) v Secretary of State for the Environment, Food and Rural Affairs* [2015] UKSC 28, at [30]–[31] and [35], the SC made a mandatory order requiring the Secretary of State to prepare new air quality plans for London and to deliver the plans to the European Commission by the end of the year.

Quashing and prohibiting orders

Remitting the matter back to the decision-maker

18–030 *[Add to end of para]*

In cases involving administrative bodies or tribunals, the matter will generally be remitted to the same decision-maker unless that would cause reasonably perceived unfairness to the affected parties, or would damage public confidence in the decision-making process. There is no set list of factors relevant to this assessment, but the presence of actual or apparent bias will make remission inappropriate. The reviewing court should consider all the circumstances and apply the usual meaning of fairness which is understood in judicial review proceedings. The position of political bodies such as local authorities may be different given their policy-making functions.[84a]

[84a] These principles are derived from *HCA International Ltd v Competition and Markets Authority* [2015] EWCA Civ 492, at [65]–[72].

Substituting a decision

18–032 *[Add to end of n.86]*

In *R. (on the application of the Governing Body of the London Oratory School) v Schools Adjudicator* [2015] EWHC 1155 (Admin) at [9], the HC remitted the impugned decision to the School's Adjudicator, being "far from sure that there is only one outcome to any fresh determination" and having regard to the fact that the Adjudicator, unlike the HC, could make a fresh decision on material available to her at the time of the new decision. The court considered that substitution was appropriate in the exceptional circumstances of the case in *Blast 106 Limited's Application* [2015] NICA 16 at [37].

Theoretical issues and advisory declarations

[Add to n.110 after first sentence]   18–042

As cited and discussed by the HC in *R. (on the application of Williams) v Secretary of State for the Home Department* [2015] EWHC 1268 at [55] (appeal outstanding).

DISCRETION IN GRANTING AND WITHHOLDING REMEDIES

[Add new title and new para.18–049A after 18–049]   18–049A

Substantially different outcome

The Criminal Justice and Courts Act 2015 (which has effect from April 13, 2015) defines the circumstances in which the High Court *must* refuse relief. Section 84 of the Act provides that the High Court must refuse to grant relief on an application for judicial review, and may not make any award under the Senior Courts Act 1981 s.31(4), if "it appears to the court to be highly likely that the outcome for the applicant would not have been substantially different if the conduct complained of had not occurred".[127a] The Court has a limited discretion to award a remedy even if the "no difference" test is made out where it "considers that it is appropriate to do so for reasons of exceptional public interest". If the court awards a remedy on grounds of exceptional public interest, it must certify that this condition is satisfied. The concept of "highly likely" is novel, and marks a significant departure from the test of inevitability previously applied at common law as a basis for refusing a remedy.[127b] It appears that the judge will be required to consider the significance of the alleged legal defect to the decision in question and speculate as to what the outcome would have been if the defect had not occurred. The courts have historically sought to avoid engaging in such questions.[127c] The constitutional implications of this aspect of the Act have been strongly criticised.[127d]

[127a] Criminal Justice and Courts Bill 2014 cl.70, inserting a new subs.2A into s.31 of the Senior Courts Act 1981. In *R. (on the application of Bokrosova) v Lambeth London Borough Council* [2015] EWHC 3386 (Admin); [2016] P.T.S.R. 355 at [88], recognising that s.31(2A) does not expressly impose a burden of proof on a defendant, the HC held that "in accordance with general principle . . . he who asserts must prove". In that instance, s.31(2A) did not require the HC to refuse relief.

[127b] See para.18–056. In *R. (on the application of Williams) v Powys County Council* [2016] EWHC 480 (Admin) at [25], the HC determined that s.31(2A) applied, albeit in a case which is likely to have satisfied the common law threshold of inevitability, the HC holding that "[i]t is more than 'highly likely': it is in my judgment clear that the . . . decision would have been the same with or without the asserted error."

[127c] See n.148. In *R. (on the application of Logan) v Havering London Borough Council* [2015] EWHC 3193 (Admin) at [55], the HC held *per curiam* that any consideration of whether s.31(2A) applied "should normally be based on material in existence at the time of the decision and not simply post-decision speculation by an individual decision-maker. Any other course runs the risk of reducing the importance of compliance with duties of procedural fairness and statutory or other requirements that certain matters be taken into account and others disregarded." The HC was concerned that the efficacy of judicial review could be undermined by a "draconian" modification of constitutional principles: if a decision-maker's declaration that obedience of the law would have made no difference led to the court refusing permission or to claimants being deterred from bringing proceedings. The Court speculated that the provision may have been intended to apply only to "somewhat trivial procedural failings", suggesting that the legislative history be reviewed to determine its scope.

[127d] See, e.g. B. Jaffey and T. Hickman, "Loading the Dice in Judicial Review: The Criminal Justice and Courts Bill 2014", UK Const L. Blog (February 6, 2014), *http://ukconstitutionallaw.org/2014/02/06/ben-jaffey-and-tom-hickman-loading-the-dice-in-judicial-review-the-criminal-justice-and-courts-bill-2014/*.

Claimant has suffered no harm

18–056 *[Delete all text in para.18–056 and substitute]*

In some cases, the court has withheld a remedy from a claimant on the basis that he has been caused no harm (the term "prejudice" is often used) by the unlawful act of the public authority.[146] Under this head, a minor technical breach of a statutory requirement may be too insignificant to justify relief.

The court has also taken into account the fact that the public authority would have made the same decision even if the legal flaw had not occurred.[147] The Criminal Justice and Courts Act 2015 has replaced this discretion with a requirement to refuse relief if "it appears to the court to be highly likely that the outcome for the applicant would not have been substantially different if the conduct complained of had not occurred".[147a] In the past, the Law Commission, academic commentators and the courts have all warned of the difficulties and risks in prejudging decisions, including overstepping the bounds of the court's reviewing functions.[148]

[147a] See para.18–049A.

Nullity and ultra vires and discretion

[Add to end of n.151]   18–058

See further, D. Feldman: "Error of Law and Flawed Administrative Acts" [2014] C.L.J. 275 and V.S. Nadhamuni, "Suspending Invalidity While Keeping Faith with Nullity: An analysis of the Suspension Order Cases and their Impact on our Understanding of the Doctrine of Nullity" [2015] P.L. 596.

CHAPTER 19

MONETARY REMEDIES IN JUDICIAL REVIEW

PROCEDURAL ISSUES

Civil claim or judicial review?

Public law issues must be decided to determine damages claim

[Add to end of n.22]   19–009

This paragraph and para.19–025 were found to be "fully justified by
authority" in *Tchenguiz v Director of the Serious Fraud Office* [2014] EWCA
Civ 472 at [14]. The case concerned the question whether a concession that
search orders had been unlawful in public law proceedings prevented the
defendant from relying on defences to a private law claim. The CA found
that the defendant was entitled to resist the private law claim.

DEFENDANTS IN MONETARY CLAIMS RELATING TO
JUDICIAL REVIEW

[Add to n.29 before "In Adams v Law Society . . ."]   19–012

This decision was applied to render the Ministry of Justice vicariously liable
for injury caused to an employee by a prisoner working in a prison kitchen
in *Cox v Ministry of Justice* [2016] UKSC 10; [2016] A.C. 660 at [20]–[29].
In contrast, the Chief Constable was not vicariously liable for acts of personal
harassment carried out by one of his officers in relation to the officer's
former partner in *Allen v Chief Constable of Hampshire* [2013] EWCA Civ
967 at [28]–[35].

[In n.35 delete "NHS Act 1977 s.125 as amended by National Health Service 19–013
and Community Care Act 1990 sch.2" and substitute]

NHS Act 2006 s.69

[In n.35 delete "[2012] EWCA Civ 981 at [20]–[23] the CA" and
substitute]

[2015] UKSC 2; [2015] A.C. 1732, the SC

[Add to end of n.35]

The SC allowed the claim under art.2 of the ECHR to proceed on the basis that it raised questions of fact (precisely what the call-handler had heard) which could not be determined by way of summary judgment.

The Crown as a defendant

19–016 *[Add to end of n.51]*

In *R. (on the application of Black) v Secretary of State for Justice* [2016] EWCA Civ 125; [2016] 3 W.L.R. 28, the CA held that relevant provisions of the Health Act 2006 which prohibited smoking in many public places were not intended to apply to the Crown to give a prisoner a cause of action for failure to provide access to a confidential help-line to report infringements. The CA emphasised that the test of necessary implication was a strict one and there was no basis for holding that the statutory purpose would be wholly frustrated in the present case if the Crown was not liable (at [30]–[35]).

[In n.53 delete "[2011] EWHC 1676 (QB) at [95]–[109]" and substitute]

[2013] UKSC 41; [2014] A.C. 52 at [89]–[96]

[In n.53 delete "in such a case (R. (on the application of Smith . . . at [19]–[20]" and substitute]

in relation to the activities of its armed forces overseas where they exercise sufficient control over the relevant area (*Al-Skeini v UK* (2011) 53 E.H.R.R. 18 at [130]–[150] and *Mohammed (Serdar) v Ministry of Defence* [2015] EWCA Civ 843; [2016] 2 W.L.R. 247 at [64]–[68]).

Judicial Immunity from civil liability

19–018 *[Add to end of n.60]*

See further, J. Murphy, "Rethinking Tortious Immunity for Judicial Acts" (2013) 33 L.S. 455 (arguing that the same test for liability should apply to superior court judges as in the tort of misfeasance in public office).

[Add to end of n.61]

In *Webster v Ministry of Justice* [2015] EWCA Civ 742; [2016] Q.B. 676 at [31]–[35] and [47], the CA upheld the strike out of proceedings under the HRA relating to the conduct of a criminal trial on the basis that although the trial judge's conduct was open to criticism, it did not constitute bad faith as required by s.9 and did not contain "gross and obvious irregularity" in a way which could give rise to claim under art.5 of the ECHR.

[Add to n.63 after ". . . power to make binding decisions"]

In *Singh v Reading BC* [2013] EWCA Civ 909; [2013] 1 W.L.R. 3052 at [43]–[46] and [70]–[72], the CA declined to follow *Heath* and held that the immunity did not apply to a claim for constructive dismissal by a former employee where the allegation was that the employer had placed undue pressure on another employee to produce an untrue witness statement and in *Daniels v Chief Constable of South Wales* [2015] EWCA Civ 680 at [40]–[48], the CA held that absolute immunity did not extend to failures to make proper disclosure of documents in the course of prosecutions against police officers. *Singh* and *Daniels* emphasise that absolute immunity is confined to protecting witnesses in the course of giving evidence and should only be extended where necessary to ensure that the protection of witnesses is not lost. In *P v Commissioner of Police for the Metropolis* [2016] EWCA Civ 2; [2016] I.R.L.R. 301 at [20]–[25], the CA held that *Heath* remained good law and, as such, a police officer's claim for unlawful discrimination arising from the police misconduct panel's mishandling of her disability discrimination claim was barred by the principle of judicial immunity.

[In n.64 delete "P. Milmo . . . (2008)" and substitute]

R. Parkes and A. Mullis et al, *Gatley on Libel and Slander*, 12th edn (2013)

Tribunals

[Add to end of n.85]   19–023

Heath was not followed in *Singh v Reading BC* [2013] EWCA Civ 909; [2013] 1 W.L.R. 3052 at [43]–[46], but was affirmed and applied in *P v Commissioner of Police for the Metropolis* [2016] EWCA Civ 2; [2016] I.R.L.R. 301.

The reason for immunity

[Delete "the immunity of the Crown" and substitute]   19–024

Judicial immunity

[In n.88 delete "10th edn (2009), p.703" and substitute]

11th edn (2014), p.697

GENERAL DIFFICULTIES

19-034 *[Add to end of n.121]*

In *Michael v Chief Constable of South Wales Police* [2015] UKSC 2; [2015] A.C. 1732, [113]–[122], *Hill* was affirmed and applied to strike out a claim of negligence about the mishandling of an emergency call. The art.2 claim was permitted to proceed to trial.

[In n.122 delete "20th edn (2010), para.2–105—119" and substitute]

21st edn (2014), paras 14–54—14–64

19-035 *[Add to end of n.123]*

See further, *Furnell v Flaherty* [2013] EWHC 377 (QB).

[In n.124 delete "4th edn (2006), pp.72–77" and substitute]

8th edn (2013), pp.70–83

19-036 *[In n.129 delete "20th edn (2010), paras 1–008, 5–117, 8–041" and substitute]*

21st edn (2014), para.1–08—1–09 and Ch.14

19-037 *[In notes 137 and 138 delete "20th edn (2010) Ch.2 and para.2–170" and substitute]*

21st edn (2014) Ch.2 and para.2–173 respectively

NEGLIGENCE

[In n.139 delete "12th edn (2010)" and substitute]

13th edn (2014)

19-038 *[In n.140 delete "20th edn (2010)" and substitute]*

21st edn (2014)

[Add to end of n.140]

Applying *Caparo*, it was not fair, just and reasonable to impose a duty of care on officers engaged in apprehending a suspected drug dealer on the street in relation to a bystander who suffered physical injury as a result of negligence by the officers (*Robinson v Chief Constable of West Yorkshire* [2014] EWCA Civ 15 at [44]–[51]). Similarly, there was no duty of care owed by a police force to a member of the public who made an emergency call which was mishandled leading to a delayed police response during which time the victim was murdered (*Michael v Chief Constable of South Wales Police* [2015] UKSC 2; [2015] A.C. 1732 at [113]–[122]); and there was no voluntary assumption of responsibility by the police towards witnesses in the course of obtaining and preserving evidence which could lead to the imposition of a duty of care not to disclose their addresses (*CLG v Chief Constable of Merseyside* [2015] EWCA Civ 836 at [22]–[24]). The SC decided that the question of whether it was fair, just and reasonable to impose a duty of care in relation to the deaths of British troops in Iraq arising from a failure to provide suitable equipment should be determined on the evidence at trial, but indicated that the defence of combat immunity should be narrowly construed (*Smith v Ministry of Defence* [2013] UKSC 41; [2014] A.C. 52 at [89]–[101]). The SC held it was fair, just and reasonable to impose a non-delegable duty of care on a school in relation to severe brain damage suffered by a pupil during a school swimming lesson (*Woodland v Swimming Teachers Association* [2013] UKSC 66; [2014] A.C. 537 at [25]). In contrast, a local authority does not owe a non-delegable duty of care to children it has responsibly placed in foster care in relation to assaults on the children by foster carers. In placing the children with foster parents, the local authority was discharging, not delegating, its duty (*Armes v Nottinghamshire CC* [2015] EWCA Civ 1139; [2016] Q.B. 739 at [24]–[25]). The registrar of companies owes a duty of care to companies to take reasonable care to ensure that when entering a winding-up order it is entered against the correct company's name: *Sebry v Companies House* [2015] EWHC 115 (QB); [2016] 1 W.L.R. 2499. In that case, the registrar's error had catastrophic consequences for the company.

[In n.142 delete "20th edn (2010), para.1–042" and substitute]

21st edn (2014) para.1–043

[Add to end of n.148] 19–041

See further, D. Nolan, "Varying the Standard of Care in Negligence" [2013] C.L.J. 651.

[In n.152 delete "20th edn (2010)" and substitute] 19–043

21st edn (2014)

[In n.154 delete "strongly doubted in . . . 863 at [47]" and substitute]

distinguished in *MacDonald v Aberdeenshire Council* [2013] CSIH 83; 2014 S.C. 114 at [42]

19–045   *[In n.172 delete "20th edn (2010)" and substitute]*

21st edn (2014)

[Add to end of n.172]

See further, J. Hartshorne, "Contemporary Approaches Towards Pure Economic Loss in the Law of Negligence" [2014] J.B.L. 425.

MISFEASANCE IN PUBLIC OFFICE

[Add to end of n.186]

In *Crawford Adjusters (Cayman) Ltd v Sagicor General Insurance (Cayman) Ltd* [2013] UKPC 17; [2014] A.C. 366, the PC held that there continued to be a tort of the malicious prosecution of civil proceedings where malice and the absence of reasonable cause could be shown. The tort does not apply to disciplinary proceedings: *Gregory v Portsmouth City Council* [2000] 1 A.C. 419. At the time of writing, the Law Commission is consulting on a new criminal offence of misconduct in public office based either on a breach of duty or corruption-based model and with a clear definition of public office (*Reforming Misconduct in Public Office: A Consultation Paper* (Consultation Paper No 229, September 5, 2016)).

19–049   *[Add to end of n.192]*

In *R. v Cosford (Karen)* [2013] EWCA Crim 466; [2014] Q.B. 81 at [34]–[39], the CA held that nurses working in a prison were public officers for the purposes of the tort whether or not they were also prison officers and whether employed directly by the state or through a private company since they were responsible in part for the proper, safe and secure running of the prison.

19–050   *[Add to end of n.207]*

The defendant could not rely on a "neither confirm nor deny" policy to avoid pleading a defence to a claim that undercover police officers had, as part of their work, engaged in long-term sexual relationships with those whose activities the police wished to observe (*DIL v Commissioner of Police of the Metropolis* [2014] EWHC 2184 (QB) at [40]–[43]).

BREACH OF STATUTORY DUTY

[In n.211 delete "20ᵗʰ edn (2010) and substitute]   19–051

21ˢᵗ edn (2014)

[Add to end of n.218]   19–053

In *Sebry v Companies House* [2015] EWHC 115 (QB); [2016] 1 W.L.R. 2499 at [106], Edis J considered that to create liability for breach of statutory duty by the Registrar of companies in relation to his functions under the Companies Act 2006 would be too wide in relation to the register (which was available to the whole world).

DEPRIVATION OF LIBERTY: FALSE IMPRISONMENT

[In n.228 delete "20th edn (2010) para.15–023" and substitute]

21ˢᵗ edn (2014) paras 15–023—15–048

[Delete "20th edn (2010)" and substitute]   19–055

21ˢᵗ edn (2014)

[Add to n.230]

In *P v Cheshire West and Cheshire Council* [2014] UKSC 19; [2014] A.C. 896 at [45]–[50], the SC held that deprivation of liberty in relation to a mentally incapacitated person was to be given the same meaning as under art.5 of the ECHR.

[Add to n.232]

A person may be deprived of their liberty without being aware of it: whether because they are asleep or lack mental capacity (*P v Cheshire West and Cheshire Council* [2014] UKSC 19; [2014] A.C. 896 at [35]). Confining an individual to a doorway (even if only for a few seconds) without lawful authority was a false imprisonment on the basis that "a fundamental constitutional principle is at stake" (*Walker v Commissioner of Police of the Metropolis* [2014] EWCA Civ 897; [2015 1 W.L.R. 312 at [46]). Damages were awarded in the sum of £5.

19–056 *[Add to end of n.235]*

The detention of a prisoner beyond the period when he would have been released had his case been considered speedily in accordance with art.5(4) of the ECHR does not constitute false imprisonment as his detention continues to be lawful as a matter of domestic law (*R. (on the application of Sturnham) v Parole Board* [2013] UKSC 23; [2013] 2 A.C. 254 at [15]–[16]). Similarly, the failure to provide a reasonable opportunity for a prisoner to rehabilitate himself did not directly impact on the lawfulness of his detention, but could give rise to right to compensation for frustration and anxiety under art.5(4) of the ECHR (*R. (on the application of Kaiyam) v Secretary of State for Justice* [2014] UKSC 66; [2015] A.C. 1344 at [35]–[39]). The distinction between the tortious claim for false imprisonment and a claim for breach of art.5 of the ECHR is illustrated by *Zenati v Commissioner of Police of the Metropolis* [2015] EWCA Civ 80; [2015] Q.B. 758 at [47]–[56]. In *Zenati*, the false imprisonment claim failed because his detention was authorised by a judicial authority, but the art.5 claim was allowed to proceed on the basis that the police were responsible for a delay in informing the court that the prisoner's passport was genuine.

MEASURE OF DAMAGES IN TORT

19–061 *[In n.248 delete "18th edn (2011)" and substitute]*

19th edn (2014)

REFORM OF TORT LIABILITY

19–072 *[Add to end of n.283]*

See now *Michael v Chief Constable of South Wales Police* [2015] UKSC 2; [2015] A.C. 1732, n.140 above.

COMPENSATION UNDER THE HUMAN RIGHTS ACT

Principles

19–084 *[In n.309, delete "R. (on the application of Faulkner . . . [103]" and substitute]*

R. (on the application of Sturnham) v Parole Board [2013] UKSC 23; [2013] 2 A.C. 254 at [99]–[103]. The court should be provided with an agreed schedule of the relevant authorities: stating the violations of the ECHR which were established and the sum awarded; summarising the parties submissions on them; listing the authorities in chronological order; and explaining the principles which are said to derive from them.

[Add to end of n.309]

In *Sturnham* [2013] UKSC 23; [2013] 2 A.C. 254 at [29], the SC indicated that reference to the ECtHR case law is likely to diminish as the award of damages under s.8 of the HRA becomes "naturalised". The ECtHR has produced a Practice Direction on *Just satisfaction claims* dated July 1, 2014 (available at http://www.echr.coe.int/Documents/PD_satisfaction_claims_ENG.pdf). See generally, J.N.E. Varuhas, *Damages and Human Rights* (2016).

[Add to end of n.310]

The Family Court was held to have the power to award damages under s.8(2) in *Re H (A Child: Breach of Convention Rights: Damages)* [2014] EWFC 38 at [62]–[64].

[Add to end of n.313]

In contrast, in *Cyprus v Turkey* (25781/94) (2014) 59 E.H.R.R. 16 at [58], the ECtHR awarded £30bn for non-pecuniary damage suffered by the surviving relatives of the missing persons and £60bn for non-pecuniary damage suffered by the enclaved residents of the Karpas peninsula following its 2001 judgment which found violations of the ECHR in relation to Turkey's military operations in Northern Cyprus. This was the first time that just satisfaction had been awarded in an inter-state case (at [41]–[43]). The ECtHR made clear that the payment was for the benefit of the individual victims and not the Cypriot Government (at [45]–[47]).

[Add to end of n.314]

The ECtHR set out some guidance on its approach to awarding just satisfaction in *Agrokompleks v Ukraine* (App. No.23465/03) (July 25, 2013) at [76]–[81]. In *Al-Jedda v UK* (2011) 53 E.H.R.R. 789 at [114], the ECtHR stated that its function was not "akin to a domestic tort mechanism court in apportioning fault and compensatory damages . . . [i]ts guiding principle is equity, which above all involves flexibility". The focus of the domestic court should be on the practice of the ECtHR, which tends not to provide "articulated statements of principle" in relation to awards (*R. (on the application of Sturnham) v Parole Board* [2013] UKSC 23; [2013] 2 A.C. 254 at [13],

[31]–[32]). The domestic court should focus on ECtHR cases involving applicants from the UK or countries with a comparable cost of living (*Sturnham* [2013] UKSC 23; [2013] 2 A.C. 254 at [38]–[39]). It is questionable whether this should apply to the nonpecuniary elements of loss.

[Add to end of point (d) in para.19–084]

The ECtHR's case law on awards for loss of opportunity is inconsistent.[317a]

[317a] *McGregor on Damages*, 19th edn (2014) paras 48–057 to 48–064. In *Sturnham* [2013] UKSC 23; [2013] 2 A.C. 254 at [13], the SC held that damages should be awarded where it is established on the balance of probabilities that a violation of art.5(4) has resulted in the detention of a prisoner beyond the date when he would otherwise have been released.

[Add to end of n.319]

Sturnham [2013] UKSC 23; [2013] 2 A.C. 254 at [41], [53]–[54]. *McGregor on Damages*, 19th edn (2014) para.48–055 has a useful table of ECtHR awards for nonpecuniary losses.

[Add to end of n.320]

Claims for damages under arts 3 and 8 of the ECHR brought under s.7 of the HRA relating to the conduct of undercover police officers in entering into intimate physical relationships with the claimants had to be brought before the Investigatory Powers Tribunal established by the Regulation of Investigatory Powers Act 2000 and not in the High Court (*AKJ v Commissioner of Police of the Metropolis* [2013] EWCA Civ 1342; [2014] 1 W.L.R. 285 at [37]–[43]). The common law claims for deceit, assault, misfeasance in public office and negligence were permitted to proceed before the High Court and the stay granted below was lifted (at [65]).

Individual Convention rights

Article 3 (prohibition of torture, inhuman and degrading treatment)

19–088 *[Add to n.326]*

In *DSD v Commissioner of Police of the Metropolis* [2014] EWHC 2493; [2015] 1 W.L.R. 1833, awards of £22,500 and £19,000 in damages were made to two rape victims for violations of art.3 on the basis of serious systemic failings and operational failures by the police in relation to their investigative duty. The quantum was not challenged in the unsuccessful appeal in *DSD v Commissioner of Police of the Metropolis* [2015] EWCA Civ 646; [2016] Q.B. 161.

Article 5 (right to liberty and security)

[Delete all text in para.19–091 and substitute]   19–091

In *R. (on the application of Sturnham) v Parole Board*,[334] the Supreme Court held that where it was demonstrated on a balance of probabilities that a violation of art.5(4) has resulted in the detention of a prisoner beyond the date when he would otherwise have been released, damages should be awarded with pecuniary losses being compensated in full. Nonpecuniary losses for frustration and anxiety should be awarded if sufficiently severe and this will usually be the case where the delay was of three months or more.

[334] [2013] UKSC 23; [2013] 2 A.C. 254 at [67]–[76]. The SC applied *Sturnham* to hold that prison authorities had a duty to afford prisoners sentenced to imprisonment for public protection a reasonable opportunity to rehabilitate themselves which may include the provision of courses and facilities (*R. (on the application of Kaiyam) v Secretary of State for Justice* [2014] UKSC 66; [2015] A.C. 1344 at [35]–[39]). This duty is ancillary to the scheme of art.5 and a breach of it did not render the detention unlawful, but may entitle a prisoner to compensation for frustration and anxiety.

[Add to end of para.19–093]   19–093

The Supreme Court reduced this sum on appeal to £6,500.

[In n.336 delete "(appeal pending)" and substitute]

(CA) and [2013] UKSC 23; [2013] 2 A.C. 254 at [87] (SC).

[Add to end of n.356]   19–099

In *OAO Neftyanaya Kompaniya Yukos v Russia (Just Satisfaction)* (2014) 59 E.H.R.R. SE12, the ECtHR made its highest award of just satisfaction in the sum of £1.9bn in a First Protocol, art.1 case.

[Add new heading and new para.19–100A after para.19–100]   19–100A

First Protocol, art.3 (right to free elections)

In *Firth v United Kingdom*,[358a] the ECtHR confirmed that a declaration that the automatic ban on voting by prisoners violated the right to free elections constituted just satisfaction and declined to award any compensation.

[358a] (App. No.47784/09) (August 12, 2014). Following *Firth*, the ECtHR rejected further claims for legal costs and non-pecuniary losses arising out of the same issues in *McHugh v UK* (App. No. 51987/08) (February 10, 2015) at [17]: the judgment in *Firth* was clear and the applicants did not require legal assistance to submit their applications which were dealt with under a simplified procedure.

Appendices

C.   *[Insert new version of s.29(6) of the Senior Courts Act 1981]*
        [Insert new version of s.31 of the Senior Courts Act 1981]
        [Insert new version of s.31A of the Senior Courts Act 1981]
E.   *[Insert new version of s.4(5)(f) of the Human Rights Act 1998]*
F.   *[Insert new version of CPR 54]*
HA.   *[Insert Civil Procedure Rules: Practice Direction 54E – Planning Court Claims]*
I.   *[Insert new version of Pre-action Protocol for Judicial Review]*
J.   *[Substitute new internet address]*
K.   *[Substitute new internet address]*
        [Insert new version of N462 Acknowledgment of Service]
L.   *[Substitute new internet address]*
        [Insert new version of N463 Application for Urgent Consideration]
M.   *[Substitute new internet address]*
N.   *[Substitute new internet address]*

APPENDIX C

[Insert new version of s.29(6) of the Senior Courts Act 1981]

29 Mandatory, prohibiting and quashing orders.[1]

(1) The orders of mandamus, prohibition and certiorari shall be known instead as mandatory, prohibiting and quashing orders respectively.

(1A) The High Court shall have jurisdiction to make mandatory, prohibiting and quashing orders in those classes of case in which, immediately before 1st May 2004, it had jurisdiction to make orders of mandamus, prohibition and certiorari respectively.[2]

(2) Every such order shall be final, subject to any right of appeal therefrom.

(3) In relation to the jurisdiction of the Crown Court, other than its jurisdiction in matters relating to trial on indictment, the High Court shall have all such jurisdiction to make [mandatory, prohibiting or quashing orders][3]

as the High Court possesses in relation to the jurisdiction of an inferior court.

(3A) The High Court shall have no jurisdiction to make mandatory, prohibiting or quashing orders in relation to the jurisdiction of the Court Martial in matters relating to–

(a) trial by the Court Martial for an offence; or

(b) appeals from the Service Civilian Court.[4]

(4) The power of the High Court under any enactment to require justices of the peace or a judge or officer of [the county court[5]

to do any act relating to the duties of their respective offices, or to require a magistrates' court to state a case for the opinion of the High Court, in any case where the High Court formerly had by virtue of any enactment jurisdiction to make a rule absolute, or an order, for any of those purposes, shall be exercisable by [mandatory order][6].

---

[1] Words substituted by Civil Procedure (Modification of Supreme Court Act 1981) Order 2004/1033 art.3(e) (May 1, 2004)

[2] S.29(1)–(1A) substituted for s.29(1) by Civil Procedure (Modification of Supreme Court Act 1981) Order 2004/1033 art.3(a) (May 1, 2004)

[3] Words substituted by Civil Procedure (Modification of Supreme Court Act 1981) Order 2004/1033 art.3(b) (May 1, 2004)

[4] Substituted by Armed Forces Act 2006 c. 52 Sch.16 para.93 (October 31, 2009)

[5] Words substituted by Crime and Courts Act 2013 c. 22 Sch.9(3) para.52(1)(b) (April 22, 2014: substitution has effect as SI 2014/954 subject to savings and transitional provisions specified in 2013 c.22 s.15 and Sch.8 and transitional provision specified in SI 2014/954 arts 2(c) and 3)

[6] Words substituted by Civil Procedure (Modification of Supreme Court Act 1981) Order 2004/1033 art.3(c) (May 1, 2004)

(5)   In any statutory provision–
  (a)   references to mandamus or to a writ or order of mandamus shall be read as references to a mandatory order;
  (b)   references to prohibition or to a writ or order of prohibition shall be read as references to a prohibiting order;
  (c)   references to certiorari or to a writ or order of certiorari shall be read as references to a quashing order; and
  (d)   references to the issue or award of a writ of mandamus, prohibition or certiorari shall be read as references to the making of the corresponding mandatory, prohibiting or quashing order.[7]

(6)   In subsection (3) the reference to the Crown Court's jurisdiction in matters relating to trial on indictment does not include its jurisdiction relating to [requirements to make payments under regulations under section 23 or 24 of the Legal Aid, Sentencing and Punishment of Offenders Act 2012[9]/[8]

---

[7] Substituted by Civil Procedure (Modification of Supreme Court Act 1981) Order 2004/1033 art.3(d) (May 1, 2004)
[8] Added by Access to Justice Act 1999 c. 22 Sch.4 para.23 (April 2, 2001 subject to transitional provisions specified in SI 2001/916 Sch.2 para.2)
[9] Words substituted by Legal Aid, Sentencing and Punishment of Offenders Act 2012 c. 10 Sch.5(1) para.21 (April 1, 2013 subject to saving and transitional provisions as specified in SI 2013/534 regs 6–13)

[Insert new version of s.31 of the Senior Courts Act 1981]

31 Application for judicial review

(1)   An application to the High Court for one or more of the following forms of relief, namely—

(a)   a mandatory, prohibiting or quashing order;[1]

(b)   a declaration or injunction under subsection (2); or

(c)   an injunction under section 30 restraining a person not entitled to do so from acting in an office to which that section applies,

shall be made in accordance with rules of court by a procedure to be known as an application for judicial review.

(2)   A declaration may be made or an injunction granted under this subsection in any case where an application for judicial review, seeking that relief, has been made and the High Court considers that, having regard to—

(a)   the nature of the matters in respect of which relief may be granted by [mandatory, prohibiting or quashing orders][2];

(b)   the nature of the persons and bodies against whom relief may be granted by such orders; and

(c)   all the circumstances of the case,

it would be just and convenient for the declaration to be made or the injunction to be granted, as the case may be.

(2A) The High Court—

(a)   must refuse to grant relief on an application for judicial review, and

(b)   may not make an award under subsection (4) on such an application,

if it appears to the court to be highly likely that the outcome for the applicant would not have been substantially different if the conduct complained of had not occurred.

(2B) The court may disregard the requirements in subsection (2A)(a) and (b) if it considers that it is appropriate to do so for reasons of exceptional public interest.

(2C) If the court grants relief or makes an award in reliance on subsection (2B), the court must certify that the condition in subsection (2B) is satisfied.[3]

(3)   No application for judicial review shall be made unless the leave of the High Court has been obtained in accordance with rules of court; and the court shall not grant leave to make such an application unless it

---

[1] Substituted by Civil Procedure (Modification of Supreme Court Act 1981) Order 2004/1033 art.4(a) (May 1, 2004)

[2] Words substituted by Civil Procedure (Modification of Supreme Court Act 1981) Order 2004/1033 art.4(b) (May 1, 2004)

[3] Added by Criminal Justice and Courts Act 2015 c. 2 Pt 4 s.84(1) (April 13, 2015: insertion has effect subject to transitional provisions specified in SI 2015/778 art.4 and Sch.2 para.6)

considers that the applicant has a sufficient interest in the matter to which the application relates.

(3C) When considering whether to grant leave to make an application for judicial review, the High Court—

    (a)   may of its own motion consider whether the outcome for the applicant would have been substantially different if the conduct complained of had not occurred, and

    (b)   must consider that question if the defendant asks it to do so.

(3D) If, on considering that question, it appears to the High Court to be highly likely that the outcome for the applicant would not have been substantially different, the court must refuse to grant leave.

(3E) The court may disregard the requirement in subsection (3D) if it considers that it is appropriate to do so for reasons of exceptional public interest.

(3F) If the court grants leave in reliance on subsection (3E), the court must certify that the condition in subsection (3E) is satisfied.[4]

(4)   On an application for judicial review the High Court may award to the applicant damages, restitution or the recovery of a sum due if–

    (a)   the application includes a claim for such an award arising from any matter to which the application relates; and

    (b)   the court is satisfied that such an award would have been made if the claim had been made in an action begun by the applicant at the time of making the application.[5]

(5)   If, on an application for judicial review, the High Court quashes the decision to which the application relates, it may in addition–

    (a)   remit the matter to the court, tribunal or authority which made the decision, with a direction to reconsider the matter and reach a decision in accordance with the findings of the High Court, or

    (b)   substitute its own decision for the decision in question.

(5A) But the power conferred by subsection (5)(b) is exercisable only if–

    (a)   the decision in question was made by a court or tribunal,

    (b)   the decision is quashed on the ground that there has been an error of law, and

    (c)   without the error, there would have been only one decision which the court or tribunal could have reached.

(5B) Unless the High Court otherwise directs, a decision substituted by it under subsection (5)(b) has effect as if it were a decision of the relevant court or tribunal.[6]

---

[4] Added by Criminal Justice and Courts Act 2015 c. 2 Pt 4 s.84(2) (April 13, 2015: insertion has effect subject to transitional provisions specified in SI 2015/778 art.4 and Sch.2 para.6)

[5] Substituted by Civil Procedure (Modification of Supreme Court Act 1981) Order 2004/1033 art.4(c) (May 1, 2004)

[6] S.31(5)–(5B) substituted for s.31(5) by Tribunals, Courts and Enforcement Act 2007 c. 15 Pt 7 s.141 (April 6, 2008)

(6) Where the High Court considers that there has been undue delay in making an application for judicial review, the court may refuse to grant—
    (a)   leave for the making of the application; or
    (b)   any relief sought on the application,
if it considers that the granting of the relief sought would be likely to cause substantial hardship to, or substantially prejudice the rights of, any person or would be detrimental to good administration.

(7) Subsection (6) is without prejudice to any enactment or rule of court which has the effect of limiting the time within which an application for judicial review may be made.

(8) In this section *"the conduct complained of"*, in relation to an application for judicial review, means the conduct (or alleged conduct) of the defendant that the applicant claims justifies the High Court in granting relief.[7]

---

[7] Added by Criminal Justice and Courts Act 2015 c. 2 Pt 4 s.84(3) (April 13, 2015: insertion has effect subject to transitional provisions specified in SI 2015/778 art.4 and Sch.2 para.6)

[Insert new version of s.31A of the Senior Courts Act 1981]

31A Transfer of judicial review applications to Upper Tribunal

(1)   This section applies where an application is made to the High Court–

    (a)   for judicial review, or

    (b)   for permission to apply for judicial review.

(2)   If Conditions 1, 2 and 3[2] are met, the High Court must by order transfer the application to the Upper Tribunal.[3]

(3)   If Conditions 1 and 2[4] are met, but Condition 3 is not, the High Court may by order transfer the application to the Upper Tribunal if it appears to the High Court to be just and convenient to do so.

(4)   Condition 1 is that the application does not seek anything other than–

    (a)   relief under section 31(1)(a) and (b);

    (b)   permission to apply for relief under section 31(1)(a) and (b);

    (c)   an award under section 31(4);

    (d)   interest;

    (e)   costs.

(5)   Condition 2 is that the application does not call into question anything done by the Crown Court.

(6)   Condition 3 is that the application falls within a class specified under section 18(6) of the Tribunals, Courts and Enforcement Act 2007. [. . .][5]][1]

---

[1] Added by Tribunals, Courts and Enforcement Act 2007 c. 15 Pt 1 c.2 s.19(1) (November 3, 2008)

[2] Words substituted by Crime and Courts Act 2013 c. 22 Pt 2 s.22(1)(a) (November 1, 2013: substitution has effect as SI 2013/1725 as amended by SI 2013/2200 subject to savings and transitional provisions specified in 2013 c.22 s.15 and Sch.8).

[3] Repealed by Crime and Courts Act 2013 c. 22 Pt 2 s.22(1)(b) (November 1, 2013: repeal has effect as SI 2013/1725 as amended by SI 2013/2200 subject to savings and transitional provisions specified in 2013 c.22 s.15 and Sch.8).

[4] Words substituted by Crime and Courts Act 2013 c. 22 Pt 2 s.22(1)(c) (November 1, 2013: substitution has effect as SI 2013/1725 as amended by SI 2013/2200 subject to savings and transitional provisions specified in 2013 c.22 s.15 and Sch.8).

[5] Repealed by Crime and Courts Act 2013 c. 22 Pt 2 s.22(1)(d) (November 1, 2013: repeal has effect as SI 2013/1725 as amended by SI 2013/2200 subject to savings and transitional provisions specified in 2013 c.22 s.15 and Sch.8).

APPENDIX E

[Insert new version of s.4(5)(f) of the Human Rights Act 1998]

4.—Declaration of incompatibility

(1) Subsection (2) applies in any proceedings in which a court determines whether a provision of primary legislation is compatible with a Convention right.

(2) If the court is satisfied that the provision is incompatible with a Convention right, it may make a declaration of that incompatibility.

(3) Subsection (4) applies in any proceedings in which a court determines whether a provision of subordinate legislation, made in the exercise of a power conferred by primary legislation, is compatible with a Convention right.

(4) If the court is satisfied—

    (a) that the provision is incompatible with a Convention right, and

    (b) that (disregarding any possibility of revocation) the primary legislation concerned prevents removal of the incompatibility,

it may make a declaration of that incompatibility.

(5) In this section *"court"* means — [

    (a) the Supreme Court;][1]

    (b) the Judicial Committee of the Privy Council;

    (c) the [Court Martial Appeal Court][2];

    (d) in Scotland, the High Court of Justiciary sitting otherwise than as a trial court or the Court of Session;

    (e) in England and Wales or Northern Ireland, the High Court or the Court of Appeal [;][3]

    (f) the Court of Protection, in any matter being dealt with by the President of the Family Division, the [Chancellor of the High Court][4]

or a puisne judge of the High Court.[3]

(6) A declaration under this section (*"a declaration of incompatibility"*)—

    (a) does not affect the validity, continuing operation or enforcement of the provision in respect of which it is given; and

    (b) is not binding on the parties to the proceedings in which it is made.

---

[1] Substituted by Constitutional Reform Act 2005 c. 4 Sch.9(1) para.66(2) (October 1, 2009).

[2] Words substituted by Armed Forces Act 2006 c. 52 Sch.16 para.156 (October 31, 2009).

[3] Added by Mental Capacity Act 2005 c. 9 Sch.6 para.43 (October 1, 2007).

[4] Word substituted by Crime and Courts Act 2013 c. 22 Sch.14(3) para.5(5) (October 1, 2013: substitution has effect as SI 2013/2200 subject to savings and transitional provisions as specified in 2013 c.22 s.15 and Sch.8).

APPENDIX F

[Insert new version of Civil Procedure Rules Part 54]

PART 54 – JUDICIAL REVIEW AND STATUTORY REVIEW
Rules 54.1—54.20 have not been repealed but have been moved into a new
Part 54 Section I.[1]

Scope and interpretation
54.1–(1) [This Section of this Part][2]
contains rules about judicial review.
(2) [In this Section][3] —
- (a) a *"claim for judicial review"* means a claim to review the lawfulness of—
  - (i) an enactment; or
  - (ii) a decision, action or failure to act in relation to the exercise
  of a public function.
- [. . .][4]
- (e) *"the judicial review procedure"* means the Part 8 procedure as
modified by [this Section][5];
- (f) *"interested party"* means any person (other than the claimant and
defendant) who is directly affected by the claim; and
- (g) *"court"* means the High Court, unless otherwise stated.

(Rule 8.1(6)(b) provides that a rule or practice direction may, in relation to
a specified type of proceedings, disapply or modify any of the rules set out
in Part 8 as they apply to those proceedings)

---

[1] Existing rules 54.1–54.20 are moved into a new Part 54 Section I by Civil Procedure
(Amendment) Rules 2003/364 Sch.1(1) para.1 (April 1, 2003 being the commencement date for
2002 c.41 Part 5).
[2] Words substituted by Civil Procedure (Amendment) Rules 2003/364 rule 5(a) (April 1, 2003
being the commencement date for 2002 c.41 Part 5).
[3] Words substituted by Civil Procedure (Amendment) Rules 2003/364 rule 5(b)(i) (April 1,
2003 being the commencement date for 2002 c.41 Part 5).
[4] Revoked by Civil Procedure (Amendment No. 5) Rules 2003/3361 rule 12 (May 1, 2004).
[5] Words substituted by Civil Procedure (Amendment) Rules 2003/364 rule 5(b)(ii) (April 1,
2003 being the commencement date for 2002 c.41 Part 5).

Who may exercise the powers of the High Court

54.1A–(1) A court officer assigned to the Administrative Court office who is—

    (a)   a barrister; or

    (b)   a solicitor,

may exercise the jurisdiction of the High Court with regard to the matters set out in paragraph with the consent of the President of the Queen's Bench Division.

(2)   The matters referred to in paragraph (1) are—

    (a)   any matter incidental to any proceedings in the High Court;

    (b)   any other matter where there is no substantial dispute between the parties; and

    (c)   the dismissal of an appeal or application where a party has failed to comply with any order, rule or practice direction.

(3)   A court officer may not decide an application for—

    (a)   permission to bring judicial review proceedings;

    (b)   an injunction;

    (c)   a stay of any proceedings, other than a temporary stay of any order or decision of the lower court over a period when the High Court is not sitting or cannot conveniently be convened, unless the parties seek a stay by consent.

(4)   Decisions of a court officer may be made without a hearing.

(5)   A party may request any decision of a court officer to be reviewed by a judge of the High Court.

(6)   At the request of a party, a hearing will be held to reconsider a decision of a court officer, made without a hearing.

(7)   A request under paragraph (5) or (6) must be filed within 7 days after the party is served with notice of the decision.[1]

---

[1] Added by Civil Procedure (Amendment No.2) Rules 2012/2208 rule 9(b) (October 1, 2012).

When this [Section]² must be used

54.2–The judicial review procedure must be used in a claim for judicial review where the claimant is seeking—

   (a)   a mandatory order;

   (b)   a prohibiting order;

   (c)   a quashing order; or

   (d)   an injunction under [section 30 of the Senior Courts Act 1981]³ (restraining a person from acting in any office in which he is not entitled to act).¹

---

¹ Existing rules 54.1–54.20 are moved into a new Part 54 Section I by Civil Procedure (Amendment) Rules 2003/364 Sch.1(1) para.1 (April 1, 2003 being the commencement date for 2002 c.41 Part 5).

² Words substituted by Civil Procedure (Amendment) Rules 2003/364 rule 5(c) (April 1, 2003 being the commencement date for 2002 c.41 Part 5).

³ Words substituted by Constitutional Reform Act 2005 c. 4 Sch.11(1) para.1(2) (October 1, 2009).

When this [Section][2] may be used

54.3–(1) The judicial review procedure may be used in a claim for judicial review where the claimant is seeking—

(a)   a declaration; or

(b)   an injunction.

([Section 31(2) of the Senior Courts Act 1981][3]

sets out the circumstances in which the court may grant a declaration or injunction in a claim for judicial review)

(Where the claimant is seeking a declaration or injunction in addition to one of the remedies listed in rule 54.2, the judicial review procedure must be used)

(2)   A claim for judicial review may include a claim for damages [, restitution or the recovery of a sum due][4] but may not seek [such a remedy][5] alone.

([Section 31(4) of the Senior Courts Act 1981][3] sets out the circumstances in which the court may award damages [, restitution or the recovery of a sum due][6] on a claim for judicial review)[1]

---

[1] Existing rules 54.1–54.20 are moved into a new Part 54 Section I by Civil Procedure (Amendment) Rules 2003/364 Sch.1(1) para.1 (April 1, 2003 being the commencement date for 2002 c.41 Part 5).

[2] Words substituted by Civil Procedure (Amendment) Rules 2003/364 rule 5(c) (April 1, 2003 being the commencement date for 2002 c.41 Part 5).

[3] Words substituted by Constitutional Reform Act 2005 c. 4 Sch.11(1) para.1(2) (October 1, 2009).

[4] Words inserted by Civil Procedure (Amendment No. 5) Rules 2003/3361 rule 13(a)(i) (May 1, 2004).

[5] Words substituted by Civil Procedure (Amendment No. 5) Rules 2003/3361 rule 13(a)(ii) (May 1, 2004).

[6] Words inserted by Civil Procedure (Amendment No. 5) Rules 2003/3361 rule 13(b) (May 1, 2004).

Permission required

54.4–The court's permission to proceed is required in a claim for judicial review whether started under this [Section][2] or transferred to the Administrative Court.[1]

---

[1] Existing rules 54.1–54.20 are moved into a new Part 54 Section I by Civil Procedure (Amendment) Rules 2003/364 Sch.1(1) para.1 (April 1, 2003 being the commencement date for 2002 c.41 Part 5).

[2] Word substituted by Civil Procedure (Amendment) Rules 2003/364 rule 5(d) (April 1, 2003 being the commencement date for 2002 c.41 Part 5).

Time limit for filing claim form
54.5–[(A1) In this rule—

"the planning acts" has the same meaning as in section 336 of the Town and Country Planning Act 1990;

[*"decision governed by the Public Contracts Regulations 2015"* means any decision the legality of which is or may be affected by a duty owed to an economic operator by virtue of regulations 89 or 90 of those Regulations (and for this purpose it does not matter that the claimant is not an economic operator); and]³

"economic operator" has the same meaning as in [regulation 2(1) of the Public Contracts Regulations 2015]⁴.]²

(1) The claim form must be filed—
    (a) promptly; and
    (b) in any event not later than 3 months after the grounds to make the claim first arose.

(2) The time [limits]⁵ in this rule may not be extended by agreement between the parties.

(3) This rule does not apply when any other enactment specifies a shorter time limit for making the claim for judicial review.

[(4) Paragraph (1) does not apply in the cases specified in paragraphs (5) and (6).

(5) Where the application for judicial review relates to a decision made by the Secretary of State or local planning authority under the planning acts, the claim form must be filed not later than six weeks after the grounds to make the claim first arose.

(6) Where the application for judicial review relates to a decision governed by [the Public Contracts Regulations 2015]⁷, the claim form must be filed within the time within which an economic operator would have been required by [regulation 92]⁸ of those Regulations (and disregarding the rest of that regulation) to start any proceedings under those Regulations in respect of that decision.]⁶]¹

---

¹ Existing rules 54.1–54.20 are moved into a new Part 54 Section I by Civil Procedure (Amendment) Rules 2003/364 Sch.1(1) para.1 (April 1, 2003 being the commencement date for 2002 c.41 Part 5).
² Added by Civil Procedure (Amendment No. 4) Rules 2013/1412 rule 4(a)(i) (July 1, 2013: insertion has effect subject to transitional provision specified in SI 2013/1412 rule 5(2)).
³ Definition substituted by Public Contracts Regulations 2015/102 Sch.6(2) para.11(2)(a) (February 26, 2015: substitution has effect subject to savings and transitional provisions specified in SI 2015/102 Pt 5).
⁴ Words substituted by Public Contracts Regulations 2015/102 Sch.6(2) para.11(2)(b) (February 26, 2015).
⁵ Word substituted by Civil Procedure (Amendment No. 4) Rules 2013/1412 rule 4(a)(ii) (July 1, 2013: substitution has effect subject to transitional provision specified in SI 2013/1412 rule 5(2)).
⁶ Added by Civil Procedure (Amendment No. 4) Rules 2013/1412 rule 4(a)(iii) (July 1, 2013: insertion has effect subject to transitional provision specified in SI 2013/1412 rule 5(2)).

[7] Words substituted by Public Contracts Regulations 2015/102 Sch.6(2) para.11(3)(a) (February 26, 2015: substitution has effect subject to savings and transitional provisions specified in SI 2015/102 Pt 5).
[8] Words substituted by Public Contracts Regulations 2015/102 Sch.6(2) para.11(3)(b) (February 26, 2015: substitution has effect subject to savings and transitional provisions specified in SI 2015/102 Pt 5).

Claim form

54.6–(1) In addition to the matters set out in rule 8.2 (contents of the claim form) the claimant must also state—

   (a)   the name and address of any person he considers to be an interested party;

   (b)   that he is requesting permission to proceed with a claim for judicial review; [. . .][2]

   (c)   any remedy (including any interim remedy) he is claiming [; and][3]

   [(d)   where appropriate, the grounds on which it is contended that the claim is an Aarhus Convention claim.

(Rules 45.41 to 45.44 make provision about costs in Aarhus Convention claims.)][4]

(Part 25 sets out how to apply for an interim remedy)

(2)   The claim form must be accompanied by the documents required by [Practice Direction 54A][5].][1]

[1] Existing rules 54.1–54.20 are moved into a new Part 54 Section I by Civil Procedure (Amendment) Rules 2003/364 Sch.1(1) para.1 (April 1, 2003 being the commencement date for 2002 c.41 Part 5).
[2] Word revoked by Civil Procedure (Amendment) Rules 2013/262 rule 18(a) (April 1, 2013: revocation has effect subject to transitional provisions specified in SI 2013/262 rule 22(8)).
[3] Punctuation substituted by Civil Procedure (Amendment) Rules 2013/262 rule 18(b) (April 1, 2013: substitution has effect subject to transitional provisions specified in SI 2013/262 rule 22(8)).
[4] Added by Civil Procedure (Amendment) Rules 2013/262 rule 18(c) (April 1, 2013: insertion has effect subject to transitional provisions specified in SI 2013/262 rule 22(8)).
[5] Words substituted by Civil Procedure (Amendment No.2) Rules 2009/3390 rule 29(b) (April 6, 2010).

Service of claim form

54.7–The claim form must be served on—
- (a) the defendant; and
- (b) unless the court otherwise directs, any person the claimant considers to be an interested party,

within 7 days after the date of issue.[1]

---

[1] Existing rules 54.1–54.20 are moved into a new Part 54 Section I by Civil Procedure (Amendment) Rules 2003/364 Sch.1(1) para.1 (April 1, 2003 being the commencement date for 2002 c.41 Part 5).

Judicial review of decisions of the Upper Tribunal

54.7A–(1) This rule applies where an application is made, following refusal by the Upper Tribunal of permission to appeal against a decision of the First Tier Tribunal, for judicial review—
- (a) of the decision of the Upper Tribunal refusing permission to appeal; or
- (b) which relates to the decision of the First Tier Tribunal which was the subject of the application for permission to appeal.

(2) Where this rule applies—
- (a) the application may not include any other claim, whether against the Upper Tribunal or not; and
- (b) any such other claim must be the subject of a separate application.

(3) The claim form and the supporting documents required by paragraph (4) must be filed no later than 16 days after the date on which notice of the Upper Tribunal's decision was sent to the applicant.

(4) The supporting documents are—
- (a) the decision of the Upper Tribunal to which the application relates, and any document giving reasons for the decision;
- (b) the grounds of appeal to the Upper Tribunal and any documents which were sent with them;
- (c) the decision of the First Tier Tribunal, the application to that Tribunal for permission to appeal and its reasons for refusing permission; and
- (d) any other documents essential to the claim.

(5) The claim form and supporting documents must be served on the Upper Tribunal and any other interested party no later than 7 days after the date of issue.

(6) The Upper Tribunal and any person served with the claim form who wishes to take part in the proceedings for judicial review must, no later than 21 days after service of the claim form, file and serve on the applicant and any other party an acknowledgment of service in the relevant practice form.

(7) The court will give permission to proceed only if it considers—

    (a) that there is an arguable case, which has a reasonable prospect of success, that both the decision of the Upper Tribunal refusing permission to appeal and the decision of the First Tier Tribunal against which permission to appeal was sought are wrong in law; and

    (b) that either—

        (i) the claim raises an important point of principle or practice; or

        (ii) there is some other compelling reason to hear it.

(8) If the application for permission is refused on paper without an oral hearing, rule 54.12(3) (request for reconsideration at a hearing) does not apply.

(9) If permission to apply for judicial review is granted—

    (a) if the Upper Tribunal or any interested party wishes there to be a hearing of the substantive application, it must make its request for such a hearing no later than 14 days after service of the order granting permission; and

    (b) if no request for a hearing is made within that period, the court will make a final order quashing the refusal of permission without a further hearing.

(10) The power to make a final order under paragraph (9)(b) may be exercised by the Master of the Crown Office or a Master of the Administrative Court.[1]

---

[1] Added by Civil Procedure (Amendment No.2) Rules 2012/2208 rule 9(c) (October 1, 2012).

Acknowledgment of service

54.8–(1) Any person served with the claim form who wishes to take part in the judicial review must file an acknowledgment of service in the relevant practice form in accordance with the following provisions of this rule.

(2) Any acknowledgment of service must be—
   (a) filed not more than 21 days after service of the claim form; and
   (b) served on—
      (i) the claimant; and
      (ii) subject to any direction under rule 54.7(b), any other person named in the claim form,
         as soon as practicable and, in any event, not later than 7 days after it is filed.

(3) The time limits under this rule may not be extended by agreement between the parties.

(4) The acknowledgment of service—
   (a) must—
      (i) where the person filing it intends to contest the claim, set out a summary of his grounds for doing so; and
      [(ia) where the person filing it intends to contest the application for permission on the basis that it is highly likely that the outcome for the claimant would not have been substantially different if the conduct complained of had not occurred, set out a summary of the grounds for doing so; and[2]
      (ii) state the name and address of any person the person filing it considers to be an interested party; and
   (b) may include or be accompanied by an application for directions.

(5) Rule 10.3(2) does not apply.
   [(Section 31(3C) of the Senior Courts Act 1981 requires the court, where it is asked to do so by the defendant, to consider whether the outcome for the claimant would have been substantially different if the conduct complained of had not occurred.)][3]][1]

---

[1] Existing rules 54.1–54.20 are moved into a new Part 54 Section I by Civil Procedure (Amendment) Rules 2003/364 Sch.1(1) para.1 (April 1, 2003 being the commencement date for 2002 c.41 Part 5).
[2] Added by Civil Procedure (Amendment No. 2) Rules 2015/670 rule 7 (April 13, 2015: insertion has effect subject to saving provision specified in SI 2015/670 rule 12(2)).
[3] Added by Civil Procedure (Amendment No. 2) Rules 2015/670 rule 8 (April 13, 2015: insertion has effect subject to saving provision specified in SI 2015/670 rule 12(2)).

Failure to file acknowledgment of service

54.9–(1) Where a person served with the claim form has failed to file an acknowledgment of service in accordance with rule 54.8, he—

    (a)   may not take part in a hearing to decide whether permission should be given unless the court allows him to do so; but

    (b)   provided he complies with rule 54.14 or any other direction of the court regarding the filing and service of—

        (i)   detailed grounds for contesting the claim or supporting it on additional grounds; and

        (ii)   any written evidence,

may take part in the hearing of the judicial review.

(2)   Where that person takes part in the hearing of the judicial review, the court may take his failure to file an acknowledgment of service into account when deciding what order to make about costs.

(3)   Rule 8.4 does not apply.[1]

---

[1] Existing rules 54.1–54.20 are moved into a new Part 54 Section I by Civil Procedure (Amendment) Rules 2003/364 Sch.1(1) para.1 (April 1, 2003 being the commencement date for 2002 c.41 Part 5).

Permission given

54.10–(1) Where permission to proceed is given the court may also give directions.

[(2) Directions under paragraph (1) may include—

    (a)   a stay of proceedings to which the claim relates;

    (b)   directions requiring the proceedings to be heard by a Divisional Court.][2]

(Rule 3.7 provides a sanction for the non-payment of the fee payable when permission to proceed has been given)[1]

---

[1] Existing rules 54.1–54.20 are moved into a new Part 54 Section I by Civil Procedure (Amendment) Rules 2003/364 Sch.1(1) para.1 (April 1, 2003 being the commencement date for 2002 c.41 Part 5).

[2] Substituted by Civil Procedure (Amendment No.3) Rules 2010/2577 rule 3 (October 20, 2010).

Service of order giving or refusing permission

54.11–The court will serve—

    (a)   the order giving or refusing permission; and

    [(ai) any certificate (if not included in the order) that permission has been granted for reasons of exceptional public interest in accordance with section 31(3F) of the Senior Courts Act 1981; and][2]

    (b)   any directions,

on—

       (i)   the claimant;

       (ii)   the defendant; and

       (iii) any other person who filed an acknowledgment of service.][1]

---

[1] Existing rules 54.1–54.20 are moved into a new Part 54 Section I by Civil Procedure (Amendment) Rules 2003/364 Sch.1(1) para.1 (April 1, 2003 being the commencement date for 2002 c.41 Part 5).

[2] Added by Civil Procedure (Amendment No. 2) Rules 2015/670 rule 9 (April 13, 2015: insertion has effect subject to saving provision specified in SI 2015/670 rule 12(2)).

Permission decision where court requires a hearing

54.11A–(1) This rule applies where the court wishes to hear submissions on—

    (a)   whether it is highly likely that the outcome for the claimant would not have been substantially different if the conduct complained of had not occurred; and if so

    (b)   whether there are reasons of exceptional public interest which make it nevertheless appropriate to give permission.

(2)   The court may direct a hearing to determine whether to give permission.

(3)   The claimant, defendant and any other person who has filed an acknowledgment of service must be given at least 2 days' notice of the hearing date.

(4)   The court may give directions requiring the proceedings to be heard by a Divisional Court.

(5)   The court must give its reasons for giving or refusing permission.[1]

---

[1] Added by Civil Procedure (Amendment No. 2) Rules 2015/670 rule 10 (April 13, 2015: insertion has effect subject to saving provision specified in SI 2015/670 rule 12(2)).

Permission decision without a hearing

54.12–(1) This rule applies where the court, without a hearing—

    (a)   refuses permission to proceed; or

    (b)   gives permission to proceed—

        (i)   subject to conditions; or

        (ii)   on certain grounds only.

(2)   The court will serve its reasons for making the decision when it serves the order giving or refusing permission in accordance with rule 54.11.

(3)   [Subject to paragraph (7), the]² claimant may not appeal but may request the decision to be reconsidered at a hearing.

(4)   A request under paragraph (3) must be filed within 7 days after service of the reasons under paragraph (2).

(5)   The claimant, defendant and any other person who has filed an acknowledgment of service will be given at least 2 days' notice of the hearing date.

[(6)   The court may give directions requiring the proceedings to be heard by a Divisional Court.]³

[(7)   Where the court refuses permission to proceed and records the fact that the application is totally without merit in accordance with rule 23.12, the claimant may not request that decision to be reconsidered at a hearing.]⁴]¹

---

[1] Existing rules 54.1–54.20 are moved into a new Part 54 Section I by Civil Procedure (Amendment) Rules 2003/364 Sch.1(1) para.1 (April 1, 2003 being the commencement date for 2002 c.41 Part 5).

[2] Word substituted by Civil Procedure (Amendment No. 4) Rules 2013/1412 rule 4(b)(i) (July 1, 2013: substitution has effect subject to transitional provision specified in SI 2013/1412 rule 5(1)).

[3] Added by Civil Procedure (Amendment No.3) Rules 2010/2577 rule 4 (October 20, 2010).

[4] Added by Civil Procedure (Amendment No. 4) Rules 2013/1412 rule 4(b)(ii) (July 1, 2013: insertion has effect subject to transitional provision specified in SI 2013/1412 rule 5(1)).

Defendant etc. may not apply to set aside

54.13–Neither the defendant nor any other person served with the claim form may apply to set aside an order giving permission to proceed.¹

---

[1] Existing rules 54.1–54.20 are moved into a new Part 54 Section I by Civil Procedure (Amendment) Rules 2003/364 Sch.1(1) para.1 (April 1, 2003 being the commencement date for 2002 c.41 Part 5).

Response

54.14–(1) A defendant and any other person served with the claim form who wishes to contest the claim or support it on additional grounds must file and serve—

(a) detailed grounds for contesting the claim or supporting it on additional grounds; and

(b) any written evidence,

within 35 days after service of the order giving permission.

(2) The following rules do not apply—

(a) rule 8.5(3) and 8.5(4) (defendant to file and serve written evidence at the same time as acknowledgment of service); and

(b) rule 8.5(5) and 8.5(6) (claimant to file and serve any reply within 14 days).[1]

---

[1] Existing rules 54.1–54.20 are moved into a new Part 54 Section I by Civil Procedure (Amendment) Rules 2003/364 Sch.1(1) para.1 (April 1, 2003 being the commencement date for 2002 c.41 Part 5).

Where claimant seeks to rely on additional grounds

54.15–The court's permission is required if a claimant seeks to rely on grounds other than those for which he has been given permission to proceed.[1]

---

[1] Existing rules 54.1–54.20 are moved into a new Part 54 Section I by Civil Procedure (Amendment) Rules 2003/364 Sch.1(1) para.1 (April 1, 2003 being the commencement date for 2002 c.41 Part 5).

Evidence

54.16–(1) Rule 8.6(1) does not apply.

(2)　No written evidence may be relied on unless—

    (a)　it has been served in accordance with any—

        (i)　rule under this [Section][2]; or

        (ii)　direction of the court; or

    (b)　the court gives permission.[1]

---

[1] Existing rules 54.1–54.20 are moved into a new Part 54 Section I by Civil Procedure (Amendment) Rules 2003/364 Sch.1(1) para.1 (April 1, 2003 being the commencement date for 2002 c.41 Part 5).

[2] Word substituted by Civil Procedure (Amendment) Rules 2003/364 rule 5(d) (April 1, 2003 being the commencement date for 2002 c.41 Part 5).

Court's powers to hear any person

54.17–(1) Any person may apply for permission—

    (a)　to file evidence; or

    (b)　make representations at the hearing of the judicial review.

(2)　An application under paragraph (1) should be made promptly.[1]

---

[1] Existing rules 54.1–54.20 are moved into a new Part 54 Section I by Civil Procedure (Amendment) Rules 2003/364 Sch.1(1) para.1 (April 1, 2003 being the commencement date for 2002 c.41 Part 5).

Judicial review may be decided without a hearing

54.18–The court may decide the claim for judicial review without a hearing where all the parties agree.[1]

---

[1] Existing rules 54.1–54.20 are moved into a new Part 54 Section I by Civil Procedure (Amendment) Rules 2003/364 Sch.1(1) para.1 (April 1, 2003 being the commencement date for 2002 c.41 Part 5).

Court's powers in respect of quashing orders

54.19–(1) This rule applies where the court makes a quashing order in respect of the decision to which the claim relates.

[(2) The court may—

(a)

(i) remit the matter to the decision-maker; and

(ii) direct it to reconsider the matter and reach a decision in accordance with the judgment of the court; or

(b) in so far as any enactment permits, substitute its own decision for the decision to which the claim relates.

(Section 31 of the Supreme Court Act 1981[3]

enables the High Court, subject to certain conditions, to substitute its own decision for the decision in question.)][2] [. . .][4]][1]

---

[1] Existing rules 54.1–54.20 are moved into a new Part 54 Section I by Civil Procedure (Amendment) Rules 2003/364 Sch.1(1) para.1 (April 1, 2003 being the commencement date for 2002 c.41 Part 5).

[2] Substituted by Civil Procedure (Amendment No.2) Rules 2007/3543 rule 7(b) (April 6, 2008).

[3] Section 31 is amended by section 141 of the Tribunals, Courts and Enforcement Act 2007 (c. 15).

[4] Revoked by Civil Procedure (Amendment No.2) Rules 2007/3543 rule 7(c) (April 6, 2008).

Transfer

54.20–The court may—

(a) order a claim to continue as if it had not been started under this [Section][2]; and

(b) where it does so, give directions about the future management of the claim.

(Part 30 (transfer) applies to transfers to and from the Administrative Court)[1]

---

[1] Existing rules 54.1–54.20 are moved into a new Part 54 Section I by Civil Procedure (Amendment) Rules 2003/364 Sch.1(1) para.1 (April 1, 2003 being the commencement date for 2002 c.41 Part 5).

[2] Word substituted by Civil Procedure (Amendment) Rules 2003/364 rule 5(e) (April 1, 2003 being the commencement date for 2002 c.41 Part 5).

General

54.21–(1) This Section applies to Planning Court claims.

(2)   In this Section, *"Planning Court claim"* means a judicial review or statutory challenge which—

    (a)   involves any of the following matters—

        (i)   planning permission, other development consents, the enforcement of planning control and the enforcement of other statutory schemes;

        (ii)   applications under the Transport and Works Act 1992;

        (iii)   wayleaves;

        (iv)   highways and other rights of way;

        (v)   compulsory purchase orders;

        (vi)   village greens;

        (vii)   European Union environmental legislation and domestic transpositions, including assessments for development consents, habitats, waste and pollution control;

        (viii)   national, regional or other planning policy documents, statutory or otherwise; or

        (ix)   any other matter the judge appointed under rule 54.22(2) [considers appropriate][2]; and

    (b)   has been issued or transferred to the Planning Court.

(Part 30 (Transfer) applies to transfers to and from the Planning Court.)[1]

---

[1] Added by Civil Procedure (Amendment No. 3) Rules 2014/610 rule 3 (April 6, 2014).
[2] Words inserted by Civil Procedure (Amendment No. 6) Rules 2014/2044 rule 9 (October 1, 2014).

Specialist list

54.22–(1) The Planning Court claims form a specialist list.

(2)   A judge nominated by the President of the Queen's Bench Division will be in charge of the Planning Court specialist list and will be known as the Planning Liaison Judge.

[(3)   The President of the Queen's Bench Division will be responsible for the nomination of specialist planning judges to deal with Planning Court claims which are significant within the meaning of Practice Direction 54E, and of other judges to deal with other Planning Court claims.][2]][1]

---

[1] Added by Civil Procedure (Amendment No. 3) Rules 2014/610 rule 3 (April 6, 2014).
[2] Added by Civil Procedure (Amendment No. 5) Rules 2014/1233 rule 4 (June 5, 2014).

Application of the Civil Procedure Rules

54.23–These Rules and their practice directions will apply to Planning Court claims unless this section or a practice direction provides otherwise.[1]

---

[1] Added by Civil Procedure (Amendment No. 3) Rules 2014/610 rule 3 (April 6, 2014).

Further provision about Planning Court claims

54.24–Practice Direction 54E makes further provision about Planning Court claims, in particular about the timescales for determining such claims.[1]

---

[1] Added by Civil Procedure (Amendment No. 3) Rules 2014/610 rule 3 (April 6, 2014).

APPENDIX G

[There has been a re-issue of Practice Direction Part 54A dated January 5, 2015 which is in identical terms to that set out in Appendix G of the main work.]

APPENDIX HA

[Insert Civil Procedure Rules: Practice Direction 54E – Planning Court Claims]

PRACTICE DIRECTION 54E – PLANNING COURT CLAIMS
This Practice Direction supplements Part 54.

General
1.1 This Practice Direction applies to Planning Court claims.
1.2. In this Practice Direction "planning statutory review" means a review under the provisions listed in paragraph 1.1(a) to (e) of PD8C.

How to start a Planning Court claim
2.1 Planning Court claims must be issued or lodged in the Administrative Court Office of the High Court in accordance with Practice Direction 54D.
2.2 The form must be marked the 'Planning Court'.

Categorisation of Planning Court claims
3.1 Planning Court claims may be categorised as 'significant' by the Planning Liaison Judge.
3.2 Significant Planning Court claims include claims which—
   (a) relate to commercial, residential, or other developments which have significant economic impact either at a local level or beyond their immediate locality;
   (b) raise important points of law;
   (c) generate significant public interest; or
   (d) by virtue of the volume or nature of technical material, are best dealt with by judges with significant experience of handling such matters.
3.3 A party wishing to make representations in respect of the categorisation of a Planning Court claim must do so in writing, on issuing the claim or lodging an acknowledgment of service as appropriate.
3.4 The target timescales for the hearing of significant (as defined by paragraph 3.2) Planning Court claims, which the parties should prepare to meet, are as follows, subject to the overriding objective of the interests of justice—
   (a) applications for permission to apply for judicial review are to be determined within three weeks of the expiry of the time limit for filing of the acknowledgment of service;

       (b)   oral renewals of applications for permission to apply for judicial review are to be heard within one month of receipt of request for renewal;

       (c)   applications for permission under section 289 of the Town and Country Planning Act 1990 are to be determined within one month of issue;

       (d)   substantive statutory applications, including applications under section 288 of the Town and Country Planning Act 1990, are to be heard within six months of issue; and

       (e)   judicial reviews are to be heard within ten weeks of the expiry of the period for the submission of detailed grounds by the defendant or any other party as provided in Rule 54.14.

3.5   The Planning Court may make case management directions, including a direction to any party intending to contest the claim to file and serve a summary of his grounds for doing so.

3.6   Notwithstanding the categorisation under paragraph 3.1 of a Planning Court claim as significant or otherwise, the Planning Liaison Judge may direct the expedition of any Planning Court claim if he considers it to necessary to deal with the case justly.

APPENDIX I

[Replace current version of Pre-action Protocol for Judicial Review]

Pre-Action Protocol for Judicial Review

INTRODUCTION

1   This Protocol applies to proceedings **within England and Wales only**. It does not affect the time limit specified by Rule 54.5(1) of the Civil Procedure Rules (CPR), which requires that any claim form in an application for judicial review must be filed promptly and in any event not later than 3 months after the grounds to make the claim first arose. Nor does it affect the shorter time limits specified by Rules 54.5(5) and (6), which set out that a claim form for certain planning judicial reviews must be filed within 6 weeks and the claim form for certain procurement judicial reviews must be filed within 30 days.[1]

2   This Protocol sets out a code of good practice and contains the steps which parties should generally follow before making a claim for judicial review.

3   The aims of the protocol are to enable parties to prospective claims to—
    (a)   understand and properly identify the issues in dispute in the proposed claim and share information and relevant documents;
    (b)   make informed decisions as to whether and how to proceed;
    (c)   try to settle the dispute without proceedings or reduce the issues in dispute;
    (d)   avoid unnecessary expense and keep down the costs of resolving the dispute; and
    (e)   support the efficient management of proceedings where litigation cannot be avoided.

4   Judicial review allows people with a sufficient interest in a decision or action by a public body to ask a judge to review the lawfulness of—
    •   an enactment; or
    •   a decision, action or failure to act in relation to the exercise of a public function.[2]

---

1. The court has a discretion to extend time. It cannot be taken that compliance with the protocol will of itself be sufficient to excuse delay or justify an extension of time, but it may be a relevant factor. Under rule 54.5(2), judicial review time limits cannot be extended by agreement between the parties. However, a court will take account of a party's agreement 'not to take a time point' so far as concerns delay while they were responding to a letter before claim. Return to footnote 1.
2. Civil Procedure Rule 54.1(2). Return to footnote 2.

5   Judicial review should only be used where no adequate alternative remedy, such as a right of appeal, is available. Even then, judicial review may not be appropriate in every instance. Claimants are strongly advised to seek appropriate legal advice as soon as possible when considering proceedings. Although the Legal Aid Agency will not normally grant full representation before a letter before claim has been sent and the proposed defendant given a reasonable time to respond, initial funding may be available, for eligible claimants, to cover the work necessary to write this. (See section 3 for more information.)

6   This protocol will not be appropriate in very urgent cases. In this sort of case, a claim should be made immediately. Examples are where directions have been set for the claimant's removal from the UK or where there is an urgent need for an interim order to compel a public body to act where it has unlawfully refused to do so, such as where a local housing authority fails to secure interim accommodation for a homeless claimant. A letter before claim, and a claim itself, will not stop the implementation of a disputed decision, though a proposed defendant may agree to take no action until its response letter has been provided. In other cases, the claimant may need to apply to the court for an urgent interim order. Even in very urgent cases, it is good practice to alert the defendant by telephone and to send by email (or fax) to the defendant the draft Claim Form which the claimant intends to issue. A claimant is also normally required to notify a defendant when an interim order is being sought.

7   All claimants will need to satisfy themselves whether they should follow the protocol, depending upon the circumstances of the case. Where the use of the protocol is appropriate, the court will normally expect all parties to have complied with it in good time before proceedings are issued and will take into account compliance or non-compliance when giving directions for case management of proceedings or when making orders for costs.[3]

8   The Upper Tribunal Immigration and Asylum Chamber (UTIAC) has jurisdiction in respect of judicial review proceedings in relation to most immigration decisions.[4] The President of UTIAC has issued a Practice Statement to the effect that, in judicial review proceedings in UTIAC, the parties will be expected to follow this protocol, where appropriate, as they would for proceedings in the High Court.

9   **Alternative Dispute Resolution**
The courts take the view that litigation should be a last resort. The parties should consider whether some form of alternative dispute

---

3. Civil Procedure Rules Costs Practice Directions 44–48. Return to footnote 3.
4. See the Direction made by the Lord Chief Justice dated August 21, 2013 (as amended on October 17, 2014), available in the UTIAC section of the www.justice.gov.uk website. Also, the High Court can order the transfer of judicial review proceedings to the UTIAC. Return to footnote 4.

resolution ('ADR') or complaints procedure would be more suitable than litigation, and if so, endeavour to agree which to adopt. Both the claimant and defendant may be required by the court to provide evidence that alternative means of resolving their dispute were considered. Parties are warned that if the protocol is not followed (including this paragraph) then the court must have regard to such conduct when determining costs. However, parties should also note that a claim for judicial review should comply with the time limits set out in the Introduction above. Exploring ADR may not excuse failure to comply with the time limits. If it is appropriate to issue a claim to ensure compliance with a time limit, but the parties agree there should be a stay of proceedings to explore settlement or narrowing the issues in dispute, a joint application for appropriate directions can be made to the court.

10   It is not practicable in this protocol to address in detail how the parties might decide which method to adopt to resolve their particular dispute. However, summarised below are some of the options for resolving disputes without litigation which may be appropriate, depending on the circumstances—

- Discussion and negotiation.
- Using relevant public authority complaints or review procedures.
- Ombudsmen – the Parliamentary and Health Service and the Local Government Ombudsmen have discretion to deal with complaints relating to maladministration. The British and Irish Ombudsman Association provide information about Ombudsman schemes and other complaint handling bodies and this is available from their website at www.bioa.org.uk. Parties may wish to note that the Ombudsmen are not able to look into a complaint once court action has been commenced.
- Mediation – a form of facilitated negotiation assisted by an independent neutral party.

11   The Civil Justice Council and Judicial College have endorsed The Jackson ADR Handbook by Susan Blake, Julie Browne and Stuart Sime (2013, Oxford University Press). The Citizens Advice Bureaux website also provides information about ADR: http://www.ad viceguide.org. uk/england/law_e/law_legal_system_e/law_taking_legal_action_e/ alternatives_to_court.htm. Information is also available at: http:// www.civilmediation.justice.gov.uk/

12   If proceedings are issued, the parties may be required by the court to provide evidence that ADR has been considered. A party's silence in response to an invitation to participate in ADR or refusal to participate in ADR might be considered unreasonable by the court and could lead to the court ordering that party to pay additional court costs.

13   **Requests for information and documents at the pre-action stage**

Requests for information and documents made at the pre-action stage should be proportionate and should be limited to what is properly necessary for the claimant to understand why the challenged decision has been taken and/or to present the claim in a manner that will properly identify the issues. The defendant should comply with any request which meets these requirements unless there is good reason for it not to do so. Where the court considers that a public body should have provided relevant documents and/or information, particularly where this failure is a breach of a statutory or common law requirement, it may impose costs sanctions.

14   **The letter before the claim**
In good time before making a claim, the claimant should send a letter to the defendant. The purpose of this letter is to identify the issues in dispute and establish whether they can be narrowed or litigation can be avoided.

15   Claimants should normally use the suggested standard format for the letter outlined at Annex A. For Immigration, Nationality and Asylum cases, the Home Office has a standardised form which can be used. It can be found online at:https://www.gov.uk/government/publications/chapter-27-judicial-review-guidance-part-1

16   The letter should contain the date and details of the decision, act or omission being challenged, a clear summary of the facts and the legal basis for the claim. It should also contain the details of any information that the claimant is seeking and an explanation of why this is considered relevant. If the claim is considered to be an Aarhus Convention claim (see Rules 45.41 to 45.44 and Practice Direction 45), the letter should state this clearly and explain the reasons, since specific rules as to costs apply to such claims. If the claim is considered appropriate for allocation to the Planning Court and/or for classification as "significant" within that court, the letter should state this clearly and explain the reasons.

17   The letter should normally contain the details of any person known to the claimant who is an Interested Party. An Interested Party is any person directly affected by the claim.[5] They should be sent a copy of the letter before claim for information. Claimants are strongly advised to seek appropriate legal advice when considering proceedings which involve an Interested Party and, in particular, before sending the letter before claim to an Interested Party or making a claim.

18   A claim should not normally be made until the proposed reply date given in the letter before the claim has passed, unless the circumstances of the case require more immediate action to be taken. The claimant should send the letter before claim in good time so as to enable a response which can then be taken into account before the time limit for

5. See Civil Procedure Rules, Rule 54.1(2). Return to footnote 5.

issuing the claim expires, unless there are good reasons why this is not possible.

19   Any claimant intending to ask for a protective costs order (an order that the claimant will not be liable for the costs of the defendant or any other party or to limit such liability) should explain the reasons for making the request, including an explanation of the limit of the financial resources available to the claimant in making the claim.

20   **The letter of response**
      Defendants should normally respond within 14 days using the standard format at Annex B. Failure to do so will be taken into account by the court and sanctions may be imposed unless there are good reasons.[6] Where the claimant is a litigant in person, the defendant should enclose a copy of this Protocol with its letter.

21   Where it is not possible to reply within the proposed time limit, the defendant should send an interim reply and propose a reasonable extension, giving a date by which the defendant expects to respond substantively. Where an extension is sought, reasons should be given and, where required, additional information requested. This will not affect the time limit for making a claim for judicial review[7] nor will it bind the claimant where he or she considers this to be unreasonable. However, where the court considers that a subsequent claim is made prematurely it may impose sanctions.

22   If the claim is being conceded in full, the reply should say so in clear and unambiguous terms.

23   If the claim is being conceded in part or not being conceded at all, the reply should say so in clear and unambiguous terms, and—
      (a)   where appropriate, contain a new decision, clearly identifying what aspects of the claim are being conceded and what are not, or, give a clear timescale within which the new decision will be issued;
      (b)   provide a fuller explanation for the decision, if considered appropriate to do so;
      (c)   address any points of dispute, or explain why they cannot be addressed;
      (d)   enclose any relevant documentation requested by the claimant, or explain why the documents are not being enclosed;
      (e)   where documents cannot be provided within the time scales required, then give a clear timescale for provision. The claimant should avoid making any formal application for the provision of documentation/information during this period unless there are good grounds to show that the timescale proposed is unreasonable;

---

6. See Civil Procedure Rules, Practice Direction – Pre-Action Conduct and Protocols, paragraphs 2–3. Return to footnote 6.
7. See Civil Procedure Rules, Rule 54.5(1). Return to footnote 7.

(f)   where appropriate, confirm whether or not they will oppose any application for an interim remedy; and

(g)   if the claimant has stated an intention to ask for a protective costs order, the defendant's response to this should be explained.

If the letter before claim has stated that the claim is an Aarhus Convention claim but the defendant does not accept this, the reply should state this clearly and explain the reasons. If the letter before claim has stated that the claim is suitable for the Planning Court and/ or categorisation as "significant" within that court but the defendant does not accept this, the reply should state this clearly and explain the reasons.

24   The response should be sent to all Interested Parties[8] identified by the claimant and contain details of any other persons who the defendant considers are Interested Parties.

A LETTER BEFORE CLAIM

SECTION 1. INFORMATION REQUIRED IN A LETTER BEFORE CLAIM

1 Proposed claim for judicial review

To
(Insert the name and address of the proposed defendant – see details in section 2.)

2 The claimant
(Insert the title, first and last name and the address of the claimant.)

3 The defendant's reference details
(When dealing with large organisations it is important to understand that the information relating to any particular individual's previous dealings with it may not be immediately available, therefore it is important to set out the relevant reference numbers for the matter in dispute and/or the identity of those within the public body who have been handling the particular matter in dispute – see details in section 3.)

4 The details of the claimants' legal advisers, if any, dealing with this claim
(Set out the name, address and reference details of any legal advisers dealing with the claim.)

---

8. See Civil Procedure Rules, Rule 54.1(2)(f). Return to footnote 8.

5 The details of the matter being challenged
(Set clearly the matter being challenged, particularly if there has been more than one decision.)

6 The details of any Interested Parties
(Set out the details of any Interested Parties and confirm that they have been sent a copy of this letter.)

7 The issue
(Set out a brief summary of the facts and relevant legal principles, the date and details of the decision, or act or omission being challenged, and why it is contended to be wrong.)

8 The details of the action that the defendant is expected to take
(Set out the details of the remedy sought, including whether a review or any interim remedy are being requested.)

9 ADR proposals
(Set out any proposals the claimant is making to resolve or narrow the dispute by ADR.)

10 The details of any information sought
(Set out the details of any information that is sought which is related to identifiable issues in dispute so as to enable the parties to resolve or reduce those issues. This may include a request for a fuller explanation of the reasons for the decision that is being challenged.)

11 The details of any documents that are considered relevant and necessary
(Set out the details of any documentation or policy in respect of which the disclosure is sought and explain why these are relevant.)

12 The address for reply and service of court documents
(Insert the address for the reply.)

13 Proposed reply date
(The precise time will depend upon the circumstances of the individual case. However, although a shorter or longer time may be appropriate in a particular case, 14 days is a reasonable time to allow in most circumstances.)

SECTION 2. ADDRESS FOR SENDING THE LETTER BEFORE CLAIM
Public bodies have requested that, for certain types of cases, in order to ensure a prompt response, letters before claim should be sent to specific addresses.

- **Where the claim concerns a decision in an Immigration, Asylum or Nationality case (including in relation to an immigration decision taken abroad by an Entry Clearance Officer)—**
  - — The claim may be sent electronically to the following email address: UKVIPAP@homeoffice.gsi.gov.uk
  - — Alternatively the claim may be sent by post to the following Home Office postal address:
  Litigation Operations Allocation Hub
  Status Park 2
  4 Nobel Drive
  Harlington
  Hayes
  Middlesex UB3 5EY

The Home Office has a standardised form which claimants may find helpful to use for communications with the Home Office in Immigration, Asylum or Nationality cases pursuant to this Protocol, to assist claimants to include all relevant information and to promote speedier review and response by the Home Office. The Home Office form may be filled out in electronic or hard copy format. It can be found online at:https://www.gov.uk/government/publications/chapter-27-judicial-review-guidance-part-1

- **Where the claim concerns a decision by the Legal Aid Agency—**
  The address on the decision letter/notification;
  Legal Director
  Corporate Legal Team
  Legal Aid Agency
  102 Petty France
  London SW1H 9AJ
- **Where the claim concerns a decision by a local authority:**
  The address on the decision letter/notification; and
  Their legal department[9]
- **Where the claim concerns a decision by a department or body for whom Treasury Solicitor acts** and Treasury Solicitor has already been involved in the case **a copy should also be sent, quoting the Treasury Solicitor's reference, to:**
  The Treasury Solicitor,
  One Kemble Street,
  London WC2B 4TS

In all other circumstances, the letter should be sent to the address on the letter notifying the decision.[9] The relevant address should be available from

---

9. The relevant address should be available from a range of sources such as the Phone Book; Business and Services Directory, Thomson's Local Directory, CAB, etc. Return to footnote 9.

a range of sources such as the Phone Book; Business and Services Directory, Thomson's Local Directory, CAB, etc.

SECTION 3. SPECIFIC REFERENCE DETAILS REQUIRED
Public bodies have requested that the following information should be provided in order to ensure prompt response.

- **Where the claim concerns an Immigration, Asylum or Nationality case, dependent upon the nature of the case:**
  — The Home Office reference number;
  — The Port reference number;
  — The Asylum and Immigration Tribunal reference number;
  — The National Asylum Support Service reference number;
  Or, if these are unavailable:
  — The full name, nationality and date of birth of the claimant.
- **Where the claim concerns a decision by the Legal Aid Agency—** The certificate reference number.

B RESPONSE TO A LETTER BEFORE CLAIM

INFORMATION REQUIRED IN A RESPONSE TO A LETTER BEFORE CLAIM
Proposed claim for judicial review

1 The claimant
(Insert the title, first and last names and the address to which any reply should be sent.)

2 From
(Insert the name and address of the defendant.)

3 Reference details
(Set out the relevant reference numbers for the matter in dispute and the identity of those within the public body who have been handling the issue.)

4 The details of the matter being challenged
(Set out details of the matter being challenged, providing a fuller explanation of the decision, where this is considered appropriate.)

5 Response to the proposed claim
(Set out whether the issue in question is conceded in part, or in full, or will be contested. Where an interim reply is being sent and there is a realistic prospect of settlement, details should be included. If the claimant is a litigant in person, a copy of the Pre-Action Protocol should be enclosed with the letter.)

6 Details of any other interested parties

(Identify any other parties who you consider have an interest who have not already been sent a letter by the claimant)

7 ADR proposals

(Set out the defendant's position on any ADR proposals made in the letter before claim and any ADR proposals by the defendant.)

8 Response to requests for information and documents

(Set out the defendant's answer to the requests made in the letter before claim including reasons why any requested information or documents are not being disclosed.)

9 Address for further correspondence and service of court documents

(Set out the address for any future correspondence on this matter.)

C NOTES ON PUBLIC FUNDING FOR LEGAL COSTS IN JUDICIAL REVIEW

Public funding for legal costs in judicial review is available from legal professionals and advice agencies which have contracts with the Legal Aid Agency. Funding may be provided for—

- Legal Help to provide initial advice and assistance with any legal problem; or
- Legal Representation to allow you to be represented in court if you are taking or defending court proceedings. This is available in two forms—

  Investigative Help is limited to funding to investigate the strength of the proposed claim. It includes the issue and conduct of proceedings only so far as is necessary to obtain disclosure of relevant information or to protect the client's position in relation to any urgent hearing or time limit for the issue of proceedings. This includes the work necessary to write a letter before claim to the body potentially under challenge, setting out the grounds of challenge, and giving that body a reasonable opportunity, typically 14 days, in which to respond.

  Full Representation is provided to represent you in legal proceedings and includes litigation services, advocacy services, and all such help as is usually given by a person providing representation in proceedings, including steps preliminary or incidental to proceedings, and/or arriving at or giving effect to a compromise to avoid or bring to an end any proceedings. Except in emergency cases, a proper letter before claim must be sent and the other side must be given an opportunity to respond before Full Representation is granted.

Further information on the type(s) of help available and the criteria for receiving that help may be found in the Legal Aid Agency's pages on the Ministry of Justice website at:

https://www.justice.gov.uk/legal-aid

A list of contracted firms and Advice Agencies may be found at:
http://find-legal-advice.justice.gov.uk

APPENDIX J

N461 Claim Form

[Delete internet address and substitute]

http://hmctsformfinder.justice.gov.uk/courtfinder/forms/n461-eng.pdf

APPENDIX K

N462 Acknowledgement of Service

[Insert new version of N462 Acknowledgment of Service]

The form reproduced overleaf is available to download from
http://hmctsformfinder.justice.gov.uk/courtfinder/forms/n462-eng.pdf

Print form | Reset form

N462

Judicial Review
Acknowledgment of Service

In the High Court of Justice
Administrative Court

Claim No.	
Claimant(s) (including ref.)	
Defendant(s)	
Interested Parties	

Name and address of person to be served

name

address

SECTION A

Tick the appropriate box

1. I intend to contest all of the claim ☐
2. I intend to contest part of the claim ☐ } complete sections B, C, D and F

3. I do not intend to contest the claim ☐ complete section F

4. The defendant (interested party) is a court or tribunal and **intends** to make a submission. ☐ complete sections B, C and F

5. The defendant (interested party) is a court or tribunal and **does not intend** to make a submission. ☐ complete sections B and F

6. The applicant has indicated that this is a claim to which the Aarhus Convention applies. ☐ complete sections E and F

7. The **Defendant** asks the Court to consider whether the outcome for the claimant would have been **substantially different** if the conduct complained of had not occurred [see s.31(3C) of the Senior Courts Act 1981] ☐ A summary of the grounds for that request must be set out in/accompany this Acknowledgment of Service

Note: If the application seeks to judicially review the decision of a court or tribunal, the court or tribunal need only provide the Administrative Court with as much evidence as it can about the decision to help the Administrative Court perform its judicial function.

SECTION B

Insert the name and address of any person you consider should be added as an interested party.

name

address

Telephone no. | Fax no.

E-mail address

name

address

Telephone no. | Fax no.

E-mail address

SECTION C

Summary of grounds for contesting the claim. If you are contesting only part of the claim, set out which part before you give your grounds for contesting it. If you are a court or tribunal filing a submission, please indicate that this is the case.

351

SECTION D

Give details of any directions you will be asking the court to make, or tick the box to indicate that a separate application notice is attached.

If you are seeking a direction that this matter be heard at an Administrative Court venue other than that at which this claim was issued, you should complete, lodge and serve on all other parties Form N464 with this acknowledgment of service.

SECTION E

Response to the claimant's contention that the claim is an Aarhus claim

Do you deny that the claim is an Aarhus Convention claim? ☐ Yes ☐ No

If Yes, please set out your grounds for denial in the box below.

SECTION F

*delete as appropriate

*(I believe)(The defendant believes) that the facts stated in this form are true.

*I am duly authorised by the defendant to sign this statement.

(If signing on behalf of firm or company, court or tribunal)

Position or office held

(To be signed by you or by your solicitor or litigation friend)

Signed

Date

Give an address to which notices about this case can be sent to you

name

address

Telephone no.   Fax no.

E-mail address

If you have instructed counsel, please give their name address and contact details below.

name

address

Telephone no.   Fax no.

E-mail address

Completed forms, together with a copy, should be lodged with the Administrative Court Office (court address, over the page), at which this claim was issued within 21 days of service of the claim upon you, and further copies should be served on the Claimant(s), any other Defendant(s) and any interested parties within 7 days of lodgement with the Court.

3 of 4

Print form   Reset form

352

Administrative Court addresses

- Administrative Court in **London**

    Administrative Court Office, Room C315, Royal Courts of Justice, Strand, London, WC2A 2LL.

- Administrative Court in **Birmingham**

    Administrative Court Office, Birmingham Civil Justice Centre, Priory Courts, 33 Bull Street, Birmingham B4 6DS.

- Administrative Court in **Wales**

    Administrative Court Office, Cardiff Civil Justice Centre, 2 Park Street, Cardiff, CF10 1ET.

- Administrative Court in **Leeds**

    Administrative Court Office, Leeds Combined Court Centre, 1 Oxford Row, Leeds, LS1 3BG.

- Administrative Court in **Manchester**

    Administrative Court Office, Manchester Civil Justice Centre, 1 Bridge Street West, Manchester, M3 3FX.

APPENDIX L

N463 Application for Urgent Consideration

[Insert new version of N463 Application for Urgent Consideration]

The form reproduced overleaf is available to download from http://hmctsformfinder.justice.gov.uk/courtfinder/forms/n463-eng.pdf

Judicial Review
Application for urgent consideration

In the High Court of Justice
Administrative Court

This form must be completed by the Claimant or the Claimant's advocate if exceptional urgency is being claimed and the application needs to be determined within a certain time scale.

The claimant, or the claimant's solicitors must serve this form on the defendant(s) and any interested parties with the N461 Judicial review claim form.

To the Defendant(s) and Interested Party(ies)
Representations as to the urgency of the claim may be made by defendants or interested parties to the relevant Administrative Court Office by fax or email:-

For cases proceeding in

Claim No.	
Claimant(s) *(including ref.)*	
Defendant(s)	
Interested Party(ies)	

London	Fax: 020 7947 6802
	email: administrativecourtoffice.generaloffice@hmcts.x.gsi.gov.uk
Birmingham	Fax: 0121 250 6730
	email: administrativecourtoffice.birmingham@hmcts.x.gsi.gov.uk
Cardiff	Fax: 02920 376461
	email: administrativecourtoffice.cardiff@hmcts.x.gsi.gov.uk
Leeds	Fax: 0113 306 2581
	email: administrativecourtoffice.leeds@hmcts.x.gsi.gov.uk
Manchester	Fax: 0161 240 5315
	email: administrativecourtoffice.manchester@hmcts.x.gsi.gov.uk

SECTION 1 Reasons for urgency

356

SECTION 2 Proposed timetable (tick the boxes and complete the following statements that apply)

a) ☐ Urgency (including abridgement of time for AOS) is sought and should be considered within ____ hours/days
   If consideration is sought within 48 hours of issue, **you must complete Section 3 below.**

b) ☐ Interim relief is sought and the application for such relief should be considered within ____ hours/days
   If consideration is sought within 48 hours of issue, **you must complete Section 3 below.**

c) ☐ The N461 application for permission should be considered within ____ hours / days
   If consideration is sought within 48 hours of issue, **you must complete Section 3 below.**

d) ☐ If permission for judicial review is granted, a substantive hearing is sought by[enter date]

SECTION 3 Justification for request for immediate consideration

Date and time when it was first appreciated that an immediate application might be necessary.

Date	Time

Please provide reasons for any delay in making the application.

What efforts have been made to put the defendant and any interested party on notice of the application?

SECTION 4 Interim relief *(state what interim relief is sought and why in the box below)*

A draft order must be attached.

SECTION 5 Service

A copy of this form of application was served on the defendant(s) and interested parties as follows:

Defendant

☐ by fax machine to   time sent

   ┌Fax no. ──────── ┌time ────

☐ by handing it to or leaving it with

   ┌name ────

☐ by e-mail to

   ┌e-mail address ────

Date served

   ┌Date ────

Interested party

☐ by fax machine to   time sent

   ┌Fax no. ──────── ┌time ────

☐ by handing it to or leaving it with

   ┌name ────

☐ by e-mail to

   ┌e-mail address ────

Date served

   ┌Date ────

I confirm that all relevant facts have been disclosed in this application

Name of claimant's advocate

   ┌name ────

Claimant (claimant's advocate)

   ┌Signed ────

▶ Print form   ▶ Reset form

APPENDIX M

N464 Application for Directions as to Venue for Administration and Determination

[Delete internet address and substitute]

http://hmctsformfinder.justice.gov.uk/courtfinder/forms/n464-eng.pdf

APPENDIX N

N465 Response to Applicationfor Directions as to Venue for Administration and Determination

[Delete internet address and substitute]

http://hmctsformfinder.justice.gov.uk/courtfinder/forms/n465-eng.pdf

Index